W9-BER-585

What Color Is Your Parachute?

Other Books by
Richard N. Bolles

The Three Boxes of Life, and How To Get Out of Them

Where Do I Go From Here With My Life? (co-authored with John C. Crystal)

1983 Edition
Revised and Enlarged

What Color Is Your Parachute?

A Practical Manual for Job-Hunters & Career Changers

•

Richard Nelson Bolles

Ten Speed Press

Library of Congress Catalog Card No. 81-50471
ISBN 0-89815-067-1 paper
ISBN 0-89815-068-X cloth

Published by Ten Speed Press, P.O. Box 7123, Berkeley, California 94707. You may order single copies prepaid direct from the publisher for $14.95 + $.75 per copy for postage and handling (clothbound), or $7.95 + $.50 per copy for postage and handling (paper). California residents please add 6% state sales tax; Bay Area residents add 6½%.)

Beverly Anderson Graphic Design

Type set by Joanne Shwed, Mary Fran McCluskey, and Design & Type, San Francisco

Printed by Consolidated Printers, Inc., Berkeley, California

This is an annual. That is to say, it is substantially revised each year, the new edition appearing in March of that year. Those wishing to submit additions, corrections, or suggestions for the 1984 edition, should submit them prior to September 1, 1983, using the forms provided in the back of this book. (Letters reaching us after that date will have to wait for the 1985 edition.)

WHY THIS BOOK WAS WRITTEN,
COMMONLY CALLED

THE INTRODUCTION, OR PREFACE

It is late 1982, as I write. To quote Charles Dickens, it is the best of times and the worst of times.

The worst of times in forty-two years, unemployment-wise. A total of 11.3 million people – 10.1% of the civilian, non-farm labor force – are out of work, and looking. This month.

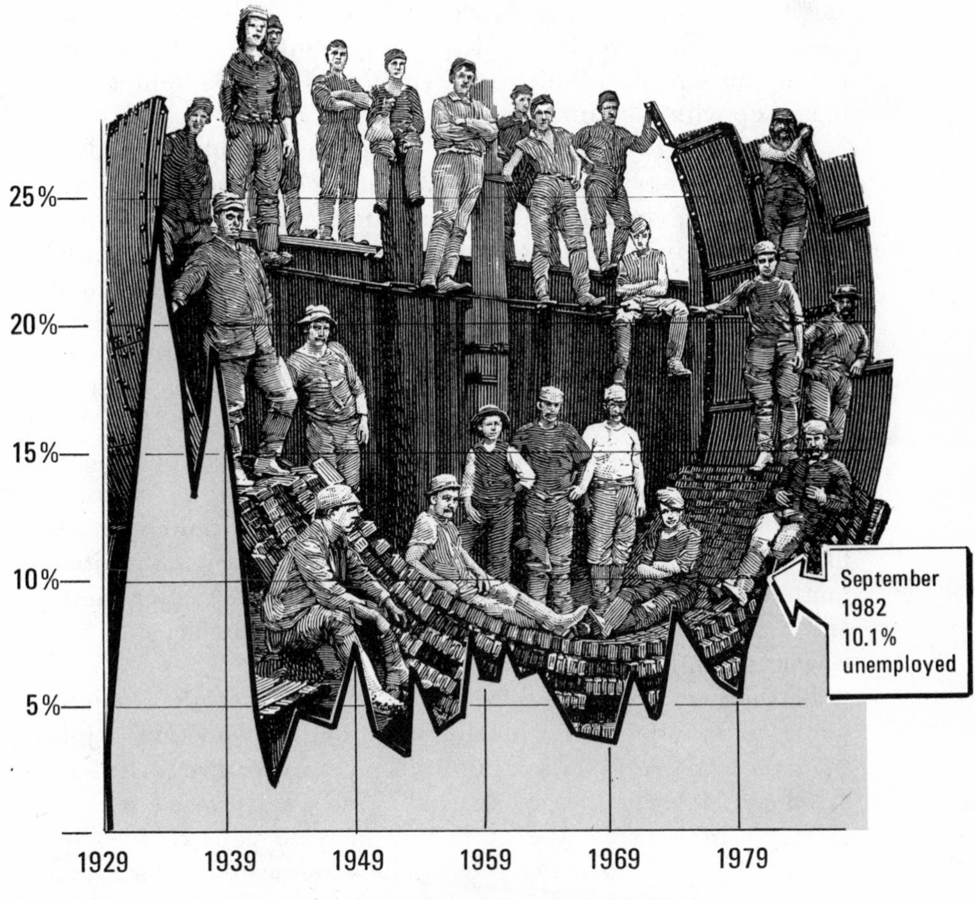

UNEMPLOYMENT RATES SINCE 1929

Since the annual rate is always between 2.5 and 4 times the monthly rate, that means at least one out of every four workers in the U.S. has been job-hunting sometime this year. Some have found a part-time job instead of the full-time job they sought – they total 6.6 million currently. Others have given up even looking – another 1.6 million – so discouraged are they at the state of the job market.

Anyone who claims he or she has an answer to tragedy of such magnitude – some kind of magical formula that, if followed, will guarantee the job-hunter will find a job – is either an idiot or a fool. Certainly, this book makes no such claim.

What this book does claim is that even in the worst of times there are at least 2 million vacancies out there; this among job-experts is common knowledge. Why such a situation exists, when so many people are desperately hunting, is due to the ponderous slowness with which employers and job-hunters get linked up with each other, under our system.

In addition to these vacancies, there are new jobs. For some businesses or organizations this is – as Dickens once said – the best of times. Notably, in the communications and professional or technical fields. The Recession/Depression we are currently in, has not even touched them. Profits are rolling in. They hear the unemployment news as only the sound of distant warfare. These organizations are flourishing, growing, – and creating new positions, new jobs – not just filling old vacancies. How many new jobs? About 1.6 million, each year.

There is no magical formula. But there *are* jobs out there. Someone is going to get those jobs. And what we know for a fact is that the *knowledgeable* job-hunter is infinitely more likely to be the one who finds those jobs than the *ignorant* job-hunter. The more you as job-hunter know about the job-hunt, and how it functions, the more you increase your chances. That is what this book is about.

Further, what we know for a fact is that the *enthusiastic* job-hunter is infinitely more likely to be the one who finds a job than the *matter-of-fact* job-hunter. The more you've identified a job you'd really love to do, and know what things are your greatest enthusiasms, the more you increase your chances of finding a job – *particularly* when jobs are scarce. Hence, the kind of careful homework suggested in this book – commonly, now, called "the Parachute process" – is not less relevant during a Recession/Depression, but more relevant and essential. That is what this book is all about.

The familiar mythology about this book (among white, college-educated, middle class people at any rate) is that the job-hunting techniques described herein only work for white, college-educated, middle class people. In point of fact, many of the key ideas in this book were first discovered among blue-collar workers, as in Harold L. Sheppard's and A. Harvey Belitsky's pioneering study of the job-hunt. In later times, we have had to *adapt* them in order to make them applicable to white, college-educated, middle class people.

The other mythology about this book is that it is a series of strategies that work well in the best of times, but not during a Recession/Depression. I have already discussed the error of that concept. Now, let me add a little history. This always has been and always will be a Recession book. Recessions only leave for a short time, and then they return. See the chart at the beginning of this Preface. This book was originally written during a Recession. It represented, from the first, an attempt to help people through a Recession. And many of the ideas in it, though modern job-hunters (typically) think *they* discovered them only in these latter days, actually are ideas that were first conceived during the Great Depression of 1929-1941. They were conceived precisely because, in that worst of times, the old ways of job-hunting just weren't working anymore.

These "new" ideas have been refined and improved upon, since; they have been added to, and made infinitely more sophisticated in their form and application. But their birthmark still shows. These are Depression strategies. In their nakedest, simplest form, they are these:

(1) *You improve your chances of finding a job once you realize that no one owes you a job:* not life, not the government, not the industry or organization you used to work for, not the community in which you live. Back in frontier days, you rode into town and had to devise or find your own job on your own. These are frontier days.

(2) *You improve your chances of finding a job once you take the label off yourself* (such as "I am a steelworker, or teacher, or auto-worker") and think instead of yourself in terms of your skills: ("I am good with my hands," "I am good at solving problems," etc.).

(3) *You improve your chances of findng a job if you know some alternative names for that job* – or some alternative jobs where you could use the same skills – rather than trying to zero in on a job that has just one name.

(4) *You improve your chances of finding a job once you*

have more than one organization you're going after; determining that "I'm going to go back to work where I used to work" and going after only one organization is self-defeating, since there is no guarantee that that organization (or industry) will *ever* hire you back again. Recessions/Depressions cause many whole industries to dwindle or die, never to rise again.

(5) *You improve your chances of finding a job once you figure out what the people who* are *working, and who do have money, are willing to spend their money to get – by way of products, goods, services, or entertainment.* On New York street corners this very year, I noticed it was orange juice and fruits when the weather was warm, umbrellas when it started to rain, gloves and scarfs as it started to get cold – and so on. Some of these vendors were making a *very* good living, indeed (I asked). Even during the Hardest of Times, millions and millions of people *are* working, have money to spend, and *will* spend it. Figure out what they are willing to spend it for, who is offering those goods or services to them in *your* city, town or geographical area, and go knock on their doors. Or, if no one is, figure out how you might.

(6) *You improve your chances of finding a job once you realize the job-hunt is essentially a hunt for information.* Everything you know about how to "find out stuff" that you want to know, is of use to you in your job-hunt. Once you know what you're looking for, asking *everyone* you meet, contacting everyone you know, is crucial.

(7) *You improve your chances of finding a job if you never put all your eggs in one basket.* Not using just one method of job-hunting; but using as many different avenues as possible. Not relying on just one source of advice; but relying on as many different sources as possible. Not looking for just one kind of job; but looking for as many different kinds (that use your best skills) as possible. Not hanging all your hopes on just one possible place of work; but approaching as many different places as possible.

(8) *You improve your chances of finding a job once you realize that going face-to-face with prospective employers is* the *most effective method of job-hunting.* It is more effective than sending letters, more effective than mailing out resumes, more effective than using the telephone, more effective than using some go-between.

(9) *You improve your chances of finding a job once you decide that you are going to be gently persistent, without being obnoxious.* Persistent about *how much* you hunt: nine to five, five days a week. Persistent about *how* you hunt: going back to the same places you visited two or three weeks ago, inasmuch as a vacancy may have developed in the meantime.

(10) *You improve your chances of finding a job if you've taken the time to learn about the places you visit, before you knock on their doors.* Asking your friends, visiting the library, taking the time to research the organization will put you way ahead of those who know nothing about the place, and show it.

(11) *You improve your chances of finding a job if you know what makes you different from (and therefore makes you stand out from) the other people who do what you do.* Are you more of a perfectionist about your craft? Are you more painstaking? Do you give more attention to detail? Do you produce higher quality work? Are you more persistent about solving problems? Are you more patient with people? If you quietly know what makes you stand out from all the others who do what you do, and can communicate this clearly during interviews with employers, you greatly increase your chances of being the one chosen, when there is a vacancy.

(12) *You improve your chances of finding a job if you go after small businesses, rather than large.* Two-thirds of all the new jobs created in the period 1969-1976 were created by businesses with twenty or less employees.

This book, in its seven chapters, only expands upon these twelve blue-collar, Hard Times strategies, and explains them in terms that even a white, college-educated, middle class person can understand.

Job-hunting is a repetitive activity, in the Western world. It isn't just now that you must job-hunt. You're going (in all likelihood) to have to do it again. And again. And again. More often when you are younger, to be sure. Less often as you get older. Still, the fact remains that the average American worker works for ten different employers during his or her lifetime. And the average job in America lasts for exactly 3.6 years. So says the National Bureau for Economic Research, the *Personnel Journal,* and the U.S. Department of Labor. The figures are probably not substantially different in other parts of the Western world.

Since job-hunting is such a repetitive activity in most of our lives, it is important that you do not depend on someone else to solve it for you, but that you learn how to do it for yourself. There is an ancient saying: "Give me a fish, and I will eat for today; teach me to fish, and I will eat for the rest of my life."

This book is an attempt to teach you how to fish with respect to the most difficult task any of us faces in this life: The Job Hunt. This book is an attempt to, in other words, empower you as job-hunter or career-changer, so that no matter how many times you have to go about this thing called the job-hunt during the years that lie ahead, you will know how to do it most effectively.

I do want to reiterate that this is not a book of *my* ideas about how you should go job-hunting. It is a distillation of the experience of literally millions of successful job-hunters. Blue-collar job-hunters. White-collar job-hunters. Pink-collar job-hunters. Male job-hunters. Female job-hunters. Minority job-hunters. Handicapped job-hunters. Teen-aged job-hunters. Middle-aged job-hunters. Highly-verbal job-hunters. Very shy job-hunters. I am not the inventor, but only the reporter, of their experience. Coming as I do from a family of journalists (my brother was the reporter who was slain in Arizona in 1976, and our father and our grandfather were journalists also) I have reported this – in my own way. I write informally, even conversationally, as you will discover. And I believe that even the gravest of situations should be salted with some humor, so you will find a considerable amount of humor in this book, both in word and picture. The light-hearted tone of so much of the book is not intended to ignore the seriousness, indeed the wretchedness, of unemployment. I have myself been through all that, so I know. But why should job manuals be dull? Hopefully the humor makes the inevitable journey of the job-hunt a little lighter, and this book more enjoyable to plow through.

My concluding plea: if you are working today, you may very well be a job-hunter tomorrow. If you are a job-hunter more than once, you will likely be a career-changer as well. Learn how to take charge of your job-hunt or yourself, and learn how to change careers without necessarily going back to college. Learn how to fish.

You know, so much is riding on your job-hunt. Not just the matter of putting bread on the table. [illegible] just the matter of using the gifts you were given. Not just the matter of your self-esteem. But the whole question of who you are, and why you are here in this world, and what it is you have to contribute to make this world a better place. If, as a result of reading this book and following its advice, the mundane task of finding a job turns out for you to be a spiritual journey as well, it will come as no surprise.

Peace, and shalom.

November 1, 1982. Dick Bolles

P.S. Given the massive influx of women into the job market during the past decade or so, no book on job-hunting these days can be insensitive to the issue of sexism in language. It was in 1960 that I myself first protested such language, but twenty-three years later we are still, as a society, without agreement on how to solve the problem. Casey Miller and Kate Swift in their excellent book *The Handbook of Nonsexist Writing* have cogently argued from history that one solution lies in using "they" as a singular pronoun ("Anyone using this beach after 5 p.m. does so at their own risk."). These authors argue that, whatever the situation may have been in the past, in the present, agreement in gender is more important than agreement in number. Thus the pronoun "they" – normally plural – should be able to also follow a singular antecedent, even as in an earlier time the solely plural "you" became both plural and single. That is the usage followed throughout this book.

P.P.S. In the annual revision, and updating, of this book, I owe a great debt of gratitude to my friend and publisher, Phil Wood, and to my layout person, a genius named Beverly Anderson – as well as to a host of others. I want also to express to John Crystal my great debt during the original inception of this work. John is not only a genius about career change, he is also very gracious and humane. When I first began the research upon which this book is based, John took the time to explain to me what is wrong with the whole job-hunting process in this country, and what could be done about it. He suggested the organizing principles for the data I was collecting, which principles became the cornerstones of chapters 5, 6 and 7 in this book.

Contents

PREFACE / PAGE *vii*

Twelve Keys to job-hunting during Hard Times

CHAPTER ONE / PAGE 1

A-JOB-HUNTING WE WILL GO

The way in which the average person, left to their own devices, normally goes about the job-hunt.

CHAPTER TWO / PAGE 9

REJECTION SHOCK

Our Neanderthal job-hunting system. The numbers game, and how well it doesn't work. People in the form of paper, and how they get screened out. What the whole numbers game is, its virtues and defects. How to use the numbers game instead of being used by it. Recruiters, ads, agencies, placement centers, clearinghouses, and other ideas. The effectiveness rate of various job-hunting methods.

CHAPTER THREE / PAGE 39

YOU CAN DO IT!

The creative minority, who they are, and how they can save your life. Their diagnosis of what's wrong with the job-hunt, and their prescription for a cure. The number of people changing careers. An overview of career and life planning. The four principles of successful job-hunting.

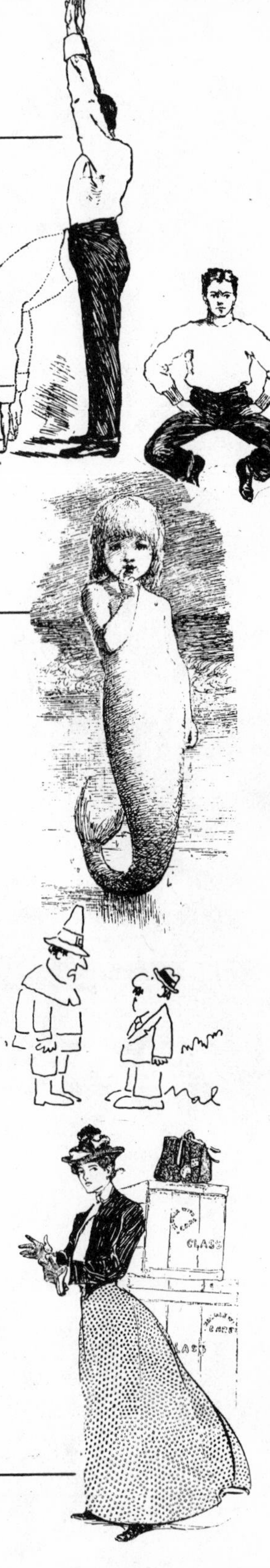

CHAPTER FOUR / PAGE 49

YOU MUST KEEP AT IT

The most important secret of successful job-hunting and career-changing. How to increase your chances of success sevenfold. The Tale of Two Job-hunters in the Same City. Job-hunting while you are still employed. Nine ways to find time while employed. Job-Hunters Anonymous. Group job-hunting. Other resources you can draw upon. Professional help for a fee, and for free. Getting support from your family or friends. How you can manage a 20,000 hour, $250,000 project.

CHAPTER FIVE / PAGE 67

ONLY YOU CAN DECIDE:
WHAT DO YOU WANT TO DO?

How to identify a second career without reschooling. How to identify what you most enjoy doing. What is going to put you ahead of the rest of the job-hunting public. How to be in control of your life, and improve your effectiveness 300%. The real meaning of "skills." How to avoid the deadend of "job descriptions." Exercises to help you know yourself, step-by-step. Interests vs. aptitudes. The salary you need.

CHAPTER SIX / PAGE 117

WHERE DO YOU WANT TO DO IT?

How many vacancies there are. How many want the job you want? How to be the sole applicant for a job. Where the jobs are. What will get you hired. Informational interviewing. How to get in to see the boss. Ways of finding out what an organization's problems are, and how you can help solve them. Thank-you letters and job-hunting success. Checklist: When Information-interviewing just doesn't seem to be working for you.

CHAPTER SEVEN / PAGE 171

YOU MUST IDENTIFY THE PERSON WHO HAS THE POWER TO HIRE YOU AND SHOW THEM HOW YOUR SKILLS CAN HELP THEM WITH THEIR PROBLEMS

Who to go see. Who to avoid. The nature of the hiring process. Why your prospective employer may fear the interview more than you. How you can help them. That old debbil: the resume. Interview checklist. Salary negotiation. How well this method works. The secret of getting hired. Postscript: When you've tried all this and still can't find a job.

APPENDIX A: DETAILED HELP / PAGE 205

THE QUICK JOB-HUNTING MAP
(Advanced Version)

APPENDIX B: RESOURCES GUIDE / PAGE 243

BOOKS, DEALING WITH:

1. The World of Work in America Today
2. Alternative Patterns of Work
3. Vocational or Career Planning
4. General Books on Job-Hunting
5. Job-Hunting Resources Especially for High School Students
6. For College Students
7. For Women
8. For Couples
9. For Minorities
10. For Handicapped Job-Hunters, including Ex-Offenders
11. For Executives and Those Interested in the Business World
12. On Your Own: Self-Employment, Part-Time Work
13. Making Your Living by Writing and Getting Published
14. Arts and Crafts, and Selling
15. Getting a Government Job
16. Volunteer Opportunities, Internships, and Organizations Dealing with Social Change
17. Mid-Life or Second Careers, on to Retirement
18. Resources Written from a Christian Perspective
19. The Nature of Your Brain and How to Stimulate Creativity and Decision-Making
20. Tuning Up Your Brain; Exercises, Images, Fantasy
21. Analysis of Skills
22. Interviewing, Resumes, etc.
23. Surviving on the Job, Surviving Burnout
24. Concerning Being Fired, Rejected, Riffed, or Laid-Off

APPENDIX C: RESOURCES GUIDE / PAGE 273

PROFESSIONAL HELP

If you're thinking of hiring a Career Counselor (Required Reading). Traps for the Unwary. Help for Anyone. Group support for the Unemployed. Help for Students or Graduates, for Women, for Clergy.

APPENDIX D / PAGE 303

WHEN MORE THAN CAREER COUNSELING IS NEEDED: BURNOUT

Symptoms. Transition burnout and its three stages. Three kinds of therapy: Courses of instruction, Short-term exploration, and Long-term psychotherapy. Guides and resources. How to choose a therapist.

APPENDIX E / PAGE 309

WHERE THE BEST JOBS ARE

Current predictions, what's wrong with them. The problems with occupational information. Questions most often asked: Should I go back to school? How do I get into an occupation that contributes toward changing our society? What can I do to create a job no one has ever heard of before, or go the self-employment route? How can I get a job in education / in government / in business / overseas?

UPDATE / PAGE 339 If a resource listed in this book has moved or is otherwise elusive, we'll try to track them down for you. And if you have a new idea/resource that helped you, we'd like to know about it.

HOTLINE / PAGE 340 If you've read this entire book and have used the Quick Job-Hunting Map on page 206 but are still having trouble, we'll see if we can suggest a resource person in your area who might be able to help you.

MAILING LIST & NEWSLETTER / PAGE 343
For counselors and other interested professionals.

INDEX / PAGE 326
AUTHOR INDEX / PAGE 335

Fairy Godmother,
where were you
when I needed you?

Cinderella

CHAPTER ONE

A Job-Hunting We Will Go

Okay, this is it.
You've been idly thinking about it, off and on, for
some time now, wondering what it would be like.
To be earning your bread in the marketplace.
Or maybe you're already out there,
And the problem is choosing another job—or career—
The old one having run out of gas, as it were.
Anyhow, the moment of truth has arrived.
For one reason or another, you've got to get at it—
Go out, and look for a job, for the first time or the twentieth.
You've heard of course, all the horror stories.
Of ex-executives working as taxi-drivers
Of former college profs with two masters degrees
working as countermen in a delicatessen.
Of women Ph.D.s who can only get a job as a secretary.
Of laid-off auto-workers waiting for the call (back to work)
that never comes.
And you wonder what lies in store for *you*.

Of course, it may be that the problem is all solved.
Maybe some friend or relative has button-holed you
and said, "Why not come and work for me?"
So, your job-hunt ends before it begins.
Or, it may be that you came into your present
career after a full life doing something else, and
You know you're welcome back there, anytime;
Anytime, they said.
And, assuming they meant it,
no problem, right?
So long as that's what you still want to do.
Or maybe you've decided this is the time to
adopt a simpler way of living,
And, so far, it's going well.
But for the vast majority of us,
that isn't how it goes.
We have to find a job, we do,
And no one's making it any easier.
We feel like Don Quixote, mounted, lance in hand; and
the job-hunt is our windmill.

Those who have gone this way before us
all tell us the very same thing:
This is how we all go about it, when our job-hunting time has come:
We procrastinate,
That's what we do.
Busy winding things up, we say.
Or, just waiting until we feel a little less 'burnt-out' and
more 'up' for the task ahead, we say.
Actually, if the truth were known,
we're hoping for that miracle,
you know the one:
that if we just sit tight a little longer,
we won't have to go job-hunting at all, because
the job will come hunting for us.
Right in our front door, it will come.
To show us we are destiny's favorites,
Or to prove that God truly loves us.
But, it doesn't, of course, and
eventually, we realize, with more than a touch of franticness,
that time and money
are beginning to run out.

Time to begin our job-hunt (or career change) in deadly earnest.
And all of our familiar friends immediately
are at our elbow, giving advice—
solicited or unsolicited, as to what it is we should do.
"Jean or Joe, I've always thought you would make a great teacher."
So we ask who they know
in the academic world,
and, armed with that name,
we go a-calling. Calling, and
sitting, cooling our heels
in the ante-room of the Dean's office,
until we are ushered in, at last:
"And what can I do for you, Mr. or Ms.?"
We tell them, of course, that we're job-hunting.
"And one of my friends thought that you..."
Oops. We watch the face change,

And we (who *do* know something about body language),
Wait to hear their words catch up with their body.
"You feel I'm 'over-qualified'? I see.
Two hundred applications, you say, already in hand
For five vacancies? I see.
No, of course I understand."
Strike-out. Back to the drawingboard. More advice, from well-meaning family or friends:
"Jean or Joe, have you tried the employment agencies?"
"Good thinking. Which ones should I try?
The ones that deal with professionals? Where are they?
Okay. Good. Down I'll go."
And down we do go.
Down, down, down, to those agencies.
The ante-room again.
And those other hopeful, haunted faces.
A new twist, however: our first bout
with The Application Form.
"Previous jobs held.
List in reverse chronological order."
Filling all the questions out. Followed by
That interminable wait.
And then, at last, the interviewer,
She of the over-cheerful countenance, and mien—
She talks to us. "Now, let's see, Mr. or Ms.,
What kind of a job are you looking for?"
"Well," we say,
"What do you think I could do?"
She studies, again, the application form;
"It seems to me," she says, "that with your background
—it is a *bit* unusual—
You might do very well in sales."
"Oh, sales," we say. "Why yes," says she, "in fact
I think that I could place you almost immediately.
We'll be in touch with you. Is this your phone?"
We nod, and shake her hand, and that is the
Last time
We ever hear from her.
Words are apparently not always to be believed;
Sometimes they are used just to soften rejection.
Strike out, number two.

Now, our original ballooning hopes that we would quickly land a job
are running into some frigid air,
So we decide to confess at last
Our need of help — to some of our more successful friends
in the business world (if we have such)
Who *surely* know what we should do, at this point.
The windmill is tiring us. What would they suggest
that Don (or Donna) Quixote should do?
"Well," say they (beaming warmly), "what kind of a job
are you looking for?"
Ah, *that*, again! "Well, you know me well, what do you think
I can do? I'll try almost anything,"
we say, now that it's four minutes to midnight, as it were.
"You know, with all the *kinds* of things I've done —"
we say; "I mean, I've done this and that, and here and there,
It all adds up to a kind of puzzling kaleidoscope; but you see things
That I don't see, so there must be *something* you can suggest!"

"Have you tried the want-ads?" asks our friend.
"Or have you gone to see Bill, and Ed, and John, and Frances and Marty?
Ah, no? Well tell them I sent you."
So, off we go—now newly armed, with new advice.
We study the want-ads. Gad, what misery is hidden in
Those little boxes. Misery in jobs which are built
As little boxes, for the large spirits of men and women.
But, nevertheless we dutifully send our resume, such as it is,
To every box that looks as though
It might not be a box.
And wait for the avalanche of replies, from bright-eyed people
Who, seeing our resume, will surely know
Our worth; even if, at this point, our worth seems increasingly
Questionable in our own eyes.
Avalanche? Not even a rolling stone. (Sorry about that, Bob.) Not a pebble.

Well, time to go see all those people that our friend said we
ought to go see.
You know: Bill, and Ed, and John, and Frances and Marty.
They seem slightly perplexed, as to why we've come,
And in the dark about exactly
Just exactly what it is they are supposed to do for us.
We try to take them off the hook; "I thought, friend of my friend,
Your company might need—of course, my experience *has*
Been limited, but I am willing, and I thought perhaps
that you..."

The interview drags on, downhill now, all the way
As our host finishes out the courtesy debt,
Not to us but to the friend that sent us; and
then it is time for us to go.
Boy, do we go! over hill and valley and dale,
Talking to everyone who will listen,
Listening to everyone who will talk
With us; and thinking that surely there must be
Someone who knows how to crack this terribly frustrating
job-market;

This job-hunt process seems the loneliest task of our lives.
And we idly wonder: is it this difficult for other people?
Well, friend, the answer is *YES.*

Are other people *this* discouraged, and desperate
And frustrated, and so low in self-esteem after
A spell of job-hunting?
The answer, again—unhappily—is
YES.

YES.

YES.

Well, yes, you do have great big teeth; but, never mind that. You were great to at least grant me this interview.

Little Red Riding Hood

CHAPTER TWO

Rejection Shock

OUR NEANDERTHAL JOB-HUNTING PROCESS

Sure, the preceding account of the job-hunt is rather bleak. But it has happened, is happening, and will continue to happen to countless millions of job-hunters in just the fashion described (or even worse). Including you and me.

Is it because we are different from other job-hunters? No. This happens to about 95% of all the people in this country who get involved in the job-hunt, at one time or other in their lives.

Let us put the matter simply and candidly: The whole process of the job-hunt in this country is Neanderthal. (Say it again, Sam.)

In spite of the fact that nearly every adult American man and, presently, some 45 million women have been or will be involved in the job-hunt at some time in their lives, we are condemned to go about the job-hunt as though we were the first person in this country to have to do it.

Year after year, our 'system' condemns man after man and woman after woman to go down the same path, face the same problems, make the same mistakes, endure the same frustrations, go through the same loneliness, and end up either still unemployed after an inordinately long period of time, or –

what is much more likely – underemployed, in the wrong field, at the wrong job, or well below the peak of our abilities. Neanderthal, indeed!

And when we turn to the "experts" in this field to say, "Show me a better way," we are chagrined to discover that the genuine experts (who *do* exist) are few and far between, and awfully difficult to find; while most of those whom the world accounts as experts (so-called "personnel people" or "human resource developers") are – in their quiet, meditative moments, and in their heart of hearts – *just as baffled by this job-hunt, and just as aware that they haven't yet come up with the answer to it, as we are.*

"Let's put it this way—if you can find a village without an idiot, you've got yourself a job."

This is never more clear than when *they themselves* are out of a job, and have to join the multitude in "pounding the pavements." You would think that they would absolutely be in their element, and know just precisely what to do. Yet the average executive (even the personnel executive) who yesterday was screening, interviewing and hiring any number of people, is just as much at a loss as anyone else *to know how to go about the job-hunt systematically, methodically, and successfully.*

Very often, the best plan they can suggest to themselves is the best plan they could suggest, in the past, to others: "The numbers game." That's right, the numbers game. It sometimes has a somewhat more sophisticated title (like, say, *systematic job search*), but in most cases this is what it comes down to, and this is what a number of experts are honest enough to call it.

THE NUMBERS GAME

In its original evolution, someone must have worked it all out, *backwards*. It wouldn't have been all that difficult. The logic would have gone like this:

For the job-hunter to get a job they really like, they need to have two or three job offers to choose among, from different employers.

In order to get those two or three offers, the job-hunter probably ought to have *at least* six interviews at different companies.

In order to get those six interviews he or she must mount a direct mail campaign, sending out *x* resumes to prospective employers, with covering letters, or whatever other kind of mail will titillate prospective employers and their screening committees (personnel department, executive secretaries, et al.) like: telegrams, special delivery letters, or whatever. So, how many is *"x"*? Well surveys have indicated that each 100 resumes sent out will get either 1-2[1], or 2-3[2] or 3-4[3] invitations for the job-hunter to come in for an interview, – the figure depending on which expert you are talking to, listening to or reading.

Consequently, the conclusion of this game is that you should send out at least 500 resumes, with some experts saying 1,000 or 1,200, and others saying that there is no limit: send out 10-15 each day, say they, keeping a card-file on them, recording each outcome – responses, completed interviews and so forth.

In a nutshell, that is The Numbers Game – the best that the personnel system in this country has been able to come up with (except for a creative minority – more about them later).

You like?

---

1. Executive Register, 72 Park Street, New Canaan, Conn. 06840, cited this figure.
2. Albee, Lou, *Job Hunting After Forty*, cites this figure (on his page 137).
3. Uris, Auren, *Action Guide for Executive Job Seekers and Employers*, cites this figure (on his page 149).

Most of the job-hunting books you can pick up at your local bookstore for five or ten bucks will sell you this game.

Most of the job counselors you can go to (paying fees up to $3,000 or higher) will sell you little more than this game – with maybe a little psychological testing and video-taped interview-role-playing thrown in.

Most of the personnel people in whose offices you may sit, will counsel you for nothing, . . . but *in this game.*

There may be a few variations here and there: and sometimes this old game is hidden under an exquisitely clever new vocabulary, so it sounds like a very different system. But if you are listening carefully to what they are saying, you will suddenly awake to realize it is, in the end, The Little Ol' Game We've All Come To Love and Know So Well: Numbers.

HOW WELL DOES IT WORK?

Now, let's face facts: no matter how much of a gamble it sounds, for *some* people this numbers game works exceedingly well. They luck in. They end up with just the job they wanted, and they are ecstatically happy about the whole thing . . . especially if they were engaged in only aimless job-hunting behavior prior to stumbling upon this plan. This works just beautifully, by contrast – *for some people.*

For other people, this numbers game works passably well. They end up with a job of sorts, and a salary, even though in retrospect it is not really the kind of work they had been hoping for, and the salary is quite a bit below what they really needed or wanted. But . . . a job is a job is a job. Parenthetically, the one thing that the job-hunt 'system' in this country does, and does exceedingly well, is scaring people to the point where they are more willing to lower their self-esteem and hence their expectations as to what they will settle for. So, the numbers game works passably, as far as some people are concerned.

But for the vast majority of people who use this 'system' (some 80-95% of them, we guess) it just doesn't work at all – and particularly for those who are trying to break into a new career. With some notable exceptions, second-careerists have the most difficulty with this system.

Thus, some job-hunters have sent out 400, 500, 600, 700, 800 resumes or more, without getting one single invitation to come in for an interview. Only the polite acknowledgement ("thank you for yours of the sixteenth. We regret . . . ") or the polite turndown ("we will however keep your resume on file (in the wastebasket!) and should anything . . . ", or – in many cases, no answer at all.

PEOPLE-IN-THE-FORM-OF-PAPER

Nor, from the *company's* point of view, is it difficult to see why. Some companies receive as many as 250,000 resumes in a year. And even small companies may receive as many as ten to fifteen a week. The employment world floats on a sea of resumes, as some experts have observed.[1] Hence, in dealing with resumes at employers' headquarters, the key word for the personnel department (and executive secretaries) is not selection, but *elimination.* (Of course, if you're agriculturally minded – or Biblically minded – you may prefer: *winnowing the crop.)* Here, to a particular organization, flows in this endless stack of People-in-the-Form-of-Paper, day after day. If you're working there, and they hand that stack to you, what do you do with it? Well, of course. You go through it, to see if you can get the stack down to more manageable size. You look to see who you can eliminate.

Who gets nominated for this dubious honor? Well, $140 a week file-clerks who are applying for a President's job. And $140,000 a year Presidents who are willing to settle for file-clerks' jobs. And resumes so poorly written you can't tell anything about the men or women behind them. And resumes so slickly written (usually by a hired professional) that you can't tell anything about the man or woman behind them. And . . . people applying for a job for which they look as though they

1. Snelling, Robert, *The Opportunity Explosion,* p. 129.

do not have the necessary qualifying experience or credentials. Indeed, the resumes that have the greatest difficulty in getting through this Screening Process are those belonging to Zig Zag people, would-be career-changers who've accumulated a lot of experience in their old Zig profession, and now are trying to Zag. Their resumes, unless they are done extremely cleverly, find this Screening Out Process is a killer.

Well, all in all, how likely is *your* resume to survive the Process? A study of a number of different companies has revealed that they send out only one invitation to an interview for every 245 resumes that they receive *on an average.* But this average represents a range between companies which consent to one interview for every 36 resumes they receive, and companies which send out only one invitation to an interview for every 1,188 resumes they receive.[1] In terms of the first process that resumes are subjected to, therefore, the Screening Out Process searches for reasons to eliminate 35 out of every 36 resumes if we are lucky; or for reasons to eliminate on up to 1,187 out of every 1,188 resumes received if we're dealing with a tough company or market.

You are of course free to doubt these statistics and decide they are simply unbelievable. Or, you may want to make your resume *the one that gets through.* Or, you may want to know a better system altogether than the Numbers Game. We will try to point out aids for all three groups: the Doubters, the System-beaters, and the Alternatives-seekers.

REJECTION SHOCK

But, first of all, every job-hunter owes it to him- or herself to *understand* the system. What it is. How it works. What its limitations are. What its out-and-out defects are.

Why? Well, first of all, to save yourself from Rejection Shock. Rejection Shock occurs when you set out to look for a job, confidently follow all the instructions that you are given about the Numbers Game (via books, articles, friends or paid professionals) only to discover that none of this works *for you* and after a lengthy period of time you are still unemployed. You then go into personal psychological Shock, characterized by a slow or

1. Deutsch, Shea & Evans, Inc. quoted on page 73 in *Electronic Design 16.*

rapid erosion of your self-esteem, a conviction that there is something wrong *with you*, leading in turn to lower expectations, depression, desperation and/or apathy. This assumes, consequently, all the proportions of a major crisis in your life, your personal relations and your family, leading to loneliness, irritability, and withdrawal, where divorce is often a consequence and even suicide is not unthinkable.[1] *(One major executive career counselor did a survey of 15,000 clients, and discovered that 75% of them were either facing, in the midst of, or just out of, a marital divorce.)*[2]

Rejection Shock also occurs when you set out to look for a job, confidently follow all the instructions you are given about the Numbers Game, only to discover that this only *partially* works for you, and after a lengthy period of time (often) you have gotten a job in which you are *under-employed.* You are in the wrong field, or at the wrong job, or well below the peak of your abilities. You go into Shock, consequently, because though you have a job you feel under-valued, ill-at-ease, underpaid and poorly-used, *and* you think you must be content with this under-employment *because you think that something is fundamentally wrong with you.* In the midst of Shock, as you are, it never occurs to you that perhaps something is fundamentally wrong with *the whole job-hunting 'system' in this country.*

A NATIONAL TRAGEDY

It should be every job-hunter's high purpose to avoid not only the obvious devil of Un-employment, but also the less-obvious devil of Under-employment, with every resource that is at your command. And, more than that, to determine to help

1. See Albee, Lou, *Job Hunting After Forty.*
2. In a study conducted by J. Frederick Marcy and Associates.

others to understand the Neanderthal 'system' in this country, so that they too may be spared the blight of these two devils.

Insiders estimate that even in Good Times 80% of our working people are Under-employed.[1] One doesn't want to even think what the figure might be during Hard Times. Certainly, in any case, this is a national tragedy. But people submit to it because they regard Under-employment as preferable to Un-employment. They prefer pounding a typewriter to pounding the pavements.

And in this instinctive fear, they are quite right. Insiders again and again announce statistics which reveal that those who regard the job-hunt as an occasion for leaping to a better job are taking a big gamble, and especially so if they are either on in years (polite euphemism) or unemployed, or both. Witness these statistics with regard to men in particular:

Of the several thousand middle-aged men who lose their jobs this month, one year from now 80% will be unemployed, under-employed (at lesser salary than before), or eking out a private income, even in Good Times, estimates one insider.[2]

Three million people are trying to get better jobs (at over $30,000 a year), and of these, 75% will not succeed in finding them – estimates another insider.[3]

A year from now, 20% of those middle-aged men who lose their jobs will still be unemployed.[4]

The cause *in large measure:* failure to understand the job-hunting system in this country.

The result: Rejection Shock.

Tragedy.

1. California State University at Fullerton, in its *CP &PC News*, reported a sixteen year study of 350,000 job applicants, which concluded that 80% were in the wrong jobs. As did Herbert Greenberg, president of Marketing Survey and Research Corporation (*The Futurist*, August, 1978).
2. Albee, *op. cit.*, p. 3.
3. John C. Crystal.
4. Albee, *op. cit.*, p. 3.

HOW TO USE THE NUMBERS GAME, INSTEAD OF BEING USED BY IT

A second reason why every job-hunter ought to understand the numbers game, in all its parts, is you may want to use *some* parts of it to *supplement* your main program outlined in chapters 4 through 7.

A study of *The Job Hunt* by Harold L. Sheppard and A. Harvey Belitsky[1] revealed that the greater the number of auxiliary avenues used by the job-hunter, the greater the job-finding success. It makes sense, therefore, to know *all* the avenues that are open to you, how they work and what their limitations are, so that you can choose *which* avenue or avenues you want to use, and *how* you want to use them. You will then be in the driver's seat about these matters, as you should be.

The parts of this game most commonly alluded to are:

- mailing out your resume
- contacting executive search firms
- answering newspaper ads
- placing newspaper ads
- going to private employment (or placement) agencies
- going to the federal/state employment agency
- contacting college placement firms
- using executive registers or other forms of clearinghouses
- making personal contacts through friends, personal referrals and so forth.

Let us look at the virtues, and defects, of each of these, in rapid succession; to see why they usually don't work — and how you might get around their limitations. I will quote some statistics as I go along, in order to *illustrate* the aforementioned defects. You will note that some of these statistics are not, ahem, *current* — to put it gently. That's because the most recent study about this-or-that part of the numbers game was done some years ago, and after seeing the depressing findings, no one has thought it useful to repeat that study since that time. And, believe me — the numbers game *hasn't* changed that much, since the studies cited. So, on with our exciting story.

---

1. In their book, *The Job Hunt: Job-Seeking Behavior of Unemployed Workers in a Local Economy.*

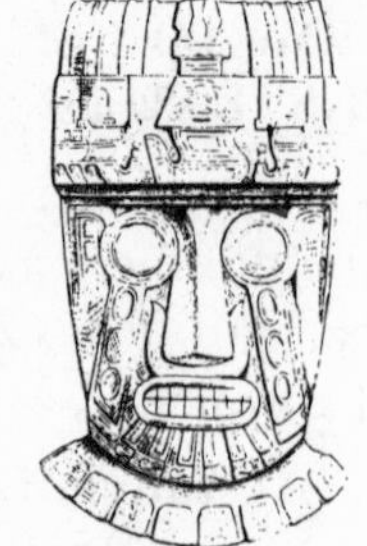

HEADHUNTERS, OTHERWISE KNOWN AS EXECUTIVE SEARCH FIRMS

If you play the numbers game, and especially if you pay someone to guide you through it, you will be told to send your resume to Executive Search firms. And what, pray tell, are *they?* Well, they are recruiting firms that are retained by employers. The very existence of this thriving industry testifies to the fact that employers are as baffled by our country's Neanderthal job-hunting 'system' as we are. Employers don't know how to find decent employees, any more than we know how to find decent employers. So, what do employers want executive recruiting firms to do? They want these firms to *hire away* from other firms or employers, executives, salespeople, technicians, or whatever, who are already employed, and rising. From this, you will realize these head-hunting firms are aware of, and trying to fill, known vacancies. That's why, in any decent scattergun sending out of your resume, you are advised – by any number of experts – to be sure and include Executive Search firms. Not surprisingly, there are even a number of enterprising souls who make a living by selling lists of such firms.

You can get lists of such firms from:

1. The American Management Association, Inc., 135 W. 50th St., New York, NY 10020, in a list entitled *Executive Employment Guide,* $2.
2. The Association of Executive Recruiting Consultants, 30 Rockefeller Plaza, New York, NY 10112 has its own list of sixty top recruiters. Also $2.
3. R.R. Bowker publishes an *Association of Executive Recruiting Consultants, 1981 Directory.* Their address is 1180 Avenue of the Americas, New York, NY 10036.
4. Consultants News, Templeton Rd., Fitzwilliam, NY 03447 has a *Directory of Executive Recruiters* which lists 2,300 search firms and offices in the U.S. and abroad. $12, prepaid. Updated annually.

The question is: do you *want* these lists, i.e., are they going to do you any good?

Well, let's say you regard yourself as an executive, and so you decide to send recruiters your resume (unsolicited – they didn't

EXECUTIVE RECRUITERS

Name: Executive recruitment consultants, executive recruiters, executive search firms, executive development specialists, management consultants.

Nicknames: head-hunters, flesh peddlers, body snatchers, talent scouts.

Number: estimated by James H. Kennedy, editor of *Consultants News*, to total 2,300.

Volume of business: they have combined billings of more than $300 million a year, currently.[1]

Number of vacancies handled by a firm: each staff member can only handle 6-8 searches at a time (as a rule)[2]; so, multiply number of staff that a firm has (if known) times six. Majority of firms

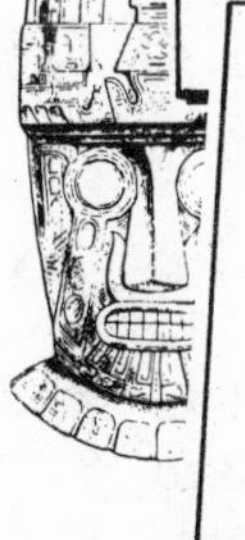

are one-two staff (hence, are handling 5-10 current openings); a few are four to five staff (20-25 openings are being searched for); and the largest have staffs handling 80-100 openings.

ask you to send it, you just sent it). The average Executive Search firm may get as many as 100 to 300 such resumes a week. Or "broadcast" letters. And, as we see above, the majority of such firms may be handling five to ten *current openings*, for which they are looking for executives who are presently employed and rising.

Well okay, that Executive Recruiter is sitting there with 100 to 300 resumes in his or her hands, at the end of that week – yours (and mine) among them. You know what's about to happen to that stack of People-in-the-Form-of-Paper. That old Elimination, Winnowing, or Screening Process again. Your chances of surviving? Well, the first to get eliminated will be those who—

1. *Business Week,* May 5, 1980.
2. Butler, L.A., *Move In and Move Up,* pp. 160-61.

a) are not presently exeuctives, or b) are not presently employed as such, or c) are not presently rising in their firm.[1]

That's why even in a good business year, many experts say to the unemployed: *Forget it!* I do think it is necessary, however, to point out that things are changing in the Executive Recruiting field. For one thing, some firms now call themselves Executive Recruiters when yesterday they would have been called Employment Agencies. These new Recruiters do indeed represent employers; but they are hungry for the names of job-hunters, and in many cases will interview a job-hunter who comes into the office unannounced or mails them a resume. I have known so-called Recruiters who truly extended themselves on behalf of very inexperienced job-hunters. So, were I job-hunting this year, I think I would get one of the aforementioned Directories, look up the firms that specialize in my particular kind of job or field, and go take a crack at them. I wouldn't have done that twelve years ago, when *Parachute* first came out. But mercy, how times change!

ANSWERING NEWSPAPER ADS

Experts will advise you, for the sake of thoroughness, to study the job advertisements in your newspaper *daily* and to study *all of them, from A to Z* – because ads are alphabetized by job title; and there are some very strange and unpredictable job titles floating around. Then you are advised that if you see an ad for which you might qualify, even three quarters, send off:

a) your resume, OR
b) your resume and a covering letter, OR
c) just a covering letter.

In short, you're still playing the Numbers Game, when you answer ads. And the odds are stacked against you just about as badly as when you send out your resume scatter-gun fashion. How badly? (Better sit down before reading further.) A comparatively recent study conducted in two sample cities revealed

1. If you want to know more about the executive recruiting world, and what it is that the job-hunter can learn from recruiters, see your library or bookstore for the excellent *Secrets of a Corporate Headhunter* by John Wareham (Atheneum, New York, 1980).

(and I quote) "that 85% of the employers in San Francisco, and 75% in Salt Lake City, did not hire any employees through want ads" in a typical year. Yes, that said *any* employees, *during the whole year.*[1] Well, then why are ads *run?* For the fascinating answer to that, read "Blind Ad Man's Bluff" in David Noer's *How to Beat The Employment Game.*[2]

NEWSPAPER ADS

Where Found:

1. In the business section of the Sunday *New York Times* and the education section; also in Sunday editions of the *Chicago Tribune* and the *Los Angeles Times.*
2. In the business section (often found with the sports section) of your daily paper; also daily *Wall Street Journal* (especially Tuesday and Wednesday's editions).
3. In the classified section of your daily paper (and Sunday's, too).

Jobs Advertised: usually those which have a clear-cut title, well-defined specifications, and for which either many job-hunters can qualify, or very few.

Number of Resumes received by Employer as Result of the Ad: 20-1,000, commonly.

Time It Takes Resumes to Come In: 48-96 hours. Third day is usually the peak day, after ad is placed.

Number of Resumes NOT Screened Out: Only 2-5 out of every 100 (normally) survive. In other words, 95-98 out of every 100 answers *are* screened out.

---

1. Olympus Research Corporation, *A Study To Test the Feasibility of Determining Whether Classified Ads in Daily Newspapers are An Accurate Reflection of Local Labor Markets and of Significance to Employers and Job Seekers.* 1973. From: Olympus Research Corporation, 1290 24th Avenue, San Francisco, CA 94122.
2. Ten Speed Press, Box 7123, Berkeley, CA 94707. $4.95. Or at your local library.

THINGS TO BEWARE OF IN NEWSPAPER ADS

FAKE ADS (positions advertised which don't exist)—usually run by placement firms or others, in order to fatten their "resume bank" for future clout with employers.

BLIND ADS (no company name, just a box number). These, according to some insiders, are particularly unrewarding to to the job-hunter's time.

PHONE NUMBERS in ads: don't use them except to set up an appointment. Period. ("I can't talk right now. I'm calling from the office.") Beware of saying more. Avoid getting screened out prematurely over the telephone.

THOSE PHRASES which need lots of translating, like:

"Energetic self-starter wanted" (= You'll be working on commission)

"Good organizational skills" (= You'll be handling the filing)

"Make an investment in your future" (= This is a franchise or pyramid scheme)

"Much client contact" (= You handle the phone, or make 'cold calls' on clients)

"Planning and coordinating" (= You book the boss's travel arrangements)

"Opportunity of a lifetime" (= No where else will you find such a low salary and so much work)

"Management training position" (= You'll be a salesperson with a wide territory)

"Varied, interesting travel" (= You'll be a salesperson with a wide territory)

Of course, you may be one who still likes to cover all bets, and if so, you will want to know how *your* resume can be the one that gets through the Screening Process. (Let's be honest: answering ads *has* paid off, for *some* job-hunters.)

Most of the experts say, *if* you're going to play this game:

1. All you're trying to do, in answering the ad, is to get invited in for an interview (rather than getting screened out). Period. So, quote the ad's specifications, and tailor your resume or case history letter (if you prefer *that* to a resume) – so that *you* fit their specifications as closely as possible.

2. Omit all else from your response (so there is no further excuse for Screening you out). Volunteer *nothing* else. Period.

3. *If* the ad requested salary requirements, some experts say ignore the request; others say, state a salary range (of as much as three to ten thousand dollars variation) adding the words "depending on the nature and scope of duties and responsibilities," or words to that effect. If the ad does not mention salary requirements, *don't you either.* Why give an excuse for getting your response Screened Out?

PLACING ADS YOURSELF

Sometimes job-hunters try to make their availability known, by placing ads themselves in newspapers or journals.

PLACING ADS

Name of Ads (Commonly): Positions wanted (by the job-hunter, that is).

Found in: *Wall Street Journal,* professional journals and in trade association publications.

Effectiveness: Very effective in getting responses from employment agencies, peddlers, salesmen, and so forth. Practically worthless in getting responses from prospective employers, who rarely read these ads. But it *has* worked for some job-hunters.

Recommendation: If you take odds seriously, you'd better forget it. Unless, just to cover all bets, you want to place some ads in professional journals appropriate to your field. Study other people's formats first, though.

Cost: Varies.

ASKING PRIVATE EMPLOYMENT AGENCIES FOR HELP

PRIVATE EMPLOYMENT AGENCIES

Number: Nobody Knows, since new ones are born, and old ones die, every week. There are probably at least 8,000 private employment or placement agencies in the U.S.

Specialization: Many specialize in executives, financial, data processing, or other specialties.

Fees: Employer; or job-hunter may pay *but only when and if hired*. Fees vary from state to state. Tax deductible. In New York, for example, a fee cannot exceed 60% of one month's salary, i.e., a $15,000 a year job will cost you $750. The fee may be paid in weekly installments of 10% (e.g., $75 on a $750 total). In 80% of executives' cases, it is the employer who pays the fee.

Contract: The application form filled out by the job-hunter at an agency *is* the contract.

Exclusive handling: Generally speaking, don't give it, even if they ask for it.

Nature of business: Primarily a volume business, requiring rapid turnover of clientele, with genuine attention given only to the most-marketable job-hunters, in what one insider has called "a short-term matching game."

Effectiveness: Some time back, a spokesman for the Federal Trade Commission announced that the average placement rate for employment agencies was only 5% of those who walked in the door. (That means a 95% failure rate, right?)

PRIVATE EMPLOYMENT AGENCIES continued

Loyalty: Agency's loyalty in the very nature of things must lie with those who pay the bills (which in most cases is the employer), and those who represent repeat business (again, employers).

Evaluation: An agency, with its dependency on rapid-turnover volume business, usually has no time to deal with *any* problems (like, career-transitions). *Possible exception for you to investigate:* a new, or suddenly expanding agency, which needs job-hunters badly if it is ever to get employers' business.

ASKING THE FEDERAL-STATE EMPLOYMENT SERVICE FOR HELP

UNITED STATES EMPLOYMENT SERVICE

Old Name: Was called USTES – United States Training and Employment Service, 2,600 offices in the country. USES (often called "Job Service") has been greatly reduced in staff and budget recently.

Services: Most state offices of USES not only serve entry level workers, but also have services for professionals. Washington, D.C. had most innovative one. Middle management (and up) job-hunters still tend to avoid it.

Nationwide Network: In any city (as a rule) you can inquire about job opportunities in other states or cities, for a particular field. Also see Job Bank (page 30).

UNITED STATES EMPLOYMENT SERVICE continued

Openings: Nine million non-agricultural job vacancies were listed with USES in 1979.

Placements: Of the 15+ million registering with USES in 1979, approximately 30% were placed in jobs. Almost half of these were blue-collar jobs, and another quarter were white-collar jobs. A survey of one area raised some question about the quality of placement, moreover, when it was discovered that 57% of those placed in that geographical area by USES were not working at their jobs anymore, just 30 days later.[1] (That would reduce the placement rate to 17%, *at best*; an 83% failure rate. It's probably closer to 13.7% placement, hence an 86.3% failure rate.)

1. The San Francisco Bay Area, for the period January 1966 thru April 1967, as reported in *Placement and Counseling In a Changing Labor Market: Public and Private Employment Agencies and Schools.* Report of the San Francisco Bay Area Placement and Counseling Survey, by Margaret Thal-Larsen. HR Institute of Industrial Relations, UC Berkeley, August, 1970.

COLLEGE PLACEMENT CENTERS

COLLEGE PLACEMENT OFFICES

Where Located: Most of the institutions of higher education in this country have some kind of placement function, however informal.

Helpfulness: Some are very good, because they understand that job-hunting will be a repetitive activity throughout the lives of their students; hence they try to teach an empowering process of self-directed job-hunting. Other offices, however, still think they have done their job if they have helped "each student find a job upon graduation," through the use of recruiters, bulletin board listings, and the like; i.e., if they help their students with this one job-hunt this one time.

Evaluation: Visit, to see whether they teach skills in "management by initiative," or only in "management by invitation." Not likely to be terribly helpful with alumni, though some, like UCLA's, are.

SUBSCRIBING TO REGISTERS OR CLEARINGHOUSES OF VACANCIES

REGISTERS OR CLEARING-HOUSE OPERATIONS

These are attempts to set up "job exchanges" or a kind of bulletin board where employer and job-hunter can meet. The private clearinghouses commonly handle both employer and job-hunter listings, charging each.

Types: federal and private; general and specialized fields; listing either future projected openings, or present ones; listing employers' vacancies, or job-hunters' resumes (in brief), or both.

Cost to Job-Hunter: ranges from free, to $75 or more.

Effectiveness: A register may have as many as 13,000 clients registered with it (if it is a private operation), and (let us say) 500 openings at one time, from employer clients. Some registers will let employer know of every client who is eligible; others will pick out the few best ones. You must figure out what the odds for you as job-hunter are. A newer register *may* do more for you than an older one.

This is a very popular idea, and new entrants in the field are appearing constantly. On the following cards, we list some examples:

REGISTERS ETC.
continued

General Clearinghouse Listing Present Vacancies: The State Employment Offices in 48 states, covering more than 300 separate labor market areas, have set up a computerized (in most cities) *job bank* to provide daily listings of job openings in that city. If every employer cooperated and listed every opening they had, each day, it would be a great concept. Unhappily, employers prefer to fill many jobs above $11,000 in more personal, informal ways. So the Job Bank remains a rather limited resource for such jobs. *Can be a helpful research instrument,* however. A summary of the job orders placed by employers at Job Banks during the previous month is published under the title of "Occupations In Demand At Job Service Offices." Available from: Superintendent of Documents, U.S. Government Printing Office, Washington, D.C. 20402.

A Clearinghouse of Newspaper Ads: The idea of someone reading on your behalf the classified sections of a lot of newspapers in this country, and publishing a summary thereof on a weekly basis (or so), is not a new idea – but it is apparently growing increasingly popular. Problem: how old the ads may be by the time you the subscriber read them. That answer will turn out to be the

REGISTERS ETC.
continued

sum of the following times: a) the time it took for the hometown paper, in which the ad first appeared, to be sent to the town in which the clearinghouse operates; plus b) the time the clearinghouse held on to the ad, – especially if it just missed "last week's" edition of the clearinghouse Report; plus c) the time it took, after insertion in the Report, before the Report came 'off the press'; plus d) the time it took for the clearinghouse's Report to get across the country to you (discount this last, if you live in the clearinghouse's backyard; otherwise give this Large Weight, especially if it is not sent First Class/Airmail – or have you forgotten about our

beloved Postal Service?); plus e) the time it takes to get your response from your town to the town in which the ad appeared. You'll recall from page 21 that most classified ads receive more than enough responses within 96 hours of the ad's first appearing; how likely an employer is to wait for you to send in your response many days, or even weeks, later, is something you must evaluate for yourself – and weigh that against the cost of the service. If you want it, there are several places offering this service. Among the most reliable: the *Wall Street Journal* publishes a weekly compilation of "career-advancement positions" from its four regional

REGISTERS, ETC.
continued

editions. $2.75, maybe $3 an issue, by the time you read this. Available on some newsstands, or order from: National Business Employment Weekly, c/o the *Wall Street Journal*, 22 Cortlandt St., New York, NY 10007.

Register for College Graduates (And Others): Career Placement Registry, a subsidiary of Plenum Publishing Corp. (with its DIALOG computerized information network), located at 302 Swann Ave., Alexandria, VA 22301, will list a mini-resume of a student in their computerized data base, for $8 (currently). It will list other applicants for $15 to $40, depending on the salary level sought. A person wishing to be listed in this system fills out a form specifying what he or she is looking for – has 500 fields to choose from, on the form. Educational background, job experience, geographic preference and salary requirements also get entered. Employers wanting a specific kind of employee then pay for a search that gives them up to twelve names. Phone: 800-368-3093.

Register for Teachers Interested in California: For bi-weekly listings of San Francisco Bay Area positions in post-secondary education, write to: P.I.P.E., 1850 Union St., San Francisco, CA 94123, or call 415-921-7673. $1.70 for current issue.

Registers in the Church: Intercristo is a national Christian organization that lists over 23,000 jobs, covering 4,600 vocational categories, available within about 700 Christian organizations in the U.S. or overseas. Their service, called Intermatch, costs the job-hunter $25. In 1979, one out of every twelve job-hunters who used this service found a job thereby. Their address is 19303 Fremont Ave. N., Seattle, WA 98133, and they have a toll-free telephone number: 800-426-1342.

OTHER REGISTERS OR CLEARINGHOUSES:

Is a thing a register or not? If job listings exist all by themselves, they tend to be legitimately called "registers." If they exist within the framework of a journal or magazine which also contains other material, they tend to be called "ads." There is a list of such journals; see Feingold, S. Norman, and Hansard-Winkler, Glenda Ann, *900,000 Plus Jobs Annually: Published sources of employment listings.* Garrett Park Press, Garrett Park, MD 20896. $8.95, prepaid. Lists more than 900 journals which carry employment want ads. The following list straddles both sides:[1]

For Social Occupations: Volunteers for Educational and Social Services, 3001 S. Congress Ave., Austin, TX 78704 publishes a list of jobs available. The National Association of Social Workers Personnel Information, 1425 H St., NW, Ste. 600, Washington, DC 20005 publishes a listing of clearinghouses, called *Job Opportunities in Social Work.* The Family Service Association of America, 44 E. 23rd St., New York, NY 10010 publishes *Social Casework*, a journal which includes listings of jobs with social agencies.

For Jobs In Criminal Justice: The *NELS Monthly Bulletin*, National Employment Listing Service, Criminal Justice Center, Sam Houston State Univ., Huntsville, TX 77341, 713-294-1692. $25 for 12 monthly issues. A non-profit service providing information on current job opportunities in the criminal justice and social services fields.

1. My thanks to my friend, John William Zehring, Director of Career Planning and Placement at Earlham College, for help with this list.

For Jobs with Youth or Children: The Child Care Personnel Clearinghouse, Box 548, Hampton, VA 23669 publishes a bi-annual list called *Help Kids.* You *must* enclose $1 for postage and handling, in order to get it, however.

For Jobs Outdoors: The Association of Interpretative Naturalists, 6700 Needwood Rd., Derwood, MD 20855 publishes a monthly listing of jobs; the list costs $10. The Natural Science for Youth Foundation, 16 Holmes St., Mystic, CT 06355 publishes a bi-monthly job-listing, called *Opportunities*; the list costs $15. Colorado Outward Bound School, 945 Pennsylvania St., Denver, CO 80203 publishes a nationwide "Jobs Clearing House" list.

One final word about registers: the very term "register," implying some sort of clearinghouse, can be misleading. The vision: one central place where you can go, and find listed every vacancy in a particular field of endeavor. *But, sorry, Virginia; there ain't no such animal.* All you'll find by going to any of these places is *A Selected List* of some of the vacancies. A smorgasbord, if you will.

So far as finding *jobs for people* are concerned, these clearinghouses and agencies (like employment agencies) really end up finding *people for jobs.* (Think about it!) Heart of gold though they *may* have, these agencies serve employers better than they serve the job-hunter.

And yet there are always *ways* of using such registers to gain valuable information for the job-hunter and to suggest places where you may wish to *start* your information interviewing (about which, more in chapter 6). So, at the least, you *may* want to consult the Federal job bank (if there is one in your city), and perhaps a relatively inexpensive Register (if there is one in your particular field), as *auxiliaries* to the main thrust of your job-search.

OTHER IDEAS

Your Resume in a Book: Some organizations circulate small booklets which are essentially mass distribution of people's resumes in concise form. Forty-Plus Clubs do this, through their *Executive Manpower Directory*. So do some of the executive registry places. Evaluation as to its worth to you as job-hunter: well, it's a gamble, just like everything else in this Numbers Game system. A real gamble, if you are trying to start a new career. You have to boil your resume down to a very few words, normally. And then decide if you stand out. If not, forget it. If yes, well . . . maybe.

OTHER IDEAS

Off-Beat Methods: Mailing strange boxes to company presidents, with strange messages (or your resume) inside; using sandwich board signs and parading up and down in front of a company; sit-ins at a president's office, when you are simply determined to work for *that* company, association, or whatever. You name it – and if it's kooky, *it's been tried*. Sometimes it has paid off. Kookiness is generally ill-advised, however. $64,000 question every employer must weigh: if you're like this *before* you're hired, what will they have to live with *afterward*?

To summarize the effectiveness of all the preceding methods in a table (you do like tables, don't you?), we may look at the results of a survey the Bureau of the Census made. The survey, made in 1972 and published in the *Occupational Outlook Quarterly* in the winter of 1976, was of ten million job-seekers. Unhappily, this ten-year-old study is valid still:

USE AND EFFECTIVENESS OF JOB SEARCH METHODS

Method	Usage*	Effectiveness Rate**
Applied directly to employer	66.0%	47.7%
Asked friends about jobs where they work	50.8	22.1
Asked friends about jobs elsewhere	41.8	11.9
Asked relatives about jobs where they work	28.4	19.3
Asked relatives about jobs elsewhere	27.3	7.4
Answered local newspaper ads	45.9	23.9
Answered nonlocal newspaper ads	11.7	10.0
Private employment agency	21.0	24.2
State employment service	33.5	13.7
School placement office	12.5	21.4
Civil Service test	15.3	12.5
Asked teacher or professor	10.4	12.1
Went to place where employers come to pick up people	1.4	8.2
Placed ad in local newspaper	1.6	12.9
Placed ad in nonlocal newspaper	.5	***
Answered ads in professional or trade journals	4.9	7.3
Union hiring hall	6.0	22.2
Contacted local organization	5.6	12.7
Placed ads in professional or trade journals	.6	***
Other	11.8	39.7

* Percent of total jobseekers using the method.
** A percentage obtained by dividing the number of jobseekers who found work using the method, by the total number of jobseekers who used the method, whether successfully or not.
*** Base less than 75,000

Well, anyway, Mr. or Ms. Job-hunter, this just about covers the favorite job-hunting system of this country *at its best.* (Except personal contacts, which we give special treatment — chapter 6.) The Numbers Game.

If it works for you, right off, *great!* But if it doesn't, you may be interested in *the other plan* – you know, the one they had saved up for you, in case all of this didn't work? Small problem: with most of the personnel experts in our country, *there is no other plan.*

And that is that.

As a rule ... he (or she) who has the most information will have the greatest success in life ...

Disraeli

CHAPTER THREE

You Can Do It!

YOU *CAN* DO IT

If you decided to hop around in this book, rather than reading it from the very beginning, the odds are great that you leaped over the preceding chapters, and decided to dig in here. Right?

So for those who have just joined us here, we will summarize what has transpired thus far in our saga. Through all the preceding pages, two facts have stood out – like Mt. Everest – above all others:

(1) In good times and bad, the whole job-hunting system in this country is a big fat gamble, in which the dice are loaded against *any* job-hunter who wants more than "just a job." *Any* job-hunter.

(2) Further, the job-hunting system in this country poses especial difficulties for *all those who seek to change careers* – and that is, according to statistical studies, four out of every five job-hunters, before their life is through.

Now, on with our story.

There are a few heroes in this country, who belong to what might be called "the creative minority" in this whole field. They are a very diverse group. Some of them live in the big city; some out in the country. Some teach and do research at universities; others are professional career counselors. But, despite these outward differences, these unsung heroes have at least two denominators in common, maybe three:

First of all, they have refused to accept the idea that the job-hunting system has to be as bad as it is, or as much of an outright gamble as it is.

Secondly, instead of just criticizing the system, they have sat down and figured out how it could be done better. (They are pragmatists, before they are theoreticians.) And, not too surprisingly, they have all come up with methods which are strikingly similar to one another.

Third, in spite of widely teaching their methods over a number of years and in a number of places to the everlasting benefit of job-hunters near and far, they have been *studiously ignored* by the "manpower/human resources development/personnel experts" in this country, from the Federal government on down (or up, depending on your point of view).

For *any* job-hunter, this creative minority and their insights are important. But when it comes time for you to seek another career, you will discover this creative minority and their insights are absolutely crucial.

THE CREATIVE MINORITY'S DIAGNOSIS

What, then, is it that makes the present job-hunting system in this country so disastrous? That was the question which the creative minority, wherever they were, first asked themselves. What are the fatal *assumptions* that are so casually made by job-hunters everywhere, to their ultimate detriment and hurt? To the creative minority, the fatal assumptions seemed to be these:

√ *Fatal Assumption No. 1: The job-hunter doesn't need to work very hard at the job-hunt, and can settle for devoting just a few hours a week to the task, since something will always turn up eventually anyway; moreover, the job-hunter can pretty well "go it alone" while hunting.* Not true, said the creative minority. There are people who have been on the unemployment rolls for two years or more because they gave their job-hunt just "a lick and a promise," confident that "something will turn up," or "I'm sure they're going to call us back soon." Common sense, as well as actual experiments, demonstrate that, on the contrary, the harder you work at the job-hunt the shorter will be the length of your unemployment – other things being equal. Experience dictates that you can't wait for something to come to you; you must go to it. Moreover, experience dictates that it is easier, by far, to keep your nose to the grindstone with respect to the job-hunt, if you solicit the company and support of other job-hunters or at least of other friends.

√ *Fatal Assumption No. 2: The job-hunter should remain somewhat loose (i.e., vague) about what he or she wants to do, so that they are free to take advantage of whatever vacancies may be available.* Good grief, said the creative minority, this is why we have so great a percentage of Under-employment in this country. If you don't state just exactly what you want to do, first of all to yourself, and then to others, you are (in effect) handing over that decision to others. And others, vested with such awesome responsibility, are either going to dodge the decision or else make a very safe one, which is to define you as capable of doing only such and such a level of work (a safe, no risk diagnosis).

√ *Fatal Assumption No. 3: The job-hunter should not spend any time identifying the organizations that might be interested in him or her (no matter in what part of the country they may be), since employers have all the initiative and the upper hand in this whole process.* Nonsense, said the crative minority. This isn't a high school prom, where the job-hunters are sitting around the edge of the dance-floor, like shy wallflowers, while the employers are whirling around out in the center of the floor, and enjoying all the initiative. In many cases, those employers are stuck with partners (if we may pursue the metaphor) who are stepping on their toes, constantly. As a result, although the employer in theory has all the initiative as to whom they choose to dance with, in actuality they are often praying *someone will pay no attention to this silly rule, and come to their rescue by cutting in.* And indeed, when someone does take the initiative with the employer, rather than just sitting on the sidelines with *I'll-be-very-lucky-if-you-choose-me* written all over their face, the employer cannot help thinking *I-am-very-lucky-that-this-one-has-chosen-me.* People who cut in are usually pretty good dancers.

√ *Fatal Assumption No. 4: Employers see only people who can write well.* Pretty ridiculous, when it's put that way. But, said the creative minority, isn't that just exactly what our present job-hunting system is based on? To get hired, you must get an interview. To get an interview, you must let the personnel department see your resume first. Your resume will be screened out (and the interview never granted) if it doesn't make you sound good. But the resume is only as good as your writing ability (or someone else's) makes it. If you write poorly, your resume is (in effect) a Fun House mirror, which distorts you out of all proportion, so that it is impossible to tell what you really look like. *However, no allowance is made for this possibility, by personnel departments, except maybe one out of a thousand.* Your resume is assumed to be an accurate mirror of you. You could be Einstein or Golda Meir, but if you don't write well (i.e., if you write a terrible resume) you will not get an interview. Employers only see people who can write well. Ridiculous? You bet it is. And, say the creative minority, this is an assumption which is long overdue for a rest. It just doesn't have to be this way.

THE CREATIVE MINORITY'S PRESCRIPTION

As soon as the fatal assumptions of the present job-hunting system in this country were accurately defined, it wasn't all that difficult to create a new prescription. Once you have said that the fatal assumptions are: that the job-hunter doesn't need to work very hard at the job-hunt, that the job-hunter should stay vague, that employers have all the initiative as to where a job-hunter works, and that employers only see people who write well, the prescription almost writes itself, as to *the new assumptions that are the key to success:*

Key No. 1: You must decide that job-hunting will be for you a full-time job (unless you are currently employed, in which case you will still give it every spare hour possible); and that you will use group support in your job-hunting as much as you can.

Key No. 2: You must decide just exactly what you want to do.

Key No. 3: You must decide just exactly where you want to do it, through your own research and personal survey.

Key No. 4: You must research in some depth the organizations that interest you and then approach the one individual or committee in each organization who has the power to hire you for the job that you have decided you want to do.

"Organization" is used here as an all-inclusive term embracing businesses, industry, colleges, government, agencies, associations, foundations, churches or whatever.

For any job-hunter who wants more than "just-a-job," is rather seeking that job which employs their abilities and interests at the highest level possible, the above prescription of the creative minority is crucial.

But for the job-hunter who is trying to strike out in some new directions, or who must of necessity do some different things than they have done heretofore, the prescription of the creative minority is careerwise *a matter of life and death.* It will be a rare career-changer, indeed, who seeks employment without paying attention to these steps in the job-hunting process, and does not wind up Un-employed or, worse, Under-employed.

THE DEMAND FOR THIS KNOWLEDGE

According to a study published by Future Directions for a Learning Society, more than 40 million Americans are – even in Good Times – in some stage of career transition or job-change.[1] It is hardly any surprise then, that social scientists and futurists as well as vocational experts are continually telling us that workers must be prepared to change careers several times in their lives.

Some careers have a certain limit, such as baseball players or opera singers, after which the person *has* to change careers. Some careers have a high "burn-out rate," such as traveling salespeople, teachers, and the like. They are jobs which some people, at least, cannot find the energy and enthusiasm to do for more than a certain number of years, after which the person *wants* to change careers. And sometimes whole careers or industries virtually get phased out by our society, such as buffalo-skinners, buggy whip makers, blacksmiths, and such. It is true there are still a few people around, who are practicing the trade; but by and large the career has been phased out by society and history. After which, those who practiced that craft are *forced* to change careers. And then, some careers are still around, affording employment to a large number of people – but historically showing a dramatic decrease in numbers, compared to those who were once thus employed. The American farmer, of old, the American automobile assembly-line worker presently,

1. Aslanian, Carol B., and Brickell, Henry M., *Americans in Transition: Life Changes As Reasons for Adult Learning.* 1980. Also: Arbeiter, Solomon; Aslanian, Carol B.; Shmerbeck, Frances A.; and Brickell, Henry M., *40 Million Americans in Career Transition; The Need for Information.* 1978.

are examples which spring instantly to mind. In which case, career change is forced upon those displaced – a bitter pill when they see others still thriving in the career they once loved.

Career change is also an issue for those who are forcibly retired, as at a certain age, but still want to work creatively at *something.* And it is an issue for those who voluntarily retire, as from the military, but at such a young age (comparatively) that they feel they *must* seek a career, still. It is too early to simply retire.

It is not difficult to understand why the number of Americans in transition at any given moment is 40 million. And the statistics in Canada and other countries are probably similar.

It has, unhappily, taken our educational system – particularly higher education – a painfully long time to become aware that its average student is going to change careers two or three times in their lifetime. We still, as a learning society, train people to do just one thing, encourage them to become specialists – and then we wonder at their agonized cry when they discover, one day, that their specialty is no longer what they can or want to do. Our country's only solution for them, at that moment, is to urge that they go back to school and get retrained all over again for another specialty. Never mind how much time it takes,

or how much money. Never mind whether they are re-tracing their steps, picking up skills which they already possess. And never mind how short-lived this new specialty of theirs may turn out to be, in terms of the market-place and its demand. This is still the solution that our country typically urges, from Congress on down, when faced with the problem of high unemployment and mandated career change. *Band-aids.*

CAREER AND LIFE PLANNING: AN OVERVIEW OF THE ART

In protest against this shortsightedness, there has grown up a field called by many names, but known generally as *career and life planning.* The purpose of this new "art" – for that is what many regard it as being, rather than a science – is to take a longer view of your life – so that you can avoid short-term, band-aid thinking. It involves building in Alternative Options into any plans that you make, from the very beginning. Like: in high school or college.

The art is really just the systematic teaching of the four principles outlined above, along with some expansion of their major ideas, and the application of them to other arenas besides work.

You can find this new art being practiced everywhere. Its popularity has snowballed in recent years. You will find it in college courses, night schools, weekend seminars, workshops, conferences, human growth centers, displaced homemakers centers, annual conventions, on tape, in books, and – like that.

Given the present course of history, it seems that career and life planning is something we are all going to have to do quite a bit of, unless we want to be helpless victims, tossed on the stormy sea of change hither and yon. Actually, it's not all that hard to get involved with career and life planning. Because, if you go about identifying *what it is you want and what it is you want to do* – not only for the immediate present but at least a little bit beyond that – you *are* doing life planning. The minute you think out, or write down, some short- or long-term goals for yourself, you are into it. Like: planning next summer's vacation. All that the art does is to systematize it, give you some tools for getting at it, and give you the benefit of other people's experience.

Unhappily, some of what passes for career planning in this country, taught by good-willed people at that, is not very well thought out at all. Some people think that just because it's called "career and life planning," it *must* be good. Let's be clear about that, right now: *there is no magic in the name.* Some people have gone away to seminars or courses billed as — well, there are a whole list of possible names:

LONG RANGE CAREER DEVELOPMENT
LONG TERM HELP IN CAREER PLANNING
FULL CAREER PLANNING
STUDYING YOUR CAREER PATTERNS
FULL CAREER PROGRAM
CRITICAL ASSESSMENT OF ONESELF AND ONE'S FUTURE
LONG RANGE ACTION PLANNING
SELF-COUNSELING AND PLANNING
SELF-CONFRONTATION AND DESIGN
DEALING WITH WHAT I WILL BECOME, AS
WELL AS WITH WHAT I WILL DO.
HUMAN RESOURCES PLANNING
VOCATIONAL DEVELOPMENT PROCESS
LONG RANGE LIFE PLANNING

Anyway, by whatever name, people attending seminars or courses in this "art" have come back "happy"— but just as confused and uncertain about what they want to do as they were before they went.

So, before we turn to our four principles — distilled from the experience of successful job-hunters and career-changers and from successful career planning *systems* — let us set this definition clearly before us, and keep it before us, as we go:

> For you, career and life planning is useless, unless at the end of your homework, you are very definite about exactly what you want to do — for the immediate future, at least.

Life is what happens while
you're making other plans.
— Tom Smothers

CHAPTER FOUR

You Must Keep At It

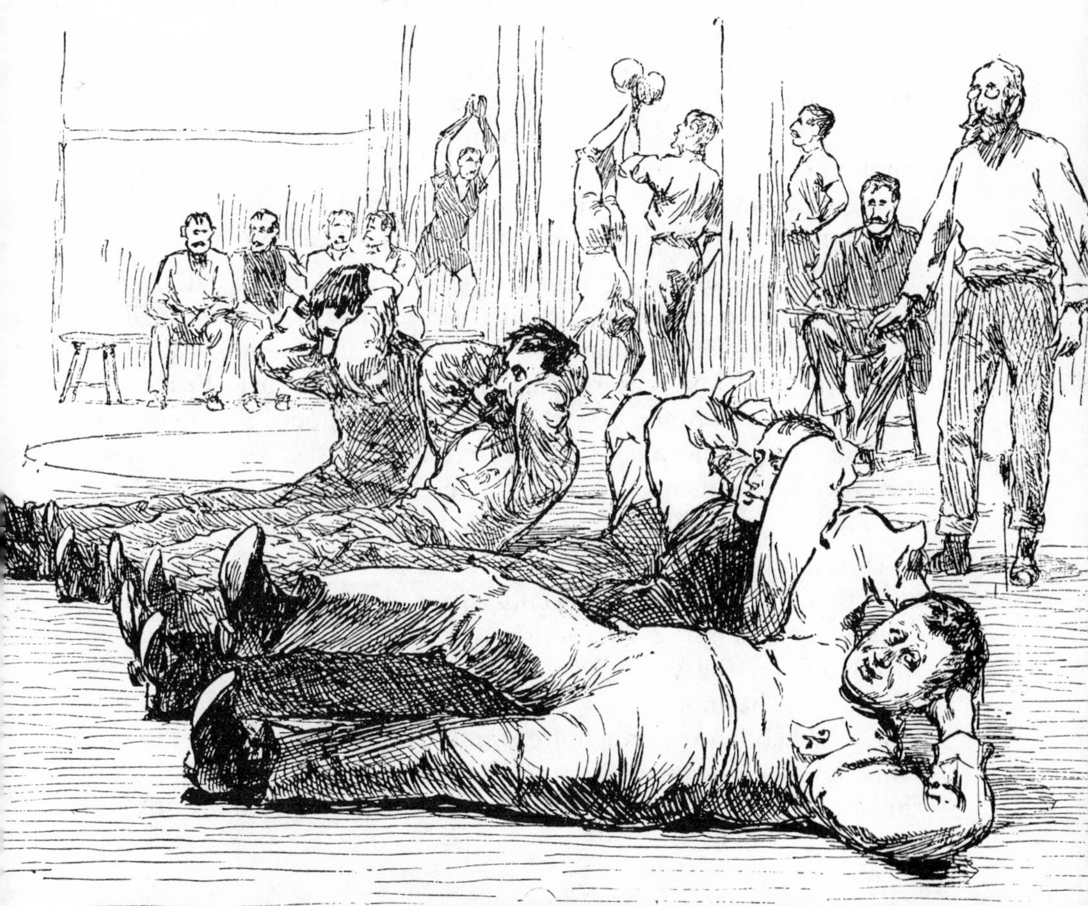

THE FIRST KEY TO CAREER PLANNING AND JOB-HUNTING

First *means* first, as in "most important." This is the first key because it is the most important. It is to this that I always point, when people say to me, "Well, you've studied successful job-hunters and successful job-hunting systems: what, in your opinion, is the most important secret of successful job-hunting or career-changing?"

The answer is simple: keeping at it. Successful job-hunters are those who keep at the task of job-hunting, with a vengeance. Successful job-hunting systems are those which have figured out a way to help the job-hunter keep at it.

I first noticed this factor, when several job-hunting systems were brought to my attention, each of which had a fantastically high success rate. I studied their characteristics, supposing that I would find certain common denominators. I did not. They were as different as night and day. Some spent all their time getting the job-hunter to do homework. Some spent all their time getting the job-hunter to turn up "leads" to prospective employers. Some spent all their time rehearsing, and video-taping, the actual hiring-interview. Yet, despite such diversity, all reported a very high success rate. Why? I asked myself.

Upon examination, it turned out that all of them had one characteristic in common, which I had at first overlooked. All of them treated job-hunting as, in itself, a full-time job. All of them had the job-hunter come in, Monday through Friday, from 9 in the morning, until 4 or 5 in the afternoon. Some even had the job-hunter punch in, on a timeclock, at the beginning of the day, and punch out, on a timeclock, at the end of each day . . . just as they might do at a real job.

Thus did I begin to suspect that it was the very act of keeping at it, that was the most important aspect of any "system." I still believe that. Simple logic would suggest that the more time you spend out on the street job-hunting, the more doors you will knock on. The more doors you knock on, the more employers you are likely to see. The more employers you get in to see, the more interviews you will have. The more interviews you have, the more job-offers you are likely to receive. The more job-offers you receive, the more likely it is that one of these will be a job you like the sound of. Thus, you accept that offer, and your job-search is successfully concluded.

Let us suppose that when you are job-hunting, you decide – on the basis of the above argument – that you will go out job-hunting from 9 a.m. to 5 p.m. every day, Monday through Friday. Within four weeks, then, you will have spent seven hours a day (an hour off for lunch) for twenty days job-hunting, or a total of 140 hours. Contrast this with the behavior of the average job-hunter, who – according to the Census Bureau – in two-thirds of the cases, spends less than five hours a week in job-search activities. In four weeks, that adds up to only twenty hours of job-hunting.[1]

Small wonder, then, that two additional studies revealed that the average job-hunter contacts only six potential employers directly in the period of a month, and in one-third of the cases, only ten potential employers in a period of seven weeks.[2]

If you decide to treat your job-hunt or career-change as a full-time job, and devote full-time to it, you will be spending seven times as many hours upon it, as do two-thirds of all job-hunters. Thus, you increase your chances of success sevenfold. Not six potential employers contacted in person during a month's time, but – potentially – forty-two. Not ten employers contacted in seven weeks time, but – potentially – seventy.

And, as you will recall from the table on page 36, applying directly to an employer is *the single most effective* method of job-hunting.

Let me give all this theory some substance by relating to you not *The Tale of Two Cities* but *The Tale of Two Job-hunters in the Same City.* Joan and Ralph were job-hunters, who lived in the same city. What was of interest was that they were both trying to change careers, to go into a field they had had no experience in, both of them had similar backgrounds, had similar degrees of expertise, and were of similar ages. And both of them were job-hunting at the same time. Joan went out every day, Monday through Friday. Eight-thirty found her leaving her

---

1. Robert G. Wegmann, "Job Search Assistance Programs: Implications for the School," in *Phi Delta Kappan*, December 1979, p. 271ff.

2. Robert G. Wegmann, "Job-Search Assistance: A Review" in the *Journal of Employment Counseling*, December 1979, p. 212.

house each morning. Nine o'clock found her knocking on the office door, without appointment, of the first employer — or potential employer – on her list. That employer would usually suggest someone else she ought to visit, and in many cases, would make an enabling phone call to prepare the way for her, while she was still there in that office. She continued calling, with an hour off for lunch, all day long. She repeated this sort of schedule each day of the week. Within ten days, she had four bona fide job offers, one of which she accepted, because it was precisely what she was looking for. Ralph, on the other hand, had been conducting his job-search for nine months, without success. He had done all the exercises in this book, knew what his skills were, and what kind of job he wanted — in the same field as Joan's – but he only devoted an hour or two to his job-hunt, two or three days each week. The rest of the time was spent on errands, cleaning house, visiting his friends, and complaining how impossible it was to find a new career in today's job market. Most of the time that he did devote to his job-hunt was spent in sending out resumes, with covering letters, and then anxiously visiting his mail box each afternoon to see if anyone had replied.

Now, I would not like to be misunderstood as claiming that if you devote full-time to your job-hunt you will have a job in ten days. Though that *does* happen. Nor would I like to be misunderstood as claiming that if you don't devote full-time to the hunt, you will be out of work nine months. Though *that* does happen. But, flukes and luck aside, there often is a direct correlation between the amount of time devoted to the job-hunt, and the speed with which you will find not just *a* job, but *the* sort of job that you are most anxious to find. And that is that.

JOB-HUNTING WHILE YOU ARE STILL EMPLOYED

All of the foregoing, of course, assumes that you are unemployed, and hence have complete freedom as to how you allot your time. But what do you do about the job-hunt or career change, if you are presently holding down a full-time job?

Good question. That is the case in which many find themselves. How many? Well, the government, bless its heart, did a study of job-hunting among employed workers about five years ago, and discovered that in a typical month (it was May of 1976) 4.2% of all employed workers, or nearly one out of every twenty, went looking for another job sometime during that month. In actual numbers, that represented 3,269,000 people who were job-hunting while still employed.[1] If the same percentage obtains today, it means 4,074,000 are employed but job-hunting.

I would like to point out two things about this finding. First of all, it means that one-third of all job-hunters are conducting the search while they are still employed. (How did that conclusion get reached? By assuming that those unemployed and seeking work are as the government says – 9,500,000 at this writing – and adding to that figure the number above of 4,074,000, which yields a total of 13,574,000 job-seekers currently – of which 4,074,000, or over one-third, are job-hunting while still employed.

Secondly, if over 4 million are thus job-hunting in a typical month, one can imagine how much larger that figure would be for an entire year. This helps to explain the statistics uncovered

1. *The Extent of Job Search by Employed Workers.* March, 1977. Special Labor Force Report 202. Published by the U.S. Department of Labor, Bureau of Labor Statistics; available from any of their regional offices.

in other studies, which reveal that the average non-agricultural firm in this country has to hire – in a typical year – as many new people as it has employees. In other words, a firm with three employees will probably have to hire two or three employees each year. A firm with 100 employees will probably have to hire 90 new employees each year. That's on the average. If you want a more detailed breakdown, this is what the study turned up: the average retail firm with say 100 employees may have to hire 136 new people each year; the average firm dealing in services and having say 100 employees may have to hire 111 new employees each year; the average financial institution, 74; the average manufacturing firm, 65; the average transportation or public utilities company, 32; and the average construction company, a whopping 202 new employees for every 100 it currently has.[1]

It is this job-hunting behavior on the part of employed workers which helps to create so many vacancies – thus increasing every job-hunter's chance of success so dramatically.

How do employed job-hunters go about their search? You guessed it: the same way unemployed job-hunters do. According to the government's study, 70% of all employed job-hunters contacted an employer directly. But, back to our original question: how do you find time to do the job-hunt if you are presently holding down a full-time job? We have asked employed job-hunters how they did it, and the sum of their advice to you – based on their experience – is:

(1) Determine to keep at it, with every spare hour you can find. Press evenings, weekends, lunch hours and the like, into the service of your job-hunt.

(2) Use evenings and weekends to do the original homework, figuring out what your skills are and what it is you want to do, as well as where you want to do it. Later on in your job-search, use evenings and the weekend also to write thank you notes, send out letters, and the like.

(3) For the actual calling upon potential employers, if they are in the city where you presently work, press your lunch hours into service. If you "brown-bag it," you will have time to

---

1. Wegmann, *op. cit.*, pp. 208-209. Wegmann quotes statistics for one quarter of the year, which I have multiplied by four. It is arguable that a quarter may not be typical; hence I have used the word "may" in describing annual hires.

make and keep one appointment, particularly if your intent is to make the interview no longer than twenty minutes – a good idea, in any case, for the exploratory or information interview. People take lunch hours at all different times: 11:15 a.m., 11:45, 12 noon, 12:30, 1 p.m. While you are on your lunch hour, somebody you want to see hasn't gone to lunch yet, or has just come back. Sometimes you can move your lunch hour – if the place where you are presently working is flexible about that — to the 11 a.m.-12 noon time slot.

(4) Press late afternoons into service. Many people you will want to see are on an executive or management level, and they often do not get away from their offices promptly at 5. It is appropriate to estimate how long it will take you to get across town to them, and ask them if they could see you that long after your quitting time, on a particular day.

(5) Press holidays into service. Holidays fall into two classes: those which everyone observes, like Christmas and New Year's Day; and those which some people observe, like Washington's Birthday, etc. In the case of the latter kind of holiday, if you have it off, you will sometimes be able to visit the people you want to see, because they do not have it off.

(6) Press Saturdays into service. Sometimes the people you want to see work on Saturday, or are occasionally willing to set up appointments for Saturday.

(7) Press your sick-leave into service. In some organizations, workers accumulate sick-leave, and have the right to take it as time off. If that is the case with you, use such days off judiciously, to visit potential employers who interest you.

(8) Press your vacations into service. If you are dead-serious about the importance of your job-hunt or career change, it is not too great a sacrifice to devote one year's vacation time to your job-hunt. This is especially important if you are trying to secure employment in a distant city. Schedule your vacation in that city, and make arrangements and appointments, by letter and phone, ahead of time (see chapter 6, on how to research a place at a distance).

(9) If you have sufficient savings, the following strategem may be one you would like to consider in addition to all the above: if you have a whole list of people and places you need to visit, and you require a concentrated period of time in which to do this, and cannot wait until your vacation time, you have the

right to ask your present employer if you can have a leave of absence without pay. So long as the time requested is no longer than a week or so, and so long as it is scheduled at the convenience of the employer (i.e., not in the week that they need you the most), this request will often be honored. You can give, as the reason, the simple truth: Personal Business.

Should you feel guilty about job-hunting while you are still employed? Well sure, if you want to. But there is no need. One-third of all job-hunters are doing the same thing: it is a common practice in our economy. Nothing odd-ball about it. Moreover, remember these simple truths: Your employer has certain rights, including the right to fire you at any time, for sufficient cause; moreover, they have the right to prepare for this act of firing ahead of time, laying the groundwork, transferring part of your work to other colleagues, etc. You, as employee, likewise have certain rights, including the right to quit at any time, for sufficient cause; moreover, you have the right to prepare for this act of quitting ahead of time, laying the groundwork through interviewing and job-searching.

JOB-HUNTERS ANONYMOUS

The secret of success for all job-hunters – employed or unemployed – is (to use my rich skills at overkill): keeping at it. Devoting every hour you can to the task. Having said that, however, we can press on to our next truth about job-hunting or career-changing. Namely: it is very difficult to mount a sustained effort when you are job-hunting all by yourself. Motivation flags, energies get diluted, and frequently – to use a common expression – we run out of gas.

It is no wonder then that during the past decade, one of the most interesting developments within the field of job-hunting has been the rapid growth of job-hunting groups. Even as we have seen, in this country, the spawning of Alcholics Anonymous, Overeaters Anonymous, and the like, so now we are seeing the springing up of a kind of Job-hunters Anonymous: job-hunters seeking out their fellow job-hunters, and banding together for the purpose of helping each other with the task.

It is as though job-hunters were saying: well, if I can't keep at this task all by myself, I'll find a support-group which will help me to keep at it.

These group-job-hunting organizations vary widely in their program, scheduling and and techniques. But all of them are indebted, in one degree or another, to:

Nathan Azrin's Job-Finding Clubs or Job Clubs, which were spawned in Carbondale, Illinois, thence New York City (Harlem), New Brunswick, Milwaukee, Wichita and Tacoma, and now in many places throughout the country;

and/or Charles Hoffman's Self-Directed Placement Corporation (SDP) which began in San Diego, then commenced similar operations in other parts of the country;

and/or Joseph Fischer's and Albert Cullen's Job Factory, in Cambridge and Worcester, Massachusetts;

and/or Forty Plus Clubs, which were founded in New York City, Philadelphia, Washington, D.C., Chicago, Milwaukee, Houston, Denver, Los Angeles, the Bay Area (Oakland) of California, and Hawaii;

and/or similar job-hunting groups, such as have existed for years – created and run by the government (as, through former CETA programs), or by various professional societies (such as IEEE, AIAA, etc.), or by various career professionals (Bernard Haldane, John Crystal, etc.).

Group-job-hunting is clearly an idea whose time has come.[1]

NATHAN AZRIN'S MODEL FOR GROUP-JOB-HUNTING

The most popular model, by far, is currently Nathan Azrin's idea of Job-Finding Clubs. The idea is being replicated throughout the country; at this writing there are 100 such clubs.

Dr. Azrin started these clubs in Carbondale, Illinois, when he was Director of Research at the Anna State Hospital in Anna, Illinois (he is currently on the staff of Nova University, in Fort Lauderdale, Florida). The idea was subsequently tested across the country by the Department of Labor, with (in my opinion) spectacular success.

If you are interested in the history of that success, you can write to the National Technical Information Service, Springfield, VA 22151, and for $5.25 they will send you Report PB 287-332:

1. The U.S. Employment and Training Administration has put out a pamphlet about all this: *Self-Directed Job Search: An Introduction.* U.S. Department of Labor, Washington, DC. 1980. Order it from the Superintendent of Documents.

"Final Report to U.S. Department of Labor: The Job Finding Club," Nathan H. Azrin, Ph.D., Principal Investigator.

If you are job-hunting or career-changing and want to become a member of a group based on the Azrin model, there are three ways you can go about doing this:

(1) You can inquire from your local federal/state employment office, and/or your county CETA office, and/or the National Office of Program Development, Robert A. Philip, Director, 202 Canterbury Dr., Carbondale, IL 62901, as to whether or not there is a Job-Finding Club already in existence in your area. If so, find its address, and go join.

(2) If there is no Club in your area, the National Office of Program Development will (for a fee) train some professional in your area in how to set up an original job club.

(3) If you and some other job-hunters in your area have no funds for such training, but want to set up a Job-Finding Club on your own, there is a manual which you can get that will give you complete instructions. It is called the *Job Club Counselor's Manual,* it is by Nathan Azrin, and is available for $14.95 from University Park Press, 233 E. Redwood St., Baltimore, MD 21202. There is also an earlier description of how to set up such a club available from the National Technical Information Service (address above), at a cost of $9.25; it is called PB 291-558, "Accompaniment to the Final Report of U.S. Department of Labor: The Job-Finding Club," Nathan H. Azrin, Ph.D., Principal Investigator.

If, as a job-hunter, you find there is no job-club or job-hunters anonymous of any kind in your community, and you decide to band together with some other job-hunters, good for

you! Even if you design your own club and your own program, it's probably going to be effective and infinitely more helpful than if you were to go about your job-hunt, or career-change, all by yourself. The mutual teamwork and support will, in all likelihood, help you to keep at the job-hunt and treat it as a full-time job – which is the point of it all.

However, there are reasons for taking Dr. Azrin's model very seriously. It is based on experience. That experience was that there were a number of problems which were defeating job-hunters – of every age, sex, race, educational and economic background. Inasmuch as Dr. Azrin is one of the original behavioral-modification psychologists in this country, he analyzed these problems, and each feature of his system was designed in response to a problem. That is to say, each feature was designed to stamp out or remove a problem. Every time you omit one of the features of his model – either through not knowing the model, or knowing it but desiring to "cut corners" – you automatically readmit the problem which that feature was designed to eliminate.

By way of illustration, his model of the Job-Finding Club is designed around the buddy system. In order to implement that system, a telephone with an extension is mandated. The point of having both the telephone and the extension, is that the buddy can listen in on your conversation with a potential employer, and give you feedback later on how you could have improved the conversation over the phone. Then, later, you can listen in on the extension, while your buddy is making similar phone calls, and later give feedback. Eliminate the "phone-with-extension" feature, and you automatically eliminate the feedback. Eliminate the feedback and you readmit the original problem: namely, that job-hunters often don't know how to handle themselves on the phone, and hence keep repeating their poor performance – precisely because no one is there to give them immediate feedback.

OTHER KINDS OF RESOURCES YOU CAN DRAW UPON

But it may be that in your case there is no group-job-hunting support system available, and you can't (or won't) get one started. Yet you still want some kind of support and help. What then?

Well, there are other kinds of help besides groups. There are individual helpers that you can turn to, and there are also books.

But to take advantage of these, there are two essential rules:

1. You must know what kind of help you need, and this is best discovered by first trying to do the job-hunt using your own resources: namely, your brain and your wits.

2. You must know what various resources can do to help you, and what they can't do.

TYPES OF RESOURCES

Let us begin by outlining the kinds of help that you might need and want:

HELP WITH PARTICULAR PARTS OF
THE JOB-HUNTING PROCESS.

- Help with deciding just exactly what it is you want to do (chapter 5):
  - A) In the way of vocation (what kind of exterior furniture do you want?)
  - B) In the way of personal growth (what to do with your interior furniture?)
- Help with informational interviewing to help you decide just exactly where you want to do it (chapter 6).
- Help with researching at length the organizations that interest you and learning how to approach the man or woman who has the power to hire you for the job you want (chapter 7).

HELP WITH THE WHOLE PROCESS OF
THE JOB-HUNT (all of the above).

Now, let us look at what resources there are, and just what they can and cannot do for you:

I. *Your own research.* This is to be preferred above all resources, for any number of reasons. First of all, knowledge which you gain for yourself is more ingrained than knowledge that is simply handed to you by others. Secondly, the job-hunt process rightly understood is itself a preparation for, and training in, skills you will need to exercise once you get the job; to deprive yourself of the opportunity to get valuable practice in these skills during the job-hunting process, is to make it just that much more difficult for yourself on the job. Thirdly, even if you pay money (and a whole lot of it) to one kind of professional agency or another, there is no guarantee that they will do the process any better than, or even as well as, you would do it yourself.

MORAL

Every investment of your money is a gamble unless you have first tried to do it on your own, know what you did find out, what you did not find out, and therefore what kind of help you now need from others.

II. *Books, pamphlets and other printed material.* If you need help this is the first resource to check out. (You already know that, or why are you reading this?) This kind of resource is inexpensive, and may give you just the extra push you need, to get past whatever bottleneck is holding you up, if information, a clue, a glimmer is all you need. If *this* book, after you have thoroughly read and tried it, just doesn't do it for you, there are a multitude of other resources listed in Appendix B.

III. *Free professional help.* People rush off to press money into the hands of paid professionals when if they would just stop to analyze exactly what they need at that moment they might discover there is professional help available at no cost. Examples of such help: your local librarian, resources at a nearby university or college, the chamber of commerce, business friends, and fellow alumni from your college or high school who live in your area (write your school and ask for their alumni list).

IV. *Professional help for a fee.* A) From a college or university. Example: vocational testing often is given for a modest fee. Recommended if you have tried all the techniques in the next chapter of this book first, without getting any satisfactory answers. Outside the college or university realm, you will want to know that there are private firms which give genuine aptitude testing (as distinct from vocational *interest* testing). The granddaddy of all such firms is Johnson O'Connor, nee Human Engineering Laboratory. They are located in major cities. You can write them at 347 Beacon St., Boston, MA 02116 to get a list of the cities, and offices. There are other such firms throughout the country, many of them staffed by former employees of Johnson O'Connor, such as Ability Potentials, Inc., 7100 Baltimore Ave., Suite 300, College Park, MD 20740.[1] B) From your own professional group. For example, if you are a clergy person there are a number of church career development centers around the country. These are able to give help in certain specific areas. Check out Appendix C. C) From the business-consultant world: (1) those which will accept anyone as a client, and (2) those which concentrate on serving specialized vocational groups.

YOUR FAMILY OR FRIENDS

Okay, you don't want to go about the job-hunt all by yourself. You've weighed the idea of a job-club, but none is available. You've weighed the idea of getting yourself a professional counselor, but you can't afford one – or you can't find one. Does this mean, then, that you are condemned to go about the job-hunt all by yourself?

Of course not. You've still got your family and you've still got your friends.

---

1. There are also books which maybe are more fun than enlightening, but try them anyway, if you wish.

Barrett, James, and Williams, Geoffrey, *Test Your Own Job Aptitude: Exploring Your Career Potential.* Penguin Books, 625 Madison Ave., New York, NY 10022. 1981. $2.50, paper.

Aero, Rita, and Weiner, Elliot, *The Mind Test.* William Morrow and Co., 105 Madison Ave., New York, NY 10016. 1981. $8.95, paper.

What do you ask of them? Very simple: we'll put it in the form of an excercise.

PRACTICAL EXERCISE (WARMUP)

Decide who you know (spouse, roommate, friend, etc.) that you can take into your confidence about this. Tell them what you need to do, the hours it will take and how much you need *them* to keep you at this task. Then put down in your appointment book a regular weekly date when they will *guarantee* to meet with you, check you out on what you've done *already*, and be very stern with you if you've done little or nothing since your previous week's meeting. The more a gentle but firm taskmaster this confidante is, the better. Tell them that it is at least a 20,000 hour, $250,000 project. Or whatever. It's also responsible, concerned, committed *Stewardship.*

Why 20,000 hours? Well, a forty-hour a week job, done for fifty weeks a year, adds up to 2,000 hours annually. So, how long are you going to be doing this new job or new career that you are looking for? Ten years? That means 20,000 hours. Longer than that? Even more hours. So, it's at least a 20,000 hour project.

Why $250,000? Well, figure it out for yourself. Say, you hope to start this new job or new career of yours at $14,000 a year. Even if you are forty years old, you still have thirty good years of work left in you. So, let us say that over that period of thirty years you get enough raises to make your annual salary somewhere between $18,000 and $20,000. Multiply this by thirty years, and you get a total earnings of something in the neighborhood of more than half a million dollars. Too extravagant, you say? You're going to start at $7,000, and have enough raises to make your annual salary only $10,000 per year? All right, even so, that adds up to $300,000 over the thirty years. If you've got more years ahead of you, or a higher potential salarywise, you're talking about even more money. So it's *at least* a $250,000 project that you're working on, with this job-hunt of yours.

HOW MUCH TIME TO DO IT RIGHT?

Considering this 20,000 hour, $250,000 project that you're electing to work on, from the point of view of a steward or manager rather than just crassly, how much time do you think a good steward or good manager should put in on such a project, to be sure that the half a million is well planned, well managed and well spent? Think carefully.

And realize that trying to get the job-hunt over with, just as fast as possible, taking short cuts wherever you can, giving the whole thing as little of your time and intelligence as you can get away with, is going to cost you money. Over the next decade or two, you can deprive yourself and your loved ones of many thousands of dollars, literally – due to your shoddy job-hunt. Not to mention your own misery, at ending up – as so many do – in a miserable excuse for a job, where you are undervalued, underused and ultimately burnt-out.

So, how much time to do it right? Only you can decide. But if you decide it is a full-time job, and you are going to devote every spare hour and day to it that you possibly can – whether you are employed or unemployed – you will be demonstrating wisdom far beyond your years. This isn't *just* a job-hunt. This is your life, man. This is your life, woman.

Get your family to help. Get your friends to help. Get your priest, pastor, rabbi, guru or whatever to help. Be in charge of this Project: Job Hunt. But don't go it alone. There is no need to.

The Inquiring Reporter asked the young woman why she wanted to be a mortician. *Because*, she said, *I enjoy working with people.*

The San Francisco Chronicle

CHAPTER FIVE

Only *You* Can Decide:

What Do You Want To Do?

THE SECOND KEY TO CAREER PLANNING AND JOB-HUNTING

We come now to the homework that you MUST do on yourself, as an essential prelude to your job-hunt. That homework begins with your getting at the issue of what it is that you want to do. I said this earlier, but let me repeat it here:

> *You have got to know what it is you want, or someone is going to sell you a bill of goods somewhere along the line that can do irreparable damage to your self-esteem, your sense of worth, and your stewardship of the talents that God gave you.*

Remember this: you live half your life at your job – whatever it may be. God's world already has *more* than enough people who can't wait for five o'clock to come, so that they can go and do what they really want to do. It doesn't need us to swell that crowd. Us . . . or anyone else. It needs people who know what they really want to do, and who do it *at* their place of work, *as* their work.

WHAT WILL HOLD YOU BACK?

Can you really sit down and figure out an alternative career for yourself, based on what you really enjoy doing – without going back to school for a million years of re-training? Or can you really define your very first career, systematically? You bet you can.

Then why is this whole country in general, and our personnel system in particular, baffled as to how to go about this whole process?

Now, that is a *very* good question, particularly when the creative minority have been crying out for years that it could be done and has been done by countless numbers of ordinary people from all walks of life. It's all very simple, they have been saying . . . and saying . . . and saying.

There are only four things that hold people back from completing this personal homework exercise successfully:

"Same career, change of career, same career... change of..."

• 1. *Lack of Purpose.* People trying to identify a first or second career for themselves are not sure what kind of things they need to be looking for.

• 2. *Lack of Tools or Instruments.* People know what kind of things they are looking for, perhaps, but they have nothing to help them go about it systematically and comprehensively.

• 3. *Lack of Motivation.* People know what kinds of things they are looking for, and they have helpful instruments so that they can do it, but the *internal push* to get at it and keep at it until it is done, is inadequate. This is usually *the* major roadblock of the four. We dealt with this in our previous chapter.

• 4. *Lack of Time.* Purpose is grasped, tools are in hand, motivation is just great, but they have waited to get at this exercise until they are actually living in Desperation Gulch (just on the outskirts of Panic City) – and the amount of time needed to do this properly just does not seem to be there. So of course the exercise is done joylessly and, often, without much profit. Food meant to be savored cannot be wolfed down, without the danger of acute indigestion. Likewise, career and life planning meant to be done with much time for reflection, cannot be telescoped without the danger of erroneous judgments and conclusions.

WHAT'S GOING TO PUT YOU AHEAD

You can sit down and work out exactly what it is that you want to do, once you resolve that *you* will not and do not lack the four prerequisites for this kind of work:

Time	Motivation	Purpose	Tools & Instruments

Of course, you aren't going to get this done just by sitting up late one or two nights. It takes longer than that. You need to make up your mind to that, before you even begin. Thoughts, like soup stock, often need to simmer for awhile – on the front burner, or on the back. So, you need to get at this homework at once, and proceed with it systematically.

Of course, the temptation is to procrastinate. And procrastination, as my grandfather used to say, sent more people to hell than whiskey.

"What do you want to do, for the rest of your life?" "Oh, I don't know; I'll figure it out when I have to."

I hate to tell you this, but the time to figure out where your parachute is, what color it is, and to strap it on, is *now* – and not when the vocational airplane that you are presently in is on fire and diving toward the ground.

But most of us typically wait until a crisis occurs. Too bad! None of us are fools. We all know that we may have to go find other work, with very short notice. But we put it off. If you have a choice, begin this homework while you are still gainfully, and somewhat happily, employed. *If you're employed, somebody wants you – and values you enough to say so, in*

the coin of the realm. If you're unemployed, there is just the breath of suspicion that perhaps no one wants you. And faced with this suspicion, many employers will choose to make no decision about you (i.e., not hire you) rather than take a gamble.

Of course, the choice may not be yours. All of a sudden you're out. You didn't see it coming. There was no warning. Or maybe there was, and you just didn't see it. Well, no sense kicking pebbles and wishing you had been wiser. You *are* unemployed. You can still do the whole process right. Just put your anger aside, stop brooding about the past, and get at this homework.

Throughout the rest of this book – here and there – you are going to find references to other books. The super-conscientious reader will, of course, want to pause at each reference, run to the library, read that book, and then continue here. Thus, the super-conscientious reader will be ninety years old before finishing *Parachute.* For most of us I recommend another plan: ignore the references to other books, do *not* go and look them up, do not bother to read them – *unless* the particular subject under discussion when that reference is given just *happens to be* your Achilles heel, and you are *desperate* for some further help with that particular area of your life. In which case, make a note to yourself and – when you're all done reading *Parachute* – you can look over those notes to see which other resources, if any, you then want to go pursue.

To illustrate what I have just said, let us suppose that you have a hunch, intuition or premonition that your problem is not that you can't get organized for your job-hunt, but rather that you can't get organized about *anything.* You may find some help in Stephanie Winston's book, *Getting Organized: The easy way to put your life in order.* (Warner Books, Inc., 75 Rockefeller Plaza, New York, NY 10019. 1978. $4.95, paper.) Stephanie is the founder and director of The Organizing Principle – an interesting job-hunt/career-change story in and of itself. Her book deals with how to organize your time, paperwork, work space, rooms in general, tasks, finances, books, clothes, etc. But, don't jot down the name of this book in your notes *unless* getting organized is *the* big problem in your life.

Practical Exercise (Cooling Down?)

If two weeks after putting down this chapter, you pick it up again, and realize you still haven't even begun this homework, deciding what it is that you want to do; and if you haven't enlisted anyone else to help you either, then face it: you're going to *have to* pay someone to aid you. Too bad, because you could do it just as well or better yourself. But better this way than no way: turn to Appendix C, choose three possible counselors or places, go ask them some questions, and then choose one. Pay them, and *get at this.*

WHAT YOU ARE LOOKING FOR

In any event, on your own — or with a *planning partner* — what is it that you are looking for, during this process? We have already indicated the long-range over-all purpose. It's worth repeating:

Career & life planning is useless, unless
at the end of the process
you are very definite about
exactly what you want to do —
at least for the immediate future.

But let's be even more specific than this. Any career and life planning that is worth its salt should help you to do the following things:

Goals

1. To become more aware of your goals in life. What do you want to accomplish before you die? What is your life's "mission," as you perceive it? (Your name isn't Cathy is it? See next page.)

You may revise this list ten times, as life goes on *(career and life planning is, ideally, an on-going continuous process — not a single event, done once and for all)*; but as you perceive it now, what are you trying to accomplish, what are you trying to become? What's unique about *you*?

Skills

2. To inventory what skills you presently have — things you do well and enjoy. This inventory needs to be taken in terms of basic units — *building blocks, if you will* — so that as time goes on, these building blocks can be arranged in different constellations. The creative minority insists this is the very heart of planning for your various careers.

Time Lines

3. To consider and identify what Peter Drucker calls the *futurity of present decisions.* Considering where you would like to go, and what you would like to do, what time spans are built into your present decisions (e.g. if school seems required, how many years before you will finish?), and what risks are built into present decisions? The purpose of your planning is not to eliminate risks (there can be no sure movement forward without them) but to be certain that the risks you take are the right ones, based on careful thought.[1]

1. If you want some help with this whole business of taking risks, there is a resource you may want to take a look at: *Risking,* by David Viscott. (Simon & Schuster, 1230 Avenue of the Americas, New York, NY 10020. 1977. $2.25.)

Who's in Control

4. To basically decide who (or what) is controlling your career planning: accident, circumstance, the stars, the system, Providence, God (how?), your family, other people or – forgive us for mentioning this possibility – You. You see, ultimately this comes down to a question of how passive you want to be about it all. (Your life, your career, where you work, the whole bag.) Now, admittedly, we have an axe to grind here: we believe

you will improve your effectiveness and your sense of yourself as a person 300% if you can learn to think (or if you already think) of yourself as *an active agent* helping to mould your own present environment and your own future, rather than a passive agent, waiting for your environment to mould you.

THE CONSTANT THREAD

But, to say that your purpose in all this homework is to find your goals, skills, time lines and who's in control, is not enough. Your deepest purpose is to identify the core of your life, the constant thread, the constancy in you that persists through all the changing world around you. As we all learned from Alvin Toffler (in *Future Shock*), change is coming at us so fast that many people are going into shock (marked by apathy, withdrawal, paralysis or galloping nostalgia).

The planning outlined thus far can help you deal with such change by identifying what in your life is unchanging: your sense of life "mission," your basic skills etc. – the things that continue relatively untouched at the core of your *inner nature.* A base of constancy is necessary in order to deal with the bombardment of change that has become the hallmark of this world in which we presently live.

You build this base of constancy by: identifying the goals, values, priorities, etc., that you already have; inventorying the basic building blocks of your skills that you already have; identifying the time spans and risks that you *must* deal with in making your present decisions; and exercising your present identity as one who moulds their fate rather than letting their fate mould them.

The secret of dealing with the shock that lies in the future for you is not that you should try to nail down every plank of that future, to spell it out and then stick to it, no matter what . . . (This is what it is going to be like, and this is what I am determined it shall be. On March 4, 1988, I will be doing exactly thus and so.) That's ridiculous, even as "the Now Generation" was so quick to point out.

Rather, the secret of dealing with the future is to nail down what you have in this present – and see the different ways in which the basic units of *that* can be rearranged, anytime you choose, into different constellations that are consistent with the goals and values that direct your inner nature.

YOU ARE AIMING AT BEING ABLE ULTIMATELY TO FILL IN THIS CHART:

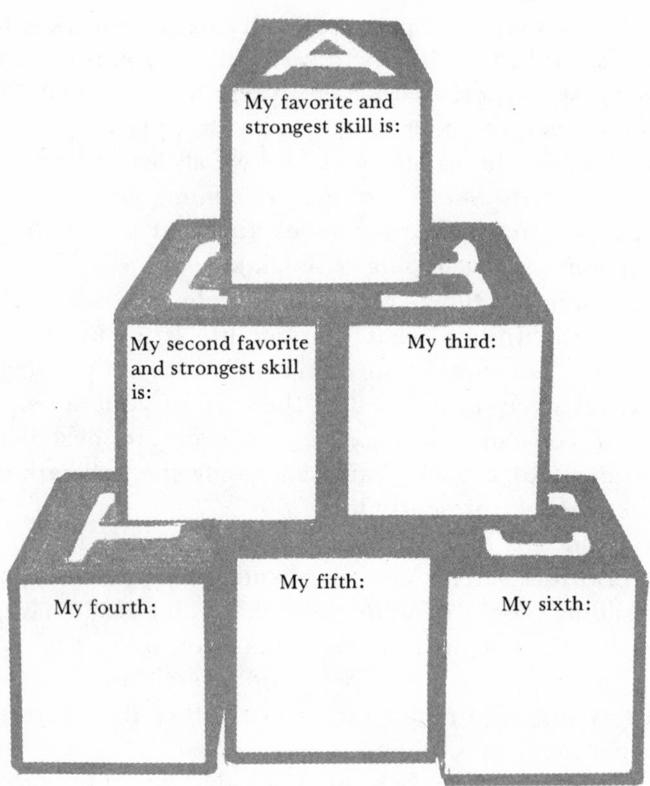

THAT BOGEY-WORD – Skills

Now, many people just "freeze" when they hear the word "skills." It begins with high school job hunters: "I haven't really got any skills," they say. It continues with college students: "I've spent four years in college. I haven't had time to pick up any skills." And it lasts through the middle years, especially when a person is thinking of changing his or her career: "I'll have to go back to college, and get retrained, because otherwise I won't have any skills in my new field." Or: "Well, if I claim any skills, I'll start at a very entry kind of level." All of this fright about the word "skills" is very common, and stems from a total misunderstanding of what the word means. A misunderstanding that is shared, we might add, by altogether too many employers, personnel departments, and other so-called "vocational experts."

By understanding the word, you will automatically put yourself way ahead of most job-hunters. And, especially if you are weighing a change of career, you can save yourself much waste of time on the (currently popular) folly called "going back to school for retraining."

So, herewith our crash-course on skills:

According to the *Bible* of vocational counseling – the fourth edition of the *Dictionary of Occupational Titles,* (U.S. Government Printing Office, Washington, DC, 1977) – skills break down, first of all, into three groups according to whether or not they are being used with Data (Information), or People or Things. (See diagram.) Thus broken down, and arranged in a

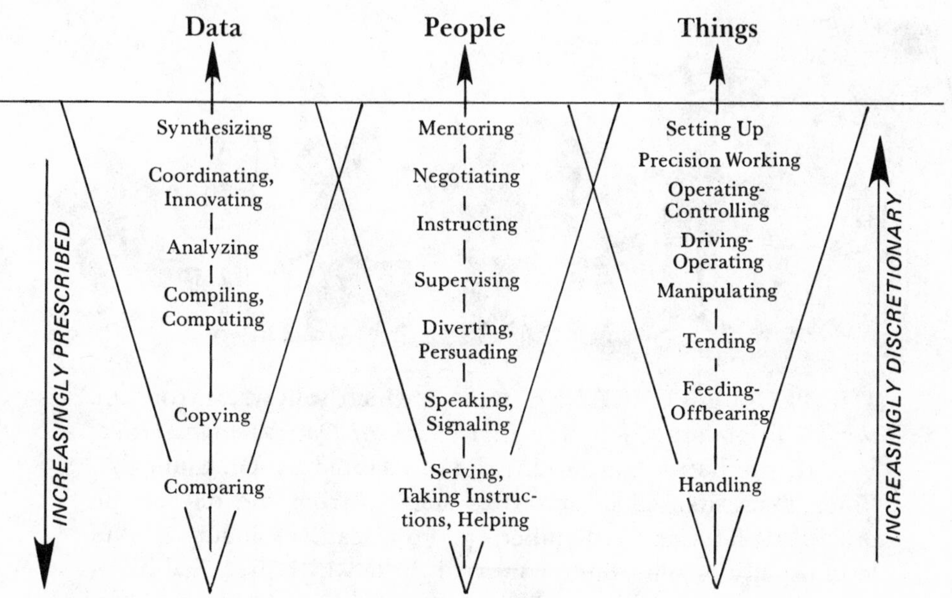

hierarchy of less complex skills (at the bottom) to more complex skills (at the top), they come out looking like inverted pyramids.

Before we explain these skills in more detail, let us look at the *most startling fact about all these skills.* It is, simply, this:

If you graded all these skills in terms of how many of their duties are prescribed in detail, i.e., by a boss, vs. how many are discretionary, i.e., left to the discretion of the employee, you would discover that the lower the skill, the *more* its duties are prescribed, with comparatively little discretion left to the employee; but, the higher the skill, the less its duties are prescribed, and the more that is left to the discretion of the employee.

This almost paradoxical meaning of the word "skill" can be easily illustrated from any, or all, of the three hierarchies on the previous page. For the sake of comparative brevity, we will take just one, namely that which deals with people. (You know, today when most people are asked what they want to do out in The World, they will almost always answer, "I want to work with people." Might as well show those of us who say this, just how varied Work with People can be.) Note, as we progress to higher levels of skills, *how it becomes harder and harder for a prospective employer (say) to draw up a job description for this skill.*

THE PEOPLE FUNCTIONS SCALE which follows, is from the *third* edition (1965) of the *Dictionary of Occupational Titles,* Vol. II, pp. 649-50, as modified and adapted by Dr. Sidney A. Fine. Thus, its skills list differs slightly from the one in the previous pictorial. Remember, as you read, each higher skill level usually or typically involves all those which preceded it.

INCREASING LEVELS OF SKILL

Beginning With
The Most Elementary Definition

TAKING INSTRUCTIONS – HELPING
Attends to the work assignment, instructions, or orders of supervisor. No immediate response or verbal exchange is required unless clarification of instruction is needed.

SERVING
Attends to the needs or requests of people or animals, or to the expressed or implicit wishes of people. Immediate response is involved.

EXCHANGING INFORMATION
Talks to, converses with, and/or signals people to convey or obtain information, or to clarify and work out details of an assignment, within the framework of well-established procedures.

COACHING
Befriends and encourages individuals on a personal, caring basis by approximating a peer- or family-type relationship either in a one-to-one or small group situation, and gives instruction, advice, and personal assistance concerning activities of daily living, the use of various institutional services, and participation in groups.

PERSUADING
Influences others in favor of a product, service, or point of view by talks or demonstrations.

DIVERTING Amuses others.

CONSULTING
Serves as a source of technical information and gives such information or provides ideas to define, clarify, enlarge upon, or sharpen procedures, capabilities, or product specifications.

INSTRUCTING
Teaches subject matter to others, or trains others, including animals, through explanation, demonstration, practice, and test.

TREATING
Acts on or interacts with individuals or small groups of people or animals who need help (as in sickness) to carry out specialized therapeutic or adjustment procedures. Systematically observes results of treatment within the framework of total personal behavior because unique individual reactions to prescriptions (chemical, behavioral, physician's) may not fall within the range of prediction. Motivates, supports, and instructs individuals to accept or cooperate with therapeutic adjustment procedures, when necessary.

continued next page

INCREASING LEVELS OF SKILL continued

SUPERVISING
Determines and/or interprets work procedure for a group of workers, assigns specific duties to them (particularly those which are prescribed), maintains harmonious relations among them, evaluates performance (both prescribed and discretionary), and promotes efficiency and other organizational values. Makes decisions on procedural and technical levels.

NEGOTIATING
Exchanges ideas, information, and opinions with others on a formal basis to formulate policies and programs on an initiating basis (e.g., contracts) and/or arrives at resolutions of problems growing out of administration of existing policies and programs, usually after a bargaining process.

MENTORING
Deals with individuals in terms of their overall life adjustment behavior in order to advise, counsel, and/or guide them with regard to problems that may be resolved by legal, scientific, clinical, spiritual and/or other professional principles. Advises clients on implications of diagnostic or similar categories, courses of action open to deal with a problem, and merits of one strategy over another.

At your public library, in the current (1977) edition of the D.O.T., as the "in crowd" calls the *Dictionary of Occupational Titles*, pp. 1369-1371 you can find similar lists for Data and Things, if you think that you prefer to work primarily with them, rather than with people.

The point of all this for you, the career-changer/job-hunter, is:

1. The lower the level of skills that you think you should claim, the more the skills can be prescribed and measured and demanded of you. In other words, you'll have to fit in. Conversely, the higher the level of skills that you can honestly claim, the less these skills can be prescribed and measured, and the more you will be free to carve out the job in the shape of *you* – making the fullest use of the special constellation of abilities that are yours.

2. The higher the level of skills that you can honestly and legitimately claim either with people, or data or things (or, in varying degree, with all three) the less likely it is that the kinds

of jobs you are thus qualified for will be advertised or known through normal channels; the more you'll have to find other ways of unearthing them – which is what the next chapter is all about.

3. Just because the opportunities for such higher level jobs or careers are harder to uncover, the higher you aim the fewer people you will have to compete with – for that job. In fact, if you uncover, as you are very likely to, a need in the organization (or organizations) which you like, a need which your skills can absolutely help solve, that organization is very likely to create a brand new job for you, which means – in effect – you will be competing with practically no one, since you will be the sole applicant, as it were.

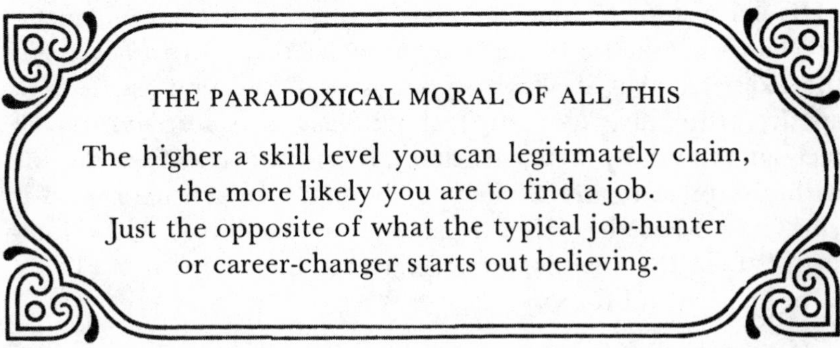

THE PARADOXICAL MORAL OF ALL THIS

The higher a skill level you can legitimately claim,
the more likely you are to find a job.
Just the opposite of what the typical job-hunter
or career-changer starts out believing.

So, now that you know you are looking for your highest level of skills, on with the homework:

- **TOOLS & INSTRUMENTS TO HELP YOU: MEMORIES, FEELINGS, AND VISIONS**

What you need, at this point, are some practical – some very practical – tools or instruments. So, we are going to list a lot of them. You may want to try every one. Or, you may want to approach them as a kind of smorgasbord, picking and choosing a few from among all those that are offered. Your problem, in that case: how to know which ones to choose?

If you have a reflective-type mind, it will have struck you already that long range planning must include some elements of your past, your present and your future.

The kinds of exercises which are available to you correspond to these three divisions of time.

To be sure, there is overlapping, but in terms of their major emphasis, we can categorize the following exercises in these terms:

YOUR MEMORIES (OF THE PAST):
Exercises No. 1, 2, 3 and 4.

YOUR FEELINGS (ABOUT THE PRESENT):
Exercises No. 5, 6, 7 and 8.

YOUR VISIONS (OF THE FUTURE):
Exercises No. 9 and 10.

You'll know which ones can best help YOU, by taking into account the following considerations:

If, because of pell-melling change or great stress, your memory has just taken a holiday, then we suggest you forget about the exercises that deal with your past. Or, if you are deep in apathy, (literally, *lack* of feelings; lack of *consciousness* of feelings would be a better description) the exercises dealing with the present aren't likely to be of too much help. And if you have what the Johnson O'Connor people call "low foresight," then the exercises that deal with the future aren't likely to be too fruitful for you.

If, on the other hand, your whole mind is having trouble, then we suggest you go get a *good* rest before you tackle *any* of these exercises. It may be, of course, that even with a good rest, your mind balks at the thought of doing a whole bunch of exercises. This sort of activity *always* turned you off in school, and – *like that.*

I need to point out that what may be surfacing here is the fact that your mind does better with pictures, and visualization, than it does with words and written exercises. Or, to use psychological jargon, the right-side of your brain (which thrives on pictures) may take precedence over the left-side of your brain (which thrives on words).[1] If so, draw, cut and paste, doodle, take pictures, rather than writing words, words, words.

---

1. For more about this subject, and for some possible help with visualizing—before you tackle any of these exercises—see the resources that are listed in the Bibliography, under the heading: # 19. The Nature of Your Brain, and How to Stimulate Creativity, and Decision-Making (p. 267).

Exercises 1, 2, 3, and 4 – involving
YOUR MEMORIES OF THE PAST

Career and life planning involves the past, as well as the present and future, because:

1. You are being encouraged to develop a holistic (rather than atomistic) approach to life, one which *builds upon* previous experiences, rather than rejecting them.
2. You are being encouraged to see that the drives which will dictate your future course have not been inactive up until now, but have been continually manifesting themselves in what you have done best, and enjoyed doing the most.
3. You are being encouraged to see that your life is a continuum, with a steady continuing core, no matter how the basic units or building blocks may need to be rearranged. The change lies in *the varying constellation* that these basic units are rearranged into (see page 76); but everything you enjoy most and do best will basically use the same building blocks that your past activities did.

In the light of all this, you need to look back and see when you were most enjoying life – and precisely what activities you were doing at that moment, what skills or talents you were employing, what kinds of tasks you were dealing with, what kinds of accomplishments were being done, and precisely what it was that was "turning you on."

Here, then, are some exercises and instruments designed to assist you in doing this (don't just read them as you go – *do* them):

Practical Exercise No. 1

A. Write a diary of your entire life. An informal essay of where you've been, what you've done. Where you were working, what you did there (not in terms of job titles – forget them – but in terms of what you feel you achieved).

B. Boast a little. Boast a lot. Who's going to see this document, besides you, God, and any twenty people that you choose to show it to? Back up your elation and sense of pride with concrete examples, and figures.

C. Describe your spare time, in each place where you lived. What did you do? What did you most enjoy doing? Any

hobbies? Avocations? Great. What skills did they use? Were there any activities in your work that paralleled the kinds of things you enjoyed doing in your leisure?

D. Concentrate both on the things you have done, and also on the particular characteristics of your surroundings that were important to you, and that you really enjoyed: green grass, the theater, golfing, warm climate, skiing, or whatever.

E. Keep your eye constantly on that "divine radar:" *enjoyable.* It's by no means *always* a guide to what you should be doing, but it sure is more reliable than any other key that people have come up with. Sift later. For now, put down anything that helped you to enjoy a particular moment or period of your life.

F. Don't try to make this diary very structured. You can bounce back and forth in time, if that's more helpful; then go back later, and use the questions above (and others later) to check yourself out. If you need further help with how you go about writing a diary like this, by all means get your hands on

Where Do I Go From Here With My Life? by that genius, John Crystal and friend.[1]

G. When your diary is all done, you may have a small book – it can run 30–200 pages. (My, you've done a lot of living, haven't you?) Now to go back over it, take a separate sheet of paper, and put two columns on it:

Things Which, On The Basis of Past Experience, I Want To Have or Use In My Future Career(s) (With Particular Attention To Skills)	Things Which, On The Basis of Past Experience, I Want To Avoid In My Future Career(s)

As you go back over the diary, each time you come to something you feel fits in the first column, put it there. Each time you come to something negative in your past that you feel fits in the second column, put that there.

H. When you come to a skill that you a) *enjoyed* AND b) *did well* (in *your* opinion), put it down in the first column *and underline it twice.*

I. When this is all done, go back over column one, looking primarily for skills. Choose the most important ones (*to you* – again, only your opinion counts) – choose 10, 9, 8, 7, 6, 5, but not less than five. Underline these three times.

J. Now rank them in order of decreasing importance to you. You can use the chart on page 76. Fill it in. Now you have your basic units.

K. What this exercise has left you with (hopefully) are: a) six or more building blocks that when woven together will form one coherent job description for you; b) a couple of lists which list (for your own private thinking, at the moment) some other things you want to have, or avoid, in your future employment.

So much for this exercise. If it helps, great. But maybe you are a high-school or college student or housewife, who feels you

1. See also: Daniel, Lois, *How to Write Your Own Life Story.* Chicago Review Press, 8320 N. Franklin, Chicago, IL 60610. 1980. $7.95, paper. Or: Johnson, Alberta W., and Rustad, Rachel, *The Storybook: A Personal Diary.* Memory Maker Series, 2434 E. Medicine Lake Blvd., Minneapolis, MN 55441. 1977. $7.50, paper.

haven't done enough yet (work-wise) for the foregoing exercise to be very profitable; if so, there is:

Practical Exercise No. 2

List all the hobbies you have done over the years, and then organize them in terms of greatest enjoyment, on down, to see what you were doing, what skills you were using, and what results you were accomplishing. This may give you a clue to what skills you enjoy using the most when no one is telling you what to do.

You can do this same exercise, of course, with your courses in school, etc.

The above exercises, to be sure, leave you a lot of freedom to go about them however you want. But perhaps you want a little more direction and help; maybe a more systematic printed-type thing; in which case, consult the various workbooks in Appendix B under #3. Vocational or Career Planning (page 250).

Why so many workbooks? Well, there is a continuing search going on for more perfect (i.e., helpful) instruments. And each inventor of a new instrument will often claim that theirs is more effective, scientific, objective, definitive, helpful and what-have-you, than anybody else's. The truth is:

Some people are more helped by one device, and other people are more helped by other devices. You have to hunt (some) until you find the one that helps *you* the most.

One systematic printed-type thing you may like, is:

Practical Exercise No. 3

Bernard Haldane in his books[1] presents a most helpful instrument for analyzing your skills. Bernard is one of the pioneers in the whole job-hunting field in this country. He has developed a very particular definition of the word "achievement," which is: "Something you yourself feel you have done well, that you have also enjoyed doing and felt proud of." His instrument has

1. Haldane, Bernard, *Career Satisfaction and Success: A Guide to Job Freedom.* 1974. Amacom, 135 West 50th Street, New York, NY 10020. P. 66ff.
Haldane, Bernard; Haldane, Jean; and Martin Lowell, *Job Power Now! The Young People's Job Finding Guide.* 1976. Acropolis Books, 2400 17th Street, N.W., Washington, DC 20009. P. 21ff.

you choose achievements from different portions of your life, fifteen, twenty or more; then has you select the ten top ones, and of these ten, prioritize the top seven. These seven are then described by you in detail, thence checked-off on a "motivated-skills" chart. Arthur Miller[1], in a slight variation on this, has you choose two achievements for each five-year period of your life. Some of the workbooks alluded to previously have lists similar to the "motivated skills" one – spinoffs from this original idea of Bernard's. Such a spinoff, or rhapsody if you will, is even to be found in The Quick Job-Hunting Map, which is in Appendix A of this book. But you may prefer to go back to the original, in which case Bernard's books (and instruments) are footnoted on page 86.

Regardless of which instrument you decide to use, where you should end up eventually is in the same place that we did on page 76. You should, that is, end up with building blocks of skills, which will form the backbone of your future job description, or your future new career.

In the previous instruments or exercises, you may be "hung up" over the idea of bragging – bragging about your achievements, accomplishments, successes, and the like. The Puritan in each of us dies hard, so it may be time for –

"A SPECIAL WORD FOR PURITANS"

Puritans come in all sizes, shapes, genders, ages, and colors. Puritans allegedly believe in God; but, what a god! A Puritan believes that God didn't intend us to enjoy anything. And that if you enjoy it, it's probably wrong for you. Let us illustrate:

Two girls do babysitting. One hates it. One enjoys it thoroughly. Which is more virtuous in God's sight? According to the Puritan, the one who hates it is more virtuous.

Two Puritans met on the street. "Isn't this a beautiful day?" said one. "Aye," said the other, "but we'll pay for it."

Puritans will talk about their failures, but hardly ever about their successes – and even then, always with a feeling that "God is going to get me, for such boasting." It's too enjoyable!

Given the Puritan's belief in God, what the Puritan fails to recognize is that enjoyment, in human life, isn't a fluke. It's

1. Miller, Arthur F., and Mattson, Ralph T., *the TRUTH about you: Discover what you should be doing with your life.* 1977. Fleming H. Revell Company, Old Tappan, NJ 07675. P. 145ff.

part of God's plan. God wants us to eat; therefore God designs us so that eating is enjoyable. God wants us to sleep; therefore God designs us so that sleeping is enjoyable. God wants to have us procreate, love, and make love; therefore God designs us so that sex is enjoyable, and love even more so. *God gives us unique (or at least unusual) skills and talents; therefore God designs us so that, when we use these, they are enjoyable.*

That is, we gain a sense of achievement from them.

So, Puritans arise; if you believe in God, believe in One who believes in you. Downgrading yourself is out — for the duration.

Practical Exercise No. 4

When you are through with all of the above exercises, you may have a lot of data about your past life at your fingertips, but be puzzled about how you use this data to make decisions concerning your future. Indeed, one of the skills some of us never got any help with when we were going through our country's vaunted school-system, is how you go about making decisions. If this is a particular hangup for you, you will want to know that the College Entrance Examination Board has published a helpful instrument which you can get for $2.50. It is entitled *Deciding.*[1] A similar book has been published particularly for women: *How to Decide, A Workbook for Women.*[2] And a newer resource you may also want to get help from is Bruce Becker's *Decisions: Getting What You Want.*[3]

Exercises 5, 6, 7, and 8 – involving
YOUR FEELINGS ABOUT THE PRESENT

Maybe your memory isn't so hot, lately. If so, of course the previous exercises aren't going to be very useful to you, whatever help they may be to others. Sooooo, we press on to the present. No need for memory, here; just feelings.

But what use, you may ask, are feelings, in trying to determine what kind of work one should do? Aren't we interested only in skills, talents, and all that? Well, not exactly. You see, studies have revealed that:

1. Your interests, wishes and happiness determine what you actually do well, more than your intelligence, aptitudes, or skills do. This is the conclusion of numerous vocational psychologists (Holland, Mierzwa, Clark, Crites) and personnel people (Snelling, and others). Strength of desire outweighs everything else, they say.

Maybe the word "feelings" or "wishes" sounds just too "fantasy-like" to your ears. OK then, borrowing a word from biology, let's speak instead of "tropisms:" things which living creatures instinctively go toward, or away from. The human animal is no exception, and we each have our own personal, unique tropisms. So, ask yourself: what do you feel drawn toward, what do you instinctively go away from? Make some lists. Your own personal tropisms may be determinative for your future career.

---

1. It may be ordered from Publications Order Office, College Entrance Examination Board, Box 592, Princeton, NJ 08540. (And if, by any chance, this is to be used in a job-hunting *group*, there is also *Deciding: A Leader's Guide*, free with each thirty copies of *Deciding.*)
2. Available from Avon Books, 959 Eighth Ave., New York, NY 10019. $4.95, paper.
3. Grosset & Dunlap, Inc., 51 Madison Ave., New York, NY 10010. 1978. $8.95, hardcover.

2. If you do work that you really feel good about, and at the highest level of skills that you can legitimately and honestly claim, you are bound to do an outstanding job, and be of genuine help to others – as the creative minority (Haldane, Crystal, and others) have long been maintaining.

3. No tests or other instruments have been devised yet, that so effectively measure what you want as just *asking you* or having you *ask yourself.* As John Holland says:

"Despite several decades of research, the most efficient way to predict vocational choice is simply to ask the person what he wants to be; our best devices do not exceed the predictive value of that method."[1]

And now, on to our exercises dealing with the present. The first one, naturally enough, simply takes Holland at his word:

Practical Exercise No. 5

This exercise consists of a very simple question indeed. Write out your answer to the question: If you could have any kind of job, what would it be? Invent your own, if need be; or ask yourself the question, among all the people you know or have seen or read about, whose job would you most like to have? And why? Forget for the moment what you think you *can* do. What do you *want* to do?

You may prefer to put the question to yourself in other forms, or with time sequences: a year from now, ten years from now, twenty years from now? Try them all.

This exercise, of course, presumes that you know what makes you happy. Maybe, however, you have a much clearer idea of what makes you unhappy (a list, as it were, of "negative tropisms" – things you instinctively want to avoid). Okay, the next exercise thrives on that awareness:

Practical Exercise No. 6

Write a detailed answer to the question: "What are the things which make me unhappy?" When you are done, analyze what you've written into two columns, with the first one sub-divided:

1. Reprinted by permission of the publisher, from Holland, John L. *The Psychology of Vocational Choice* (Ginn and Company, Waltham, MA. 1966.) Now out of print.

THINGS THAT LIE WITHIN THE CONTROL OF MYSELF		THINGS THAT LIE WITHIN THE CONTROL OF OTHERS, OR FATE, OR CIRCUMSTANCE
Things which I could change thru a change in my external environment (my job, or the place where I live)	Things which I could change thru working on my interior life (what's going on inside me)	

Check these columns over, when you are done, reviewing the second list to be sure the things listed there *really* are beyond your control or power to alter. Then go over the first list and decide whether the priority for you is to work on your *external* furniture (environment, work, etc.) or your *internal* furniture (personal growth, emotions or spiritual factors), or *both.* List concrete resolutions for yourself, with time goals beside them. Paste the list on your bathroom mirror. Read it each morning.

If you come down, very heavily, in the previous exercise, on the need to deal with your *internal* furniture, then we suggest you go to the back of this book and read Appendix D, page 303.

"WHILE YOU'RE WAITING FOR YOUR SHIP TO COME IN, WHY DON'T YOU DO SOME MAINTENANCE WORK ON THE PIER ?"

Choosing a job is primarily a question of choosing what your *external* furniture should be. Jobs are environments, mostly "people environments," and the issue is how well these correspond to, and are compatible with, your internal furniture. In the past, our society has insisted that when your external furniture and your internal got "out of sync," that you should go get your internal furniture "rearranged," as it were. A lot of people, especially the young, are getting very impatient with this "solution." But not just the young. The increased interest in second careers these days, among those who served "honorably" in their first – clergy, doctors, aerospace engineers, physicists, executives, etc. – may be traced in large part to a new realization that where the external and internal are out of synchronization, it is easier by far (and maybe more sensible) to first try altering the external. To make the environment conform to you, rather than you to the environment.[1]

If you want to take a good hard look at the external *people* environments that are most compatible with your internal furniture, there is an exercise you may like (and a book you *must* read):

Practical Exercise No. 7

Holland's *"The Self-directed Search"* in his *Making Vocational Choices: A Theory of Careers* (Prentice-Hall, 1973) helps to identify particular occupations you might be interested in, defined in terms of your preferred people-environments. Tremendously useful. If you want *"The Self-directed Search"* all by itself, this is available to professionals (get your clergy person, counselor, or placement officer to order it for you) from Consulting Psychologists Press, 577 College Avenue, Palo Alto, CA 94306, for around a dollar. (If you made the acquaintance of this popular and helpful instrument a long time ago, you may want to know that it has been rather substantially revised, beginning with the 1977 edition. One hundred and thirty-nine changes were made, together with the elimination of all graphs from the main instrument. The auxiliary "Occupa-

1. Finding a balance between the external (work) and internal (love) is explored at length in Jay B. Rohrlich's *Work and Love: the crucial balance.* (Summit Books, Simon & Schuster Bldg., 1230 Avenue of the Americas, New York, NY 10020. 1980. $10.95, hardcover.)

tions Finder" now has 500 occupational titles in it. And a complementary and important guide "Understanding Yourself and Your Career," by John L. Holland, has been issued for use with *"The Self-directed Search."*) These materials are helpful with all ages, but especially high-school students, and those entering the labor market for the first time.

If you want to do some hard thinking about the internal "You" that your work environment has got to be compatible with, in order for you to be happy, then we suggest you try the following exercise:

Practical Exercise No. 8

1. Take ten sheets of paper. Write on the top of each one the words: Who am I?
2. Then write, on each sheet, *one* answer to that question. At the end of the ten sheets, you'll have the same question written, but ten different answers.
3. Now go back over the ten again, and looking at each answer, write below it on each sheet *what turns you on* about that particular answer.
4. Go back over the ten sheets, and arrange them in order of priority. Your most important identity goes on top. Then, in order, on down to the identity that is *to you* of least importance, among the ten.

5. Finally, go back over the ten sheets, looking particularly at the answers you wrote (on each page) to *What turns you on?* and see if there are some common denominators.
6. If so, you have begun to put your finger on some things that your career (vocation, job or whatever) *must use* if you are to be truly happy, fulfilled, and effective – to the height of your powers.

Since this can be an eye-opening exercise, if you possess some degree of self-knowledge, but difficult if you don't, let us show how one person filled it out. This is not in any way to suggest the kind of answers you should give, but only to flesh out these instructions with an example from one completed exercise – (shown in box at right):

This is but one illustration. There are many other levels that the exercise can be done at. Be as wild, imaginative, and creative as you want to be with it.

And when it is done, here are some check-back questions, to be sure you have gotten all that you can out of the exercise:

CHECKBACK:
PRACTICAL EXERCISE NO. 8
CONCLUDED

7. What is it that, if I lost it, life would have no meaning? Is it included in the exercise above? If not, why not? (Think hard, and revise your answers, in the light of this new insight.)
8. Out of the ten identifications of myself, and the ten lists of things which turn me on, which of these *must* be included in any job I have? *Remember the world is already filled with people who have to wait until after 5 p.m. to do all the things they really enjoy.*

Those of you who feel there is too much emphasis on *doing* in our society, and not enough on *being*, should find the above exercise particularly up your alley.

[SAMPLE — PRACTICAL EXERCISE NO. 8]

Part 1 Who Am I?

1. A man
2. An urban dweller (and lover)
3. A loving person
4. A creator
5. A writer
6. A lover of good movies and music
7. A skilled counselor and teacher
8. An independent
9. An executive
10. An enabler

Part 2 What Turns Me On About These?

1. Taking initiative, having inner strength; being open, growing, playful
2. Excitement, variety of choices available, crowds, faces
3. Feelings, empathizing, playfulness, sex, adoration given, happiness
4. Transforming things, making old things new, familiar wondrous
5. Beauty of words, variety of images, new perspectives, new relationships of ideas, words, understandings
6. Watching people up close, merging of color, photography, music
7. Using intuition, helping, seeing totalities of people, problem solving, long-term close helpful relationships
8. Making own decisions, carrying out own plans
9. Taking responsibility, wise risks, using mind, seeing totalities of problems overall
10. Helping people to become freed-up, to be what they want to be.

Part 3 Any Common Denominators?

Variety, totalities, rearranging of constellations, dealing with a number of different things and showing relationships between them all in a new way, helping others.

Part 4 What Must My Career Use (and Include) For Me To Be Truly Happy, Used and Effective?

A variety of different things that have to be dealt with, with people, where seeing totalities, rearranging their relationships, and interpreting them to people in a new way is at the heart of the career.

Exercises 9 and 10 – involving YOUR VISIONS OF THE FUTURE

If your memory groans at the idea of trying to remember the past, and if your feelings about yourself in the present are difficult for you to put into words, there is still another family of exercises available to you – which may help you pinpoint just exactly what it is that you want to do with your life. And they are, of course, those exercises which deal with the future.

The future. It sounds far away, mystical, and mysterious. But, as someone has said,

"We ought to be interested in the future, for that is where we are going to spend the rest of our lives."

Most of us have our visions and dream our dreams. It's only when we come to our job, and what we want to do with the rest of our lives, that we think our visions and dreams should be shelved. In career planning there is a certain group of professionals, here and there, who love to play the game of getting you to say just what you want to do, and then "bringing you down to earth" by saying, "All right; now, let's get realistic." What they should ask is, "Are you *sure* this is what you really want?" because if it is, chances are you will find some way to do it. Remember the man who was called "The Great Imposter." Whatever he badly wanted to do, he found a way to do. Something of him lives in us all.

Never mind "being realistic." For every person who "over-dreams" – of doing more than their merits would justify, – there are four people who "under-dream," and sell themselves short. According to experts, 80% of the workers in this country are "under-employed," as we noted earlier. Trying to be "realistic" too early in your career planning becomes a prison for your mind. You are not going to do your homework very effectively if you try to keep one eye fixed on your dreams, and one eye fixed on what you *think* you know about the job market, e.g., "I'd like to be able to do this and that at my job, but I *know* there is no job in the world like that."

Granted, you may not be able to find a job that has all that you want. But why not aim for it, and then settle for less if and when you find out that you simply have to? Don't foreclose your future prematurely. You'd be surprised what you may be able to turn up (see the next chapter).

To be sure, dreams sometimes have to be taken in stages. If you want to be president of a particular enterprise, for example, you may have to work your way toward it through two or three steps. But it is quite possible you will eventually succeed – *if your whole heart is in your dream.*[1]

If you still doubt, then maybe you'd better do a little extra-curricular reading first, like Barbara Sher's *Wishcraft: How*

---

1. For further reading, see: Terkel, Studs, *American Dreams: Lost and Found.* Ballantine Books, Dept. AL, 201 E. 50th St., New York, NY 10022. 1981, 1980. $3.50, plus $.50 postage and handling, if ordering by mail.

to Get What You Really *Want.*[1] Whether you read this or not, when you feel that dreams once dreamed, and maybe since forgotten, are worth dusting off again, here are some exercises to help you:

Practical Exercise No. 9

Spend as much time as necessary writing an article entitled "Before I die, I want to . . . ." (Things you would like to do, before you die.) Confess them to yourself now, and maybe you can begin to make them happen.

You may prefer to write an article on a similar topic: "On the last day of my life, what must I have done or been so that my life will have been satisfying to me?" When finished, go back over it and make two lists: Things Already Accomplished, and: Things Yet To Be Accomplished. Then make a third column, beside the one called Things Yet To Be Accomplished, listing the particular *steps* that you will have to take, in order to accomplish these things that you have listed.

1 Things already accomplished.	2 Things yet to be accomplished. *(Then number them in the order in which you would like to accomplish them.)*	3 Steps needed in order to accomplish the things in column 2

As you get involved with these exercises you may notice that it is impossible to keep your focus only on your vocation, occupation, career or whatever you want to call it. You will find some dreams creeping in concerning your leisure or your lifelong learning — of places you want to visit, some things you want to learn, some experiences you want to have, that are not on-the-job. *Don't omit these.* Be just as specific and yet holistic as possible. Incidentally, you don't have to do the above exercise just once in your life. Some experts in career and life planning suggest turning the previous exercise into a continuous one, with a list posted on your office or kitchen wall — crossing out items as you accomplish them, and adding new ones as they occur to you from month to month.

---

1. Written with Annie Gottlieb, and published by Viking Press, from whom you can order it if your bookstore doesn't have it: 625 Madison Avenue, New York, NY 10022. 1979. $9.95, hardcover.

Turning from dreams (albeit, concrete, solid dreams) to visions, let us talk of goals and purposes – for these are the visions of the future which cause men and women to set their hands to present tasks. Here is an exercise to deal with the goals that drive you (and there always are such, even if for you they are presently undefined):

Practical Exercise No. 10

Think of some practical concrete task or project in your life, hopefully in the present, that you are a) doing successfully and b) enjoying immensely. (Well, besides that!) It could be at your work, at school, at home or in your spare time. But it must be one which really "turns you on." Put down this task in the center of a blank piece of 8½ x 11 paper turned on its side. Then take the following steps:

1. Begin at the lower left hand side of the page, and write the word "why?" (do/did you want to do this), and on the line above it, indented, write that reason, goal, or purpose.
2. Then write "why?" after this answer, too; and on the line above *it*, indented even more, see if you can write an even more basic reason, goal or purpose.
3. Then write "why?" after it, and on the line above . . . etc., etc., etc. Continue this exercise up the paper, until you think you have reached a purpose or goal that is rather ultimate. (You cannot think of any "why?" behind it.)
4. Now, take that most basic goal (the topmost one on the paper), and draw an arrow from it, down to the part of the paper that is beside the "task" with which you began. There, write the words "how else?" and think of what other tasks or projects would accomplish the same ultimate goal (the topmost one on your paper). In the end, your exercise will look something like this.

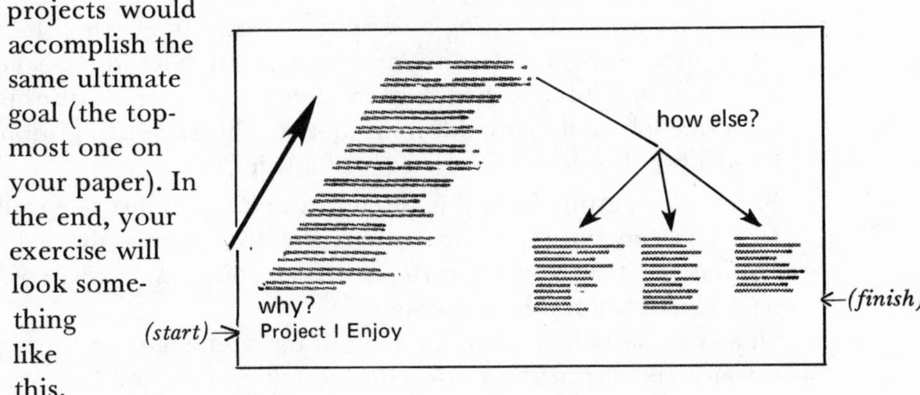

5. Repeat this schema with other projects or tasks that have really "turned you on," using a new piece of paper for each one. See if you begin to see what turns you on about life, and if you begin to see some alternate strategies (or jobs) that could accomplish the same goals. If you "run out of gas" by step four, consult some wise friend or vocational counselor (at school or wherever). This exercise, incidentally, can begin with a job you have, rather than with a task you enjoyed doing. It is particularly useful if you've lost your job, can't find any place else where you could do the same kind of work, and you're at an absolute loss to know what else to do.

IN SUMMARY: CHECK BACK

So much for our exercises. You've at least skimmed through them. Now please try them. One or two. Or (if you're the really thorough type) all of them. Do enough until they achieve your purpose – knowing exactly what you want to do. And if you draw a blank with all of them, you obviously are going to have to turn to someone for professional help. (See Appendix C.)

But let's assume you've tried some of the exercises. Here's a check list of questions to help you test how well things are going for you thus far:

Check-Back Questions:

1. Have you identified the basic building blocks (and filled the chart in, on page 76) of your strongest skills and interests? (Strongest = done best *and* enjoyed *and* feel confident about.)
Do you prefer most to be related to people, data, or things? Or all three? In what priority?
Have you avoided putting a definitive (restricting) job title on what you want to do, at least until you have done some informational interviewing? (There are many different titles for the same job, and many different jobs for the same title – don't build a box for yourself by means of a title.)

2. Are you getting locked in, in your thinking, to just one route to go in the future, or are you trying to preserve alternative options, so that you see different ways your basic skills could be utilized, and not just *one* way?
What risks are there: a) in the kind of job you might be working towards and b) in the route you are taking thereto? Have you

provided for alternative procedures, techniques and goals if those risks materialize?

When all is said and done, are you planning for a changing world, or are you assuming the world will stay still while you move? (As the experts say, *Planning without planning for change is planning for nothing but trouble.*)

3. What time spans are *built in* to the route that you have decided upon, or that you think you ought to take?

If you decide you simply *have to have* credentials, what date will you need them by, how long will it take to get them; and, when – therefore – should you start working on this? If you decide you need experience, where, how, and how long? When will you need it, how long will it take to get it, when should you start?[1]

4. Do you know what questions of life you are most earnestly seeking answers to?

Do you know now what you are after in life? Your needs? Your values? Your tropisms – the things that you instinctively (or otherwise) go *toward,* and the things you instinctively go *away from?* The things that make you happy, and the things that make you unhappy?

Which values actually hold the most attraction for you (not *should* but *do*): service, security, status, popularity, recognition, approval, affection, belongingness, acceptance, power, achievement, authority, glamour, wealth, etc.? Which rewards hold the most meaning for you?

5. In terms of the goals you are moving toward, will a change in externals (your environment, job, place of work, and so forth) be sufficient? Or do you feel that you also need some internal movement and growth? If so, in what areas?

To the extent that you can put a label on what is bothering you in your career/life at the moment, would you characterize it basically as Conflict or Frustration? Or both? Or neither? What, then? (Frustration is between an individual and their environment, and would point to the need for a new work environment. Conflict is within an individual, and points to the need for personal help and personal growth.)

---

1. If time is a continuing problem or hangup for you, you may wish to get your hands on Peter F. Drucker's *The Effective Executive.* Harper & Row, New York, NY. 1967. Excellent on time-use.

6. Do you feel that all planning of this nature is just too much work? Too long and lonely? (To sing our old song once again, how about involving your loved ones in it with you? – you might be surprised at the increased communication and its helpful benefits!)
If you don't do any planning, what will rescue you (or who) if you reach a dead-end in creativity, work and happiness? (As Ezra Pound said, *A slave is one who waits for someone else to come and free him.*)

PUTTING THE BUILDING BLOCKS TOGETHER

Okay, let's assume you pass all the above "check-backs." You know what the basic building blocks of your skills are. Now, you want to know, of course, how do you arrange them into different constellations or careers?

We begin with some basic vocabulary:

• *Jobs, positions, work, careers* are used by some people to mean different things and by other people to mean essentially the same thing. The Distinguishers vs. The Synonymists. The former generally tend to regard the word "job" as a dirty word. By job, they mean *just a job.* The Distinguishers are exquisitely careful about their vocabulary, and may look down on the Synonymists – who are not so precise. The latter feel that the framework of thinking within which a person uses particular words is of more significance and importance than the particular words they may or may not use.

• *Tasks, functions, aptitudes, abilities, skills* – another group of words used by some people to mean very different things, and by other people to mean essentially the same thing. The Distinguishers can give carefully differentiated meanings, which are all supported completely by Webster's Unabridged. The Synonymists, on the other hand, take you by the hand out onto the street and bid you listen to Everyday conversation – whereupon you discover that Everyday conversation makes no such careful distinctions between the meanings of these words, most of the time.

If you want to know the jargon, technically *a job is a flexible combination of tasks* – which can be arranged and rearranged in a number of different tantalizing ways. *A career is a flexible combination of skills* – which can be arranged and rearranged in a number of different tantalizing ways.

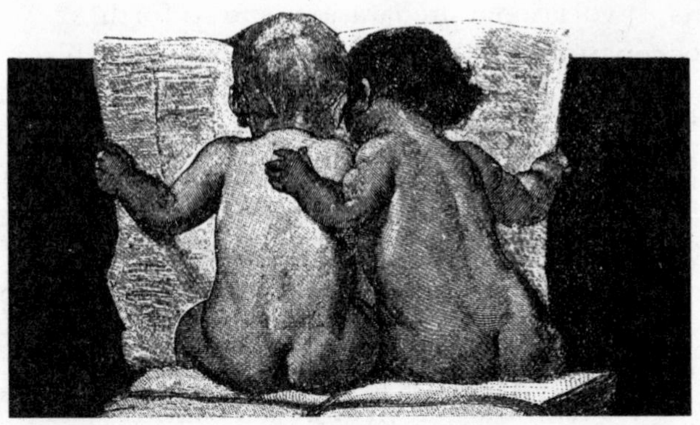

Turning Skills Into Careers

- Researching your skills involves trying to discover what different kinds of careers (i.e., constellations or arrangements of skills) are open to you; and then arranging these in order of priority *according to what you enjoy most.*

Now, beyond vocabulary:

How do you go about nailing this down?
Here are some *beginning* suggestions:

PRACTICAL AID NUMBER 1

The Dictionary of Occupational Titles, fourth edition: Superintendent of Public Documents, Washington, DC. 1977. Based on a concept of *functional job analysis*, the outgrowth of research from 1948-1959 directed by Sidney Fine,[1] this "Bible" of the vocational field lists some 20,000 job titles. Called by experts

1. Sidney's written works are described in Appendix B, p. 270.

either "the greatest single source of occupational information in the world" or "an unwieldy mishmash," you can locate occupations or jobs by a) physical demands, b) individual working conditions, c) interest, d) aptitude or skills, e) educational requirements, f) vocational preparation, and so forth.

Each occupation has been given a nine-digit code number. The first three digits are called *the occupational group* and describe The World of Work. The second three digits describe skills, i.e., what workers do with data, with people, and with things. The last three digits indicate the varying titles of occupations that have in common the first six digits.[1]

You are encouraged to go to your library, and browse in the D.O.T. for a while, to get the feel of it.

The point of all this research is to *be sure that you do not get prematurely locked into one field or occupation, but that you see how many alternative options are open to you.*

Our Canadian readers (or job-hunters in the U.S.A. who want a slightly different perspective) will want to look up in their library the *Canadian Classification and Dictionary of Occupations*, 1971. Vol. I and II. Published by Manpower & Immigration, available from Renouf's, 51 Sparks St., Ottawa, Ontario, Canada K1P 5R1 – or from: Canadian Government Publishing Centre, Supply and Services Canada, 45 Sacre-Coeur Blvd., Hull, Quebec, Canada K1A 059. $20. each volume.

PRACTICAL AID NUMBER 2

A Handbook for Job Restructuring, Superintendent of Documents, U.S. Government Printing Office, Washington, DC 20402. 1970. If your library does not have this, or they cannot get it for you on an Inter-Library Loan (ask!), then I'm afraid you're out of luck, because it's out of print. Has interesting section (pp. 30-42) on "benchmarks" of various skills or aptitudes. "Benchmarks" are typical situations where, at various levels, the skill is used. If your library can find it for you, I think you will find it at least suggestive.

---

1. Counselors and others who became accustomed to the earlier third edition (1965) of the D.O.T. may want to know that there is now a book entitled *Conversion Table of Code and Title Changes Third to Fourth Edition Dictionary of Occupational Titles.* U.S. Employment Service, 1979. Available from: Superintendent of Documents, U.S. Government Printing Office, Washington DC 20402. $7.50.

PRACTICAL AID NUMBER 3

Occupational Outlook Handbook, U.S. Department of Labor, Washington, DC. Get this at your library. It gives an outline for 300 (or so) occupations. For each one, it lists: what its future looks like, nature of the work, usual training required, employment outlook, earnings and working conditions. Helpful if you don't just want to get into occupations that're closing out; but its prophecies should be taken with a large barrel (not just "grain") of salt. There is incidentally an *Occupational Outlook Handbook for College Graduates.*

The very word "outlook" (occupational or employment) ought to make you beware. "A good outlook" for a particular industry only means, if you will stop to think about it, that there is relatively little competition for the openings that exist; i.e., that there are more openings than there are bodies to fill them. On the other hand, "a bad outlook" for a particular field, or a prediction that it is going to be 'crowded,' is only another way of saying there is going to be a lot of competition. That just means you will have to follow the techniques described in this book more faithfully, that's all. Remember, time and time again men and women have gotten positions in a place where everyone told them there was No Employment At All; and they did it by following precisely the strategies described in these chapters.

PRACTICAL AID NUMBER 4

In the course of researching your skills, we urge you to consult with one or more of the following persons, to ask them: What occupations use the skills that I have?

Your *librarian* (or business librarian); *counselors* at the appropriate department of your local State Employment office; *friends* knowledgeable in the fields that interest you; *consultants* to the fields you are interested in (for a list of people you might possibly want to consult with, see the *Training and Development Directory*, Paul Wasserman, Managing Editor, Second Edition, published by and obtainable from Gale Research Company, Book Tower, Detroit, MI 48226 – or see your friendly neighborhood library); and the like.

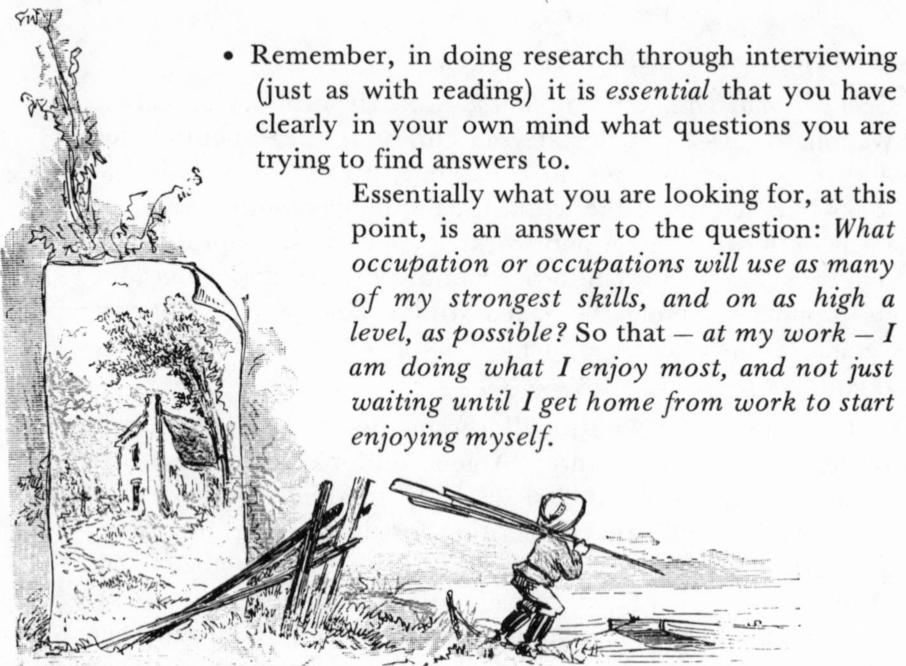

- Remember, in doing research through interviewing (just as with reading) it is *essential* that you have clearly in your own mind what questions you are trying to find answers to.

Essentially what you are looking for, at this point, is an answer to the question: *What occupation or occupations will use as many of my strongest skills, and on as high a level, as possible?* So that – *at my work* – *I am doing what I enjoy most, and not just waiting until I get home from work to start enjoying myself.*

PRACTICAL AID NUMBER 5

In the course of researching a field we urge you to consult with a number of people who are active in it. You should not be hesitant about asking for the time of important people, even heads of companies or corporations. *If they really like their own vocation,* they should be very receptive to your desire to know more about that vocation: what they do, the various kinds of tasks and skills required, and the aspects of it that they particularly enjoy.[1]

---

1. Some employers have complained that since *Parachute* got popular, they are besieged by people wanting to take their time just to discuss what they do. They fear this is happening all over the country. We have found no evidence of this. There are 14 million employing organizations in this country – many of them having countless managers, executives, department heads and others who *might* be thus approached. This inundation is happening only to a comparative few, to those with high visibility, who are well-known and/or are leaders in their field, at least in one particular geographic area. For such employers, a word of advice: set one hour each week or every other week, when you are willing to see such people *as a group*, and don't try to see every individual inquirer by themselves. Then your secretary can simply tell them: "Ms. Vice-President will be happy to talk with you. She has set aside every Monday at 4 p.m. for that kind of sharing."

You say you freeze at the very thought of tackling interviews (even an interview *only for information* with people – afraid you'll botch it up, through shyness or nervousness? Not if it's YOUR enthusiasm you're exploring – the thing in this world you're dying to know more about. But you say, "You don't know what you're asking of me. I mean, I know half the world is shy, but I've got a *terminal case* of that disease." Ah, yes, how well I know. Fortunately, there is help. First of all, a lot of research has been done on the subject of shyness by a man named Philip G. Zimbardo, and he has published his findings (and some helpful antidotes) in two paperbacks: *Shyness, What It Is, What To Do About It*, (if you're too shy to go into your book store to look for it, try ordering it by mail directly from Jove Publications, Inc., 757 Third Avenue, New York, NY 10017. 1977. $2.25 paper). AND: *The Shyness Workbook* (coauthored with Shirley L. Radl, and available from A&W Publishers, Inc., 95 Madison Avenue, New York, NY 10016. 1979. $5.95, paper).

Secondly, when you go out on your informational interviewing, *it's perfectly kosher to take somebody with you* – anyone, though I don't particularly recommend that it be your mother, or your dog Ralph.

Well, okay, but suppose you are still nervous about The Interview – even if it isn't, at this point, for the purpose of getting hired, but only for the purpose of getting some information. Well, maybe you should browse, then, for a copy of *Contact: The First Four Minutes* by Leonard and Natalie Zunin (in your library, paperback bookstore, or directly from Ballantine Books, 201 East 50th Street, New York, NY 10022; published 1972; $1.75). That should help. After all, the harder you work on this, now, the more it's going to repay you later.

Remember, it's 20,000 hours – on up – of your time that you are trying to find out about, when you explore a possible job or career for yourself. Remember also, that you *may* be coming back to some of these men and women in a different role later on (if they are in the area you want to work in), so it would be helpful to leave a good impression behind you. In other words, dress well and conduct yourself as *quietly confident that you would be an asset to any organization you ultimately decide to serve in.*

PRACTICAL AID NUMBER 6

Many, if not most, fields have professional journals. Ask your local librarian to assist you in getting your hands on these. Follow all leads that they may suggest to you, as your reading of articles and ads uncovers these, for additional information.

Again, many if not most fields have professional, trade, or union associations. Your public library has all kinds of listings of such associations – yours for the asking. Such as:

Career Guide to Professional Organizations, compiled and edited by the Staff of The Carroll Press, Box 8113, Cranston, Rhode Island 02910. 1976. $8.95, paper. Classifies nearly 2,000 organizations by occupational field, with cross-references from one career field to another. Or there is:

National Trade and Professional Associations of the United States and Canada and Labor Unions, Craig Colgate, Jr., Editor, Patricia Broida, Assistant Ed. Columbia Books, Inc., Publishers, 734 15th St., NW, Washington, D.C. 20005. Volume XV – 1980. $30, paper. Lists 6,000 national trade associations, labor unions, scientific or technical societies and other national organizations – alphabetically, geographically, by budget, by key word, and by executive/directors.

Try to see what other resources there are, in the city or town where you are: Chamber of Commerce library; university libraries; libraries at appropriate businesses, etc.

PRACTICAL AID NUMBER 7

If you decide that what you want help in researching are "alternative kinds" of work, then we suggest you look at some of what (in the old days) were called "counter-culture" directories: such as Peoples' Yellow Pages (for various cities). A couple of these are listed on page 265 in this book.

To find further sources of information in your own community, visit "new age" bookstores, food co-ops, health food stores and restaurants, laundromats, some record and bicycle shops, any place organized as a collective, communes, and groups organized around issues (such as the nuclear freeze, rape-crisis centers, etc.) – not to mention the offices of such places as the American Friends Service Committee. You will find that these places attract a goodly number of people committed to alternative kinds of work. So, at the least, look at bulletin boards there (if they have one) plus any literature they may be giving out. Braver still, talk to the staff there; the higher up they are, the more likely that they will know of other resources or contacts for you. And, at the most, get involved there – either as a volunteer, or as an employee. You will make lots of contacts (particularly if they put out some kind of newsletter or any other communication), and you can do loads of informational interviewing there.

If you prefer reading (let's, ahem, call it "boning up" prior to interviewing), see section 16 in the Bibliography at the end of this book (p.264) not to mention sections 14 and 12 (pp. 263, 261 respectively). You will find that browsing in such excellent books as *The Next Whole Earth Catalog, Second Edition,* just to see which subjects strike your fancy, may give you some helpful clues as to the direction your heart and mind are heading in.

If, among alternatives, you are also weighing alternative patterns of working, you will probably want to browse in section 2 of the Bibliography (p. 248), and contact some of the Work Option places listed in section VI, in our Appendix C Resources Guide (p.301).

PRACTICAL AID NUMBER 8

We have placed a number of notes in the back of this book, summarizing *some of the things* that other people have discovered (why shouldn't *you* benefit from their research?) about various fields. So, if you're interested particularly in:

- *business and management,*
- *social service or change,*
- *the education field,*
- *working in government,*
- *self-employment (counseling, consulting, writing, owning your own business, etc.)*
- *going back to school*

} turn to Appendix E on page 309

That section won't save you from having to do your own research, but it will give you clues, at least. Then you *must* go do your own interviewing. While going on your interviewing for information, please remember that the *woods are alive* with people who will solemnly tell you *something that ain't true* as

though they were sure of it with every fibre of their being. So, check and cross check and cross check again the information that books, people, and experts give you. Let no one build any boxes for you; and watch that you don't hand them any wood with which to build one for you.

In the end, there is virtually no information you want to know, that you cannot find out. This is a *knowledge society,* and the only limits – really – lie within you, as to the amount of commitment, diligence and perseverance you want to lavish on all this. If you feel you're not cut out for research, an absolutely invaluable book is *Finding Facts Fast: How to Find Out What You Want and Need to Know,* second edition, by Alden Todd. And subtitled: *A handbook for students, political activists, civic leaders and professionals . . . based on methods used by reference librarians, scholars, investigative reporters and detectives.*[1]

1. See your library, bookstore, or write directly to the publisher: Ten Speed Press, Box 7123, Berkeley, CA 94707. 1979, 1972. $3.95 – and is worth ten times that much. See also: Garvin, Andrew P., and Bermont, Hubert, *How to Win With Information or Lose Without It.* Bermont Books, 815 15th St. NW, Washington, DC 20005. 1980. $26.00, hardback.

PUTTING A PRICE TAG ON YOUR LIFE STYLE

Well, yes, we're going to have to talk about money, at this point. For some people, that's a *big* issue; for others, it's rather insignificant – because, well, *somehow,* they always seem to manage to survive.

But I want to emphasize that we are talking about it at this point in the process, because it will help determine at what level you should do your informational interviewing, and at what level you may end up working. In other words, leaving aside the question of what money can buy, you need to know what your minimum salary requirements are going to be, before you ever start looking around to see where you want to use your talents.

If you are one of those who doesn't care much about money or possessions, but is very big on "subsistence type living," this is going to be simple. Just figure out how much you need in order to merely subsist. Housing, food, school, household furnishings, clothing, medical – and car, gas and insurance (yes, most of the subsistence people I've met seem to have a car, for some reason or other). Things like recreation, gifts, personal stuff and – like that – are probably academic, in your case.

If you're not into 'just subsistence,' then we suggest you make up two budgets. First: the 'rock-bottom need' budget – what you need to just survive, if you found yourself (and your loved ones) between a rock and a hard place. Second: the 'I hope' budget – what you hope you will have to live on. The categories, for both budgets, of course, include:

Food—at home; Food—away;
Housing—rent/mortgage, tax, insurance;
Housing—furnishings; Housing—utilities and household supplies; Transportation—car payments, insurance, parking, gas, other maintenance, public transportation;
Clothing—purchases, maintenance;
Hairdos, toiletries;
Medical—insurance, physicians visits, other, including dental;
Education—tuition, books, loan

repayment; Recreation; Gifts, contributions; Life Insurance; Union dues; Savings; Payments on debts; Pension contribution; Social Security; federal / state income taxes.[1]

PLUS 15%

To the two budgets add 15% more, because we all habitually underestimate our needs, and by about that much. What you have now is your range: the amounts *between which* you can bargain, at the conclusion of a promising job interview, and the level at which you want to do your exploring, now.

If you're already out into the world of work, and have been for some time, you may want to fool around with making a graph of your salary history, over the years (yearly salary, plotted against time in years). If you're real good at graphs, you may want to make an overlay, of the inflation rate at the same time – that'll send you into a Depression! It may also give you the impetus to think seriously how long you want to stay where you are, without a decent further raise. Budget-making that isn't taking into account inflation, is foolishness – for individuals as well as for businesses.

---

1. Military are advised by the creative minority not to include their retirement pay in any way in their computations. That's extra, for emergencies. Clergy are advised that they probably make $30,000-40,000 – on the average – although this is hard to comprehend, until you add in all the perquisites, etc., or ask the thought-provoking question: how much would it cost to hire skilled laypersons to do *all* my work, after I leave?

The point is you must start here – *before* you ask your librarian to help you figure out what the average salaries are in a given field, to find out if you're in the right ball park. Those average salaries incidentally (for non-supervisory workers, at least), are found in a monthly government publication which every library should have, entitled "Employment and Earnings." At this writing, the average salary for all non-supervisory workers in the U.S. (on private non-agricultural payrolls) was $7.62 hourly, $266.70 weekly, and $13,868.40 annually – in case you were wondering.

Now, if you have merely *read* this chapter – at this point – don't be surprised if no blinding light has come to illuminate your path. Just reading doesn't count. Nor does putting this book under your pillow at night, and hoping you can absorb it by osmosis. No, dear friend, you've got to DO THE EXERCISES. Choose which ones you will, choose them all if you please, but DO them. That is the only way you will truly profit from this step of the process. Just reading about it won't do (unless, of course, like Archimedes, you are taking a bath while you are reading this, and you have suddenly shouted, "Eureka, I've found it!")

But, *if* you've done all the exercises, and you're *still* very hazy about what you want to do, then you will obviously need a more detailed step-by-step plan. You will find that in Appendix A, at the back of this book, in something called (with rare humor) the *Quick Job-Hunting Map.* If you set aside a full weekend (breakfast and dinner shoved under your door, while you continue to work away) you can get it done, up to the point where you need to go out and do some interviewing.

If *that* doesn't work – you just can't *get at* the *Map,* the dullest program on television looks absolutely fascinating to you, – well, you know. You are running into what we call "resistance" within yourself. Why so? Well, there are lots of reasons. Fear of change. Fear of changing your image of yourself. (We all are raised with such terrible – but familiar – self-esteem, these days, that when confronted with a chance to find out what we do positively and well, we become what I call "trembling stewards of our own excellency." It's like having a face-lift, where suddenly you are beautiful, but you are afraid to look in the mirror.) It could be lots of other things, too.

In any event, you've obviously got to go find someone to help you. Mate, relative, friend, neighbor, someone who "owes you" – whatever. Get two people, if you can, and find seven evenings when you could do "trioing." That's a method of doing Skill Identification which is more fully described in *Where Do I Go From Here With My Life?* – a detailed life-planning manual written by John C. Crystal and "a ghostwriter."[1]

And if that still doesn't work, you're going to have to go pay someone to help you. See Appendix C at the back of this book, not so much for names, as for the questions you must be sure to ask *before* you pay anyone.

When you're done, however you did it, you should be able to say what it is that you do best, what the skills are that you most enjoy using, and (maybe) what kinds of jobs or careers those skills point to. Hallelujah!

---

1. Available from your local bookstore or directly from the publisher, Ten Speed Press, Box 7123, Berkeley, CA 94707. $9.95, paper (the book, for those of you already familiar with it, has shrunk in size this year, in order to keep the price the same. No change in the contents however; just a slightly smaller print).

Students spend four or more years learning how to dig data out of the library and other sources, but it rarely occurs to them that they should also apply some of that same new-found research skill to their own benefit—to looking up information on companies, types of professions, sections of the country that might interest them.

Professor Albert Shapero
The William H. Davis Professor of The American Free Enterprise System at Ohio State University

CHAPTER SIX

Where Do You Want To Do It?

THE THIRD KEY TO CAREER PLANNING AND JOB-HUNTING

Whether it took you two weeks or two months,

whether it was done easily or only with much blood, sweat and tears,

whether you did it all on your own, or only with professional help, if you did the exercises in the previous chapter (or in the Quick Job-Hunting Map, in Appendix A) you now have identified *which skills you have that you enjoy most and do best.*

Your *priority skill* — the one you gave first place to (like, on page 76) will dictate the general kind of thing that you will be doing. Hopefully. Your *secondary* skills—the ones you gave lesser rank to (page 76, again) will help determine the more specific thing you will be doing within your general field, and perhaps give some clue as to where.

Naturally, you'll want to be narrowing this down, and also determining *at what level* your skills should (and can) be defined. But before we show you how the creative minority suggests you go about doing just that, let us look at the Third Key to your job hunt . . . career search program . . . or whatever you would like to call this whole process.

> *You have to decide what city, or what part of the country (or the world) you would like to work in.*

WHERE, OH WHERE

You probably have one of four answers immediately trembling on the tip of your tongue:

1. *I want to continue to work in the city or town where I am, because I just love it here. OR*

2. *I want to work in______, because it is my favorite spot in this country of ours. OR*

3. *I haven't the foggiest idea; I don't really care, either. OR*

4. *This is a silly exercise. Where I want to work, and where the jobs are, may be two entirely different subjects. So, why get my hopes all up, for nothing?*

Since that last answer, if true, effectively wipes out the first three, let us deal with No. 4 right off the bat—and at some length—so that we understand this whole business of what is *(laughingly)* called

The Job Market

Upon hearing this very misleading term, one has visions – instantly – of some central place, like the Stock Exchange, say, where every job opening and every job-hunter can meet each other. Such a vision may dance, like a sugar plum, in the job-hunter's head; but the reality is quite different. And, much more jolting.

When you start into the *supposed* unified job market, to conduct your own job-search campaign, you discover sooner or later that you actually face *14 million or more separate job markets* (for this is how many individual businesses, organizations, agencies, and foundations there allegedly are in this country). Every business or organization has its own way of going about the process of hiring – separate, independent of, and uncoordinated with, other businesses or organizations. Hence, each is a separate job market.

THE SOURCE OF THE MYTHOLOGY

What deludes people into thinking of the whole country as a vast single job market? Two factors, at least:

First of all, the term itself. *Market* is a metaphor, at best. By analogy with the market where we shop, we have come to speak – in the world of business – of four *markets* today:

a) the market for information; b) the market for goods and services; c) the market for capital, money, investment; d) the market for labor.

Whatever usefulness the term may have in the hands of genuine experts, as it is commonly bandied about in everyday language it often means little more than *demand,* e.g., "How's the labor market this month?" Whatever usefulness such shorthand may have among the experts, it certainly does delude the job-hunter. There is no such central market – and the generalizations made about it are downright demonic and soul-destroying to unwary and naive job-hunters.

The second factor which has deluded people into thinking of the country (as a whole) as though it were one market is the statistics that appear in the paper each month. You recall, perhaps, how an English professor once declined the word "lie":

LIES, DAMN LIES, AND STATISTICS

In any event, once a month (the first Friday of the month, usually, and published in Saturday's papers – if you care) the nation is alternately comforted or terrorized by *One statistic for the whole country*. It is published (naturally) by the U.S. Government (its Bureau of Labor Statistics). And it is, of course, The Unemployment Figure.

To understand it, you must be aware that there are actually three basic figures that are involved:

1. *The total number of people in the nation who want to work: e.g., 112,580,000 in September 1982.*
2. *The total number of people in the nation who are actually employed that month: e.g., 99,720,000 in September 1982.*
3. *The difference: e.g., 12,860,000 in September 1982.*

Actually, this last figure is divided by the government into two: those job-hunters who have gotten so discouraged they have stopped going out on the job-hunt (1,600,000 in September 1982), and those job-hunters who are still looking (11,260,000 in September 1982). The government, with a reasoning known only to itself, calls only this last figure the monthly unemployment figure. It is usually published as a percentage of the total labor force (e.g., 10.1% in September 1982).

INTIMIDATING FIGURES

Prominent press coverage is always given to *this one statistic for the whole country: the unemployment figure.* The human mind is staggered by the thought of over 11 million people being out of work. It would be even more staggered if it realized that there is good evidence that actual unemployment may be three times the government figure.[1] In one moment of unusual candor, the government admitted that during a typical year over 20% of the total labor force is out of work at some time that year . . . i.e., one of every five workers. During a Recession year (as, currently) the figure is almost certainly one out of every

1. For starters, the government itself tells us that in September 1982, 6.6 million people had made only temporary peace with their inability to find a full-time job. They had taken what is called in the government's jargon "an involuntary part-time job." In my view, that makes them job-hunters still. Add to their number the 1.6 million "discouraged workers" cited above, and you can see there are at least 8.2 million unemployed or semi-unemployed workers which the government does not publicly include in its figures.

four. The human tragedy that this represents, to each of us in the imagination of our hearts, is overwhelming.

But the media do not leave it to the imagination. Continuously, throughout the rest of the month, we are given details.

We are told industry horror stories, such as what is happening to the auto industry or to the construction/housing industry. We are told individual horror stories, such as how one family has lost its home, car, and everything – or even how some job-hunter, in total despair over the fact that society apparently does not value him or want him, takes his own life. And if the country is in one of its periodic recessions, as is the case this year, we are bombarded almost daily in the newspapers and on television, with interviews – not with successful job-hunters who were able to find a job in spite of hard times, but with unsuccessful job-hunters who describe with bitterness how they tried everything "and I still couldn't find a job." We are given statistics until they are coming out our ears. In September 1982, for example, those statistics were: every second black

WHO'S OUT OF WORK

Here are the Labor Department's unemployment figures for September 1982 compared with those for December 1981:

	Sept. 1982	Dec. 1981
All workers	10.1%	8.9%
Adult men	9.6	8.0
Adult women	8.3	7.5
White	9.0	7.8
Black	20.2	17.4
Hispanic	14.6	11.1
Teenagers	23.7	21.7
Black teenagers	48.5	42.2

Here are the Bureau of Labor Statistics' tabulations of the unemployment rate for various industries in September 1982, compared with January 1981.

	Sept. 1982	Jan. 1981
Steel and other primary metals	24.6%	9.3%
Construction	22.6	13.7
Automobile	18.7	17.7
Textiles	18.2	9.6
Lumber and wood products	17.1	10.4
Eating and drinking establishments	13.9*	12.8
Processed foods	13.4	9.9
Personal services (beauty parlors, dry cleaning, etc.)	13.2	11.8
Railroads	11.6*	8.7
Retail trade	10.1*	9.4
Government (federal, state and local)	4.9	4.4

*Not "seasonally adjusted"

teenager was out of work; every fourth teenager; every fourth construction worker; every fifth black worker; every seventh Hispanic; every seventh blue-collar worker.

Then, as if the contemporary situation weren't bad enough, there are always some handy, long-range predictions about what technology, automation, computers, and such, will do to the work place within the coming decade.

By the time that *You as Newspaper Reader or Television Viewer* are ready to become *Job Hunter,* you are convinced that it is foolish of you to venture out into the so-called Job Market, because there can't be a single job left out there.

IS NO ONE HIRING?

But then, the unemployment figure doesn't really tell us anything about vacancies – as, upon sober reflection, we must realize. It only tells us how many people we are competing with (sort of) for whatever vacancies exist. That is, *assuming we all possess the skills that the vacancies call for.*

But, how many vacancies are there?

Well, the total is actually the total of three figures:

(1) How many present jobs fall vacant? The employed are a tremendously mobile population, even in Hard Times. During the best of times, they change jobs at the rate of about 800,000 *per month* – thus leaving 800,000 vacancies behind them, of course. During the worst of times, they change jobs still – at the rate of about 300,000 *per month.* We have, then, essentially a game of musical chairs. And, of course, while those chairs are empty, you can compete for them just as well as anyone else.

(2) To this we must add the number of new jobs that are created. No one seems to know this figure. What they do know is the *net* rise, annually. That figure has varied in recent years between 2.4 million, in Good Times, to a minus 600,000 in the worst of times (like now). In an average it runs around 2 million.[1]

(3) But, of course, a net rise covers up another figure, which is the number of jobs that got phased out permanently in our society. To show you what this means, let us suppose that in a typical year 5 million jobs were phased out of our society per-

1. *New York Times,* p. 20F, Sunday, September 27, 1981.

manently, due to business failures, bankruptcies, or the fading away of certain industries. No one seems to know what the actual figure is. But let us say it was 5 million. Then, of course, if there were a *net* rise of 2 million that particular year, 7 million new jobs (hence *new* vacancies) would have had to be created in the total job market, in order to preserve that *net* increase of 2 million. A job market has to cover its losses before it can forge ahead. It is this figure, of course, that always rises during Hard Times. With the abrupt rise in bankruptcies, plant shut-downs, and so on, a vast number of jobs must be replaced even to preserve a *net* rise of zero.

If you add these three figures together: musical chairs vacancies, new vacancies due to net rise (or loss), and lost jobs replaced, you will understand why the creative minority insists that there is a *minimum* of 1 million job openings each month, even in the Hardest of Times (like now); and, of course, many more than that during Good Times.

HOW MANY WANT THE JOB THAT I WANT?

Are 11 million people, then (or whatever the unemployment figure is, in a given month) competing for these 1 million job openings each month? Well, of course you know they are not. And, for the following reasons:

1. *Musical chairs:* A lot of vacancies never have a chance to get publicized, because as soon as they exist, some employee recommends a relative; or else someone (by accident or design) walks in off the street, is interviewed, and straight-away hired.

2. *Stiff demands on the part of job-hunters:* If ever there were an era, once upon a time, when an unemployed worker was willing to take any kind of work, just so that it brought in some money, that time is no longer. Many of the unemployed these days are extremely particular about the kind of work they are willing to do. Some want only highly skilled work. Some want only very unskilled work. Some want only jobs that will pay as well as their former job did. Some want only jobs that they can truly enjoy, and will settle for nothing else, not even something that would logically be a step toward their goal. For one and all of these, until they find such jobs, they are willing

to live off savings, food stamps, welfare, or the income of whoever else in the house *is* working.[1]

3. *Stiff demands on the part of employers:* A lot of jobs call for very special skills which just may not exist in sufficient abundance, and so the jobs stay vacant for long periods of time.

4. *Low visibility:* There are a number of vacancies for which any number of qualified applicants could be found if only the employers had some way of getting the information *out*. But, particularly for jobs that are at all decent, many employers prefer not to advertise the vacancy, inasmuch as they are very particular about whom they hire. The consequence of all this? Not long ago, it was estimated that during an average year there are 750,000 management vacancies of which only 250,000 are filled by the end of the year. Jobs at other levels of responsibility exhibit similar gaps.

5. *Fictitious job-hunters:* Some people who are collecting unemployment insurance (and therefore are listed by the U.S. Government as job-hunters, which *in theory* they must be in order to collect) actually have no interest in competing for any of the 1 million vacancies that month: such persons as students between semesters, seasonal workers, production workers on temporary layoff, singers, actors and dancers awaiting a call, and people who are moonlighting (holding down full-time jobs but still collecting unemployment insurance as though they were unemployed).

I want to repeat from our previous chapter, the paradoxical nature of the word "skills" (page 76ff), and what this means for the job-hunter of today (whether student, housewife, mid-life changer or whatever):

(1) The *higher the level* of skills that you can legitimately claim, either with people, data or things (or, in varying degree,

---

1. It has been estimated that one of the reasons the current unemployment rate, the highest since the Great Depression, has not caused greater social unrest than it has, is that 60% of the unemployed have another member of their household who *is* working. This, of course, is due to the heavy influx of women into the market-place since 1950. During the Great Depression it was not so: then, when a wage-earner lost his job, it represented to his household the loss of the only income that household was receiving. Paradoxically, the largest group facing this predicament in the present Hard Times are *women* who, through whatever circumstances, are single heads of households.

". . . and give me good abstract-reasoning ability, interpersonal skills, cultural perspective, linguistic comprehension, and a high sociodynamic potential."

with all three) the less these kinds of jobs are advertised or known through normal channels; the more you'll have to find your own individual ways of unearthing them – which is what this chapter you are now reading is all about. It is written for You!

(2) Just because the opportunities for the higher level jobs (or careers) are harder to uncover, the higher you aim the less people you will have to compete with – for that job. In fact, if you uncover, as you are very likely to, a genuine need in the organization (or organizations) you like, which you can help resolve, they are very likely to create a brand new job for you, which means – in effect – *you will be competing with practically no one, since you are virtually the sole applicant,* as it were. You will, of course, hasten to point out to me that brand new jobs don't get created during Hard Times. Not true. The current year, which has seen a record number of bankruptcies, has also seen a record number of new businesses starting up.

New businesses create jobs that never existed before. And you – regardless of your age, sex, race, lack of supposed credentials, or inexperience – can go after those new jobs, *if* you pursue newer, smaller businesses, instead of the "Big Boys" that so many pin all their hopes on.[1]

Now, let me repeat:

THE PARADOXICAL MORAL OF ALL THIS

The higher a skill level you can legitimately claim, *the more likely you are* to find a job. Just the opposite of what the typical job-hunter or career-changer starts out believing.

Now, I would like to expand upon these ideas, beginning with the fact – alluded to, above – that the higher you aim, the less likely the jobs are to be advertised.

JOB MARKET DIAGRAMS NEVER INCLUDE JOBS FOR WHICH NO VACANCY EXISTS

The average job-hunter is almost sure that the job-hunting task consists – in one way or another – of unearthing *jobs which someone held before, and which are now vacant. So the job-hunter searches classified ads, employment agencies, etc.*

It rarely occurs to them that if, instead, you select the organizations or companies that interest you, and do enough research to unearth their problems (and how you can help solve them), the company may be perfectly willing to create a new job, for which no vacancy exists.

Certainly, a little reflection will tell you why all of this is so. Pretend, for a moment, that you are an executive of some company or organization. Your organization exists in order to get a certain job done, or product produced. And it's doing a pretty good job. But *naturally* you've also got problems; who doesn't? You don't publicly call them "problems," of course; you call them "challenges," "opportunities for growth," and that sort of thing. But privately, as you lay your head down on the pillow at night, you can call them by their real name: "problems." Some of them are relatively minor and perhaps of long standing – just something you've learned to live with. Others are relatively

1. A widely-cited study by Professor David Birch of my old alma mater (M.I.T.), determined that 66% of all new jobs created during a seven-year period (which included a major Recession) were created by small firms with 0-20 employees.

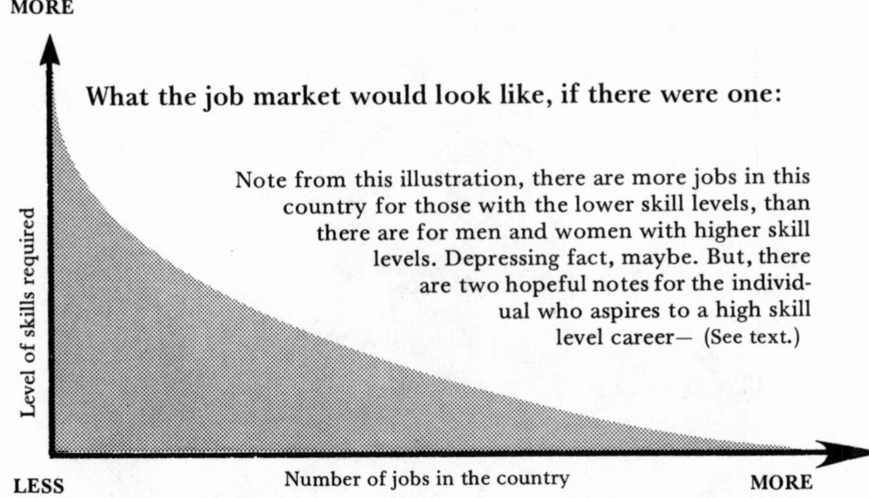

new and of major importance, maybe even in a sense *time bombs.* If you don't solve these, they're going to break your back. They're costing you money, sometimes a lot of money.

Now, naturally, your employees are aware of these problems – and some at least are trying to help you solve them. But, for one reason or another, they haven't succeeded. Then, into your office one morning comes some job-hunter who knows an amazing amount about your company or organization, including some of the major problems – excuse me, "challenges" – that you are facing. That person has analyzed them, and has skills which they believe can help solve them. Very soon, you believe they can too, but *there is no vacancy in your company. Will you go and try your darnedest to create a new job, in order to get your hands on this person? Regardless of their age, background, or whatever?* Provided you have the power (and our man or woman won't be talking to you if you don't) *you bet you will.* In fact, you may have been thinking for some time that you needed this new position, anyway. You just haven't gotten around to doing anything about it – 'til now.

KNOWLEDGE IS POWER

These facts about the nature of the "job market," the meaning of "skills," and the availability of "high level positions" seem very strange, at first.

They are contrary to what many people, posing as experts, will tell you.

They are also (nonetheless) true.

And (consequently) they work.

Time after time, again and again, men and women who have comprehended the true nature of what they were facing in the matter of "the job market" – so called – have successfully found their first job, or made the transition from one career to another, without retraining or further post-graduate courses, and in the area of the country that *they* chose.

And this, in spite of the fact that the country was in the middle of a very hard time, and the geographical area they wanted to live and work in was designated by experts as virtually a disaster area, employment-wise.

They realized, as we said earlier, that *all that the unemployment figures tell you is how many people are competing with you* for whatever vacancies there are, or for whatever new positions there might be.

But, the vacancies (or potential new positions) *are there no matter how bad the economy is.* Even during a recession, people get promoted; people move; people die; executives get tired of dealing with the same old unsolved problems and resolve to hire *anyone* capable of solving them. Young or old; male or female. Even if they're from *Mars.*

Since the vacancies or potential new jobs really are out there – regardless of where in the country one turns – you *must* choose WHERE it is you want to focus.

That means: the place where you already are (if you love it or have no choice, because of family or economic pressures) or the place where you've always wanted to be or if you are absolutely without any preference, it means something like pinning up a map of the U.S. and throwing darts (one job-hunter actually did this.)[1]

But one way or another *you* have got to do the choosing.

You should not ask another man or woman to make this decision for you, nor should you ask external events (fate, coincidence, or where the "job market" is alleged to be favorable) to decide for you.

It's your move. *Your* move.

JOB MARKET FOCUSING (THE LASER BEAM APPROACH)

Job-hunters such as yourself, dear Reader, begin by thinking there are too few job markets (and therefore, too few jobs) "out there." Thus far, in this chapter, we have argued just the opposite. There are too many. If you try to hit them all – as so many job-hunters do – you will only diffuse your energies

---

1. These two recent books can be marvelous aids in helping you evaluate prospective geographical locations: *Places Rated Almanac: Your guide to finding the best places to live in America,* by Richard Boyer and David Savageau. (Rand McNally & Co. 1981. $11.95, paper.); and *Finding Your Best Place to Live In America,* by Thomas F. Bowman, George A. Giuliana, and M. Ronald Minge. (Red Lion Books, 609 Rte. 109, West Babylon, NY 11704. 1981. $9.95, paper. Order it from the publisher if your bookstore doesn't have it.)

Another book in the same vein, except that it deals only with weather, is:Ruffner, James A., and Bair, Frank E., eds., *The Weather Almanac.* Avon Books, 959 Eighth Ave., New York, NY 10019. 1979. $6.95, paper. And a further resource, to aid you with your actual move, is: Raymond, Dr. Ronald J., Jr., and Eliot, Dr. Stephen V., with Mercer, Marilyn, *Grow Your Roots Anywhere, Anytime.* Peter H. Wyden, Inc., PO Box 151, Ridgefield, CT 06877. 1980. $12.95, hardcover.

and your effectiveness. Better, far better, to concentrate your job-hunting energies and effectiveness. This whole process might be compared to a funneling (read the diagram on page 133 at least three times, for it summarizes the heart of this chapter).

THE CRUCIAL MATTER:

What Will Get You A Job?

Suppose the time has come when you need an alternative career. As you think about the job-hunt, very well-meaning people will tell you that the only route is to go back to college: go learn some skill or profession other than the one you had, *they say*. Go back to school. Get retrained. *They say*.

The government, personnel experts, and many others think along these same lines: *retraining* always seems to be the answer. As you will discover, when that time comes, or have already discovered.

There is, of course, a reason for this:

They think there are only two things that can get you a job: experience, or credentials. They figure you've got to have one or the other.

1. EXPERIENCE. If you want to be a machinist, and you've done it for ten years, you have convincing experience. If you want to be a teacher, and you've taught for ten years, you have acquired convincing experience. In other words, if you've done a particular thing long enough, many people will not care *how* you picked up the skill in the first place. It is sufficient that you have it. You may run into problems, though, if you are changing careers. You may pick a career you would really enjoy, may possess all the skills to do it well, but how do you convince an employer of that? You have no convincing experience to prove that you are good or would be good in that career. And since all your friends tell you that experience or credentials are the only ways to get a job, you therefore assume that you must go and get:

2. CREDENTIALS. Now, to be sure, there are certain fields where people have to go back to school and get retrained before they can practice in this new occupation. Law and medicine come immediately to mind. If that is the sort of thing you want

very much to do as your next career, you're probably going to have to go the credentialing/retraining route.

It is also true that during really Hard Times there is a high premium placed upon individuals who have been trained or re-trained in certain specialties. During the current Recession/Depression, for example, we are told that it is in every way an advantage to have training or retraining in the following subjects: data processing, paralegal work, computer systems analysis, computer programming, industrial-robot production, geriatric social work, hazardous-waste management, genetic engineering, bionic medical electronics, or industrial laser processing or maintenance. That's fine. *If* any of these subjects particularly fascinates you, and *if* the occupational experts are correct. (Currently, as I write, people trained in computer programming or data processing are having difficulty finding jobs in some sections of the country – all the forecasts to the contrary notwithstanding.)

But what is patently *not* true is the assumption on the part of almost everyone – Congress, manpower experts, universities and colleges, and the man and woman on the street, – that if your old career has run out of gas for whatever reason, your *only* route to a new career lies through retraining and new credentials. This false assumption flourishes because job-hunters tend to go for General Rules, rather than Exceptions. The general rule is that if you want to get a job in a University as a full-professor, you have to possess a doctorate. But there *are* exceptions: people who are full-professors, yet possess no such credential. The general rule is that you have to be thoroughly trained in this or that specialty, if you want to do this or that thing. But there *are* exceptions. Your mission, should you choose to accept it, is to unearth individuals who are *exceptions* – ask them how *they* did it, and then learn from their experience.

For countless years now, men and women have changed careers without going back for retraining, because they didn't believe there were only two things that could get you a job: Experience or Credentials. There has got to be a third thing, they reasoned, that doesn't thus depend upon the Past; and that is, *to give a demonstration of your skills right before your prospective employer's very eyes.* Impossible, you say? Not at all. You can show an employer right in their own office that you have whatever skill you claim. Is it that you are a craftsperson of some skill, even though you've never worked a day as a craftsperson? Then, take some pictures in with you (or even a sample) of your work. But what if your skill produces no product, but is somewhat intangible? You can still demonstrate it before the employer's very eyes. This is even true of the skill that most employers want in an employee more than any other: namely, the skill of:

3. PROBLEM-SOLVING. No matter how much it may seem that different kinds of work vary on the surface, underneath they have this common base: they deal with one kind of problem or another. Universities, community organizations, businesses – all require people good at problem-solving *no matter what title may be tacked on the person they hire, in order to justify the salary. Problem-solvers get hired,* whether they are fresh out of high school, or in their retirement years, or in between.

Now, how do you prove you are a problem-solver right before the very eyes of a prospective employer? By the way you do your job-hunt, of course. Forget about producing convincing Experience from the past, or producing Credentials from the past. Just do the most thorough-going research imaginable of the particular company(ies), university(ies), organization(s) or other "job markets" *that you have chosen as most interesting to you,* BEFORE you ever go into their office to seek the job. Such thorough-going care, and research, is the mark of all good problem-solvers – and most employers will immediately sense that.

We said this third pathway is often THE KEY to getting a job when changing careers. But it is just as important when you are setting out to find your first job, or when you are job-hunting in a field where you are already experienced. Therefore, we urge this path upon *all* job-hunters: thorough-going research of every place that truly interests you; we don't mean just an hour or two in the library. This is not what we are talking about, here.

We are talking about the most thorough-going research – through library work and personal visits to organizations or individuals – that you have the patience and determination to do. Hour after hour; day after day. Phew! Lots of work, But the rewards: Wow.

JOB MARKETS IN THE UNITED STATES
14,000,000
(that's the total number of non-farm employers)

1 You narrow this down by deciding just what area, city or county you want to work in. This leaves you with however many thousands of job markets there are in that area or city. **2** You narrow this down by identifying your Strongest Skills, on their highest level that you can legitimately claim, and then thru research deciding what field you *want* to work in, above all. This leaves you with all the hundreds of businesses/ community organizations/agencies/schools/hospitals/projects/associations/ foundations/institutions/firms or government agencies there are in that area and in the field you have chosen. **3** You narrow this down by getting acquainted with the economy in the area thru personal interviews with various contacts; and supplementing this with study of journals in your field, in order that you can pinpoint the places that interest you the most. This leaves a manageable number of markets for you to do some study on. **4** You now narrow this down through further personal visits to those 'markets', with this question uppermost in your mind: *can I be happy in this place, and, do they have the kind of problems which my strongest skills can help solve for them?* **5** All of the above is called Informational Interviewing. When your II is completed, you will have a list of the companies or organizations you already visited, which still look interesting to you; and you will now carefully plan how to approach them for a job, in your case — ● *the* job.

DON'T PAY SOMEONE TO DO THIS RESEARCH FOR YOU, WHATEVER YOU DO

There are a number of reasons why *no one else* can do your job-hunting research for you; not a job-counselor, not a friend, not anyone.

1. Only *you* really know what things you are looking for, what things you want to avoid if possible; in a word, what your *tropisms* are.

2. Moreover, you need the self-confidence that comes to you as you practice this skill of researching, and you need it *before* you go after the organizations that you have chosen.

3. Most importantly, the skills you use to find a job are close to the skills you use to do the job, after you get it. Therefore, by doing all this research – or informational interviewing, as we will call it – you are increasing your qualifications for the job itself. Thus, this conclusion: the more research you do, the more qualifications you have.

Can you do this research yourself, then?

Of course you can.

If you went to high school or college, you should know exactly how to go about Researching – since you probably did lots of it there: term papers, and the like. You'd be surprised at how this skill continues to be useful, or how – if you've been out of school for some time – it all comes back, once you try to revive it.

It consists, in essence, of a careful blend of:

WRITTEN STUFF, AND PEOPLE

In researching any part of this whole process: a) your skills; b) your field; c) your geographical area; or d) your chosen places to approach for a position, you will probably be dealing *alternatively* with written material—such as books, journals, magazines, or other material which librarians and such can direct you to —and—

with *people* who are doing what it is you are researching. YOU READ until you need to talk to someone because you can't find more in books; then YOU TALK TO PEOPLE until you know you need to get back and do some more reading.

Essential to your research (in either form) is that you know:

WHAT IT IS THAT YOU ARE LOOKING FOR

When You Are Reading or Interviewing About—	Among The Things You May Be Looking For Are—
your skills	what kind of work uses *most* of these skills *together*
fields of possible work . . .	which ones you will be happiest (and therefore most effective) in, because they fit in with your total Life Mission as you perceive it
geographical area that you have chosen	the kind of places that might need your skills, in the field you have chosen
places where you might want to work	to find out if there is any reason why you might *not* want to work there; to find out what problems they have *and* which problems are both urgent ("time-bombs") and ones which your skills can help solve.

Interviewing for Information Only

Beyond mechanics, it is essential for you to remember who you are, as you are going about this whole business of researching and interviewing *for information only.* Your whole job-hunting process from here on out will divide into two parts. Let us make clear what they are:

Part I. Informational Interviewing: You are the screener. The employers and organizations are the *screenees.* You are looking them over, trying to decide which of these pleases YOU. This is for information, building of contacts, and tracking down places that interest you *only.* During this part of the process, you can even take others with you (especially if you are in high school or college and this is all new to you, or if you are a housewife coming into the market-place for the first time). After all, you are going out only to find information. You are not *yet* job-hunting. Therefore, it's perfectly okay to take someone with you, if you want to.

Part II. Interviewing for Hire: Having narrowed down the possibilities to four or five that really fascinate you, you now return to them in the fashion we shall describe in the next chapter, to seek an interview for an actual job there, doing the thing you have decided you would most like to do. At this point *and only at this point,* you now become the Screenee, and the employers or organizations or funding-sources or whatever become the Screeners. Though, of course, you are still keeping your eyes and ears open in case you see something dreadful that will put you abruptly back into the role of Screener and cause you to say, to yourself at least, "I have just learned this place really isn't for me."

In any event, the part we are talking about in this chapter is what we have called Part I, above – where you are the Screener; and is not to be confused with Part II (next chapter) where you become the screenee. If you *feel* as though you are the Screenee

in this first part of the research we are describing, you're doing something wrong – even if you have all the mechanics down pat. Just remember, as a human being you've got rights: including the right to go look at places and decide whether or not they interest you, and whether or not you like what they're doing, and whether or not you could do your most effective work there. Now, you may of course think that during Hard Times, when jobs are scarce, you lose this right. Au contraire! Think of what Hard Times mean for the employer. He or she has fewer dollars to spend, in most cases. Wants more value for what dollars they do spend. Wants people who are truly excited about working *there,* people who have taken the time to look at other places, but want most of all to work *in this place* – and know why. Such a person will give employers the most for their money. That person can be You.

There are resources to help you at this point; but resources are useless, unless you keep firmly in mind what kinds of questions you want the resources to help you with. These questions are best illustrated when surveying a far-away place. So, let's take a look at how you do that.

HOW TO SURVEY A PLACE . . . FAR AWAY OR NEAR

The Basic Principles of Information-Searching

1 *Be clear about the different kinds of information you are going to need for your job-hunt.*

To recapitulate, you are going to need information about the following (use this as a check-list):

A. WHAT SKILLS DO YOU HAVE THAT YOU HAVE ALREADY DEMONSTRATED; AND THAT YOU ENJOY?

This list must be in detail, *and* clustered into families, *and* prioritized in terms of your six or so favorites. If you failed to do any of these three steps (put them in detail, clusters, and prioritized) you will *dramatically* hamper your subsequent information-search. See Appendix A for instructions on how to do all this.

B. WHERE DO YOU WANT TO USE THESE SKILLS?

Someone who has the skill of welding can use that skill to weld the casting for a nuclear bomb, or to make a wheel for a cart. So, what do *you* want to use *your* skills with? In the service of what? To accomplish what? And in what geographical area? SIMPLY TO SAY YOU WANT TO DO WELDING (OR WHATEVER) IS NOT SUFFICIENT, AND WILL SERIOUSLY HAMPER YOUR SUBSEQUENT INFORMATION-SEARCH.

You must decide *where* you want to use the skill.

C. WHAT KINDS OF ORGANIZATIONS ARE THERE THAT YOU LIKE, IN TERMS OF THEIR GOALS, THAT EITHER ALREADY USE PEOPLE WITH YOUR SKILLS, OR OUGHT TO, AND PERHAPS COULD BE PERSUADED TO, AND THAT ARE IN THE GEOGRAPHICAL AREA (OR AREAS) YOU HAVE FOCUSED ON?

The last step above is the pre-condition for answering the other three. An overseas soldier – for example – cannot do an information-search about corporations' department of mental hygiene back here in the States, until he or she has *first* selected at least an area of the country, and two or three cities there, by name.

D. WHAT ARE THE NAMES OF SUCH ORGANIZATIONS, IN THE CITIES YOU HAVE FOCUSED UPON?

The more specific and detailed you have been in step C, above, the easier this step D will be. The more general you have been, the harder this step will be, e.g., "Corporations" is too general. In a particular city, that will turn out to be a very long list. But (for example) "Corporations with not more than 200 employees, which produce such and such a product" is a much shorter list, in any particular city (or area). Likewise, "nonprofit organizations" is too general. That again will produce a long list, if your information-search is thorough. "Nonprofit organizations dealing with . . . " what? health services, consumer protection, or what? *The more detailed you are, the easier it will be for you to do the information-search.*

E. WHAT ARE THEIR PROBLEMS, AS ORGANIZATIONS – AND PARTICULARLY "IN THE DEPARTMENTS OR AREAS WHERE I WOULD BE WORKING"?

A lot depends on the level at which you want to work. If at the clerk or secretary level, the problems are pretty predictable: absenteeism, too-long coffee or lunch breaks, not caring about the subject-matter, not accepting your supervisor's priorities about which work needs to get done first, etc. If you want to work at a higher level, the problems are likely to be correspondingly more complex. But you can figure them out – usually by asking: what would a *bad* employee in this department be like? The problems to be solved are often in the employee, rather than in the situation.

F. WHO THERE HAS THE POWER TO HIRE FOR THE LEVEL OF JOB YOU ARE AIMING AT?

It's not likely to be the Personnel Department, unless you're talking about entry-level.

MY QUESTIONS FOR INFORMATIONAL INTERVIEWING

A. What Skills Do I Have and Enjoy
B. Where Do I Want to Use These Skills
C. What Kinds of Organizations Can I Focus On—
 in terms of Goals,
 for use of my Skills,
 in my Geographical Area of Preference
D. What Are the Names of Such Organizations
E. What Are Their Problems—
 at the Level I Want To Work
F. Who There Has The Power To Hire Me

If you are researching a far-away place, set down on paper which of the above information-searches you can do right where you are, and which ones you need others' help with, in the city of your choice.

Normally, you can do the information-search on A and B, above, right where you are, since this is potentially a self-directed information-search. This was what the previous chapter was all about. As we said there, the most complete way of doing this is to fill out the *Quick Job-Hunting Map* – either the *Beginning Version,* for high school students and others who are entering the world of work for the first time, or the *Advanced Version,* for those who have had considerable experience in the world of work, or who wish to change careers. (The *Advanced Version,* as you already know, is in Appendix A, page 206.)

If, even with the *Map,* you have difficulty identifying your skills or where you want to use them, you may then: (1) Recruit your mate, or a friend, or business acquaintance there in your city where you presently are, to help you work through the map; OR (2) Use a professional career expert such as your college career-planning or placement office; or a career counselor, to be found by the methods suggested in Appendix C, at the back of this book, page 273.

Now, once A and B are done, with or without help, you are ready to go on to the other information-searches listed on the previous pages. If there is a really good library near you, or if that library (however small and limited) is on an inter-library loan system, you can do *some* research on C, *some* research on D, and some also on F.

So your two lists will *probably* come out looking like this:

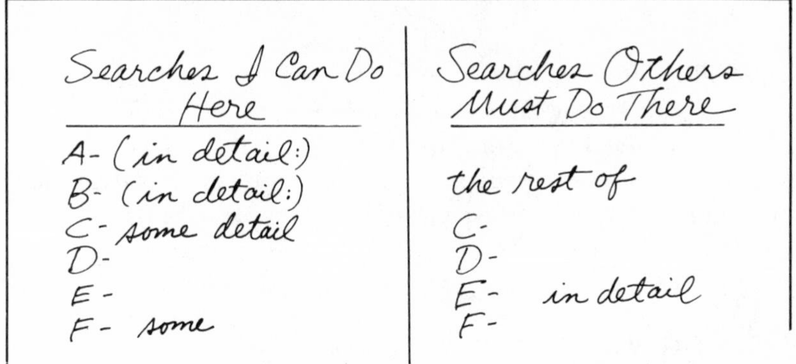

3 *Determine how much time you have before you* **absolutely** *have to find a job.*

Yes, of course it would be just dandy if you could conclude your information-search – successfully – within a month. And, many people do. But it is not *at all* unusual for a job-hunt to take nine months (something symbolic about *that*) or longer. Soooo, how much time *do* you have before you simply *must* have your next job? (This is the place to total up your savings, your mate's income if applicable, money you could borrow, cuts you could make in your expenses, and so forth, and then divide it all by your weekly expenses.) The earlier you can get started – the more lead-time you can give yourself – the better.

4 *If it is a far-away place you are interested in, figure out if there isn't* **some way** *during that time that you could go visit the city or cities of your choice.*

You can do this even if you are presently employed. Does a vacation fall within the time period you have between now and when you must finally have that job? Could you visit it on vacation? Could you take a summer job there? Go there on leave? Get sent to a convention there? Get appointed to a group or association that meets there? Think it through. You will *have* to go there, finally (in almost all cases) for the actual job interview(s). If worse comes to worse, go there a week or so ahead of that interview. Better late than never, to look over the scene in person, and do some on-site Informational Interviewing.

5 *Until you can go there, use every resource and contact you have, in order to explore the answers to C, D, E and F on page 139.*

It will be doubly-apparent by now, to one and all, how crucial it is for you to choose *by name* a city or town where you are going (a) to focus your information-search; (b) at least initially. And if it's a country-area that interests you, then at least identify that area, and the name of the city or town(s) therein. Then, with that city or town, use the following resources in your information-search:

☆ **THE DAILY OR WEEKLY NEWSPAPER THERE.**
Almost all papers will mail to subscribers anywhere in the world. So: subscribe, for a six-month period, or a year. You'd be surprised at what you can learn from the paper. Some of the answers to C, D, E and F will appear there. Additionally, from the ads and business news items, you will know what businesses are growing and expanding – hence, hiring – in that city.

☆ **THE CHAMBER OF COMMERCE, AND CITY HALL (OR THE TOWN HALL).**
These are the places whose interest it is (in most cases) to attract newcomers, and to tell them what kinds of businesses there are in town – as well as some details about them. So: write and ask them, in the beginning, what information they have about the city or town in general. Then later, don't hesitate to write back to them with more specific questions, as your target organizations become clearer in your mind.

☆ **THE LOCAL LIBRARY OR REFERENCE LIBRARIAN, IF YOUR TARGET CITY/TOWN HAS ONE.**
It is perfectly kosher to write to the library of your target city, asking for information that may be only there. If the librarian is too busy to answer, then use one of your contacts there to find out. "Bill (or Billie) I need some information that I'm afraid only the library in your town has. Specifically, I need to know about company x." Or whatever.

☆ **YOUR CONTACTS.**
Yes, of course, you know people in whatever city or town you're researching during your job-hunt-as-information-search. For openers, write to your old high school and get the alumni list for your graduating class. If you went to college, ask for

their alumni list also (for your class, at the very least). Subscribe to your college's alumni bulletin for further news, addresses, and hints. If you belong to a church or synagogue, write to the church or synagogue in your target city, and tell them that you're one of their own and you need some information. ("I need to know who can tell me what nonprofit organizations there are in that city, that deal with x.") ("I need to know how I can find out what corporations in town have departments of mental hygiene.") Or, whatever. To find further contacts, ask your family and relatives who *they* know in the target city or town of your choice. You know more people in that city, who might help you, than you think.

☆ **THE APPROPRIATE STATE, COUNTY, AND LOCAL GOVERNMENT AGENCIES, ASSOCIATIONS, ETC.**
Ask your contacts to tell you what that appropriate agency might be.[1]

6 *Regard the city or town where you presently are, as a replica of the city or town you are interested in going to (in some respects at least) — so that some of your informational interviewing can be done where you are, and then its learnings transferred.*

How do you go about doing this? Well, suppose that you are skilled in: counseling people, particularly in one-to-one situations; that you are knowledgeable about — and well-versed in — psychiatry; and that you love carpentry and plants. (You are obviously at stage C on page 139.)

What kinds of organizations does this point to?

To get at this, first translate all of your above interests into people (counseling = counselor), (psychiatry = psychiatrist), (carpentry = carpenter), (plants = gardener).

Next, ask yourself which of these persons is most likely *to have the largest overview?* This is often (but not always) the same as asking: who took the longest to get their training? The particular answer here: the psychiatrist.

1. For additional help, there are directories of national addresses and phone numbers, such as: *National Directory of Addresses and Telephone Numbers* (by Stanley R. Greenfield, available from Bantam Books, Inc., 666 Fifth Ave., New York, NY 10019, $14.95, paper). Ask your library or browse your bookstore to see what's come out recently.

In the place where you presently are, then, go to see a psychiatrist (pay them for fifteen minutes of their time – if there is no other way) or go see the head of the psychiatry department at the nearest college or university, and ask them: Do you have any idea how to put all the above together in a job? And if you don't, who might?

Eventually, you will be told by them: Yes, there is a branch of psychiatry that uses plants to help heal people.

Having found this out in the place where you live, you can then write to your target city or town to ask, What psychiatric facilities are *there,* and which ones – if any – use plants in their healing program?

Thus can you conduct your research where you are, and then transfer its learning to the place you want to go.[1]

FOCUSING DOWN: TO YOUR GEOGRAPHICAL AREA THROUGH USE OF CONTACTS

It will ultimately be *essential* for you to visit the geographical area you want to work in (or, if it is the place where you already live, to visit it *with new eyes).* You will want to talk to key individuals *who can suggest other people you might talk to, as you try to find out what organizations interest you.* You will want to define these key individuals (they are called CONTACTS) ahead of time and let them know you are coming. Your list may include: friends, college alumni (if you attended college), high school pals, church or synagogue contacts, Chamber of Commerce executives, city manager, regional planning offices, appropriate county or state offices in your area of interest, the Mayor, and high level management in particular companies that look interesting from what you've read or heard about them.[2]

When you "hit town," you will want to remember the City Directory, the Yellow Pages of your phone book, etc.

---

1. For further information on how to conduct this information search more thoroughly, see *Where Do I Go From Here With My Life?* (op. cit.) pages 102-112, 120-148, the even-numbered pages particularly.

2. A new book is out, dealing with how you locate such contacts, called *Names and Numbers: A Journalist's Guide to the Most Needed Information Sources and Contacts,* by a staff member of *The Philadelphia Inquirer* (Rod Nordland). It's expensive ($24.95, in hardcover)–so I suggest you consult your local library. It has over 20,000 listings. Many job-hunters may find it helpful during their research.

If going into a strange new geographical area is a totally new experience for you, and you have no friends there in your chosen target area, just remember there are various ways of meeting people, making friends, and developing contacts rather quickly with people who share some interest or enthusiasm of yours. There are athletic clubs, Ys, churches, charitable and community organizations, where you can present yourself and meet people from the moment you walk in the doors. You will soon develop many acquaintances, and some beginning friendships, and the place won't seem so lonely after all.

Also, visit or write your high school before you set out for this new town and find out what graduates live in the area that you are going to be visiting for the first time: they are your friends already, because you went to the same school. As I indicated earlier, all of these acquaintances, friends and key individuals have one common name: contacts. Yes, contacts, Contacts, CONTACTS. Whenever anyone writes me and says that "information interviewing may be a *great* idea for Others, but it just isn't working for Me," I know inevitably what the problem is. Namely, that this job-hunter or career-changer just hasn't made Sufficient Use of his or her contacts. So, remember this: contacts are *crucial* to the success of your informational interviewing and, ultimately, your job-hunt.[1]

Some job-hunters cultivate new contacts whenever they can. If they go to hear a speaker on some subject *that interests them,* they make it a point to join the crowd that gathers 'round the speaker at the end of the talk, and – with notebook poised – ask such questions as: "Is there anything special that people with my technical expertise can do?" And then you mention your specialty: computer scientist, health professional, chemist, writer, or whatever. Very useful information may thus be turned up. You can also ask if you can contact the speaker for further information – "and at what address?" Conventions,

1. An interesting study about contacts has been published, and you may find some helpful ideas in it. The book is called *Getting a Job: A Study of Contacts and Careers,* by Mark S. Granovetter, and if your library doesn't have it, it can be ordered from Harvard University Press, c/o Uniserv Inc., 525 Great Rd., Rt. 119, Littleton, MA 01460. 1974. $7.95, hardcover. See also: Lipnack, Jessica, and Stamps, Jeffrey, *Networking: The first report and directory – People connecting with people, linking ideas and resources.* Doubleday & Co., 245 Park Ave., New York, NY 10017. 1982. $15.95, paper.

likewise, afford rich opportunities to make contacts. Says one college graduate: "I snuck into the Cable Advertisers Convention at the Waldorf in N.Y.C. That's how I got my job."

You *may* want to put a modest-sized advertisement in the paper once you are in your chosen geographical area (or in the place where you currently live, if that is where you intend to do your job-hunting), saying you would like to meet with other people who are following the job-hunting techniques of *What Color Is Your Parachute?* That way you'll form a kind of 'job-hunters anonymous,' where you can mutually support one another in your hunt.

Your search: for places that need your skills. Your aide: your contacts (and that includes *everyone* you know or meet during a typical day or week: people on the street, in the market, in the stores you patronize, the places you regularly visit, and so on). Your purpose: not to find out if particular organizations want you, but rather, whether or not *you* want them.

FOCUSING DOWN: TO KINDS OF PLACES IN THAT AREA

Suppose you've decided that, let us say, being a consultant uses more of your skills than anything else. The question you then face is: should I be a consultant in education, in business, in nonprofit organizations, in fund-raising, or what? It is important, as you are identifying what you like to do, that you identify in what *kinds* of places you might enjoy doing this.

It is the same with any other career or occupation. You want to teach, let us say. Do you want to teach at a university, a college, a junior college, a business school, in private industry (some corporations, such as IBM for example, make large use of teachers), or where? The purpose of this stage of your informational interviewing is to look at *all the options,* so that you can choose the one you prefer the most – along with some 'plan Bs.'

You are looking for the organizations or places (colleges, associations, small businesses, institutions, agencies, etc.) where you would be *happiest* working. Why? Because the more you enjoy *what* you are doing and *where* you are doing it, the better you are going to use the talents which God gave you.[1]

Here are *the kinds of questions* that you are (hopefully) trying to find the answers to, as you do your informational interviewing:

☐ 1. Do I want to work for a company, firm, agency, college, association, foundation, small business, the government, or what?

☐ 2. Do I want to work for an older and larger organization, or get in on the ground floor of a new and smaller one, with growth possibilities? (During Hard Times, look *hard* at the new and smaller ones.)

☐ 3. Do I want to advance rapidly? If so I need an organization with solid plans for expansion – overseas or at home.

☐ 4. Do I want to work for a "going concern" or for "a problem child" type of operation? As the experts say, *a company in trouble* is a company in search of leadership. The same goes for foundations, agencies, etc. If that is your cup of tea (well, is it?), you can probably find such places without too much investigation. Some experts say if you go for such a challenge, give yourself a time limit, say 3 to 5 years, and then if you can't solve it, get out. The average job in this country only lasts 3.6 years, anyway.

---

1. If you are not at all familiar with the business world, and want a detailed breakdown of management functions and sub-functions, so that you will gain a better idea of where you might want to target yourself, there is the *Common Body of Knowledge for Management Consultants,* available in your library or (for $13 or so) from the Association of Consulting Management Engineers, Inc., 230 Park Ave., New York, NY 10017.

☐ 5. Other questions: *your own personal ones* – what do I want to accomplish with my skills? what working circumstances do I want?[1] what opportunities? what responsibilities? what kinds of job-pressures am I willing to exist under, and do I feel capable of handling? kinds of people I want to work with? starting salary? salary five years from now? promotion opportunities? (Keep these always in mind.)

So much for *the kinds* of questions. Now, what resources are there in your local library, that can help you find answers?

WRITTEN RESOURCES

Some tools for helping you to identify organizations' problems, names of people who have the power to hire, and the like, are listed below. Many of these directories issue new editions annually. They should all be available in your local library.

American Men and Women of Science.
American Society of Training and Development Directory.
Who's Who in Training and Development, Suite 305,
600 Maryland Ave., SW, Washington, DC 20024.
Better Business Bureau report on the organization
(call the BBB in the city where the organization is located).
Business Information Sources, by Lorna M. Daniels.
University of California Press, Berkeley, CA 94720.
Annotated guide to business books and reference sources.
Career Guide to Professional Associations, Garrett Park Press,
Garrett Park, MD 20766. $18.95, postpaid.
Chamber of Commerce data on the organization
(visit the Chamber there).
College library (especially *business school* library), if there
is one in your chosen area.

---

1. A wonderful book to help you sort out your feelings about this whole matter is Fritz Steele's *The Sense of Place.* CBI Publishing Co., Inc., 51 Sleeper St., Boston, MA 02210. 1981. Hardcover. There is also *So This is Where You Work: A Guide to Unconventional Working Environments,* by Charles A. Fracchia. Penguin Books, 625 Madison Ave., New York, NY 10022. 1979. $9.95, paper. And: *People in Places: Experiencing, Using and Changing the Built Environment,* by Jay Farbstein and Min Kantrowitz. Prentice-Hall, Englewood Cliffs, NJ 07632. 1978. $4.95, paper. And: *Worksteads: Living and Working in the Same Place,* by Jeremy Joan Hewes. Doubleday and Co., Inc., 245 Park Ave., New York, NY 10017. 1981. $9.95, paper.

Company/college/association/agency/foundation *Annual Reports.* Get these directly from the Personnel Department or publicity person at the company, etc., or from the Chamber or your local library.

Contacts Influential: Commerce and Industry Directory. Businesses in particular market area listed by name, type of business, key personnel, etc. (Contacts Influential, Market Research and Development Services, 321 Bush St., Ste. 203, San Francisco, CA 94104, if your library doesn't have it.)

Directory of Corporate Affiliations. (National Register Publishing Co., Inc.)

Directory of Information Resources in the United States. (Physical Sciences, Engineering, Biological Sciences) Washington, DC. Library of Congress.

Dun & Bradstreet's Million Dollar Directory. Very helpful.

Dun & Bradstreet's Middle Market Directory. Very helpful.

Dun & Bradstreet's Reference Book of Corporate Managements.

Encyclopedia of Associations, Vol. I, National Organizations, Gale Research Co. Lists organizations that are in the business of giving out information.

Encyclopedia of Business Information Sources (2 volumes). 4th Ed. Gale Research Co.

Fitch Corporation Manuals.

F & S Indexes (recent articles on firms).

F & S Index of Corporations and Industries. Lists "published articles" by industry and by company name. Updated weekly.

Fortune Magazine's 500.

Fortune's Plant and Product Directory.

The Foundation Directory.

How to Reach Anyone Who's Anyone, by Michael Levine. Price/Stern/Sloan Publishers, Inc., 410 N. La Cienega Blvd., Los Angeles, CA 90048. 1980. $4.95, paper.

Industrial Research Laboratories of the United States, R.R. Bowker Co., 1180 Ave. of the Americas, New York, NY 10036. 1977. $65.

In-House Training and Development Programs Directory, Andrea Pedolsky, ed. Gale Research Co. 1981. Describes programs in hundreds of companies and schools nation-wide.

Investor, Banker, Broker Almanac.

MacRae's Blue Book.

Moody's Industrial Manual (and other Moody manuals).

National Directory of Addresses and Telephone Numbers, by Stanley R. Greenfield. Bantam Books, Inc.

National Recreational Sporting and Hobby Organizations of the U.S., Columbia Books, Inc., 777 14th St., NW, Washington, DC 20005. 1981.

National Trade and Professional Associations of the United States and Canada and Labor Unions. Garrett Park Press, Garrett Park, MD 20766. Available from Columbia Books, Inc. (see above).

Plan Purchasing Directory.

Register of manufacturers for your state or area (e.g., *California Manufacturers Register).*

Research Centers Directory, 6th ed. Gale Research Co. Also: *New Research Centers,* updating the original 1979 volume.

Standard and Poor's Corporation Records.

Standard and Poor's Industrial Index.

Standard and Poor's Listed Stock Reports (at some brokers' offices).

Standard and Poor's Register of Corporations, Directors and Executives. Key executives in 32,000 leading companies, plus 75,000 directors.

Telephone Contacts for Data Users. Customer Services Branch, Bureau of the Census. 301-449-1600 for statistical information on any subject.

Thomas' Register of American Manufacturers. Thomas Publishing Co.

United States Government Manual. Or call the Federal Information Center of the General Services Administration at 202-755-8660 to find the names of experts in any field. For help on a question no one seems to know the answer to, try the National Referral Center at the Library of Congress, 202-287-5670.

Value Line Investment Survey, from Arnold Bernhard and Co., 5 E. 44th St., New York, NY 10017. (Most libraries have a set.)

Walker's Manual of Far Western Corporations and Securities.

Who's Who in Finance and Industry, and all the other *Who's Who* books. Useful once you have the name of someone-who-has-the-power-to-hire, and you want to know more about them.

If all of this seems like an embarrassment of riches to you, and you don't know where to begin, there's even a guide to all these directories: If you don't know which directory to consult, see—

Klein's *Guide to American Directories,*
or Gale Research Company's *Directory of Directories*
or (when you are about to throw up your hands in despair,
remember
there's a person who knows how to use all these books):
your friendly neighborhood librarian.

Besides these directories, some other resources may also be worth perusing. Periodicals: *Business Week, Dun's Review, Forbes, Fortune,* and the *Wall Street Journal;*

Trade Associations and their periodicals; Trade journals.

There are also excellent surveys of key companies, e.g., Moskowitz, Milton; Katz, Michael; and Levering, Robert, ed., *Everybody's Business, An Almanac: The irreverent guide to corporate america.* Harper and Row, 10 E. 53rd St., New York, NY 10022. 1980. $9.95, paper.

You will want to note, also, that some libraries – particularly in large cities – have special sections devoted to careers. In Chicago, for example, there is a Business Information Center at the Chicago Public Library, 425 N. Michigan Ave., 11th floor, which publishes a list of its "Career Information Sources," and a list of the resources available from its "Business/Science Technology Division," – including computer-assisted searches for information. New York City's Mid-Manhattan Public Library (at 40th St. and Fifth Ave.) also has a "Job Opportunities Information Center." Other libraries (increasingly) have similar resources. If you are timid about exploring your library's resources, walk up to the reference librarian and ask for help. The point of all this is, libraries are not just for scholars. Libraries are also for job-hunters, and career-changers. Whatever it is that you want to know, in many cases is there.

Of course, despite this wealth of material, you cannot simply hide yourself away in the libraries all the time. (Don't you wish!) This information out of books *must* be supplemented by talks with *insiders*—brokers, college alumni, friends, anyone you know who has friends within the particular organizations you are interested in, who can give you helpful insights. Use every contact you know, once names of organizations that interest you begin to surface in your notes.

FOCUSING DOWN: GETTING ACQUAINTED

In visiting the geographical area where you most want to work (whether it is where you already are, or not), and conducting your own personal and organizational survey of the area, you are trying to go from one person to another, building a chain of links in which each contact you see refers you to another (and hopefully sets up the appointment for you, or at least allows you to use their name).

Let's listen to an actual job-hunter describe the process:

"Suppose I arrived cold in some city, the one place in all the world I want to live – but with no idea of what that city might hold as a match and challenge for my 'personal-talent bank.' I have an economic survey to make, yes; but I also have an equally or more important personal survey to accomplish. Can this city meet my peculiarly personal needs? To find out, I meet Pastors, bankers, school principals, physicians, dentists, real estate operators, et al. I would be astonished if opportunities were not brought to my attention, together with numerous offers of personal introduction to key principals. All I would be doing is forging links (referrals) in a chain leading to my eventual targets. *The referral is the key.*"

People who haven't tried this are understandably afraid: afraid important men or women won't have time to see them, afraid they won't be able to get past the secretary or receptionist, etc. But, as was said above, referral (by one of your contacts) is the key.

Let's listen to John Crystal, a master in this field, describe this informational interviewing process:

"If you really are interested in highway-carrier operations and really do know quite a bit about it, for instance, and you get to Charlotte, NC, where you learn that one small, new company is doing something really innovative and intelligent in *your* field I would guess that the chances are that its President is just as fascinated by the subject as you are. And if you called him up – Oh, yes, the secretary, well this goes for her or him too – and told him the simple truth about that shared interest – if he asks if you are job hunting tell him the truth, *No, not at the moment,* – but that you are *in truth* impressed by what you have heard about his bright ideas, and that you want to hear more about them, and that you just possibly might have a suggestion or two based on your own experience which he might find useful – Well, he just might invite you to lunch. And if he wants to offer you a job after a while, and many do, it's strictly *his* idea. And you do not accept it although you are always polite enough to say that you will be glad to consider it and perhaps talk it over with him again later on, after you have decided precisely what you want to do, where, with whom, etc. The key to the whole thing is this: treat the other person just as you would like to be treated yourself."

If this whole process described on these pages has been followed religiously (so to speak) you will have at the end of your initial informational interviewing:

1. A *list* of places in your chosen geographical area *that interest you, and that look as though they have problems your skills can help solve.*

What you then want to do further research about is:

2. *Identifying in detail what those problems are,* for the manageable number of organizations you have now identified in list No. 1 above.

AN ORGANIZATION'S PROBLEMS

All organizations have money – to one degree or another. What you are looking for are *problems* – specifically, *problems that your skills can help solve. What problems are bugging this organization? Ask; look. (If you are talking to people within a company or organization that looks as though it might be interesting to you, ask them ever so gently:* What is the biggest challenge you are encountering here?)

The problem does not have to be one that is bothering only *that* organization. You may want to ask what problem is common to the whole industry or field – low profit, obsolescence, inadequate planning, etc.? Or if there is a problem that is common to the geographic region: labor problems, minority employment, etc. All you really need is one major problem that you would truly delight to help solve.

Some of these questions above will be relevant for you; others will not. *If you are "going after" a college, for example, some of these may have to be ignored, and some adapted.*

Again, some of these questions are general in nature, and you will try to answer them about *any* organization you approach. Other questions are very specific, requiring detailed research, and you will have to keep at it, searching, digging, interviewing, until you find out.[1] But the skills you are sharpening up will more than repay you the time spent, a thousandfold. If this whole question of an organization's problems is a difficult con-

1. If you are totally new to all of this, these two books will help you: *How to Find Information About Companies,* Donna M. Jablonski, ed. (Washington Researchers, 918 16th St., NW, Washington, DC 20006) and *A Business Information Guidebook* by Oscar Figueroa and Charles Winkler (Amacom, 135 W. 50th St., New York, NY 10020. 1980. $9.95, paper.) If the organization is large enough to have an annual financial report, that report may help you see what the organization's challenges are –provided you know how to read it. These resources may help: *How to Read a Financial Report* (Merrill Lynch Pierce Fenner and Smith, Inc., 1 Liberty Plaza, New York, NY 10080. 1979.); *What Else Can Financial Statements Tell You?* (American Institute of Certified Public Accountants, 1211 Avenue of the Americas, New York, NY 10036.); and *Understanding Financial Statements* and *Investors Information Kit* (both available from New York Stock Exchange, Inc., Publication Section, 11 Wall St., New York, NY 10005.)

cept for you to grasp, just think of five stores you've patronized during the past year, where something went wrong for you as a customer. What was it? You weren't waited on, when it was your proper turn? You weren't told all the information you needed to know, in order to make an intelligent choice? The person with whom you were dealing insisted on going by the rule book, no matter what common sense and compassion would otherwise dictate? The person with whom you were dealing had some small amount of power but was misusing that power for all it was worth? The organization had installed a computer where a person used to be, and the person between you and the computer seemed to be taking orders from it, rather than vice versa? The organization had, in a word, lost the human touch? Or what? You will quickly realize, you are more aware of an organization's problems than you thought you were.[1]

YOU'LL LIKE THIS JOB, EXCEPT EVERY NOW AND THEN, WHEN THEY DUMP A LOT OF PAPER WORK ON YOU.

1. If you want some more Basic Training, before you dive into this phase of your active informational interviewing, you can choose from the following: *The Handbook of Business Problem Solving,* Kenneth J. Albert, ed. (McGraw Hill Book Co., 1221 Avenue of the Americas, New York, NY 10020. 1980. $24.95, hardcover.); *Life in Organizations: Workplaces as People Experience Them,* Rosabeth Moss Kanter and Barry A. Stein, eds. (available from Basic Books, Inc., 10 E. 53rd St., New York, NY 10022. 1979. $17.50, hardcover. Or see your library.); *Quality is Free: The Art of Making Quality Certain,* by Philip B. Crosby (McGraw Hill Book Co., New York, NY. 1979. $12.50, hardcover.); and *The Briarpatch Book: experiences in right livelihood and simple living,* from the Briarpatch Community (available from New Glide Publications, 330 Ellis St., San Francisco, CA 94102. 1978. $8.00, paper.)

RULES FOR FINDING OUT IN DETAIL THE NEEDS OR PROBLEMS OF AN ORGANIZATION

Rule No. 1: *You don't need to discover the problems of the whole organization (unless it's very small); you only need to discover the problems that are bugging the-person-who-has-the-ultimate-responsibility (or power) -to-hire-you.* The conscientious always bite off more than they can chew. If they're going to try for a job at the Telephone Company, or IBM or the Federal Government, or General Motors or – like that – they assume they've got to find out the problems facing that whole organization. *Forget it!* Your task, fortunately, is much more manageable. Find out what problems are bugging, bothering, concerning, perplexing, gnawing at, the-person-who-has-the-power-to-hire-you. This assumes, of course, that you have first *identified* who that person is. If you did a thorough information-search, of course, you probably have already met that person, in the course of gathering your information. So they are more to you than just a name. If it's a committee of sorts that actually has the responsibility (and therefore Power) to hire you, you will need to figure out who that one individual is (or two) who sways the others. You know, the one whose judgment the others respect. How do you find that out? By using your contacts, of course. Someone will know someone who knows that whole committee, and can tell you who their *real* leader is. It's not necessarily the one who got elected as Chairperson.

Rule No. 2: *Don't assume the problems have to be huge, complex and hidden. The problems bothering the-person-who-has-the-power-to-hire-you may be small, simple, and obvious.* If the job you are aiming at was previously filled by someone (i.e., the one who, if you get hired, will be referred to as "your predecessor") the problems that are bothering the-person-who-has-the-power-to-hire-you may be uncovered simply by finding out (through those among your contacts who know your prospective boss) what bugged him or her about your predecessor. Samples:

"They were never to work on time, took long lunch breaks, and were out sick too often"; OR

"They were good at typing, but had lousy skills over the telephone"; OR

INTERVIEWING FOR INFORMATION ON AN ORGANIZATION'S PROBLEMS

☐ If it's a decent-sized company, send for their annual report to stockholders; granted it's a public relations piece, it still may help quite a bit. If the organization is too small to have an annual report, use your contacts to try to find people who know a lot about it. Then, after your information gathering, you will want to weigh the following questions:

IF IT IS A LARGE COMPANY:

☐ How does this organization rank within its field, or industry? Is this organization family owned? If so, what effect has that on promotions? Where are its plants, offices or branches? What are all its projects or services? In what ways have they grown in recent years? New lines, new products, new processes, new facilities, etc? Existing political situations: imminent proxy fights, upcoming mergers, etc? What is the general image of the organization in peoples' minds? If the organization sells stock, what has been happening to it (see an investment broker and ask).

QUESTIONS TO BE ASKING YOURSELF REGARDLESS OF THE COMPANY'S SIZE:

☐ What kind of *turnover of staff* have they had? What is the attitude of employees toward the organization? Are their faces happy, strained, or what? Is promotion generally from within, or from outside? How long has the chief executive been with the organization?

☐ Do they encourage their employees to further their educational training? Do they help them pay for it?

☐ How do *communications* work within the organization? How is information collected, and by what paths does it flow? What methods are used to see that information gets results – to what authority do people respond there? Who reports to whom?

☐ Is there a "time-bomb" – a problem that will kill the organization, or drastically reduce its effectiveness and efficienciency if they don't solve it real fast?

"They handled older people well, but just couldn't relate to the young"; OR

"I never could get them to keep me informed about what they were doing"; etc.

Sometimes, it's as simple as that. In your research you may be thinking to yourself, Gosh, this firm has a huge public relations problem; I'll have to show them that I could put together a whole crash P.R. program. That's the huge, complex and hidden problem that you think the-person-who-has-the-power-to-hire-you *ought to be concerned about.* But, in actual fact, what they *are* concerned about is whether (unlike your predecessor) you're going to get to work on time, take assigned lunch breaks, and not be out sick too often. Don't overlook the Small, Simple and Obvious Problems which bug almost every employer.[1]

Rule No. 3: *In most cases, your task is not that of educating your prospective employer, but of trying to read their mind.* Now, to be sure, you may have uncovered – during your information-search – some problem that the-person-who-has-the-power-to-hire-you is absolutely unaware of. And you may be convinced that this problem is *so crucial* that for you even to mention it will instantly win you their undying gratitude. Maybe. But don't bet on it. Our files are filled with sad testimonies like the following:

"I met with the V-P, Marketing in a major local bank on the recommendation of an officer, and discussed with him a program I devised to reach the female segment of his market, which would not require any new services, except education, enlightenment and encouragement. His comment at the end of the discussion was that the bank president had been after him for three years to develop a program for women, and he wasn't about to do it because the only reason, in his mind, for the president's request was reputation enhancement on the president's part . . . "

Inter-office politics, as in this case, or other considerations may prevent your prospective employer from being receptive

1. For further boning up, browse through *Management: Tasks, Responsibilities, Practices* by Peter F. Drucker, Harper & Row, 1973; and *Work in America,* Report of a Special Task Force to the Secretary of Health, Education, and Welfare, M.I.T. Press, 1973—at your local library.

to Your Bright Idea. In any event, you're not trying to find out what *might* motivate them to hire you. Your research has got to be devoted rather to finding out what *already does* motivate them *when they decide to hire someone for the position you are interested in.* In other words, you're trying to find out What's Already Going On In Their Mind. In this sense, your task is more akin to a kind of mind-reading than it is to education. (Though *some* people-who-have-the-power-to-hire are *very* open to being educated. You have to decide whether you want to risk testing this.)

Rule No. 4: *There are various ways of finding out what's going on in their mind: don't try just one way.* We will give a kind of outline, here, of the various ways. (You can use this as a checklist.)

A *Analyzing the Organization at a Distance and Making Some Educated Guesses.*

1. If the organization is expanding, then they need:
   a. More of what they already have; OR
   b. More of what they already have, but with different style, added skills, or other pluses *that are needed;* OR
   c. Something they don't presently have: a new kind of person, with new skills doing a new function or service.
2. If the organization is continuing as is, then they need:
   a. To replace people who were fired (find out why; what was lacking?); OR
   b. To replace people who quit (find out what was prized about them); OR

c. To create a new position (yes, this happens even in organizations that are not expanding – due to
   1) Old needs which weren't provided for, earlier, but now must be, even if they have to cut out some other function or position.
   2) Revamping assignments within their present staff.

3. If the organization is reducing its size, staff or product/service, then they
   a. Have not yet decided which staff to terminate, i.e., which functions to give low priority to (in which case *that* is their problem, and you may be able to help them identify which functions are "core-functions"); OR
   b. *Have* decided which functions or staff to terminate (in which case they may need multi-talented people or generalists able to do several jobs, i.e., functions, instead of just one, as formerly).

B *Analyzing the problems of the-person-who-has-the-power-to-hire-you by talking to them directly, during your preliminary information-interview.*

Why guess at what's going on in their mind, when you can find out directly by including them in your information survey? When you are in an interview, listen carefully to the employer you are talking to. The greatest problem every employer faces is finding people who will listen and take them seriously. If you listen, you may find the employer discusses their problems – giving you firmer grounds to which you can relate your skills.

C *Analyzing the problems of the-person-who-has-the-power-to-hire-you by talking to their "opposite number" in another organization which is similar (not to say, almost identical) to the one that interests you.*

If, for some reason, you cannot approach – at this time– the organization that interests you (it's too far away, or you don't want to tip your hand yet, or whatever), what you can do is pick a similar organization (or individual) where you are – and go find out what kind of problems are on their mind. (If you are interested in working for, say, a senator in another state, you can talk to a senator's staff here where you are, first; the problems are likely to be similar.)

D *Analyzing the problems of your prospective employer by talking to the person who held the job before you – OR by talking to their "opposite number" in another similar/identical organization.*

Nobody, absolutely nobody, knows the problems bugging a boss so much as someone who works, or used to work, for them. If they still work for them, they may have a huge investment in being discreet (i.e., not as candid as you need). Ex-employees are not necessarily any longer under that sort of pressure. Needless to say, if you're trying to get the organization to create a new position, there is no "previous employee." But in some identical or similar organization *which already has this sort of position,* you can still find someone to interview.

E *Using your contacts/friends/everyone you meet, in order to find someone who*

1. Knows the organization that interests you, or knows someone who knows;
2. Knows the-person-who-has-the-power-to-hire-you, or knows someone who knows;
3. Knows who their opposite number is in a similar/identical organization;
4. Knows your predecessor, or knows someone who knows;
5. Knows your "opposite number" in another organization, or knows someone who knows.

F *Supplementary Method: Research in the library*, on the organization, or an organization similar to it; research on the individual-who-has-the-power-to-hire-you, or on their opposite number in another organization, etc. (Ask your friendly librarian or research librarian for help—tell them what you're trying to find out.)

Rule No. 5: *Ultimately, this is a language-translation problem. You're trying to take your language (i.e., a description of your skills), and translate it into their language (i.e., their priorities, their values, their jargon, as these surface within their concerns, problems, etc.).* You should be aware to begin with that most of the-people-who-have-the-power-to-hire-you for the position that you want DO NOT like the word "problems," as I said earlier. It reminds them that they are mortal, have hangups, haven't solved something yet, or that they overlooked something, etc. "Smartass" is the word normally reserved for someone who comes in *and shows them up*. (This isn't true of everybody, but it's true of altogether too many.) Since you're trying to use *their* language, speak of "an area you probably are planning to move into" or "a concern of yours" or "a challenge currently facing you" or *anything* except: "By the way, I've uncovered a problem you have." Use the word *problems* in your own head, but don't blurt it out with your prospective employer, *unless you hear them use it first.*

Beyond this, your goal is to be able to speak of Your Skills in terms of *The Language* of Their Problems. Here are some examples, in order to bring this all home:

The person who has the power to hire you, was bugged by or concerned about:	**You therefore use language which emphasizes that you:**
Your predecessor had all the skills, but was too serious about *everything.*	have all the skills (name them) *plus* you have a sense of humor.
This place is expanding, and now needs a training program for its employees.	have the skills to do training, and in the area they are concerned about.
All the picayune details they have to attend to, which they would like to shovel off on someone else.	are very good with details and follow up. (That had better be true, or don't say it.)
This magazine probably isn't covering all the subjects that it should, but that's just a gnawing feeling, and they've never had time to document it, and decide what areas to move into.	have done a complete survey of its table of contents for the last ten years, can show what they've missed, and have outlined sample articles in those missing areas.

It all looks, at first sight, as though this whole informational interviewing process were an awful lot of hard work. And, at first, it certainly may feel that way. Self-inventory, meaningful skills, career and life planning, job markets – looking back later, you may admit there were times you were tempted to forget

TRAVELS WITH FARLEY by Phil Frank (c) 1982 Field Enterprises, Inc. Courtesy of Field Newspaper Syndicate

the whole thing, and just go about the transition process and job-hunt in the old haphazard way that so many others do it. But, you told yourself, *that way lies madness.* So, you kept at it. And now, you've begun to notice something: you're enjoying it. No telling just when it happened. But, you began to notice it is *fun* to go around and talk to people. Maybe because they aren't on the spot (yet), and neither are you. And you begin to notice it is *fun* to do the research in your local library, college, or whatever.

Maybe we enjoy talking to higher-ups and finding out that it isn't so difficult as the books *(with their long chapters on the art of conducting interviews)* make interviewing out to be. Maybe we enjoy the renewed sense of self-confidence that we are picking up, in non-stress situations. Maybe a detective hides within the breast of each one of us.

Well, you with the soul of a detective, you *are* solving a mystery. Namely: in what environment will this hardy plant called *you* thrive, grow, and bloom the best? Or: if you're instinctively religious, a better form of the question for you might be, in what place can your service to the Lord or this global village best continue – without the danger of burying your talents in the ground?

That's the mystery you are unraveling.

Sure, it's fun. It's dealing with YOU. And by focusing down, in this fashion, you are increasingly able to concentrate your energies in an effective fashion.

You are acting as though the organization that gets you will be darned lucky. You are even beginning to feel this is true. And, what is most strange, you are absolutely right.

THANKS

Hopefully you will remember each night to sit down and write a brief note to each person you saw that *day*. This is *one of the most essential steps in the whole job-seeking process – and the one most overlooked by job-seekers.* Every professional counsels this, and yet job-hunters overlook it continually. *It should be regarded as basic to courtesy, not to mention kindness, that we thank people who help us along the way.* Call them "bread and butter notes." Or whatever. We all ought to be most serious about this business of saying Thank You. Letters along the way also serve secondary purposes, such as underlining things we said, adding or correcting impressions we left behind us, and confirming our understanding of things the people we talked to said.

Don't forget secretaries, either. Get their names. Thank them for their help. They will appreciate you, and remember you. If you go to see their boss again, greet them by name (you did jot it down, didn't you?).

After all, you are presenting yourself as one who has one of the most sought-after skills in the world today: Knowing how to treat people as persons. Prove it, please – day by day. You'll get pleasure from it. And, what's more:

It just may get you the job. (According to one survey, job-hunting success was more related to this "thank you note" process than any other factor.) Indeed, we know of one woman who was actually told that she was hired because she was the only interviewee who sent a thank-you note after the interview.

Looking Back:

WHEN INFORMATION-INTERVIEWING JUST DOESN'T SEEM TO BE WORKING FOR YOU

You say that you've tried informational interviewing, and while it seems like a wonderful idea in theory, it just isn't working for You? Here is a checklist to help you find where the trouble lies:

☐ Did you do your homework regarding Your Self, so that you know exactly what your skills are? *If not, go to Appendix A, and do the Quick Job-Hunting Map. If you set aside a full weekend, undisturbed, you can get it done.*

☐ Are you following the pattern for informational interviewing, that is outlined on pages 237–240 in the Map? *If not, that may explain your problem. In which case, You Know What You Must Do.*

☐ Are you sending letters asking for appointments? *Unless your interviewees are in a faraway city, don't. Use the phone instead; or, in some cases, it pays to just stop by, without an appointment, and try "pot-luck."*

☐ Are you clear in your own head that you are in a Pre-Job-hunt phase, when you are doing informational interviewing; or do you *really* feel that informational interviewing is just an extra-clever, extra devious way of hoodwinking the employer into thinking you are not a job-hunter, when in reality you are? *If the latter is the case, then you have utterly failed to understand the purpose of informational interviewing. In which case, you had better re-read pages 237–240 five times. For, if you secretly think you are job-hunting at this*

point, then you have become the screenee; when, with genuine informational interviewing, you are in an earlier pre-job-hunt phase, where you are the screener.

☐ If you're having trouble getting in, are you making it clear to the person you want to interview (or their receptionist), that you *only need fifteen (or, at the most, twenty) minutes* of their time? And are you sticking to that self-imposed limit, religiously? *If not, no wonder you can't get in. Every employer or information-source dreads becoming the semi-captive of a two-hour talker; and unless you have reassured them that You Are Brief, you are under suspicion of being a Possible THT.*

☐ If you're having trouble getting in, are you using your contacts to "get by" whoever it is that is screening you out? *If not, why not? Contacts are not merely to be saved for the final job-hunt phase. You can use them during the informational interviewing phase, as well. If you're trying to get information out of a certain place, and that place is guarded like Fort Knox, try this: for a week, ask EVERYONE you meet: "Do you know someone who works at (and here name the place you are trying to get in, to interview for information)? Or do you know anyone who knows someone who does?" See what happens. (Of course, it doesn't always work; but you'd be surprised how many times it* does.)

☐ If after you get in, you are tongue-tied as to what to say, then obviously you're not clear as to what information you're looking for. *In which case, refer back to question #2 above, or read Billingsley's book* (listed at the end of The Quick Job-Hunting Map).

P.S. A Brief Footnote for Employers, Regarding Informational Interviewing: There are more than 14 million employing-organizations in this country, and heaven-only-knows how many managers or People-Who-Are-Information-Sources, within those more than 14 million. So, most of you have *not* run into Informational Interviewing, and where you have, you have been delighted to find someone who shares your enthusiasm for a particular field or job, and are more than willing to give a helping hand to someone who is up-and-coming, especially if they know what they need to ask you, even as someone once gave you a helping hand. However, as we mentioned in the last chapter, a few of you are in highly-obvious organizations, or positions, where people who want information are going to be given your name, again and again. And so, you few will be receiving (over the years) more calls or drop-ins, looking for information, than you can bear. For you, a suggestion: why not schedule one hour a week, or every two weeks, or once a month, when you are willing to sit down and talk with anyone and everyone who wants some information from you about your career field, or your organization, or your particular job? That way, when anyone calls for an informational interview, you can give them an appointment for this particular time you have set aside on your schedule; and thus take care of everyone at once, because you will be doing group interviewing, instead of individual interviewing.

You're a bunch of jackasses. You work your rear ends off in a trivial course that no one will ever care about again. You're not willing to spend time researching a company that you're interested in working for. Why don't you decide who you want to work for and go after them?

Professor Albert Shapero
(again) to his students

CHAPTER SEVEN

You must identify the persons who have the power to hire you and show them how your skills can help them with their problems.

THE FOURTH KEY TO CAREER-PLANNING AND JOB-HUNTING

As you go through all this intensive research concerning the places where you might like to work, you achieve two results:

1. *Your list gets smaller,* as you discover some of the places that interested you (even after visiting them) *did not have the kind of problems or difficulties that your strongest skills could* a) solve; and b) let you enjoy doing so, during the process.

2. You get to know *a great deal* about the remaining organizations, including – most specifically – *their problems, and what you can do to help solve them.*

Organizations (including hospitals, colleges, and everything else) love to be loved. You are going to be a very rare bird when you walk in their front door. You loved them enough to find out a lot of information about them. *You know far more than you are ever going to have to use,* at least during the hiring process. But the depth of your knowledge will pay off in your quiet sense of competence. You know they have problems – oops, excuse me, "challenges" – and you know you can help solve them.

This fact will be of great interest – most of the time – to the person you go to see, provided you have taken the trouble to identify, learn about, and ask to see *the top executive whose responsibility it is to solve the particular problems that you have zeroed in on.*

That is the person you are going to need to approach, by name, by appointment: the person who has the interest, the responsibility and the motivation for hiring *this problem solver: Y-O-U...*

You are going to ask to see that person only, and you are going to generally avoid

THAT ORGANIZATION'S PERSONNEL DEPARTMENT

This advice has been given historically since job-hunting manuals were first written, by the likes of Albee, Crystal, Haldane, Harper, Kent, Miller, Miner, Shapero, Snelling, Townsend, and Uris – to name just a few.

The advice has always been strongly stated by them all:

> The personnel department in most companies, they say, is at the bottom of the social and executive totem pole; it rarely hears of middle-high level vacancies even within its own company; when it does know of the vacancies, it rarely has power to hire except for entry level; in almost all other cases it can only screen out applicants, and refer those who survive, on up to higher executives; therefore it is in the job-hunter's interest (generally speaking) to skip over this extra screening-out process. In other words, avoid this department like the plague.

I myself first echoed the above advice some thirteen years ago, and now that it is the year of our Lord 1983, I am bound to say that I do not think things have changed much. But I do think they have changed *a little.* That is to say, job-hunters who have successfully concluded their job-hunt have written to tell me of an anonymous personnel department here or there that did *not* see itself as an extra screening-out step in the job-hunting process, but was – au contraire – the very model of helpfulness to them. The personnel director sat down with them and helped them figure out just exactly where "upstairs" they might fit in, and then sent them on up with an introductory note, "kicking the door open for them" as it were. Bravo! I say.

You may therefore want to keep an open mind about the *possibility* that a particular company's personnel department is like the one I have just described, and – if you are in an extreme risk-taking mood – follow your intuition and your hunches about whether or not *this* is a personnel department to seek, or to avoid. Going in there merely to pick up their annual report, and any other printed material they have, which you should do in any event, gives you a chance to look the place over and decide. Apart from visiting it briefly, merely to pick up such literature, you will probably still find it (generally speaking) wise to avoid that department. I know too many stories about people who have been turned down by a particular company's personnel department, who then went back to square one, found out who, in that very same company, had the power to hire for the position they wanted, went to that woman or man, and got hired – ten floors up from the personnel department that had just rejected them.

If not the personnel department, what then? Well, you are going to have to do enough research – using the directories listed on pages 148–151 and your contacts – to figure out who has the responsibility for hiring in the division, department or whatever that you are interested in. If you can't figure out, despite all your best efforts, who that person is, there is a simple rule you would do well to remember: *when in doubt, go too high rather than too low on the organizational chart.* You will probably be referred "down"; but if you go too low, you will rarely be referred "up."

It will help you further if you learn something about that person-who-has-the-power-to-hire. Once you have their name, look them up in *Poor's Register, Who's Who in Commerce and Business,* or any other of the *Who's Who* directories, and consult your friendly neighborhood research librarian as well for any clippings or other file material they may have on your target person. Further, consult every acquaintance, friend, relative you know – i.e., all your Contacts – to see what they may know about him or her. . . before you ever go to meet them for a potential hiring interview.

WELL, YOU WANT TO SEE THEM, BUT DO THEY WANT TO SEE YOU?

This is the question that bothers almost everyone new to the job-hunt. We sort of just assume the answer is no. But, on the contrary,

Ten to one the answer is yes. Whether they are young or older; male or female.

First of all, you may have already met, during the process of your Informational Interviewing within your chosen geographical area and field.

They may have liked you.

They may even have offered you a job (this happens) during your informational interviewing process. And, as indicated earlier, we hope you responded to any such offer with nothing but the Absolute Truth: you were flattered, you would certainly keep it in mind, but at this point you weren't ready to say yet just exactly where it was that you wanted to work. But now you *are* ready, and you call to tell them so.

On the other hand, maybe the two of you didn't meet before.

Even so, they are very likely interested in meeting you. The odds are ten to one you've figured out someone who'll refer you, and act as your link to this person; but even lacking that referral you still can tell them that *you want to talk to them (for twenty minutes) about some of the challenges facing their organization, and what you've discovered that might be helpful to them.*

That's a switch!

Most of the time, when they do interviewing (for hiring, or otherwise) people are there to ask what that employer can do for them. You know: "How much vacation do you give, and what fringe benefits do you offer?"

Now, you offer to come in and tell them what *you* can do for *them.*

Are they interested?

The odds are ten to one that they are.

(If they are not, maybe you'd better re-evaluate whether you really want to work for this kind of person. And if you decide you still do, maybe you're going to have to convince them that they should hire you – even if they have to establish a new function or position, at a senior level, just for you.)

THIS PERSON YOU ARE GOING TO SEE IS JUST LIKE YOU, BUT UNDER REAL STRESS

The creative minority in this field have correctly pointed out that one of the reasons the hiring process in America today (at least beyond the $20,000 level) is so difficult, is because of the great stress involved for the executive who is interviewing.

Let's look at some of those sources of stress:

1. The odds are very great that the executive who does the interviewing was hired because of what they could contribute

to the company, and not because they were such a great interviewer. In fact, their gifts in this arena may be rather miserable.

2. They can't entrust the process to someone else, because they have to live with whoever gets hired afterwards. So, hiring-interviews for above-entry-level positions have a heavy accent of "I wish I could get someone else to do this for me, but I can't afford to take that chance."

3. If the person-with-the-power-to-hire makes a mistake, they are going to rub shoulders with that mistake, day by day. They don't usually hire someone, and then never see that new employee again. An executive who has the responsibility of hiring for this position is given or takes that responsibility (customarily) away from the personnel department *because this position is directly under them and they're going to have to live with whoever is hired, day by day.*

4. If they hire a mistake, it's going to make them look very bad with their superiors, board of directors, stockholders, or whoever it is that they report to.

5. If they hire a mistake and they aren't the chief executive yet, this could cost them a promotion personally – since they have proved they have bad judgment; and maybe their department is getting botched up – to boot.

6. If they hire a mistake, it's going to cost a lot of money. The costs of terminating their "mistake," going through the long hiring process for the replacement, and then training that replacement, totaled about $6,000 for a claims adjuster, $44,100 for an average salesperson, and $186,100 for a sales manager – according to a study done in an insurance company some ten years ago.[1] Heaven only knows what those costs have risen to in 1983. You can probably double these amounts without fear. In any event, my point: mistakes in hiring cost the employer *money.*

Not bad. In one twenty-minute interview (or even several of same), this hapless interviewer can botch up part of the organization, cost the organization a great deal of money, lose their own promotion, be called to account, and acquire a whole new set of ulcers. No wonder hiring is such a stressful situation for the employer, not just the job-hunter.

---

1. Flamholtz, Eric G., "Human Resources Accounting: Measuring Positional Replacement Costs," *Human Resource Management,* Spring 1973, Vol. 12, No. 1, pp. 8-16.

A person could be forgiven for wanting never to do it. But hiring is unavoidable. Experts estimate good corporation presidents spend 25% of their time (of necessity) in looking for new talent within the ranks, and outside.

Failing to get rid of the responsibility entirely, a president (or whoever) could be forgiven for praying at least for a new way to do it – *one with much less stress built in.*

YOU OFFER A PLEASANT LOW STRESS INTERVIEW

This is where you come in.

You are following the suggestions of the creative minority, who all are united in this: *create a situation where you and the-person-with-the-power-to-hire-you-for-a-position-you-want, can get a look at each other – without having to make a big decision* at that time.

If this person met you during your Informational Interviewing, or while you were developing what Bernard Haldane calls "remembrance and referral" contacts, they had a chance to see you in a low stress situation. It is a form of talent *window shopping.*

You came into their office on one mission – Mr. or Ms. Researcher, or Surveyor or whatever; but the interviewer had a chance to look at you surreptitiously as Mr. or Ms. Possible-Human-Resource-for-My-Organization.

All the creative minority who have studied the career transition process and the job-hunt are agreed in this: any way you can let an executive windowshop you, without your putting them on the spot, will create *a very favorable* situation for you. That's precisely what your Informational Interviewing (hopefully) did.

With this clue firmly in your hand, now that you have chosen this organization as one of the top ones you would like to work for, and are returning to discuss being hired, you may be able to think up an even more inventive approach to the-person-with-the-power-to-hire, in each organization. If so, more power to you. Your essential mission, however, is to show them how your skills can help them with their "problems."

But let's be very clear about one thing: as I said in the previous chapter, you must show this person how your skills can help them with their problems *as they perceive them.* I cannot stress this strongly enough. You may think you perceive a prob-

"I'll tell you why I want this job. I thrive on challenges. I like being stretched to my full capacity. I like solving problems. Also, my car is about to be repossessed."

lem that they are absolutely blind to, in that organization; but if so, you are going to have to delicately and very skillfully explore how they perceive that particular problem area, before you hit them over the head with your brilliant insight into it all.

We ourselves have had would-be job-hunters approach *us* for a job and confidently tell us that we desperately needed a person with such and such skills (which they just happened to possess) in order to accomplish – and then they proceeded to lay out some goals and priorities for our organization (the National Career Development Project) which we had already looked at and rejected, as part of our program. But they didn't know that, *because they hadn't done their homework.* So be aware, when you sit across the table from the person you'd most like to work for, that it is crucial for you to relate your skills to what's going on in *their* head, not merely to what's going on in *yours.* If I'm in trouble for lack of a creative artist in my organization, and you walk in and show me you have genuine skills in that area, you are interpreting your skills in terms of my problems. But if I have long since decided I don't need any help with art work, and you try to sell me on the idea that I need such help (namely, you), you are falling into the pitfall of interpreting your skills in terms of *your* problems, not mine. I, as employer, will lose interest in you from that point on, and at an accelerating rate.

THAT OLD DEBBIL: THE RÉSUMÉ

You are waiting breathlessly, no doubt, for me to mention somewhere along in here that you are going to need a resumé. Well, over the years I have tended to downplay the whole subject of resumés, largely because my interviews with successful job-hunters year after year have revealed that a large proportion of them never used a resume in getting their job. And never intend to. I said this once to a group of college counselors, many of whom were devoting large blocks of time in their job-hunting classes to teaching their students how to write a resumé. When I sat down afterward, I found myself next to the personnel director for a huge public utility company, which employed thousands of people. He leaned across to me. "I listened to what you said about resumés," he began. I waited for the axe to fall. However he went on: "I've been trying to tell these counselors for years to get off this obsession they have with resumés. I'll interview anyone. But I don't read resumes. Haven't read one in five years. I can't tell a thing about a candidate from a resumé. I was so glad you said what you did. Maybe they'll listen if they hear it from you."

Well, the subject of resumés *is* loaded. So, perhaps we ought to briefly summarize what we know about resumés.

> **RÉ-SU-MĒ rez-ə-mā** n [F. *resume* fr. pp. of *resumer* to resume, summarize] SUMMARY *specif:* a short account of one's career and qualifications prepared typically by an applicant for a position.
>
> —Webster's

Resumes can serve four different functions: they can be a SELF-INVENTORY, preparing you before the job-hunt to recall all that you've accomplished thus far in your life; they can be an EXTENDED CALLING-CARD, whose purpose is to get you invited in for an interview, by the employer(s) to whom you send that 'calling card'; they can be an AGENDA FOR AN INTERVIEW, affording the interviewer a springboard from which to launch his or her inquiry about you, after you have been invited in; and, finally, resumes can be a MEMORY-

JOGGER FOR THE EMPLOYER AFTER THE INTERVIEW, or for a whole committee – if a group is involved in the hiring decision.

It is as EXTENDED CALLING-CARD that the resume is most often used. Indeed, as calling-card it may be sent out to hundreds of prospective employers. Its lack of effectiveness in this role is well-known. I cited the statistics in chapter 2. Only one job-offer is tendered for every 1470 resumes that the average company receives. What is not so well-known, is the tremendous damage done to your self-esteem by dependency upon resumes. This damage is created by the following facts:

a) *some* job-hunters do actually get an interview, and subsequently a job, because they sent out resumes.

b) *many, many more* job-hunters do *not* get a job by means of a resume. In fact, many do not even get one invitation to an interview, in spite of sending out 800 or 900 resumes.

c) the ones who do get a job thereby talk a lot about it; the ones who find their resumes don't work for them, rarely say much. Consequently, there is a widespread *mythology* in our culture that "resumes usually work."

d) Therefore, when resumes don't work at all for a particular job-hunter, he or she usually assumes something is drastically *wrong with them.*

The result: plummeting self-esteem. It is not that a method has been tried, and failed. It is that a method *which you think works for almost everyone else* has not worked for you. Hence, depression. Paralysis. Etc. Well, you can see why I disbelieve in resumes as extended calling cards. How then *do* I think you are going to get in for an interview? I think you are going to get in by the methods that I have been hammering at, throughout the preceding pages: the ones we KNOW are most effective:

a) *COMMITMENT. Devoting eight hours a day, five days a week, to the job-hunt.*

b) *GOING FACE-TO-FACE. Knocking on the door, personally, at every organization that looks the least bit interesting to you.*

c) *USING CONTACTS. When you find a place you like, or are curious about, but you can't get an interview there, asking every person you know if they know someone who works there, and can get you an invitation to an interview.*

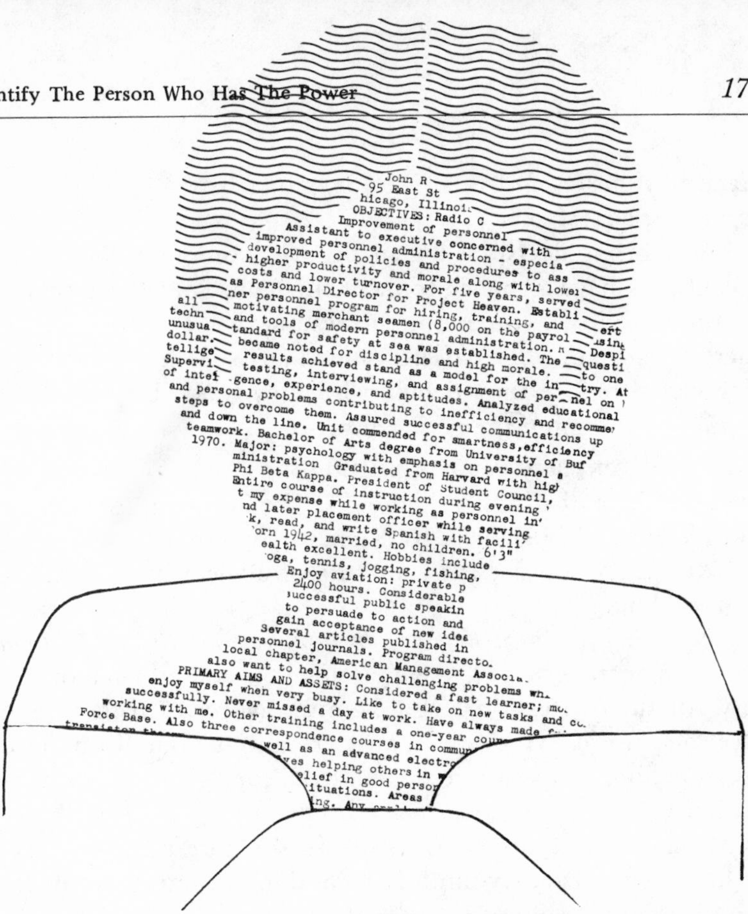

I believe in these three strategies because I know they work.

Given the fact that the resume AS EXTENDED CALLING-CARD is not very effective, what can we say about its other three roles? Well, I believe the exercises in chapters 5 and 6 (or the *Quick Job-Hunting Map*) really supplant any need for it as SELF-INVENTORY. And your own research about organizations that interest you really supplants any need for it as AGENDA FOR AN INTERVIEW. But, after talking with countless numbers of successful job-hunters, I am bound to say that I believe a resume may be very useful *after* the interview as A MEMORY-JOGGER FOR THE EMPLOYER.

It is an ancient wise-saying in the employment field: "A resume is something you should never send ahead of you, but always leave behind you." I believe that. Further, I believe it is often – if not always – wise *not* to carry a resume into an interview, but to say truthfully, "I don't have one with me, but I can mail one to you tonight." Then go home, construct a resume tailored exactly to the skills needed in the job you both just discussed, type it up *very* neatly, or run it over to a professional place post-haste, and then send it, along with a thank-you note as a cover letter.

Many hiring decisions are made by a committee and you do not always have a chance to meet them all. So, I think there is a genuine need sometimes for the resume as memory-jogger. Further, oftentimes you may be called back for three or four more interviews, before they decide who they want. The resume, left behind, will remind them who you are.

If you want any help in putting the resume together, there are a number of useful guidebooks. The best of these, by a long shot, is *Who's Hiring Who,* by Richard Lathrop.[1]

Now, there are a couple of bits of advice that I would like to underline:

Never put anything negative in your resume that would cause you to be screened out. Save confessions and excruciating honesty for the confessional. E.g., omit "divorced," if that be your case, because it may imply "quitter" about your future in that organization. (Say "three dependents" or "single" and leave it at that.)

Never lie; but do select your truths carefully, as Bernard Haldane says. Don't volunteer something negative. Confessions are for the confessional, not for the resume.

The most important quality needed in your resume, besides neatness and clarity, is that YOU should shine through it all. One job-hunter, for example, found this clever but truthful way of describing her period of job-hunting: "Job-Hunter (Self-Employed) January 1982 - January 1983.

- Developed and executed all phases of marketing and advertising for product.
- Targeted markets and identified the needs of diverse consumers

---

1. See the bibliography at the end of the *Quick Job-Hunting Map,* in Appendix A. There are also these recently published helps:

Jackson, Tom, *The Perfect Resume.* Anchor Press/Doubleday. Garden City, NY 11530. 1981. $6.95, paper.

Parker, Yana, *Damn Good Resume Guide.* 2928 Derby St., Berkeley, CA 94705. 1981. $4.50, paper.

Resume Service, *Resumes That Work.* Coles Publishing Co., Ltd., Toronto, Canada. 1979. $4.95, paper.

Williams, Eugene, *Increase Your Employment Opportunities with the Audiovisual Portfolio.* Competent Associates, Box 6745, Washington, DC 20020. 1980. $12.95, paper. Focuses on teachers, but has wider application.

- Developed sales brochure
- Designed packaging, and upgraded visual appeal of product
- Scheduled and conducted oral presentations"

If you have followed faithfully the techniques suggested by the creative minority (as outlined in these chapters), your resume will show it. Don't, whatever you do, just copy and adapt someone else's resume. It will be self-evident to the reader that you didn't go through the processes in these chapters. In the competitive game that job-hunting (alas) is, *that* will earn you four demerits.

INTERVIEWS FOR HIRE

Many job-hunting books devote a whole chapter or two or three to this subject. We are giving it relatively brief coverage here. There are reasons:

By going through the Practive Field Survey (see the *Quick Job-Hunting Map* in Appendix A for details), and then Informational Interviewing (chapter 6), you are getting hours and hours of practice in interviewing, such as the best video-tape classes will not give you. You will get constant helpful experience in talking with relatively high-level people, which – after all – is what we really mean by that dreadful word, *interviewing.*

> Most importantly, interviewing in our view is not something that waits for you at the end of the job-hunting process. It is a thread that runs throughout that process.

Still, you may feel in need of a little bolstering at this point, so let us take a look at the basic principles that successful job-hunters keep in mind as they reach this stage of the process:

You begin by thinking about your interviewer. Here you have two choices. You can be optimistic and assume that your interviewer is thoroughly trained *in interviewing,* knows exactly what it is that he or she needs to know, and knows exactly how to ask the proper questions that will elicit this information. In some cases, this will be true.

Alternatively, you can assume that the interviewer may be as uncomfortable with this process as you are, and as ill-equipped to know how to find out what he or she wants to know, as the newest college graduate just coming into the job-market. With the majority of interviewers you will face, particularly in smaller companies or organizations, this is the more realistic assumption.

Given this reality, it is as important for you to guide the interview — at least half of the time — as it is for the employer to guide it. The essence of the interview, from your point of view, is that you have come to make the employer a proposal:

1. Help me to understand the job completely and thoroughly.

2. Once I understand it, I will tell you if I think my skills truly match the job.

3. If they do, I will try to persuade you to hire me, because I will bring to this job both enthusiasm and effectiveness.

From the employer's point of view, the essence of the interview is contained in three questions that they are dying to ask you.[1] Whether they come right out with these questions, or beat around the bush, will depend on their expertise. In any event, you should know in any successful interview (whether steered by you or by them) these three *will* need to be addressed:

1. WHY ARE YOU HERE? Why have you chosen this particular place to come to? If you've done all the research recommended earlier in this book, and followed the steps in funneling (p. 133) you'll *know* the answer. If you haven't, you won't.

2. PRECISELY WHAT CAN YOU DO FOR ME? You will talk about their problems to the degree that you have been able to guess at them, and also listen very carefully to what they have to say. If new factors are revealed, field them as best you can; all the while showing how your skills can help with those problems. Within this category of questions, be prepared also for the particular form of: after you got this job, if you did, how would you start out?

3. HOW MUCH IS IT GOING TO COST ME? They probably have a range in mind (with a two to three thousand dollar variation), if you're seeking a job above the lowest level. If you have done your research thoroughly, you probably have some idea at least of what that range is. Therefore, you will need to quote it at this point, adding that money isn't everything and you are interested in the opportunity and challenge as well.

As can be seen, the research we have exhorted you to do in these chapters previously, is absolutely key to your successful

1. I am indebted to my friend John Crystal for this insight.

Study Shows Neatness Pays Off In Job Hunt

STANFORD, Calif. (UPI) – Neat, well-dressed college graduates have a better chance to land a job than those who appear in jeans or refuse to wear a bra, according to a Stanford University study.

The wearing of jeans, shorts, sandals, of dispensing with bras creates an impression ranging from "mildly" to "strongly negative," the survey shows.

Applicants who use jargon, have dirty fingernails or fiddle with objects on the desk also earned negative ratings, according to the study by two Stanford students who received doctoral degrees in educational counseling and guidance.

The researchers, Jane Anton and Michael Russell, questioned more than 100 recruiting officers from 17 different industry groups, ranging from accounting and aerospace to government and utilities.

They found that a male creates a mildly positive impression if he wears a sport coat, shirt, tie and slacks. But he creates a stronger impression if he wears a suit.

And the shorter, more neatly trimmed the hair and beard on males, the better the impression on recruiters.

Applicants considered "assertive, intelligent, independent and inquisitive" registered only a mildly positive influence in job interviews.

– *Cincinnati Enquirer,* 10/23/75

conduct of a hiring interview, and the fielding of these sorts of questions. *You will be at a disadvantage precisely to the degree that you have tried to cut corners or short-circuit the whole process described in these chapters (4-7).*

Do remember to look professional. Have a good-looking suit or dress on, a decent haircut or coiffure, clean fingernails, dentally cleaned teeth, deodorant, shined shoes, no smoking or pre-drinking – clean breath. It may seem like a silly game to you, but it's a game with very high stakes, in which you want to be the winner.[1]

---

1. If you are a male, and want to take a hard look at your appearance to see how it can influence the interview for better or for worse, you may find John T. Molloy's famous *Dress for Success* helpful. (Warner Books, 75 Rockefeller Plaza, New York, NY 10019. 1975. $3.95, paper). He has a similar (but more controversial) book out for women: *The Women's Dress for Success Book* (same publisher, same price).

His books are representative of a whole fast-growing field called Personal Image Consultancy. How many are in this field may be gauged from the fact that the *1979 Directory of Personal Image Consultants* (Editorial Services Co., 1140 Avenue of the Americas, New York, NY 10036. $10.95) lists 85 such firms, in 20 states and 38 cities, even back then.

There are certain questions no employer is any longer allowed to ask you – unless they are BFOQ's – "bona fide occupational qualifications."

Here are some interview guidelines that one major California company has drawn up for its managers and supervisors:

	THEY CAN DO OR ASK	THEY CAN*NOT* DO OR ASK
Your sex–	Notice your appearance.	Make comments or take notes unless sex is a BFOQ.
Marital status–	Status after hiring, for insurance purposes.	Are you married? Single? Divorced? Engaged? Living with anyone? Do you see your ex-spouse?
Children–	Numbers and ages of children after hiring, for insurance purposes.	Do you have children at home? How old? Who cares for them? Do you plan more children?
Physical data–	Explain manual labor, lifting, other requirements of the job. Show how it is performed. Require physical examination.	How tall are you? How much do you weigh? Do you have any physical or mental handicaps?
Criminal record–	If security clearance is necessary, can be done prior to employment.	Have you ever been arrested, convicted or spent time in jail?
Military–	Are you a veteran? Why not? Any job-related experience?	What type of discharge do you have? What branch did you serve in?
Age–	Age after hiring. "Are you over 18?"	How old are you? Estimate age.
Housing–	If you have no phone, how can we reach you?	Do you own your home? Do you rent? Do you live in an apartment or a house?
Religion–		What is your religious background?

As a job applicant, what can you do if you are asked one of these illegal questions? The Wall Street Journal pointed out you have three courses of action:

"1. Answer the question and ignore the fact that it is not legal.

"2. Answer the question with the statement: 'I think that is not relevant to the requirements of the position.

"3. Contact the nearest Equal Employment Opportunity Commission office.

"Unless the violation is persistent, is demeaning, or you can prove it resulted in your not being employed, number three should probably be avoided. The whole area is still relatively new; many interviewers are just not totally conversant with the new code requirements.

"Answer number two is probably, in most circumstances, the best to give. There are times when it may cost you the job, but are you that interested in working for someone who is all that concerned about your personal life?"

And now for some final thoughts about this whole matter.

Whatever the interviewer may ask about Your Past, (like, why did you leave your last job?) remember the only thing they can possibly be really interested in is The Future (like, under what circumstances might you leave me?).

Never volunteer negative information about yourself.

Never accept a job on the spot, or reject one. And, unless you are talking with a very "liberated" employer, do not say, I need to talk with my mate (it implies you are not a decision maker on your own. Just say, "I need some time to weigh this."[1]

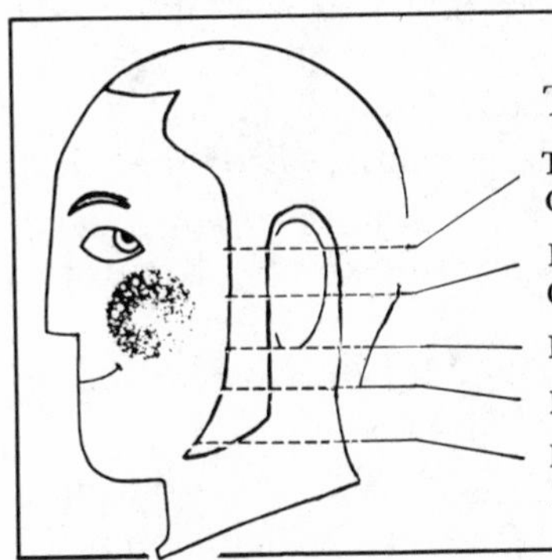

The Sideburn Chart

The Military, Bankers, Doctors, Government Leaders

Federal Employees, Firemen, Policemen, Clergymen in General, Conservative Professors

Professional Athletes, Episcopal Clergymen

Liberal Newspapermen Under 30

Hippies, Social Rebels, Way Out Professors, Free Thinkers, Latin Lovers

By permission, from *The Missionary*, Episcopal Diocese of Northern California

SALARY NEGOTIATION

A woman was once describing her very first job to me. It was at a soda fountain. I asked her what her biggest surprise at that job was. "My first paycheck," she said. "I know it sounds incredible, but I was so green at all this, that during the whole interview for the job it never occurred to me to ask what my salary

1. For further reading on the subject of Interviewing: see the bibliography on that subject in Appendix B, p. 270.

"Let's talk salary. How does 'astronomical' sound to you?"

would be. I just took it for granted that it would be a fair and just salary, for the work that I would be doing. Did I ever get a shock, when my first paycheck came! It was so small, I could hardly believe it. Did I ever learn a lesson from that!" Yes, and so may we all.

AT ITS SIMPLEST LEVEL

To speak of salary negotiation is to speak of a matter which can be conducted on several levels. The simplest kind – as the above story reminds us – involves remembering to ask during the job-hiring interview what the salary will be. And then stating whether, for you, that amount is satisfactory or not. *That* much negotiation, everyone who is hunting for a job must be prepared to do.

It is well to recognize that you – or the students or clients that you are trying to teach about job-hunting, if you are a career counselor – are at a disadvantage if salary negotiation is approached on this simplest level, however. A figure may be named, and you are totally unprepared to say whether this is a fair salary for that particular job, or not. You just don't know.

AT ITS NEXT HIGHEST LEVEL

Hence, you may prefer to do a little research *ahead* of time. Before you ever get in there, for that interview. This is taking salary negotiation to its next highest level. Visit the library in your community, before you interview for hiring. There are five smashing new books out, that give an overview of the whole subject of salaries. They are: Thelma Kandel's *What Women Earn*. (The Linden Press, Simon & Schuster, 1230 Avenue of the Americas, New York, NY 10020. 1981. $6.95, paper.) And: John W. Wright's *The American Almanac of Jobs and Salaries.* (Avon Books, 959 Eighth Ave., New York, NY 10019. 1982. $9.95, paper.) And: Stern, Edward L., *Salary Guide and Job Outlook.* (Hilary House Publishers, 1033 Channel Dr., Hewlett Harbor, NY 11557. 1981. $5.95, paper.) And: David Harrop's *Paychecks: Who Makes What? The Book That Tells You What Everybody Earns.* (Harper & Row, 10 E. 53rd St., New York,

WEEKLY EARNINGS

By Industry Division and Major Manufacturing Group

(Gross averages, production or nonsupervisory workers on private nonagricultural payrolls)

Industry Division and Group	Annual average			1981			1982	
	1979	1980	1981	June	Sept.	Nov.	Jan.	June
TOTAL PRIVATE:								
Current dollars	$219.91	$235.10	$255.20	$254.88	$259.74	$262.20	$255.95	$266.70
Constant (1977) dollars		172.74	170.13	170.49	168.88	169.71	164.70	
MINING	365.07	397.06	439.19	420.04	450.85	461.32	456.89	$451.08
CONSTRUCTION	342.99	367.78	398.52	395.81	396.31	414.78	385.95	427.11
MANUFACTURING								
Current dollars	269.34	288.62	318.00	320.39	322.32	325.54	312.38	333.59
Constant (1977) dollars		212.06	212.00	214.31	209.57	210.71	201.02	
Durable goods	290.90	310.78	342.91	346.72	346.26	351.68	336.28	$359.17
Lumber and wood products	239.16	252.18	270.90	280.06	271.36	269.93	248.71	286.50
Furniture and fixtures	195.82	209.17	226.94	229.51	226.58	230.51	204.10	236.88
Stone, clay, and glass products	284.28	306.00	335.76	342.37	346.32	345.87	325.38	361.42
Primary metal industries	371.77	391.78	437.81	439.68	457.78	440.67	431.23	443.39
Fabricated metal products	278.80	300.98	330.46	335.78	330.70	337.64	323.19	349.27
Machinery except electrical	305.98	328.00	360.33	361.27	361.98	372.28	360.25	369.86
Electric and electronic equipment	254.70	276.21	304.04	303.91	307.68	311.63	304.04	318.75
Transportation equipment	350.58	379.61	424.95	432.63	418.55	438.19	414.34	464.39
Instruments and related products	251.74	275.40	300.17	296.13	306.64	313.34	306.10	325.56
Miscellaneous manufacturing	195.16	211.30	231.25	230.88	234.14	241.35	229.48	247.81
Nondurable goods	236.19	255.45	280.74	281.64	287.78	288.56	277.65	297.22
Food and kindred products	250.17	271.95	294.97	294.18	300.89	302.88	302.63	312.44
Tobacco manufactures	253.46	294.89	344.54	359.98	352.15	350.75	332.48	393.67
Textile mill products	188.26	203.31	218.59	218.56	221.34	224.62	179.71	220.60
Apparel and other textile products	149.32	161.42	177.07	180.41	177.41	180.43	155.40	181.63
Paper and allied products	303.74	330.85	365.50	364.66	386.64	376.05	374.18	384.89
Printing and publishing	260.25	279.36	305.11	301.69	313.04	314.07	312.31	319.92
Chemicals and allied products	318.44	344.45	379.39	377.31	395.84	391.87	394.94	405.96
Petroleum and coal products	409.97	422.18	491.62	491.99	512.82	499.10	514.51	557.05
Rubber and miscellaneous plastics products	241.79	260.80	288.55	292.03	289.41	291.67	283.88	305.20
Leather and leather products	154.03	168.09	183.63	189.74	183.24	187.03	172.83	194.88
TRANSPORTATION AND PUBLIC UTILITIES	325.58	351.25	382.18	381.52	390.04	393.96	388.85	398.19
WHOLESALE AND RETAIL TRADE	164.96	176.46	190.95	190.51	194.49	192.68	191.89	199.32
WHOLESALE TRADE	247.93	267.96	292.20	289.11	296.45	300.69	300.13	309.21
RETAIL TRADE	138.62	147.38	158.03	158.17	162.17	158.54	157.47	164.65
FINANCE, INSURANCE, AND REAL ESTATE	190.77	209.60	229.05	225.63	230.04	236.02	237.47	241.15
SERVICES	175.27	190.71	208.97	206.99	211.25	216.78	219.32	222.36

(*Monthly Labor Review*, August 1982)

NY 10022. 1980. $5.95, paper.) For readers interested in other countries, there is also: Harrop, David, *World Paychecks: Who makes what, where, and why.* (Facts on File Publications, 460 Park Ave. S., New York, NY 10016. 1982.) Beyond these sorts of overviews, there are other resources you can turn to:

• If it's a non-supervisory job, you can find out what a 'ballpark figure' for a particular industry might be by having the reference librarian, or general librarian, find a chart for you similar to the one on page 187. Just add approximately 7% for each year that has elapsed.

• If it's a supervisory job, or one at a higher level than non-supervisory, you will find that the College Placement Council, with some frequency publishes reports on salaries being offered in various industries to college graduates. While this is of primary interest to such graduates, the "Salary Surveys" of the Council do give some guidance, at least, to other job-hunters. See your library, or the career counseling and placement office of a nearby college — rather than buying the Survey, as it is available only to members of the Council and/or to subscribers to their Journal Publications Group. (Average cost: $30-35.)

• If the job you're looking for information about is not in either of the above sorts of places, there is always the *Occupational Outlook Handbook* in your local library, which has the best available information on earnings in the most popular occupations. You will discover that the only trouble with such information is that it covers all geographic regions in the U.S., all industries, and all periods of economic fluctuations. In other words, the figures are very general.

Your library may have more detailed information for your particular region, regarding the occupation that you are interested in. Witness the following example:

AVERAGE WEEKLY EARNINGS OF LEAD DRAFTSMEN

$295.00	Detroit, Michigan
226.00	Dayton, Ohio
215.50	Chicago, Illinois
206.00	Houston, Texas
193.00	Seattle, Washington
189.50	Columbus, Ohio
175.00	Salt Lake City, Utah
173.00	Scranton, Pennsylvania
172.50	Raleigh, North Carolina
162.50	Little Rock, Arkansas

REGION	
$213.50	North Central
202.00	Northeast
199.00	West
192.00	South
204.00	United States

These figures are now outdated but they show *comparative* differences at least.

The figures show the fluctuation from region to region may be quite wide. Though it is important to remember that this depends on the particular occupation that you are interested in. For lead draftspersons, Detroit may pay more than any other city. With regard to other occupations, however, Detroit may be at the bottom of the list.

Such regional differences in salary reflect, of course, a variety of factors, such as differences in cost of living, differences in supply and demand, etc. Supply and demand has exercised a big influence on salaries particularly in Alaska, among the various "trades" – as a result of the building of the Alaskan pipe-line or gas-line. So short a preparation as an "oil field technology" course at the Alaska Skill Center in Seward, Alaska, has resulted in relatively easy placement at Prudhoe Bay and Cook Inlet there. This situation may continue in the early 1980s. But similar regional differences in supply and demand, if not as dramatic, occur in other regions, and with other professions.

If your librarian simply cannot find for you, or help you find, the salary information that you want, remember that almost every occupation has its own association or professional group, whose business it is to keep tabs on what is happening salary-wise within that occupation or field. For people interested, by way of example, in the guidance and counseling field, there is the American Personnel and Guidance Association. And it has published a modest volume entitled, "Compen$ation *(sic)* in the Guidance and Counseling Field." Other associations have similar data (in most cases) at their fingertips. To learn the association or professional group for the field or occupation you are interested in, consult the *Encyclopedia of Associations, Vol. 1,* at your library.

In reviewing any information about "average earnings," you will want to remember *every* occupation has a vast *range,* as shown in the chart on the next page.

MORE SOPHISTICATED YET

Some job-hunters – you, perhaps, or the clients/students you are helping – may want to get beyond these "ball-park figures" into more detailed salary negotiation. They – or you – may want to walk in on an interview knowing exactly what That Place pays for a job. Why? Well, for one thing, it may be too low for you – and thus you are saved the necessity of wasting your precious time on that particular place. Secondly, and more

EARNINGS WITHIN OCCUPATIONS VARY WIDELY

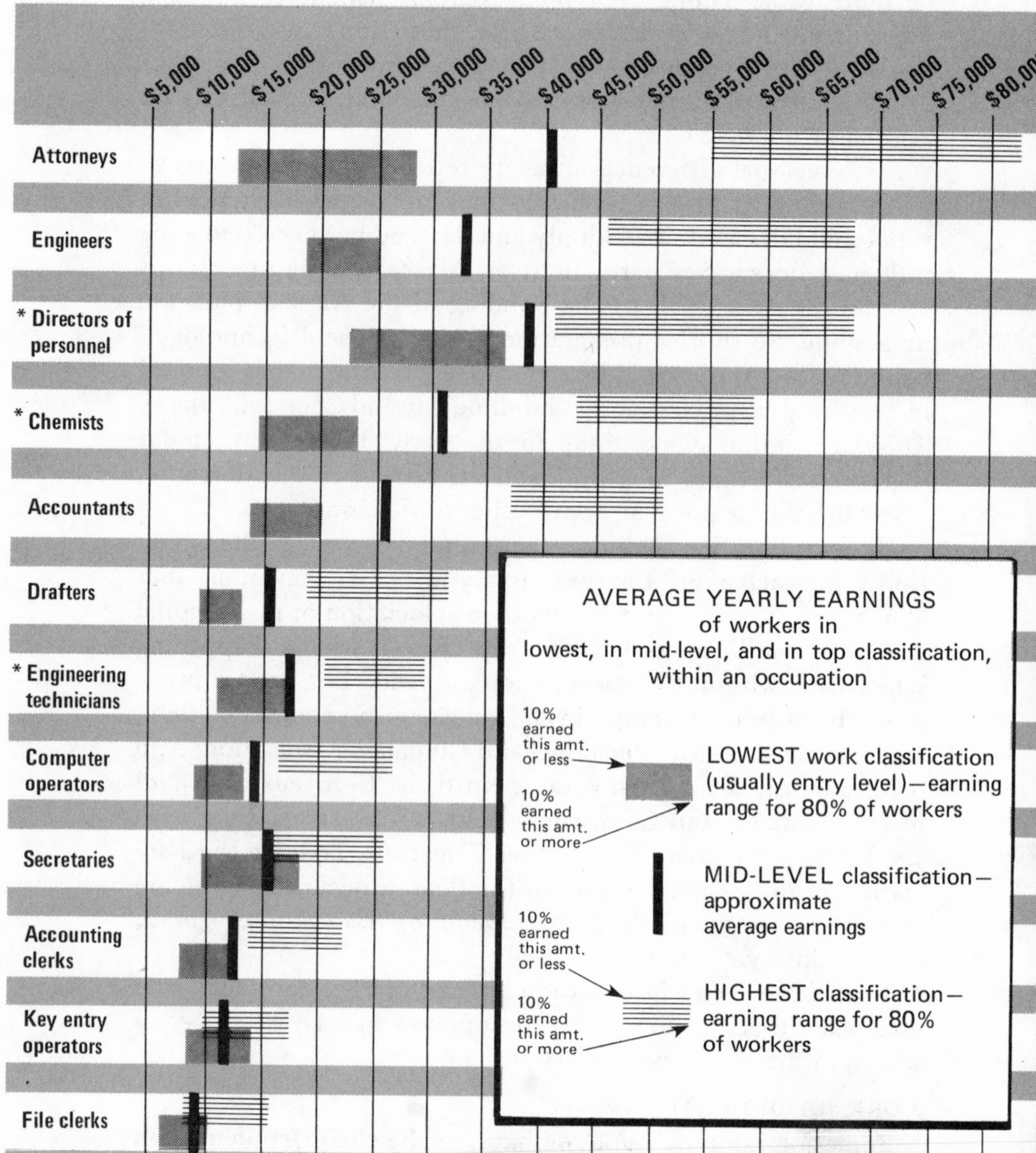

* Top earnings in these occupations are understated because an additional higher work level was surveyed but the data obtained were insufficient to warrant publication.
Source: Based upon data contained in a Bureau of Labor Statistics bulletin, *National Survey of Professional Administrative, Technical, and Clerical Pay, March 1981.*
A summary of this survey appears in BLS press release 81-326, "White-Collar Salaries, March 1981," June 26, 1981. (*Occupational Outlook Quarterly*, Fall 1981)

importantly, many places have – as John Crystal has so insistently pointed out – a *range* in mind. And if you know what that range is, you can negotiate for a salary that is nearer the top of the range, than the bottom.

So, let us say that you have done some extensive homework – such as is represented by *The Quick Job-Hunting Map* or by the process described in *Where Do I Go From Here With My Life?* And you have gotten your search, by means of the Information Survey, down to three or five places that really interest you. You know in general what sort of position you are aiming at, in those particular places – and you are ready to go back and visit them in The Interview for Hiring – *as soon as you know what the salary range is, that they probably have in mind for the position that interests you* (whether that position already exists, or is one you are going to ask them to create). How do you find out what the salary is, or should be, by way of range?

It's relatively easy to define, as – again – John Crystal has pointed out. The rule of thumb is that you will, generally speaking, be paid more than the person who is below you on the organizational chart, and less than the person who is above you. There are – needless to say – exceptions to this rule: people who don't quite fit in the organizational chart, such as researchers financed by a grant, or consultants. Consequently they may be paid much more than the people who are theoretically above them. But In General, the Rule of Thumb is true.

This makes the matter of salary *research* which precedes salary negotiation relatively (I said "relatively") simple. If through your own information search you could discover who is or would be above you on the organizational chart, and who is or would be below you, and what they are paid, you would know what your salary range is, or would be.

It works out like this:

<table>
<tr><td colspan="8">IF THE PERSON BELOW YOU MAKES:</td></tr>
<tr><td>a)</td><td>$6240</td><td>or</td><td>b)</td><td>$10,000</td><td>or</td><td>c)</td><td>$22,000</td></tr>
<tr><td colspan="8">AND THE PERSON ABOVE YOU MAKES:</td></tr>
<tr><td>a)</td><td>$7800</td><td>or</td><td>b)</td><td>$13,500</td><td>or</td><td>c)</td><td>$27,000</td></tr>
<tr><td colspan="8">YOUR RANGE WILL BE SOMETHING LIKE:</td></tr>
<tr><td>a)</td><td>$6400–
7600</td><td>or</td><td>b)</td><td>$10,500–
12,500</td><td>or</td><td>c)</td><td>$23,000–
26,000</td></tr>
</table>

So, how do you find this out?

For openers, you do all the kinds of library research that I alluded to, above. Then you go to work on your contacts: you know, everybody who knows you well enough even to misspell your name. Moreover, you pick up a copy of the annual report and any other literature available on that company or organization. Your goal, of course (to go into Overkill) is to discover:

The Names of the people above and below you, if you were to be hired at that organization. And:

What they make.

You will be surprised at how much of this information *is* in the annual report, or in books available at your library. When those sources produce all they can for you, and you are still short of what you want to know, go to your contacts. You are looking for Someone Who Knows Someone who either is working, or has worked, at that particular place or organization that interests you.

If you absolutely run into a blank wall on that particular organization (everyone who works there is pledged to secrecy, and they have shipped all their ex-employees to Siberia), then seek out information on their nearest *competitor* in the same geographic area (e.g., if Bank of America is inscrutable, try Wells Fargo as your research base; or vice-versa).

You will be surprised at how often perseverance and legwork pay off, in this. And if your enthusiasm flags along the way, just picture yourself sitting in the interview for hiring, and now you're at the end of the interview (the only proper place for discussion of salary to take place, anyway). The prospective employer likes you, you like them, and then they say: "How much salary were you expecting?" (Employers *love* to toss this ball to you.) Because you have done your homework, and you know the range, you can name a figure near or at the top of the range – based on your anticipated performance in that job: i.e., "Superior."

But suppose you *didn't* do your research. Then you're Shadow-Boxing in the Dark – as they say. If you name a figure way too high, you're out of the running – and you can't backtrack, in most cases ("Sorry, we'd like to hire you, but we just can't afford you.") If you name a figure way too low, you're also out of the running, in many cases ("Sorry, but we were hoping for someone a little more, ah, professional.") And if you're in the right range, but at the bottom of it, you've just

gotten the job – *but needlessly lost as much as $2,000 a year that could have been yours.*

So, salary research/salary negotiation – no matter how much time it takes – pays off handsomely. Let's say it takes you a week to ten days to run down this sort of information on the three or four organizations that interest you. And let us say that because you've done this research, when you finally go in for the hiring interview you are able to ask for and obtain a salary that is $2,000 higher in range, than you would otherwise have known enough to ask for. In just three years, you'll have earned $6,000 extra, because of that research. Not bad pay, for ten days' work![1]

AT ITS MOST SOPHISTICATED LEVEL

Job-hunters with incredibly-developed bargaining needs, always ask how salary negotiation is conducted at its most sophisticated level. It is my personal conviction that Most Job-Hunters will not operate at this level, and therefore do not need this sort of information. But in case you do, or in case you are simply dying out of curiosity, it is completely described in *Where Do I Go From Here With My Life?* pages 140-142. As honed to a fine point by John Crystal, the most sophisticated salary negotiation goes like this:

1. For further reading see: Chastain, Sherry, *Winning the Salary Game.* John Wiley and Sons, Inc., 605 Third Ave., New York, NY 10158. 1980.

You do all the steps described immediately above: i.e., you discover what the range would be. Let us say it turns out that the range is one that varies two thousand dollars. You then "invent" a new range, for yourself, that "hooks" on the old one, in the following fashion:

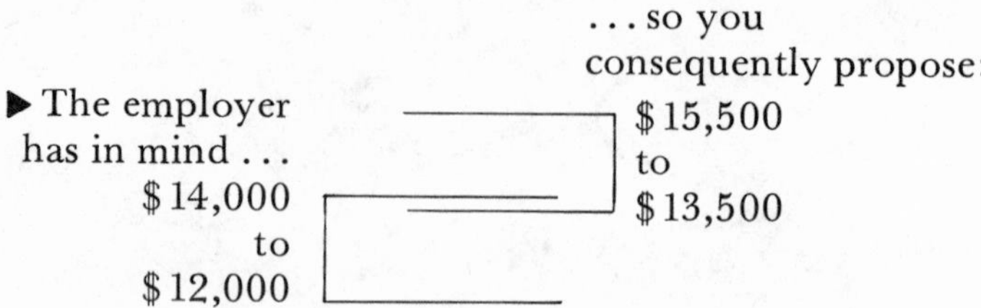

And when the employer says, "What kind of a salary did you have in mind?" you respond, "I believe my productivity is such that it would justify a salary in the range of $13,500 to $15,500." This keeps you, at a minimum, near the top of their range; and, at a maximum, challenges them to go beyond the top that they had in mind, either immediately – or in terms of future raises. (Don't be afraid to ask "When?")

FRINGES

In all your research, and ultimate negotiation, do not forget to pay attention to so-called "fringe benefits." In a recent year, it was calculated that such 'fringes' as life insurance, health benefits or plans, vacation or holiday plans, and retirement programs, added up to 25% of manufacturing workers' salary, e.g., if an employee received $800 salary per month, the fringe benefits were worth another $200 per month. So, if the employee who is beneath you on the organizational chart gets $700 plus benefits, and the employee who is above you gets $1100 plus benefits, while you during the hiring interview are offered $800 *and no benefits,* you will need to negotiate for more than $1000 salary, in order to make up for that lack of benefits.

Of course, if you don't need that extra money – or you couldn't care less that the person below you makes more than you do – great! But just in case you do, I thought I'd mention it.

FINALLY, THE MATTER OF THOSE RAISES

Salary negotiation, during the hiring interview, is more than just a matter of negotiation for your Starting Salary. It is ultimately a matter of negotiating for your Yearly or Semi-yearly Raises, as well. "When, and under what circumstances, can I expect to have my salary raised?" needs not only to be asked, but to be put in writing – if there is a letter of agreement, or any kind of contract forthcoming from your would-be employer. The Road to Hell is paved with Promises that are unwritten, and which altogether too many employers *conveniently* forget once you are hired. Moreover, employers Leave, and their successor or their own boss may disown unwritten promises ("I don't know what caused them to say that to you, but they clearly exceeded their authority, and we can't be held to that.")

Against That Day, it will pay you to keep a diary, weekly, of your achievements at work, so that when time for discussing raises comes around, you can document – with a one or two page summary – just exactly what you have accomplished there, and why you deserve that raise. . . as Bernard Haldane explains in his classic *How To Make A Habit of Success* (Acropolis Books, Ltd., 2400 17th St. NW, Washington, DC 20009. $4.95).

PROMOTION

We hope *promotion* is not for you a distasteful concept. After all, it means wider responsibility (hopefully), and not just more prestige. It means a widening scope for your desire to be truly helpful to people, and not just (hopefully) an illustration of *The Peter Principle.* Women, in particular, should remember that they are generally much more underpaid than men, that the average woman would require a 70% pay raise, to bring her up to the level of a similarly qualified man.

Do not forget also, that in only twenty-five of the last one hundred years has the cost of living declined and the U.S. dollar gained in buying power. The annual rate of inflation lately has been between 5% and 15% annually. During the period 1973-1978, inflation totaled 47%, in actual fact. Were it to continue at the same rate for the next five years (actually, it has already gone higher), a person who made $11,804 in 1978 (incidentally, the median earning that year for the nation's 69.4 million full-time workers) would *have* to earn $17,352 in 1983, just in order to have the very same purchasing power.

So you see, what our society calls "promotion" is necessary *just in order to stand still.* Lack of promotion automatically means going backward – in terms of purchasing power for you and your loved ones.

And this says nothing of promotion as an opportunity for you to operate in increasing spheres of influence and helpfulness.

The end of the matter is this: if, during the hiring interview, you negotiate only for your initial position and salary, you are likely to lose a great deal.

When and only when you're sure they want you, and they have made a firm offer, by all means negotiate. And when (and if) it's resolved to your satisfaction, (again) *get it in writing, please. Please. Please.*

WHAT MAKES YOU GET CHOSEN?

While you're waiting to see if you get chosen, from among all the applicants that company or organization was considering, what's going on in the employer(s)' mind? We asked a number of employers, or would-be employers, that very question: if you had seventeen applicants, *all* of whom were equally able to do the job, but you could only choose one of them, how would you decide which one to pick? What would you look for?

These were their collective answers, in order of importance or frequency:

(1) I would ask myself, does this prospective employee *fit in* with the people who are already here? Does this person share compatible perspectives, exhibit integrity, manifest a desire to work as part of a team, and have similar values and sense of humor?

(2) I would ask myself, does this prospective employee give the feeling of great *enthusiasm for this particular job*? How much does he or she seem to *want* it?

(3) I would ask myself, does this prospective employee have an *appearance* that I like? This is an intangible thing, and I can't define it, but it has to do with my intuition about the person, their face, the way they dress, and how reliable or stable I feel them to be, beneath all the externals. I look for a quiet self-confidence.

(4) I would ask myself, does this prospective employee give me the feeling that he or she would give that *extra boost of energy* to their work that I like to see, rather than just trying "to get by." I think this is dependent on how much the prospective employee truly has their own individual goals, toward which they are striving.

(5) Finally, I would ask myself, does this prospective employee seem to have a genuine *enthusiasm for our organization* and what it is trying to do? Does he or she seem to like its goals, appreciate its style, and want to work for its success?

Well, there it is. If you get chosen, it will probably be because you *stood out* from the other applicants, in these five areas. And – of course you know – you stand out in these five areas, precisely *because* you have carefully done the homework in chapters 5 through 7.

DOES THIS WHOLE PROCESS ALWAYS WORK?

Of course not. This is job-hunting, not magic. As Nathan Azrin has well said, job-hunting is more like choosing a mate than like buying a car.

Even in the best of times, no one can absolutely guarantee you a job exactly where you want it, doing exactly what you want, at the salary you want. But *most* people who follow the method set forth in these last four chapters get very close – with perhaps some compromises – and *some* succeed in virtually every particular, even in the worst of times.

This method is, in any event, so far superior to the traditional form of the job-hunt, that it ought to be taught to every job-hunter in this country, and especially to those who are working at *any* job above the most menial level. It needs to be taken particularly seriously by job-hunters during hard times, when jobs are especially scarce.

With the traditional numbers game, as you will recall, a job-hunter had to send out 300-500 resumes, in order to get 3-5 interviews, and one or two job offers – assuming they were lucky.

On the other hand, with this method, you might have the same experience as did one man (among many we could cite): 107 places that looked interesting in the geographical area he chose, 297 letters sent to them (and 126 phone calls) followed by a visit to the area where he had 45 low-stress interviews as part of his informational interviewing, resulting in 35 job offers – including exactly the job he wanted.

For job-hunters in the process of career transition, this method is infinitely superior to any other – particularly if you are trying to avoid not merely un-employment but the even greater danger of under-employment.

FOR THOSE WHO LOVE TO COVER EVERY BASE

If you are by any chance uncomfortable with putting all your eggs in one basket, i.e., with committing yourself to the approach described in chapters 4-7 here, and to that approach only, if you feel there might be some merit to answering classified ads, visiting agencies, etc., you may perhaps be interested in the advice offered by Bernard Haldane, who recommends that no more than 20% of one's time be allocated to these other methods, in view of the fact that barely 20% of the jobs above entry level are filled through these other methods. *Many going through the job-hunt prefer, however, to give all their time to the method set forth in these pages – and have done so with great success; so you may want to take this into account in planning your own strategy.*

Remember, in going about all this, you have a tremendous advantage over other job-hunters – and job-hunting is, sad to say, at the present time a very competitive business.

You know how to get hired.

In Candide's world, it may be otherwise. But, in this world it remains true:

The person who
gets hired is not necessarily
the one who can do that job best;
but, the one who *knows the most about*
how to get hired.

AND THE SEARCH GOES ON— FOR MORE THAN SKILLS —

In closing, I would like to add a personal word to You, dear reader. Once you have been hired, you will wonder what your next goal should be. It is easy to think that the answer is this: mastering your job. Proving that you were worth hiring. Demonstrating that you are truly competent at your craft.

Well, of course, that is true. But it seems to me so obvious and .... well, so easy. If you did identify your truest skills, and did identify the place where you could use those skills most happily and effectively, proving you are competent now that you have the job will be as easy as falling off a log.

There is a harder task, a less obvious task, to set as your goal, once you are hired. It is, in a word, the demonstration of the fact that you have character, integrity, or whatever other old-fashioned word you want to use. It is the quiet manifestation, in everything you do, that you are a particular Kind of person, a person of principle, inspiring of trust – not merely a person who is technically proficient, but utterly devoid of that old-fashioned quality called character. Phillips Brooks, the author of "O Little Town of Bethlehem," in a sermon preached a century ago was describing the latter kind of worker: he spoke about men, but the truth applies equally to women.

"There was something imperfect in the development of their humanity, as it always seemed. They were the men of unsymmetrical culture; the men in whom some one power was overgrown and the rest were sluggish; the men who did not impress you with largeness of life, but with special, almost mechanical dexterity of action; the men whom you might call upon for certain tasks which require certain skill, but whom you could not trust with that entire confidence which can only rest on character. In one word, they were not kingly men, not men who in any regal way, according to the old idea of a king, represented their race. Men with sharp, ingenious tools in their hands, but no crowns upon their heads."

The metaphors are from another age, but I'm sure you catch their meaning. If you want a goal, once you are hired, let it be this: beyond mastering the job itself, seek to be a special kind of Person: one who has character, and exhibits it in everything done there, at work. Stand there at your craft, or sit there at your desk, not merely with sharp ingenious tools in your hands, but – as the old phrase says – with a crown upon your head.

Shalom.

DO YOU KNOW WHERE I'M RESIDING? BORED CITY, THAT'S WHERE
JIM DAVIS

BUT NOT FOR LONG. WITH A POSITIVE MENTAL ATTITUDE I CAN WHIP IT

I THINK I'LL MAKE A LATERAL MOVE TO SELF-PITY
12-5
© 1980 United Feature Syndicate, Inc.

Postscript
WHEN YOU'VE TRIED ALL THIS AND YOU STILL CAN'T FIND A JOB

Some readers, of course, will read this section first of all, before they've even browsed through the rest of the book. Well – and I say it gently – I'm not really talking to You. You need to go read the book and do the homework on yourself, and go out there and try the methods described in chapters 4-7 – methods distilled from the experience of countless thousands of successful job-hunters and career-changers.

I'm talking here to those who have read the book, slavishly done all the exercises, gone out and spent dozens of hours doing informational interviewing, with the result: Noth-ing.

I've been there myself. So I know it is tempting to think that the problem lies somewhere Out There. It's the Economy. Or the Recession. Or the State of the World. Or the Universe. You're having a run of bad luck. Your karma is turning upon you. You've somehow invoked the displeasure of your Creator.

After meeting job-hunters who have been out of work one, two, three or four years, I have become convinced of this one truth: you've got to redouble your efforts, and try harder to deal with the things that *are* within your control. Never mind what's going on Out There. Even in the worst of times, the problem isn't that you're too Old. Some senior citizens are still finding meaningful work. The problem isn't that you are too Young. Some teenagers are still finding work. The problem isn't that you're Black. Some Blacks are still finding work. The problem isn't that you're inexperienced. Some inexperienced people are still finding work. The problem isn't that you were laid-off. Some of your fellow workers who were laid-off with you have still found work. What are they doing, that you're not?

Well, they were just lucky, you say: *in the right place at the right time. Pure luck.* Well, as someone has said, luck favors the prepared mind. So: prepare your mind. That's what this book is all about.

Well, they knew the right people, you say. *Someone kicked the door open for them.* Well, then you need to redouble your efforts to cultivate the people you already know, and find ways to make new friends in your community, so that they can kick the door open for you.

Or, *they weren't as choosy as you are,* you say. *They were willing to take anything.* Well, if you're getting down toward your last dollar, maybe you'd better be willing to abandon the hunt for the dream job (for the moment at least) and settle for a temporary stop-gap job that will at least bring in some bread.

Well, they could forgive and forget what was done to them, the way they were laid-off after all those years they gave that company; but I can't so easily forget all that. Sure. And in your anger you can subtly botch up every interview, misread every exercise, and trip yourself up throughout the job-hunt, so that it comes a cropper. And you can live out, as many years as you choose, a job-less life which cries out to the company that laid you off: See what you did to me.

Or, alternatively, you can talk out the anger with some trusted friend or confidant, and let go of the past, so that you can have a better and brighter future.

If you want more practical pointers, I'll share with you some of the things I've observed from countless interviews, phone-calls and letters, over the years.

● *Job-hunters who have tried all this and still can't find a job often have put a label on themselves which cripples their job-hunt.* Like: "I am an auto-worker." Not true. There was no such tag on your arm when your mother brought you into the world. You are A Person, with auto-working experience. You are A Person with auto-working skills. But that experience and those skills can be put to good use in other fields of endeavor, if all the auto-working jobs have dried up. Go out job-hunting as A Person, not as "an auto-worker" – or "a construction worker," or as any other label.

● *Job-hunters who have tried all this and still can't find a job often are devoting precious little time to their job-hunt,* usually because they have falsely concluded that these are hard times and there simply are no jobs out there. Successful job-hunters devote eight hours a day to their job-hunt, day in and day out. That's a simple unavoidable fact. They treat the job-hunt as though it were itself a full-time job. If you're trying to get by with only an hour or so a day, then it is not surprising that you can't find a job.

● *Job-hunters who have tried all this and still can't find a job often are sending out paper (resumes, by the bushel) instead of going out themselves, face to face.* Nobody likes rejection, and the job-hunt is in and of itself inevitably a process of rejection. Tom Jackson has brilliantly symbolized the job-hunt as NO NO NO NO NO NO NO NO NO NO NO NO NO NO NO NO NO NO YES. The more NOs you get out of the way, he says, the closer you are to that YES. So, you need to stop sending out paper, and go out yourself, knock on the door of any organization that looks interesting to you, ask if they have a job that could use your skills – and get another one of those inevitable NOs out of the way, so that you are closer to the inevitable YES.

● *Job-hunters who have tried all this and still can't find a job often are trying too hard to "go it alone."* If they live alone, they don't talk much with their friends about the job-hunt. If they have a mate, they can be pretty close-mouthed about what's going on inside them. "Don't want to depress the family," they compassionately say. Well, if the family feels really *shut off* from you during the job-hunt, *that* will depress them more than anything. Moreover, bottled-up emotions – frustration, depression, anger or rage – will inevitably botch-up the way you conduct interviews, the way you present yourself, and the way you come across to people. So, find someone – hopefully your loved ones or friends – with whom you can *talk* the emotions out, instead of having to *act* the emotions out.

● *Job-hunters who have tried all this and still can't find a job often are extremely pessimistic about their chances of finding a job.* "Well of course I'm pessimistic," you may say; "you would be too, in my place." That raises an interesting point. You can always find two job-hunters who are rather identical in age, experience, and the length of time they've been trying to find employment: yet one will be optimistic still, while the other is pessimistic in the extreme. And when you revisit them a month or so later, the optimistic one has found work, while the pessimistic one is looking still. This happens too often to be mere coincidence. There is a connection. It is commonly called "self-fulfilling prophecy" – a term I cordially hate. But the phenomenon is well-demonstrated: what you believe, helps to determine what happens. So, a long period of job-hunting, frustrating as it may be, is precisely the time that you need to work – hard – on what you believe. If you are religious by instinct, it is time to recover your faith. If you are a believer in prayer, it is time to pray much – not merely that you will find employment, but more to the point that you can remain *optimistic* because you are praying as though everything depended on God, but going out every weekday as though everything depended on You. If you are not religious, work on what belief system you do have: Karma, gratitude to the Universe, or whatever. It has been said that in *every* experience we have, there are two sets of data: things which encourage us, are hopeful, and are cause for gratitude AND things which discourage us, are productive of hopelessness, and make us bitter. The optimist, it is said, is one who focuses on the first set of data, giving little time or energy to the second. The pessimist is one who focuses on the second set of data, giving little time or energy to the first. Thus, optimism can be nourished within us, each day, by focusing our attention on those factors throughout the day which are encouraging, hopeful and cause for gratitude. And where optimism is nourished, the job-hunt is inevitably affected for the better.

I repeat: beyond all mechanics of the job-hunt, all techniques, and all "secrets": what you believe will happen, helps to determine what does happen.

Appendices

Stundenring
Colur des
Nördl. Polar-Kreis
Col. des des Krebses
Colur
Axe
Wendekreis
Sommer
Hori
Erde
zont
Aequator
Steinbock
Horizont
West
Ekliptik
Winter
Solstitium
Aequator
Herbst-
Wende
Südl.
Aequin
octiums
Süd

Appendix A

The Quick Job-Hunting Map

A fast way to help

ADVANCED VERSION*

For the undecided college student or the housewife going back to work, or the mid-career changer, or the man or woman whose job has been terminated, or anyone else facing obstacles in the job hunt

*Those entering the job-market for the first time, and desiring a simpler skill-list than we have provided here, are referred to *The Three Boxes of Life*, in which the Beginning Version of the Quick Job-Hunting Map may be found. Or that version may be ordered separately, by writing directly to Ten Speed Press, P.O. Box 7123, Berkeley, CA 94707. $1.25 + $.50 for postage and handling.

Introduction: What You Need To Know Before You Go Job-Hunting

You need to know, basically, that there are two methods of job-hunting. The first, or traditional, method is the one everybody knows about: want-ads, employment agencies, recruiters, resumés, etc. This method works very well for *some job-hunters.* In case you want to know what the odds are, before you start, a survey of ten million job-seekers by the Bureau of the Census[1] revealed that for every 100 who use:

a) classified-ads in the daily or weekly papers, 24 find a job thereby; 76 out of the 100 don't.

b) private employment agencies, 24 (again) find a job thereby; 76 out of the 100 don't.

c) the Federal/State Employment Service, 14 find a job thereby; 86 out of the 100 don't.

d) their school or college placement office, 22 find a job thereby; 78 out of the 100 don't.

e) Civil Service examinations, 13 find a job thereby; 87 out of the 100 don't.

f) friends, relatives, teachers, etc., 22 find a job thereby; 78 out of the 100 don't.

In a separate study, of those who send out resumés,[2] it was found that employers made one job-offer to a job-hunter for every 1470 resumés they received, on an average. That means that 1469 out of every 1470 resumés do not result in a job.

Fortunately, there is a second method of job-hunting. Which is *dreadfully* important for you to know, if the first method doesn't work for you. In fact, many many job-hunters prefer to begin with this second method, without even waiting to see whether or not they are successful using the first or traditional method. The success rate of this second method, in records kept for over 13 years,[3] is that 86 out of every 100 job-hunters who use it find a job thereby; only 14 out of every 100 don't.

In order to go about your job-hunt using this second method, you are going to have to do a bit of homework on yourself before setting out to pound the pavements. This homework has three parts, which we have symbolized throughout this MAP under the figures of a cart, a horse, and a road:

---

1. Published in the *Occupational Outlook Quarterly,* Winter, 1976.
2. Summarized in "Tea Leaves: A New Look at Resumés," Ten Speed Press, Box 7123, Berkeley, Calif. 94707.
3. By John C. Crystal, author of *Where Do I Go from Here with My Life?,* Ten Speed Press.

a • **THE CART** is the symbol of pages 209 through 231 in this MAP. These pages are to help you identify:

What skills you have and most enjoy using.
Skills are the basic building-blocks of jobs. You have picked up a lot of marketable skills regardless of how young you are, and regardless of whether you have worked a lot outside your home, or not. But you need to identify *what* skills you have, and—more importantly—which of these you *enjoy*.

b • **THE HORSE** is the symbol of pages 232 through 236. These pages are to help you identify:

Where you want to use your skills.
Your skills, by themselves, are like a cart sitting in the middle of a road. The cart needs to be hooked up to something. Your skills need to be hooked up with the *kinds* of places you would most like to use those skills. Only you can say *where* you want to use your skills. For example, if you are good at (and enjoy) welding, do you want to weld a wheel, or the casing of a nuclear bomb? You must decide.

c • **THE ROAD** is the symbol of pages 237 through 241. These pages are to help you put it all together, and are to show you:

How to identify the kind of job you want,
once you've decided the *What* and the *Where.*

How to identify the kind of organizations which have that sort of job,
in your chosen geographical area.
How to get hired there.

We have chosen the road as the symbol of this third part of your homework, because if you don't know how to identify the job, and the organization, and get hired there, it's like leaving the cart and the horse simply standing in the middle of the road.

This Job-Hunting MAP,* then, is devoted to helping you do this homework, in three steps, in order to go about job-hunting *the second way*—using the Method that works for 86 out of every 100 persons who use it. How long will it take? Who can say? If you devote a whole weekend to the task, you should be able to work through the whole MAP to page 236. After that, you will need to go see people. Some people, using this MAP, have found a job in a week. Others have taken nine months. One thing for sure: used conscientiously, this MAP will greatly *shorten* the time your job-hunt (or career-change) takes. If your job-hunt isn't Quick, it will at least be Quicker than it would be, otherwise.

---

*Using the excellent insights of John Crystal, John Holland, and Bernard Haldane, (see Bibliography, pp. 244-245), to whom we are all indebted.

What Skills You Have and Most Enjoy Using

Generally speaking, all skills divide into six clusters or families. To see which ones you are *attracted to,* try this exercise:

Below is an aerial view of a room in which a two-day (!) party is taking place. At this party, people with the same or similar interests have (for some reason) all gathered in the same corner of the room—as described below:

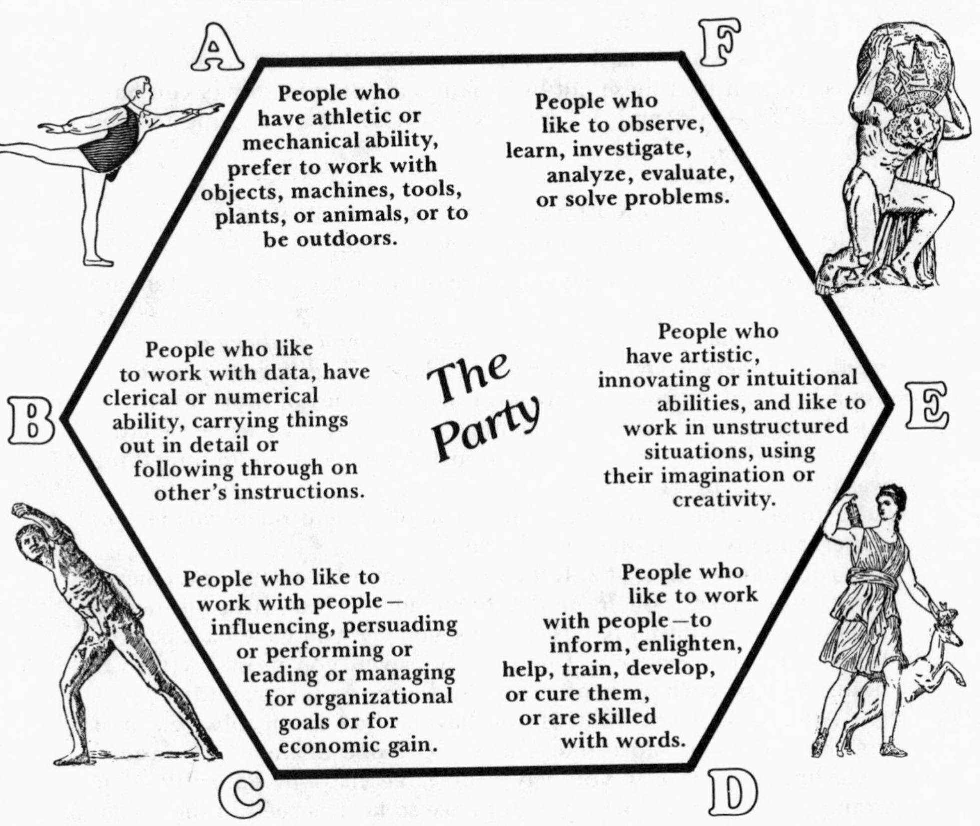

(1) Which corner of the room would you instinctively be drawn to, as the group of people you would most *enjoy* being with for the longest time? (leave aside any question of shyness, or whether you would have to talk with them.) Write the *letter* for that corner here:

____

(2) After fifteen minutes, everyone in the corner you have chosen, leaves for another party crosstown, except you. Of the groups *that still remain* now, which corner or group would you be drawn to the most, as the people you would most *enjoy* being with for the longest time? Write the letter for that corner here:

____

(3) After fifteen minutes, this group too leaves for another party, except you. Of the corners, and groups, which remain now, which one would you most enjoy being with for the longest time? Write the letter for that corner here:

____

(4) Now, underline the skills in each corner that you like best.

If you don't like parties, think of this as a library, or bookstore, with different book-sections: which one would you be most attracted to, etc.? Or think of it as a job-fair, with the employers grouped into different sections, etc.

However you think of it—party, library, job-fair—it should end up giving you a GENERAL idea about what skills you have—for it is based on the theories of Dr. John L. Holland about skill groupings, and on the idea that we are attracted to People, Books, Jobs which use the skills we *already have* and most enjoy.

GETTING DETAILED

But now you must have MORE DETAILED ideas about your skills. We can find these out by looking at different things you have ALREADY done—and, for the next exercise, you are going to need SEVEN.

So, please take

SEVEN BLANK PIECES OF PAPER
(lined or unlined, any size)

You have a choice as to what you write on these seven sheets. Here are three ways you can go:

First Choice: You can describe the seven *most satisfying accomplishments or achievements* you have ever done—in different periods of your life, and in your leisure or learning times or working times. Just be sure each accomplishment is one where you were *the active 'agent' who did the thing,* rather than just someone to whom something was done. (Being given a prize, etc. *won't do,* unless you say what you DID to earn the prize.) Put one accomplishment on each piece of paper, and give each one a brief title.

Alternative Choice #2: If the word "accomplishment" or "achievement" just makes you *freeze* ("Achievement? Who—little ol' me?"), then here is an alternative. Describe seven *jobs* you have had, paid or unpaid, full or part-time. Describe the seven you most ENJOYED doing. One on each piece of paper. And: give each a brief title.

Alternative Choice #3: If you haven't had seven jobs yet, or if you had seven or more, but hated every one of them, try instead describing seven *roles* you have (or have had) in your life. For example, if all your working experience so far has been in the home, and you are a married woman with children let us say, your seven roles might be: wife, mother, cook, homemaker, volunteer worker, student, citizen, etc. One role on each piece of paper; a brief title above each.

TALK, TALK, TALK

Now, go back over each sheet of paper, and be SURE you have described each achievement/job/role in enough detail, so that you can see what it is you really did.

How much detail? Well, let's take an example. This WON'T DO: "The Halloween Experience. I won a prize on Halloween for dressing up as a horse."

This WILL DO:

SAMPLE

"My Halloween Experience When I Was Seven Years Old. Details: When I was seven, I decided I wanted to go out on Halloween dressed as a horse. I wanted to be the front end of the horse, and I talked a friend of mine into being the back end of the horse. But, at the last moment he backed out, and I was faced with the prospect of not being able to go out on Halloween. At this point I decided to figure out some way of getting dressed up as the whole horse, myself. I took a fruit basket, and tied some string to both sides of the basket's rim, so that I could tie the basket around my rear end. This filled me out enough so that the costume fit me, by myself. I then fixed some strong thread to the tail so that I could make it wag by moving my hands. When Halloween came I not only went out and had a ball, but I won a prize as well."

SORT OF MEMORIZING

When you have finished writing out ALL SEVEN accomplishments/jobs/roles in detail, and each has a title, turn to page 212 and write the seven titles in, at the top of the SKILLS INVENTORY. Then, read over the seven sheets of paper two or three times, to be sure each story is very clear in your mind. So much so, that the title alone will recall the whole story to you.

ONE BY ONE

● MANY PEOPLE, incidentally, have found all of this is much easier for them, *if they don't write all seven accomplishments/jobs/roles at the same time,* but WRITE ONLY ONE, "run it through" the SKILL INVENTORY (pages 212-230). THEN write the next one, run it through the Inventory, THEN write the next one, etc. People who do it this way say they have a better idea of *which* accomplishments to choose, and *how* to write them up, as a result.

Your Functional/Transferable Skills Inventory

Webster's dictionary says: "**function**: *one of a group of related actions contributing to a larger action.*" And, "**transferable**: *usable in any occupational field.*" You are now about to take each experience of your own (your accomplishment/job/role), by title, and do an Inventory of it.

DIRECTIONS. This Skills Inventory is essentially a Coloring Book.

- Let's try it out with the sample we just saw on the previous page. We write the title in at the top: "The Halloween Experience". Then we start down the grid. (The letters, such as A^1, correspond to the letters of the Party exercise which you did on page 209. A^1 and A^2 correspond to the A-corner of the Party, etc.)
- The first "paragraph" or "box" of skill words has: "Designing____; Molding____; Shaping____;" etc. So we ask ourselves, did we—in doing the Halloween Experience—use ANY or ALL of those skills? The answer is: "Yes". So, we do two things:
  (a) We *color in* the square (sort-of) next to that paragraph, to indicate "this experience used one or more of these skills in this paragraph; AND THEN
  (b) We *underline*, within the paragraph, the skill(s) used. In the case of the Halloween Experience, it was "designing"—so, we underline it. (We have put it in italics here, so as not to confuse you when you come to your own underlining.)
- Then we go on to the next "paragraph", which begins with "Preparing____; Clearing____;" etc. We ask ourselves, did we use ANY or ALL of these skills, in doing the Halloween Experience? The answer is "No" so we leave it blank and go on to the next. The answer there is "No" also.
- We go on to the paragraph which begins with "Handling/fingering/feeling____;" etc. We ask ourselves the same question again, and here the answer is "Yes". So: (a) We *color in* the square.
  (b) We *underline*, within the paragraph, the skills used in the Halloween Experience. Several here appear relevant: "Handline, Manual dexterity, and Manipulating". We underline, therefore, these words (we have italicized them, again, so as not to confuse you). And so on to the end of page 230.

Sample: The Halloween Experience

1 2 3 4 5 6 7

Additional thoughts that occur to me about other times when I used these skills

A[1]

Machine or Manual Skills

I can do because I did do:

Skill Paragraphs	sample	1	2	3	4	5	6	7	Additional experiences
*Designing*____; Molding____; Shaping; Developing____; Composing____(e.g., type)									
Preparing____; Clearing____; Building____: Constructing____; Assembling____; Setting Up____; Installing____; Installation of ____; Laying____									
Lifting/Pushing/Pulling/Balancing____; Carrying____; Unloading/Moving/Shipping____; Delivering____; Collecting____									
Handling/fingering/feeling____; Keen sense of touch; Keen sensations; Finger dexterity (as in typing, etc.); *Manual*/hand *dexterity*; Handling____; *Manipulating*____; Weaving/Knitting; Handicrafting/craft skills; Making models									
Precision-working; Punching____; Drilling____; Tweezer dexterity; Showing dexterity or speed									
Washing; Cooking/culinary skills									
Feeding____; Tending____									
Controlling/Operating____; Blasting____; Grinding____; Forging____; Cutting____; Filling____; Applying____; Pressing____; Binding____; Projecting____									
Operating tools; operating machinery (e.g. radios); operating vehicles/equipment; Driving____; Switching____									
Fitting____; Adjusting____; Tuning____; Maintaining____; Fixing/Repairing____; Masters machinery against its will; Trouble-shooting____									
Producing____									
Other skills which you think belong in this family but are not listed above:									

and I used the above skills with:

Machine or Manual Skills continued	sample	1	2	3	4	5	6	7	Additional experiences
Tools (specify kinds):									
Work aids (what kinds?):									
Trees/stones/metals/other:									
Machines/equipment/vehicles:									
Processed materials (kinds?):									
Products being made (kinds?):									
Other:									

A2

Athletic/ Outdoor/ Traveling Skills

I can do because I have proven:

	sample	1	2	3	4	5	6	7	Additional experiences
Motor/Physical coordination & agility; *Eye-Hand-Foot coordination*; Walking/Climbing/Running									
Skilled at general sports: Skilled in small competitive games; Skilled at ___(a particular game)									
Swimming: Skiing/ Recreation; Playing. Hiking/ Backpacking/Camping/Mountaineering; Outdoor survival skills; Creating, planning, organizing outdoor activities; Traveling									
Drawing samples from the earth; Keen oceanic interests; Navigating									
Horticultural skills; Cultivating growing things; Skillful at planting/nurturing plants; Landscaping and groundskeeping									
Farming; Ranching; Working with animals									
Other skills which you think belong in this family, but are not listed above:									

B[1]

Detail/ Follow-through Skills

I can do because I did do:

Following-through; Executing____; Ability to follow detailed instructions; *Expert at getting things done*; Implementing decisions; Enforcing regulations; Rendering support services; Applying what others have developed; Directing production of ____ (kind of thing)									
Precise attainment of set limits, tolerances or standards; Brings projects in on time, and within budget; Skilled at making arrangements for events, processes; Responsible; Delivering on promises, on time.									
Expediting____; Dispatching____; Consistently tackles tasks ahead of time; Adept at finding ways to speed up a job; Able to handle a great variety of tasks and responsibilities simultaneously and efficiently; *Able to work well under stress, and still improvise*; Good at responding to emergencies									
Resource expert; Resource broker; Making and using contacts effectively; Good at getting materials; Collecting things; Purchasing____; Compiling____									
Approving____; Validation of information; Keeping confidences or confidential information.									
A detail man or woman; Keen and accurate memory for detail; Showing careful attention to, and keeping track of, details; Focusing on minutiae; High tolerance of repetition and/or monotony; Retentive memory for rules and procedures (e.g. protocol); *Persevering*____									
Checking____									
Explicit, ordered, systematic manipulation of data; Good at the processing of information; Collates data accurately, comparing with previous data; Tabulation of data; Keeping records (time, etc.); Recording____(kinds of data)									
Facilitating/Simplifying other people's finding things; Orderly organizing of data or records									

	sample	1	2	3	4	5	6	7	Additional experiences
Organizing written and numerical data according to a prescribed plan; Classification skills; Classifying materials expertly; Filing; Filing materials; Retrieving data									
Clerical ability; Typing; Operating business machines and data processing machines to attain organizational and economic goals; Copying; Reproducing materials									
Other skills which you think belong in this family, but are not listed above:									

B²

Numerical/ Financial/ Accounting/ Financial (Money) Management Skills

I can do because I did do:

	sample	1	2	3	4	5	6	7	Additional experiences
Numerical ability; Expert at learning and remembering numbers; number memory; Remembering statistics accurately, for a long period of time									
Counting; Taking inventory; Calculating; Computing; Arithmetical skills; High accuracy in computing /counting; Rapid manipulation of numbers; Rapid computations performed in head or on paper									
Managing money; Financial planning and management; Keeping financial records; Accountability									
Appraising____; Economic research and analysis; Doing cost analysis; Effective Cost Analyses, Estimates, Projections, and Comparisons; Financial/ Fiscal Analysis and Planning/Programming									
Developing a budget; Budget Planning, Preparation, Justification, Administration, Analysis and Review									
Extremely economical; Skilled at Allocating Scarce Financial Resources									
Preparing financial reports; Bookkeeping; Doing accounting; Fiscal Cost Audits, Controls, and Reductions									
Using numbers as a reasoning tool; Very sophisticated mathematical abilities; Effective at solving statistical problems									
Others which you think belong in this family of									

C1

Influencing/ Persuading Skills

I can because I did:

- Develop rapport / trust; Inspiring trust in the minds and hearts of others; Encouraging people
- Helping people identify their own intelligent self-interest
- Persuading____; Expert in reasoning persuasively / developing a thought; Debating, Influencing the attitudes or ideas of others
- Promoting____; (Face to face) Selling of tangibles/ intangibles; Selling ideas or products without tearing down competing ideas or products; Selling an idea, program or course of action to decision-makers; Developing targets/building markets for ideas or products; Fund-raising / money-raising
- *Recruiting talent or leadership*; Attracts skilled, competent creative people; *Enlisting*; Motivating others; Mobilizing____; Stimulating people to effective action
- Getting diverse groups to work together; Wins friends easily from among diverse or even opposing groups or factions; Adept at conflict management
- Arbitrating / mediating between contending parties or groups; Negotiating to come jointly to decisions; Bargaining; Crisis intervention; reconciling____
- Renegotiating____; Obtaining agreement on policies, after the fact
- Charting mergers; Manipulating____ to achieve____; Arranging financing
- Other skills which you think belong in this family, but are not listed above:

and I used the above skills with:

- Opinions
- Attitudes
- Judgments, Decisions
- Products
- Money
- Other:

C2 Performing Skills

I can do because I did do:

	sample	1	2	3	4	5	6	7	Additional experiences
Getting up before a group; Very responsive to audiences' moods or ideas; Diverting; Contributes to others pleasure consciously; Performing									
*Demonstrating*___ (products, etc.); *Modelling*___; Artistic (visual) presentations									
Showmanship; *A strong theatrical sense*; Poise in public appearances									
Addressing large or small groups; (Exceptional) speaking ability/articulateness; Public address/public speaking/oral presentations; Lecturing; Stimulating people/stimulating enthusiasm; Poetry reading									
Playing music; Making musical presentations; Singing; Dancing									
Making people laugh; Understands the value of the ridiculous in illuminating reality									
Acting; Making radio and TV presentations/films									
Public sports									
Conducting and directing public affairs and ceremonies; Conducting musical groups									
Other skills which you think belong in this family, but are not listed above:									

C3 Leadership Skills

I can do because I did do:

	sample	1	2	3	4	5	6	7	Additional experiences
Initiating___; Able to move into totally new situations on one's own; Able to take the initiative or first move in developing relationships; Skilled at striking up conversations with strangers									
Driving initiative; Continually searches for more responsibility; Persevering in acquiring things (like____)									
Excellent at organizing one's time; *Unusual ability to work self-directedly, without supervision*; (Very) self-directed at work									

		sample	1	2	3	4	5	6		Additional experience
	Unwillingness to automatically accept the status quo; Keen perceptions of things as they could be, rather than passively accepting them as they are; Promoting and bringing about major changes, as change agent; Planning for/and effecting/initiating change; *Sees and seizes opportunities*									
	Sees a problem and acts immediately to solve it; Deals well with the unexpected or critical; Very decisive in emergencies; Adept at confronting others with touchy or difficult personal matters									
	Showing courage; No fear of taking manageable risks; Able to make hard decisions; Adept at policy making; Able to terminate projects/people/processes when necessary									
	Leading others; guiding____; Inspiring, motivating and leading organized groups; Impresses others with enthusiasm and charisma; Repeatedly elected to senior posts; Skilled at chairing meetings									
	Deft in directing creative talent; Skilled leadership in perceptive human relations techniques									
	Other skills which you think belong in this family, but are not listed above:									
C4 *Developing/ Planning/ Organizing/ Executing/ Supervising/ Management Skills*	Planning____; Planning and development____; Planning on basis of lessons from past experience; A systematic approach to goal-setting									
	Prioritizing tasks; Establishing effective priorities among competing requirements; Setting criteria or standards; Policy-making; Policy formulation or interpretation									
	Designing projects; Program development/Programming; Skilled at planning and carrying out well-run meetings, seminars or workshops									
	Organizing____; Organizational development; Organizational analysis, planning and building; adept at organizing, bringing order out of chaos with masses of (physical) things									

	Developing/Planning/Organizing/Executing/ Supervising/Management Skills, continued	sample	1	2	3	4	5	6	7	Additional experiences
I can do because I did do:	Organizing others, bringing people together in cooperative efforts; Selecting resources; Hiring; *Able to call in other experts/helpers as needed*; Team-building; Recognizing and utilizing the skills of others; Contracting/Delegating____									
	Scheduling____; Assigning____; Setting up and maintaining on-time work-schedules; Coordinating operations/details; Arranging/Installing____									
	Directing others; Making decisions about others; Supervising others in their work; Supervising and administering____									
	Managing/Being responsible for others' output; Management____; Humanly-oriented technical management; Real property, plant and facility, management; R & D Program and Project Management; Controlling____									
	Producing____; Achieving____; Attaining____									
	Maintaining____; Trouble-shooting____; Recommending____									
	Reviewing____; Makes good use of feed-back; Evaluating____; Recognizes intergroup communication gaps; Judging people's effectiveness									
	Other skills which you think belong in this family, but are not included above:									
and I used those skills with:	*Individuals*									
	Personnel									
	Groups									
	Organizations									
	Management systems									
	Office procedures									
	Meetings									
	Projects/Programs									
	Educational events									

D[1]

Language/ Reading/ Writing/ Speaking/ Communications Skills

I can do because I did do:

	sample	1	2	3	4	5	6	7	Additional experiences
Reading; Love of reading voraciously or rapidly; Love of printed things; Relentlessly curious									
Comparing____; Proofreading____; Editing effectively____; Publishing imaginatively____									
Composing____(kinds of words)									
Communicating effectively; Expresses self very well; Communicates with clarity; Making a point and cogently expressing a position; Thinking quickly on one's feet; Talking/Speaking; Encouraging communication									
Defining____; Explaining concepts; Interpreting____; Ability to explain difficult or complex concepts, ideas and problems									
Translating____; Verbal/linguistic skills in foreign languages; Linguistics; Teaching of languages; Adept at translating jargon into relevant and meaningful terms, to diverse audiences or readers									
Summarizing____; Reporting accurately; Very explicit and concise writing; Keeping superior minutes of meetings									
Outstanding writing skills; Ability to vividly describe people or scenes so that others can visualize; Writes with humor, fun and flair (related to *Diverting*, below); Employs humor in describing experiences, to give people courage to embrace them									
Uncommonly warm letter composition; Flair for writing reports; Skilled speech-writing									
Promotional writing; Highly successful proposal writing for funding purposes; Imaginative advertising and publicity programs									
Other skills which you think belong in this family, but are not listed above:									

and I used those skills with:	*Language / Reading / Writing / Speaking Communications Skills continued*	sample	1	2	3	4	5	6	7	Additional experiences
	Ideas									
	Feelings									
	Facts									
	Articles									
	Reports/Newsletters									
	Brochures/catalogs/journals									
	Books									
	Other:									

D[2]

Instructing/ Interpreting/ Guiding/ Educational Skills

I can because I have:		sample	1	2	3	4	5	6	7	Additional experiences
	Proven myself to be very knowledgeable; Having a commitment to learning as a life-long process									
	Briefing____; Informing____; Enlightening ✓; Explaining ✓; Instructing____; Teaching____; In-Service training									
	(Unusually) skillful teaching; Fosters a stimulating learning environment; Creating an atmosphere of acceptance; Patient teaching; Adept at inventing illustrations for principles or ideas; Down to earth; Adept at using visual communications (charts, slides, chalkboards, etc.); Instills love of the subject; Conveys tremendous enthusiasm									
	Coaching about____(finances, etc.); Advising/aiding people in making decisions; Giving advice about ____; Giving insight concerning____									
	Encouraging____; (cf. Influencing/Persuading Family of Skills, above)									
	Adept at two-way dialogue; Communicates effectively; Ability to hear and answer questions perceptively; Acceptance of differing opinions; (Keen) ability to help others express their views; Consulting									

		sample	1	2	3	4	5	6	7	Additional experiences
	Enabling/Facilitating personal growth and development; Helping people make their own discoveries in knowledge; Helping people to develop their own ideas or insights; Clarifying goals and values of others; Counseling; Putting things in perspective; Brings out creativity in others; Shows others how to take advantage of a resource									
	Group-facilitating; Discussion group leadership; Group dynamics; Behavioral modification									
	Empowering____; Training and Development____; Training someone in something; Designing educational events; Organization and administration of inhouse training programs									
	Other skills which you think belong in this family, but are not listed above:									
and I used those skills with:	Information									
	Ideas / Generalizations									
	Values / standards									
	Goals / decisions									
	Other									
D3 *Serving/ Helping/ Human Relations Skills*	Relates well in dealing with the public/public relations									
	Servicing____; Customer relations and services; Attending____; Adjusting____(e.g. bills); Referring (people)____									
	Rendering services to____; Being of service; Helping and serving____									
	Sensitivity to others; Interested in/manifesting keen ability to relate to people; Intense curiosity about other people—who they are, what they do; Remembers people and their preferences; Adept at treating									

I can because I did:	*Serving/Helping* *Human Relations Skills continued*	sample	1	2	3	4	5	6	7	Additional experiences
	people fairly; Listening intently and accurately; A good trained effective listener; Good at listening and conveying awareness; Consistently communicates warmth to people; Conveying understanding, patience and fairness; Readily establishes warm, mutual rapport with____; Able to develop warmth over the telephone									
	Interpersonal competencies; (Unusual) perception in human relations; Expertise in interpersonal contact; Keen ability to put self in someone else's shoes; Empathy: instinctively understanding how someone else feels; Understanding; Tact, Diplomacy and Discretion; Effective in dealing with many different kinds of people/Talks easily with all kinds of people									
	Caring for/Nursing children or the handicapped; Watching over____; Love of children; Guiding____									
	Administering a household; Hostessing; Shaping and influencing the atmosphere of a particular place; Providing comfortable, natural and pleasant surroundings; Warmly sensitive and responsive to people's feelings and needs in social or other situations; Anticipating people's needs									
	Works well on a teamwork basis; Has fun while working, and makes it fun for others; Collaborates with colleagues skillfully; Treats others as equals, without regard to education, authority, or position; Refuses to put people into slots or categories; Ability to relate to people with different value systems; Motivates fellow workers; Expresses appreciation faithfully; Ready willingness to share credit with others									
	Takes human failings/limitations into account; Able to ignore undesirable qualities in others; Deals patiently and sympathetically with difficult people; Handles super-difficult people in situations, without stress; Handles prima donnas tactfully and effectively; Works well in a hostile environment									

	Serving/Helping *Human Relations Skills continued*	sample	1	2	3	4	5	6	7	Additional experiences
	Nursing____; Skillful therapeutic abilities; Curing____; Gifted at helping people with their personal problems; Raises people's self-esteem; (Thorough) understanding of human motivations; Understands family relationships and problems; Aware of people's need for supportive community; Adept at aiding people with their total life adjustment/Mentoring									
	Unusual ability to represent others; Expert in liaison roles; Ombudsmanship									
	Other skills which you think belong in this family, but are not included above:									
and I used those skills with:	Children									
	The young									
	Adolescents									
	Adults or *Peers*									
	The aging									
	All age groups									
	Other:									
E[1] *Intuitional and Innovating Skills*	Imagining____; Highly imaginative; *Possessed of great imagination, and the courage to use it*									
	Ideaphoria/Continually conceiving, developing and generating ideas; Conceptual ability of the highest order; Being an idea man or woman; Inventing; *Inventive; Ability to improvise on the spur of the moment*									
	Innovating; Having many innovative and creative ideas; Creative, perceptive effective innovator; *Willing to experiment with new approaches*; Experimental with ideas, procedures, and programs; Strongly committed to experimental approaches; Demonstrating continual originality; Love of exercising the mind-muscle									

I can do because I did do:	*Intuitional and Innovating Skills continued*	sample	1	2	3	4	5	6	7	Additional experiences
	Synthesizing perceptions, etc.; Seeing relationships between apparently unrelated factors; Integrating diverse elements into a clear coherent whole; Effective dissolution of barriers between ideas or fields; Ability to relate abstract ideas; Balancing factors/Judging/Showing good judgement									
	Deriving things from others' ideas; Improving____; Updating____; *Adapting*____; Reflection upon____; Sees the theoretical base in a practical situation; Significant theoretical modeling; *Model developing*; Developing____; Formulating____; Developing innovative program ideas									
	Generating ideas with commercial possibilities; Able to see the commercial possibilities of abstract ideas or concepts; Applying____; Applying theory; Applied research; Creating products; Entreprenurial									
	Form perception; Perception of patterns and structures; *Visualizing shapes*; Graphing and reading graphs; Visualizing in the third-dimension; Able to read blueprints									
	Spatial memory; Memory for design; Able to notice quickly (and/or remember later) most of the contents of a room; Remembering____; Memory for faces									
	Showing foresight; Recognizing obsolescence before compelling data is yet at hand; Instinctively gathering resources even before the need for them becomes clear; Forecasting									
	Perceiving intuitively; Color-discrimination (of a very high order)									
	Other skills which you think belong in this family, but are not listed above:									
	__________									

E²

Artistic Skills

I can because I did:

	sample	1	2	3	4	5	6	7	Additional experiences
Shows strong sensitivity to, and need for, beauty in the environment; Adept at coloring things; instinctively excellent taste									
Expressive; Exceptionally good at facial expressions used to express or convey thoughts, without (or, in addition to) words; Ability to use the body to express feelings eloquently; Uses voice tone and rhythm as unusually effective tool of communication; Skilled in telephone-voice; Can accurately reproduce sounds (e.g., foreign languages spoken without accent); Mastery of all forms of communication									
Good sense of humor/*playfulness*									
Creative imagining/Creating original____; Operates well in a free, unstructured, unsupervised environment; Bringing new life to traditional (art) forms; Translating____; Restoring____									
Aware of the value of symbolism, and deft in its use; Skilled at symbol formation (words, pictures, and concepts); Visualizing concepts; Creating poetry, or poetic images; Designing and/or using audio-visual aids; Photographing									
Visual & spatial designing; Artistic talent (drawing, etc.); Illustrating; Mapping; Drafting/Mechanical drawing									
Fashioning/Shaping things; *Making*____; Designing in wood or other media; Redesigning structures; Styling____; Decorating____									
Writing; Playwriting; Assisting in/directing the planning, organizing and staging of theatrical productions									
Musical knowledge and taste; Tonal memory; Uncommon sense of rhythm, Exceedingly accurate melody recognition; Composing									
Other skills which you think belong in this family, but are not listed above:									

and I used those skills with:	*Artistic Skills continued*	sample	1	2	3	4	5	6	7	Additional experiences
	Colors									
	Spaces									
	Shapes, faces									
	Handicrafts									
	Arts, drawing, paints									
	Fashion, jewelry, clothing, furs, furniture									
	Music									
	Other:									

F[1]

Observational/ Learning Skills

I can do because I did do:

Skill	sample	1	2	3	4	5	6	7	Additional experiences
Observing____; (Highly) observant of people/data/things; (Keen) awareness of surroundings									
Reading____ (e.g., dials); Adept at scanning radar or other sophisticated observational systems; Estimating____ (e.g., speed)									
Listening skillfully; Hearing accurately; Keen sense of smell; (Tremendously) sensitive sense of tasting									
Perceptive: Perceiving____; Detecting____; Discovering____; A person of perpetual curiosity/discovery, delighting in new knowledge; Continually seeking to expose oneself to new experiences; Highly committed to continual personal growth and learning; Learns from the example of others; Learns quickly									
Alert in observing human behavior; Studying other people's behavior perceptively; Perceptive in identifying and assessing the potential of others; Recognizes and appreciates the skills of others									
Appraising____; Assessing____; Screening applicants; Realistically assessing people's needs; Accurately assessing public moods; *Quickly sizes up situations* and instinctively understands political realities									

		sample	1	2	3	4	5	6	7	Additional experiences
	Exceptional intelligence, tempered by common sense									
	Other skills which you think belong in this family, but are not listed above:									
and I used those skills with:	Data (what kinds?)									
	People (any special kinds?)									
	Ideas									
	Behavior									
	Procedures									
	Operations									
	Phenomena									
	Instruments									
	Other									

		sample	1	2	3	4	5	6	7	Additional experiences
F2 *Research/ Investigating/ Analyzing/ Systematiz-ing/ Evaluating Skills*	Anticipates problems before they become problems; Recognizing need for more information before a decision can be made intelligently; Skilled at clarifying problems or situations									
	Surveying___; Interviewing___; Adept at gathering information from people by talking to them; Researching resources, ways and means; Researching personally, through investigation and interviewing; Inquiring									
	Inspecting___; Examining___; Surveying organizational needs; Researching exhaustively; Collecting information/Information gathering; Academic research and writing									
	Analyzing___; Dissecting___; *Breaking down principles into parts*; Adept at atomizing/breaking down into parts; Analyzing community needs, values, and resources; Analyzes communication situations; Analyzing manpower requirements; Analyzing performance specifications									

	Research / Investigating / Analyzing / Systematizing / Evaluating Skills continued	sample	1	2	3	4	5	6	7	Additional experiences
I can because I did:	Diagnosing___; Organizing/Classifying___; Identifies elements, relationships, structures, and organizing principles of organizations to be analyzed; Isolating elements; *Able to separate 'wheat from chaff'*; Reviewing large amounts of material, and extracting essence; Perceiving and Defining Cause & Effect relationships; Ability to trace problems, ideas, etc. to their source									
	Grouping___; Perceiving common denominators; Systematizing/Organizing material/information in a systematic way									
	*Testing*_____ (e.g. an idea, or hypothesis)									
	Determining/Figuring out___; Solving___; Problem-solving; Trouble-shooting									
	Reviewing/Evaluating___; Screening___(e.g., fund proposals); Critiquing___; Evaluating by measurable or subjective criteria; Accurately evaluating___ (e.g., programs administered by others; experiments; loan applications; papers; quizzes; work; records; staff; program bids; evidence; options; qualifications; etc.)									
	Decision-making skills; Re-evaluating									
	Other skills which you think belong in this family, but are not listed above:									
and I used those skills with:	People (what kinds?)									
	Data (what kinds?)									
	Things (what kinds?)									
	Ideas (theoretical, abstract, symbolic, systematic?)									
	Articles, artifacts, or processes									
	Matter (inert or moving) or Energy									
	Phenomena (physical, biological, scientific, mathematical, or cultural?)									
	Other:									

PATTERNS AND PRIORITIES

When you've finished this whole Inventory, for all seven of your accomplishments/achievements/jobs/roles or whatever, you want to look for PATTERNS and PRIORITIES.

a) For Patterns, because it isn't a matter of whether you used a skill once only, but rather whether you used it repeatedly, or not. "Once" proves nothing; "repeatedly" is very convincing.

b) For Priorities, because the job you eventually choose may not be able to use all of your skills. You need to know *what you are willing to trade off, and what you are not.* This requires you to know what your priorities are: i.e., which skills, or family of skills, are most important to you.

PHOTO-COPY, DOUBLE-COLOR, PRIORITIZE

We therefore suggest you tear out the preceding pages of the Skills Inventory, *arrange to photo-copy the opposite side of each page,* and then spread them all out on a table or on the floor.

Now you have a complete "aerial view" of all the skills you have. At this point, we suggest you use a second color (like red) and go back over all the "squares" you colored in. Ask yourself, do I enjoy this skill/these skills still today? If the answer is "Yes" DOUBLE-COLOR that particular square. And DOUBLE-UNDERLINE, in red, the particular skills you ENJOY, in each corresponding Skill Paragraph.

When you are all done, look at the total "aerial view" of your skills, to see which family of skills has the most DOUBLE-COLOR (say, red); put it up at the top of the table or floor lay-out. Which family of skills has the next most DOUBLE-COLOR? Put it next. Thus, you will quickly see which skills are most important to you.

Enter the results on the diagram on page 236.

Now it is time to go on to the second part of your homework, and consider:

Where You Would Most Enjoy Using These Skills

Where You Would Most Enjoy Using These Skills

It is, of course, nice to 'stay loose' and be willing to use your skills any place that there is a vacancy. Unfortunately, experts say that 80% of all the vacancies which occur in this country, above entry level, are never advertised through any of the channels or avenues that job-hunters traditionally turn to.

So, you're going to have to approach any place and every place that looks attractive to you.

So, you can't rule out any place that looks interesting to you, because it's just possible they have a vacancy that you don't know about. Or will develop one *while you're there.* Or will decide (since they may be expanding) to create a job just for you.

You can't, of course, go visit EVERY place that looks interesting. Hence, the importance of this part of your homework. You've GOT to "cut the territory down" to some manageable size, by using:

SIX PRINCIPLES OF EXCLUSION, FOR NARROWING DOWN THE AREA YOU NEED TO FOCUS ON

1. *First Principle for Narrowing Down the Organizations You Will Need to Visit:* WHAT STATE, CITY OR AREA DO YOU MOST WANT TO WORK IN? If it's where you presently live, get a city (or county) street map, decide the longest time or distance you are willing to commute, and then cut a piece of string *that length,* stick a pencil through one end, a pin at the other, put the pin at the place where you presently live, and swing an arc with the pencil. That gives you the area where you will go job-hunting. If it's not where you presently live, decide on the name of the city or place you'd most like to work, followed by two alternatives (in case). Enter your answer on page 236.

2. *Second Principle for Narrowing Down the Organizations You Will Need to Visit:* WHERE, WITHIN THAT GEOGRAPHICAL AREA, DO YOU WANT TO WORK, IN TERMS OF SPECIAL KNOWLEDGES? Consider all the subjects you know quite a bit about, knowledges you picked up in the home, in your leisure, in school, or on the job. On a blank sheet of paper, list them all. Then prioritize them, using the grid on the next page.

PRIORITIZING GRID

LIST, COMPARE

Here is a method for taking (say) ten items, and figuring out which one is most important to you, which is next most important, etc.

1 *2*
1 *3*   2 *3*
1 *4*   2 *4*   3 *4*
1 *5*   2 *5*   3 *5*   4 *5*
1 *6*   2 *6*   3 *6*   4 *6*   5 *6*
1 *7*   2 *7*   3 *7*   4 *7*   5 *7*   6 *7*
1 *8*   2 *8*   3 *8*   4 *8*   5 *8*   6 *8*   7 *8*
1 *9*   2 *9*   3 *9*   4 *9*   5 *9*   6 *9*   7 *9*   8 *9*
1 *10*   2 *10*   3 *10*   4 *10*   5 *10*   6 *10*   7 *10*   8 *10*   9 *10*

Make a list of the items and number them. *In the case of Specific Knowledges, make a list of ten subjects you know quite a bit about, then number them 1 thru 10.* Now, look at the first line of this grid. You see a 1 and a *2* there. So, compare items one and two on your list. Which one is more important to you? *State the question any way you want to: in the case of Specific Knowledges, you might ask yourself: if I was being offered two jobs, one which used knowledge # 1, and one which used # 2, other things being equal, which would I prefer?* Circle it. Then go on to the next pair, etc.

CIRCLE, COUNT

Total Times Each Number Got Circled:

1____ 2____ 3____ 4____ 5____ 6____ 7____ 8____ 9____ 10____

When you are all done, count up the number of times each number got circled, all told. Enter these totals in the spaces just above.

RECOPY

Finally, recopy your list, beginning with the item that got the most circles. This is your *new #1.* Then the item that got the next most circles. This is your *new #2.*

In case of a tie (two numbers got the same number of circles), look back on the grid to see when you were comparing those two numbers there, which one got circled. That means you prefer That One over the other; thus you break the tie.

P.S. If you need to compare any list that has more than ten items to it, just keep adding new rows to the bottom of the grid. Thus: 1 *11*   2 *11,*   etc.   Until you have all the numbers compared.

You will need to use the above grid several times, in the course of completing this map. Just copy it on a separate piece of paper each new time you need to use it.

Once you have listed, in the order of their priority, the special knowledges you most enjoy using, list them in the appropriate place on page 236. Also, get together with two or three of your friends and have them suggest the kinds of places where such special knowledges might be useful on the job.

3. *Third Principle for Narrowing Down the Organizations You Will Need to Visit:* WITHIN THE ORGANIZATIONS WHICH USE THE SPECIAL KNOWLEDGES YOU CARE THE MOST ABOUT, WHAT KINDS OF PEOPLE WOULD YOU LIKE TO BE SURROUNDED BY—

a) Defined, first of all, in terms of skills? *(Here enter your answers—spelled out—from The Party Exercise, on page 209. List the three corners you liked best, in order, plus the words you underlined in each of those three corners.)*

b) Defined, secondly, in terms of characteristics: e.g., competent, friendly, etc. If you have trouble thinking of characteristics, think of the *kinds* of people who turn you off, then list their opposites, here. Prioritize this list—using the grid, on page *233*. Enter the answers in the appropriate place on page 236.

4. *Fourth Principle for Narrowing Down the Organizations You Will Need to Visit:* WITHIN ORGANIZATIONS THAT USE YOUR FAVORITE SPECIAL KNOWLEDGES, AND HAVE PEOPLE WITH THE SKILLS AND CHARACTERISTICS YOU LIKE BEST, WHAT GOALS/PURPOSES/VALUES DO YOU WANT THAT ORGANIZATION TO BE TRYING TO ACHIEVE?

a) Working primarily on the mind—trying to bring more truth into the world? OR working primarily with the emotions—trying to bring more beauty or love into the world? OR working primarily with the moral will—trying to bring more justice, honesty, perfection, etc. into the world? OR: what?

b) Producing a product, making money, offering services, making better bodies, reducing mortality, or what?

List all your answers to both a) and b), prioritize them (using the grid on page 233), then list your answers in order of priority at the appropriate place on page 236.

5. *Fifth Principle for Narrowing Down the Organizations You Will Need to Visit:* YOU WILL DO YOUR BEST AND MOST EFFECTIVE WORK WITHIN ONE OF THE ABOVE ORGANIZATIONS THAT ALSO HAS WHAT SORT OF WORKING CONDITIONS:

a) Outdoors, indoors, with large windows, indoors anywhere?

b) In an organization with more than 500 employees, 300 or so, 100, less than 50, less than 10, or—what?

c) What sort of dress code, supervision, openness to change, use of authority, and—what else?

d) List distasteful working conditions you have endured in the past on the job/at school/at home, and then state the opposite of these—in more positive form.

List all your answers to a), b), c) and d) above on a separate blank sheet of paper, prioritize them all together (using the grid on page 233), then list your answers at the appropriate place on page 236.

6. *The Sixth, and Final, Principle for Narrowing Down the Organizations You Will Need to Visit:* IN THE ORGANIZATIONS DESCRIBED BY YOUR ANSWERS TO THE ABOVE QUESTIONS, WHAT KIND OF RESPONSIBILITY DO YOU WANT, AND (TO PUT IT ANOTHER WAY) AT WHAT SALARY LEVEL?

a) Do you want to work alone, OR in tandem with one other co-worker, OR as a member of a team, OR as a supervisor, boss or owner, OR—what?

b) How much, and what kinds, of initiative would you like to be able to take on the job?

c) What's the minimum salary you could stand? What's the maximum you hope for/would like to get?

Enter this information at the appropriate place on page 236. together with any other thoughts you have, related to this question.

And Now, To Put It All Together:

All the information gathered so far, on the subject of

WHAT (skills do I have, and most enjoy using); and

WHERE (do I want to use those skills)

must now be summarized, all together, on the diagram on the next page:

The Flower:

A PICTURE OF THE JOB I AM LOOKING FOR

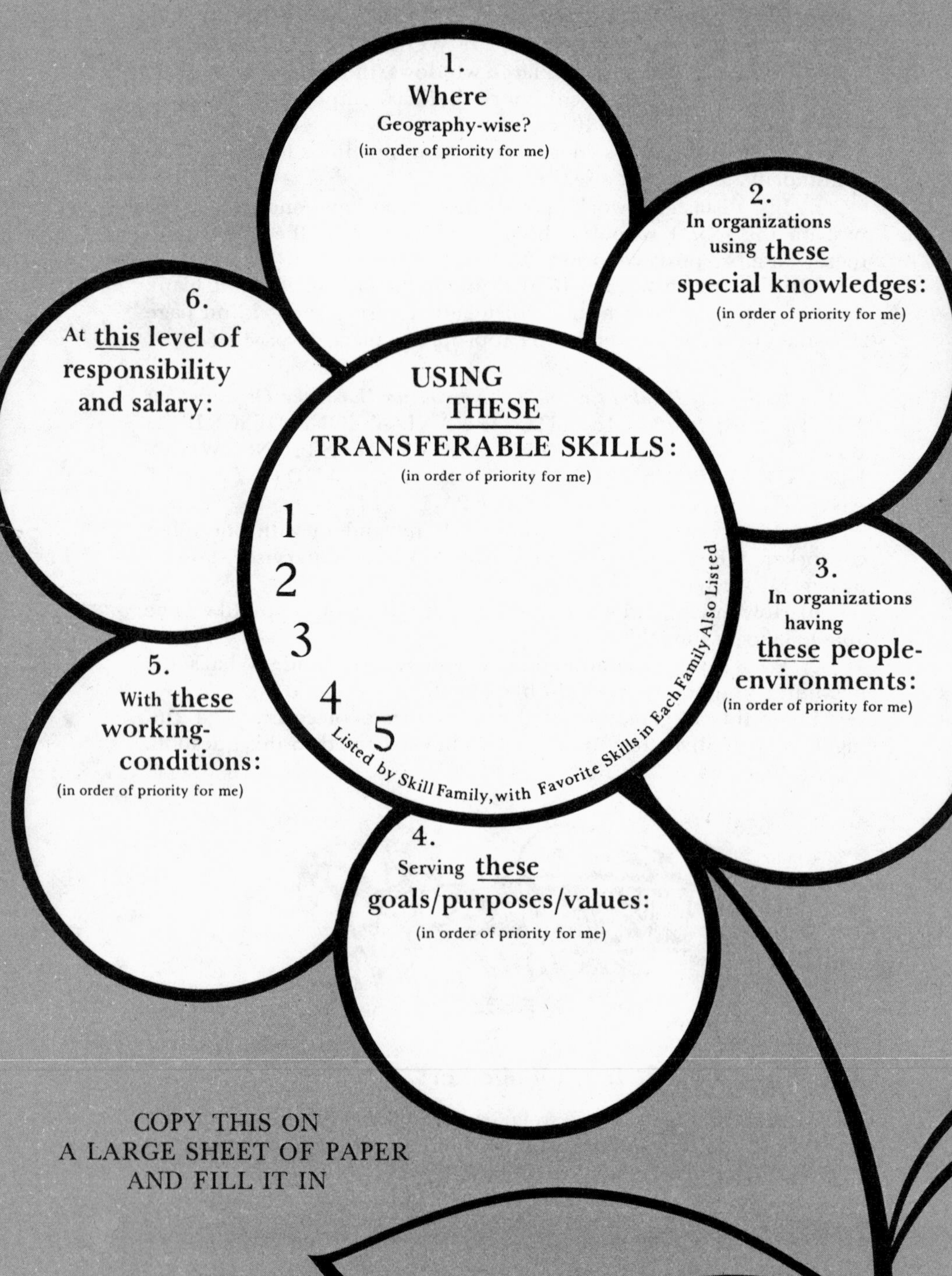

COPY THIS ON
A LARGE SHEET OF PAPER
AND FILL IT IN

Now, on to the third part of your homework:

How to identify the job you have just drawn a picture of, by name or by title;

How to identify the kind of organizations which have such a job;

How to get hired there.

There are three steps to the HOW part of your homework:

● *The First Step on the Road to Your Job:*

PRACTICE INTERVIEWING

You need to go out and practice talking to people. Just for practice. In a non-job, low-stress, practice interview situation—just for information. You can take someone with you, if you want. If you're shy, maybe you want to take someone with you who is more at ease with people than you are; and watch how he/she does it. Anyway, by yourself, or with someone:

Your task here is to go out and talk with somebody. Somebody at *A Place That Fascinates or Interests You*—like, say, an airport (how does it get run), a toy-store, a television station, or whatever; OR somebody who has *The Same Hobby or Leisure-Activity That You Do*—like, say, skiing, gardening, painting, music, color, or whatever; OR somebody who is working on *Some Issue That Fascinates or Interests You*—like, say, affirmative action, or ecology, or assertiveness, or lower taxes, or whatever. Use your phone book (the Yellow Pages) or friends to find the kind of person you're looking for: e.g., for skiing, try a ski-supply store, or instructor.

When you find him or her, talk about your mutual enthusiasm. If you don't know what else to ask them, here are four suggestions:

1. How did you get into this work? Or: How did you get interested in this?

2. What do you like best about doing this?

3. What do you like least about doing this?

4. Where else could I find people who share this enthusiasm, or interest, or are interested in this issue?

Then go visit the people they suggest, and ask them (if nothing else) the same four questions. Keep at this, practice it as long as you need to, until you feel comfortable talking to people.

Then, on to the next step.

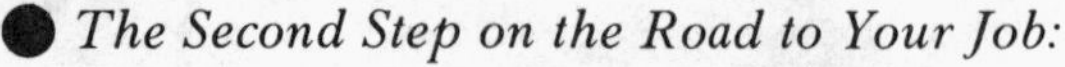

● *The Second Step on the Road to Your Job:*

INFORMATION INTERVIEWING TO PUT IT ALL TOGETHER

Once you feel comfortable interviewing people, you are ready to go find what kind of job, and organizations, that PICTURE OF THE JOB I AM LOOKING FOR points to.

THE SIMPLER FLOWER

So, begin with that picture (page 236). Take a large piece of blank paper (like, shelf paper or notebook paper 8½ x 11″) and

a) COPY THE OUTLINE of the flower (one centerpiece, six petals around its outside). Then:

b) COPY YOUR TWO most favorite skills onto the centerpiece of this New flower. Copy them off the Flower on page 236.

c) COPY THE TWO most important items on each of the six petals (e.g., your two top special knowledges, your two top people-environments, your two top goals/values, etc.)

d) On this *Simpler Flower* you will now have 12-14 items, all together. Make a list of these on the margin of your diagram, and prioritize them (using a blank copy of the prioritizing grid on page 233; and asking the question in the case of each pair, "If I had two job offers and they were both the same, except that one gave me (here name the first factor you are comparing) and the other gave me (here name the second factor you are comparing), which job would I take?")

e) NOW NUMBER THE 12-14 FACTORS ON THIS Simpler Flower in the order of priority or importance to you.

f) THEN FILL IN THE BLANKS BELOW WITH THE CORRESPONDING ITEM off your "Prioritized Simpler Flower": e.g., each time a 1. occurs below, copy your first—or most important—factor there.

THE INTERVIEWS FOR INFORMATION ONLY

1— *On my first information interview(s) I'm going to go see someone whose job uses/is characterized by*

1. ______________________________

and I'm going to ask him/her what kind of jobs they know about which use:

1. ______________________________ *AND*

2. ______________________________

2 *On my second information interview(s) I'm going to go see the kind of person suggested to me in my first interview(s) above, namely, someone whose job uses/is characterized by*

1. ______________________________ AND

2. ______________________________

and I'm going to ask him/her what kind of jobs they know about which use:

1. ______________________________ *AND*

2. ______________________________ *AND*

3. ______________________________

And if they don't know, I'll ask them who they think does.

3 – *On my third information interview(s) I'm going to go see the kind of person suggested to me in my second interview(s) above, namely, someone whose job uses/is characterized by*

1. ______________________________ *AND*

2. ______________________________ *AND*

3. ______________________________

and I'm going to ask him/her what kind of jobs they know about which use:

1. ______________________________ *AND*

2. ______________________________ *AND*

3. ______________________________ *AND*

4. ______________________________

And if they don't know, I'll ask them who they think does.

4 – *On my fourth information interview(s), I'm going to go see the kind of person suggested to me in my third interview(s) above, namely, someone whose job uses/is characterized by*

1. ______________________________ *AND*

2. ______________________________ *AND*

3. ______________________________ *AND*

4. ______________________________

and I'm going to ask him/her what kind of jobs they know about which use:

1. ______________________________ *AND*

2. ______________________________ *AND*

3. ______________________________ *AND*

4. ______________________________ *AND*

5. ______________________________

And if they don't know, I'll ask them who they think does.

5 – *On my fifth information interview(s), etc.*

(You can surely finish this diagram for yourself, on a separate sheet of blank paper.)

If at any time during this informational interviewing, you can't get to see someone who actually holds the job you are interested in holding, ask to talk to his/her superior or boss, rather than to a co-worker or someone under him/her.

Whenever you run into a stone-wall, use your contacts (friends, family, school alumni, former employers, etc.) for suggestions as to where you can turn next.

● *The Third and Last Step on the Road to Your Job:*

In the course of the above interviewing, you will not only discover the kind of job(s) you would most like to have, but you will—in the course of your interviewing—inevitably discover what organizations have such jobs, as you will have to visit those organizations in the course of your informational interviewing.

Now, your task is TO RETURN TO THE TWO OR THREE ORGANIZATIONS YOU LIKED THE BEST and tell them so—together with why (your chance to discuss all the factors on The Flower Picture of the job you are looking for).

You are now, but only now, coming to visit them as Job-hunter. Whether they have a vacancy or not, is immaterial. You are going to seek out in each organization among your top three or so, the person who has the power to hire (not the personnel department); and you are going to tell him or her

a • what impressed you about their organization, during your information survey (stage 2),

b • what sorts of challenges, needs or "problems" (go slow in using this latter word with sensitive employers) your survey suggested exists in this field in general, and with this place in particular—that intrigue you.

c • what skills seem to you to be needed, in order to meet those challenges or needs in his or her organization.
d • the fact that you have these skills (here use the information summarized on the Map, page 236).

They, for their part, will have four basic questions they will want to know the answers to, about YOU:
a • why are you here (i.e., why did you pick out their organization)?
b • what can you do for them (i.e., what are your skills and special knowledges)?
c • what kind of person are you (i.e., what are your goals/values, self-management, etc.)?
d • how much are you going to cost them (your salary *range*—maximum, minimum)?

They may ask you directly about these, or they may try to find them out by just letting the interview happen.

Hopefully, this will lead to your being offered the job. If it does not, go on to the next place you liked the best.

For further information about any part of the above process, reread chapters 4-7.

Good luck, Peace, and Shalom.

IF YOU WANT ADDITIONAL HELP

Bernard Haldane Associates' Job and Career Building, by Richard Germann and Peter Arnold. 1981, 1980. Ten Speed Press, Box 7123, Berkeley, CA 94707. $6.95 + $.75 postage and handling.

Who's Hiring Who? by Richard C. Lathrop. 1977. At your local bookstore, or order directly from Ten Speed Press, Box 7123, Berkeley, CA 94707. $5.95 + $.75 postage and handling.

Making Vocational Choices: A Theory of Careers, by John L. Holland. 1973. Order directly from Prentice-Hall, Inc., Englewood Cliffs, NJ 07632. $4.95, paperback.

Where Do I Go From Here With My Life? by John C. Crystal and Richard N. Bolles. 1974. Ten Speed Press, Box 7123, Berkeley, CA 94707. $9.95 + $.75 postage and handling.

Job Power Now! The Young People's Job Finding Guide, by Bernard Haldane, Jean Haldane and Lowell Martin. 1976. At your local bookstore or order directly from Acropolis Books Ltd., 2400 17th St. NW, Washington, DC 20009. $4.95, paperback.

My son, be admonished:
of making many books there is no end;
and much study is a weariness of the flesh.

Ecclesiastes

Appendix B
Resources Guide:

Books

BOOKS are an inexpensive way of getting information, advice, coaching, and supervision.

Books are an inexpensive way of transporting *Someone Knowledgeable* into your living room or library for an hour's conversation or two, with you.

On the other hand:

Books are also large blocks of black print, often boring, sometimes filled with misinformation delivered with a pontifical ring—which may, *however unwittingly*, lead the reader down some primrose path. Most of us have a tendency to believe that if something is *in print*, it must be true. But you'd be amazed at how easily misinformation can get into print.

So, if you decide you want to read additional books to help you with your job-hunt or career-change, choose with caution and read with care. The job-hunt you save will be your own.

HIGHLY RECOMMENDED

Lathrop, Richard, *Who's Hiring Who?* Ten Speed Press, Box 7123, Berkeley, CA 94707. 1977. $5.95, paper. Simply excellent resource. Now back in print, revised and improved. Used more often by our readers than any other book (besides *Parachute*).

Holland, John L., *Making Vocational Choices: A theory of Careers*. Prentice-Hall, Inc., Englewood Cliffs, NJ. 1973. $15.95. Despite its incredible rise in price, many of our readers continue to find this one of the most helpful supplementary resources to *Parachute*, including as it does John Holland's instrument (The Self-Directed Search) for determining the people-environments that you prefer. (We recommend, however, that after you have arrived at your final 'people-environment code,' you do not at that point turn back to the sample Occupations Finder, included in the book, since this is in my view a rather limited classification including as it does only the most common (and hence, most traditional) occupations. Instead, we recommend you use the translation of the Holland 'code' into the 'codes' of the 1965 Dictionary of Occupation Titles [p. 136f in Holland's book] in order to find out *clues*; and then we urgently recommend you go on your own information-gathering expeditions around town, as we suggested on page 135ff, asking people who are in the D.O.T. occupations that "go with" your Holland 'people-environment': "What *other* occupations are there that enable you to work with the same kind of people?" You will begin to discover some very unbelievable ways in which people make their living, while at the same time being surrounded by the kinds of people that appeal to *you*. Thus, when you begin to focus down on the kinds of occupations that interest you, you will be doing so from among a multitude of possibilities. Confucius say: When you choose a card, be sure it is from a full deck.)

Greiner, Peggy, et al., *Moving On: A guide for career and life planning*. Ulrich's B.B.M., Box D-1. Ann Arbor, MI 48106. 1982. $6.25, postpaid.

Crystal, John, and Bolles, Richard N., *Where Do I Go From Here With My Life? The Crystal Life Planning Manual*. 1974. A more detailed step-by-step explanation of the process described in chapters 5-7 of *Parachute*. From: Ten Speed Press, Box 7123, Berkeley, CA 94707. $9.95, paper.

Bolles, Richard N., *The Quick Job-Hunting Map: a fast way to help*. For the undecided college student or the housewife going back to work, or the mid-career changer, or the man or woman whose job has been terminated, or anyone else facing obstacles in the job-hunt. Ten Speed Press, Box 7123, Berkeley, CA 94707. 1979. $1.25. Specify Beginning Version or Advanced Version. The Advanced Version is on page 206 of this book.

If you dislike books, but like to listen to audio-cassettes, you may want to know that an overview (nothing more) of *Parachute* is available on two cassettes:

Bolles, Richard N., *A Skills Approach to Career Choice*. Available from the State Bar of Texas, Sales Desk—Career Tape, Box 12487, Austin, TX 78711. 1977. $12.00 postpaid; audio-cassette.

Bolles, Richard N., *How to Choose and Change Careers*. #20247. Psychology Today Cassettes, Box 278, Pratt Station, Brooklyn, NY 11205. $10.95, plus applicable state tax; audio-cassette.

Incidentally, the latter also has a cassette of:

Azrin, Nathan, *The Psychology of Job-Hunting. #20207. Same address, same price.*

Our Canadian readers will want to note that a number of the previous books—by Bolles, Lathrop, Crystal, etc.—as well as other (Canadian-oriented) publications, may be procured from the UNIVERSITY AND COLLEGE PLACEMENT ASSOCIATION (of Canada), 43 Eglinton Ave. E., Suite 1003, Toronto, Ontario M4P 1A2. Just ask for their publication list, related to Career Planning, Placement, Recruitment and Employment.

Jackson, Tom, *Guerrilla Tactics in the Job Market* (revised). Bantam Books, 666 Fifth Ave., New York, NY 10103. 1980. $2.95, paper.

Figler, Howard E., *The Complete Job Search Handbook: Presenting the Skills You Need to Get Any Job, And Have A Good Time Doing It.* Holt, Rinehart and Winston, 383 Madison Ave., New York, NY 10017. 1979. $5.95, paper. Tries to identify twenty skills the job-hunter needs in order to pull off a job hunt *successfully*.

Sheppard, Harold L., and Belitsky, A. Harvey, *Promoting Job Finding Success for the Unemployed*. (Summarizing part of the author's book: *The Job Hunt: Job-Seeking Behavior of Unemployed Workers in a Local Economy*. The Johns Hopkins Press, Baltimore, MD. 1966.) The W.E. Upjohn Institute, Kalamazoo, MI. 1968. Excellent pioneer research study on blue collar workers and successful job-hunting.

Germann, Richard, and Arnold, Peter, *Bernard Haldane Associates' Job and Career Building*. Ten Speed Press, Box 7123, Berkeley, CA 94707. 1981, 1980. $6.95, paper. A detailed description of how to find a job, once you know what it is you want to do.

Billingsley, Edmond, *Career Planning & Job Hunting for Today's Student: The Nonjob Interview Approach*. Goodyear Publishing Co., Inc., Santa Monica, CA 90401. 1978. $9.50, paper. A first-rate workbook, dealing in great detail, and step-by-step, with the process described in chapters 6 and 7 of *Parachute*.

Miller, Arthur F., and Mattson, Ralph T., *The Truth About You: Discover what you should be doing with your life*. Fleming H. Revell Co., Tappan, NJ. 1977. $6.95, hardcover. I like this a lot.

Stanat, Kirby W., with Patrick Reardon, *Job-Hunting Secrets & Tactics*. Published by Westwind Press, A Division of Raintree Publishers Ltd. Distributed by: Follett Publishing Co., 1010 W. Washington St., Chicago, IL 60607. 1977. $4.95, paper. Points out all the strengths and weaknesses of "the numbers game." Excellent tips.

Haldane, Bernard, *How to Make a Habit of Success*. Acropolis Books, Ltd., 2400 17th St. NW, Washington, DC 20009. $4.95, paper. One of the pioneer books in this field, first published in 1960.

Haldane, Bernard, and Jean, and Martin, Lowell, *Job Power: The Young People's Job Finding Guide*. Acropolis Books Ltd., 2400 17th St. NW, Washington, DC 20009. 1980. $4.95, paper. Undoubtedly the best book available for high school students.

Noer, David, *How to Beat the Employment Game*. Ten Speed Press, Berkeley, CA 94707. 1978. $4.95, paper. He tells the truth about the numbers game. Highly recommended.

Campbell, David P., *If you don't know where you're going, you'll probably end up somewhere else*. Argus Communications, Niles, IL. 1974. $1.95, paper.

Irish, Richard K., *Go Hire Yourself An Employer*. Anchor Press (Doubleday & Co., Inc.), New York, NY. 1978, 1973. $2.95, paper.

Edlund, Sidney and Mary, *Pick Your Job and Land It*. Sandollar Press, Santa Barbara, CA 93101. 1938. $4.95, paper. A classic among job-hunting books, still (mercifully) available.

FOR SPECIAL REFERENCE OR BROWSING

When *Parachute* was first published (in 1970) I had no difficulty whatsoever keeping up with the other books in this field. A good bookstore would have only about seven titles; a good library only about twenty. In little more than a decade, however, the task of "keeping up" has become virtually impossible. Largely as a consequence of *Parachute's* popularity and success (it has been, at this writing, on the *New York Times* bestseller list for the better part of four years, and on many other bestseller lists for comparable periods), publishers have become aware that books in this field are popular, and (in their jargon) "will sell"; consequently there has been an explosion of publishing in this field. Many books that are fine books, but nevertheless would not have ever seen the light of day, have thus been able to find a publisher. That is the good news. However: many books that are very bad, and would never have seen the light of day in another era, have also found a publisher. That is the bad news.

I hate to tell you this, but in my moderately-humble opinion there are a lot more books in the latter category than in the former. But *anyway*, I have compiled here a sampling of what's available. There are some gems that are missing, I'm sure. Even so, this is probably one of the most comprehensive and up-to-date bibliographies you're likely to find in this field.

So, begin by deciding in what area you want more help. In order to make this guide more usable, I have broken it down into a number of categories; namely:

1. The World of Work in America Today
2. Alternative Patterns of Work
3. Vocational or Career Planning
4. General Books on Job-Hunting
5. Job-Hunting Resources Especially for High School Students
6. For College Students
7. For Women
8. For Couples
9. For Minorities
10. For Handicapped Job-Hunters, including Ex-Offenders
11. For Executives and Those Interested in the Business World
12. On Your Own: Self-Employment, Part-Time Work
13. Making Your Living by Writing and Getting Published
14. Arts and Crafts, and Selling
15. Getting a Government Job
16. Volunteer Opportunities, Internships, and Organizations Dealing with Social Change
17. Mid-Life or Second Careers, on to Retirement
18. Resources Written from a Christian Perspective, or Directed at Clergy
19. The Nature of Your Brain and How to Stimulate Creativity and Decision-Making
20. Tuning Up Your Brain, and Increasing Your Powers: Exercises, Images and Fantasy
21. Analysis of Skills
22. Interviewing, Resumes, etc.
23. Surviving on the Job, Surviving 'Burnout,' and/or Getting Promoted
24. Concerning Being Fired, Rejected, Riffed, or Laid-Off

In the earlier editions of *Parachute*, I listed books in the most haphazard order imaginable. But, now I list the books—within each category—in the order of their publishing (or copyright) date, starting with the most recent books at the head of the list, and thence working back, in time. There are exceptions—usually within sub-sections.

Since *Parachute* is revised annually, this now enables me to put the new books at the beginning of each category, and drop the older books from the end of each category, yearly.

So, look over these resources to see what you can find that looks as though it might be helpful to *you. If you find a recent book listed here and think you might like to buy it, check out the possibility that it has been issued in paperback by the time this falls into your hands. If you are looking for one of the older books—in any category—and you simply cannot find it, it may well be out of print. In which case, see if your local library has a copy of it. If they do not, and you really want to be persistent, ask them to get it for you on inter-library loan. Or write directly to the publisher, whose address we have usually listed after each book, to see if you can still order it directly from them.*

Admittedly, not all readers of this book will have found their way back here into this bibliography. *As almost everyone knows, the only people who usually read bibliographies are:*

- people who want to know what some other good books are in the general field that they have been trained in; or
- people who are knowledgeable in the subject, and want to see what new books have appeared that they may not be aware of; or
- people who question seriously the scholarship and/or orthodoxy of the author, and want to scrutinize the bibliography as a test of their command of the field; or
- speed-reading graduates who have run through three libraries already, and are desperate for some new fodder for a long winter's night.

I will offer no comment on any of these prospective users of *this* bibliography, except to say that yours truly is a speed-reading dropout.

1. THE WORLD OF WORK IN AMERICA TODAY

Raines, John C.; Berson, Lenora E.; and Gracie, David McI., ed., *Community and Capital in Conflict: Plant Closings and Job Loss.* Temple University Press, Broad and Oxford Sts., Philadelphia, PA 19122. 1982, hardcover.

Kidron, Michael, and Pluto Press, *The State of the World Atlas.* Simon and Schuster, 1230 Avenue of the Americas, New York, NY 10020. 1981. $9.95, paper.

Ouchi, William, *Theory Z: How American Business Can Meet the Japanese Challenge.* Addison-Wesley, Jacob Way, Reading, MA 01867. 1981. $12.95, hardback.

O'Toole, James; Scheiber, Jane L.; and Wood, Linda C., eds., *Working: Changes and Choices.* Human Sciences Press, 72 Fifth Ave., New York, NY 10011. 1981. $12.95, paper. Includes a section on the changing notion of a career, by *Parachute's* author.

Raelin, Joseph A., *Building a Career: The effect of initial job experiences and related work attitudes on later employment.* W.E. Upjohn Institute for Employment Research, 300 S. Westnedge Ave., Kalamazoo, MI 49007. 1980. $4.50, paper.

U.S. Dept. of Labor, Bureau of Labor Statistics, *Handbook of Labor Statistics.* Supt. of Documents, U.S. Govt. Printing Off., Washington, DC 20402. $9.95, paper.

U.S. Dept. of Labor, Employment and Training Admin., *Selected Characteristics of Occupations Defined in the Dictionary of Occupational Titles.* Supt. of Documents, U.S. Govt. Printing Off., Washington, DC 20402. 1981. Paper.

U.S. Dept. of Labor, Employment and Training Administration, *Guide for Occupational Exploration.* Supt. of Documents, U.S. Govt. Printing Off., Washington, DC 20402. Stock #029-013-0080-2. 1979. Paper.

Bureau of Labor Statistics, *Occupational Outlook Handbook,* Supt. of Documents, U.S. Govt. Printing Off., Washington, DC 20402. $9, paper. 670-page encyclopedia of careers, covering hundreds of occupations and 35 major industries.

Reprints available from the *Occupational Outlook Handbook,* 1980-1 Edition: *Tomorrow's Jobs* (overview); particular occupational outlooks, for such jobs as *Metalworking, Printing, Clerical, Banking Service, Construction, Sales,* etc. Supt. of Documents, GPO, Washington, DC 20402. $1.25 each.

Maurer, Harry, *Not Working: Unemployed Men and Women Talk About How They Survive, Cope, and Even Prosper*. New American Library, 1633 Broadway, New York, NY 10019. 1981. $6.95, paper.

Cluster, Dick, and Rutter, Nancy, *Shrinking Dollars Vanishing Jobs: Why the Economy Isn't Working for You*. Beacon Press, Boston, MA. 1980. $5.95, paper (or hardcover).

Best, Fred, *Flexible Life Scheduling: Breaking the Education-Work-Retirement Lockstep*. Praeger Publishers, 521 Fifth Ave., New York, NY 10017. 1979. $8.95, paper.

Miller, Ann R., et al., eds., *Work, Jobs, and Occupations: A Critical Review of the Dictionary of Occupational Titles*. National Academy Press, 2101 Constitution Ave. NW, Washington, DC 20418. 1980. Paper.

U.S. Dept. of Labor and the U.S. Dept. of Health and Human Services, *Employment and Training Report of the President*. Superintendent of Documents, U.S. Govt. Printing Off., Washington, DC 20402. Paper.

U.S. Dept. of Labor Employment and Training Administration, *Exchange Earnings for Leisure: Findings of an Exploratory National Survey on Work Time Preferences*. For sale by the Superintendent of Documents, U.S. Govt. Printing Off., Washington, DC 20402. Paper.

Edwards, Patsy B., *Leisure Counseling Techniques*. Constructive Leisure, 511 N. La Cienega Blvd., Los Angeles, CA 90048. $11.95 per copy, postpaid (add 6% sales tax in California), paper.

Lathrop, Richard, *The Job Market*. The National Center for Job-Market Studies, Box 3651, Washington, DC 20007. 1978. $4.85, paper. What would happen if we decreased the length of the job-hunt in America, and other iconoclastic ideas which are also eminently sensible.

Miller, Gale, *Odd Jobs: The World of Deviant Work*, Prentice-Hall, Englewood Cliffs, NJ 07632. 1978. $4.95, paper.

Schrank, Robert, *Ten Thousand Working Days*. The MIT Press, 28 Carleton St., Cambridge, MA 02142. 1978. $5.95, postpaid.

Terkel, Studs, *Working*. Avon Paperback, New York, 1975. $3.50, paper. A classic.

Herzberg, Frederick, *Work and The Nature of Man*. New American Library, 1633 Broadway, New York, NY 10019. 1973, 1966. $1.50, paper. A classic on motivation.

Work in America. Special Task Force to the Secretary of Health, Education, and Welfare, administered by the W.E. Upjohn Institute for Employment Research. MIT Press (Cambridge, MA). 1973. Or: Available from National Technical Information Service, U.S. Dept. of Commerce, Springfield, VA 22151. December 1972. PB 214779. $6.75. Another classic.

2. ALTERNATIVE PATTERNS OF WORK

People are discovering there are all kinds of alternatives to the traditional nine to five, Monday through Friday job. Job-sharing with another worker, flex-time, where

you decide which hours of the day you want to work, the four-day work week, holding down three to five small jobs rather than one full-time job, working long and hard two or three days a week, then having the other days to yourself, etc. If such alternatives appeal to you, do your informational interviewing with people who have already gone that route, first; and then with smaller employers, who are often more open than are larger employers, to new patterns of work.

Omsted, Barney and Smith, Suzanne, *Job Sharer's Handbook: Working Less, Enjoying It More*. Viking-Penguin, 625 Madison Ave., New York, NY 10022. 1983.

Best, Fred, *Work Sharing: Issues, Policy Options and Prospects*. The W.E. Upjohn Institute for Employment Research, 300 W. Westnedge Ave., Kalamazoo, MI 49007. 1981. $5.00, paper.

Job Sharing in the Public Sector. New Ways to Work, 149 Ninth St., San Francisco, CA 94103. A survey of job-sharing programs in various public agencies. 1979. *New Ways to Work*, incidentally, in addition to the various publications contained on this list, issues two newsletters or journals. One is called "New Ways to Work Newsletter," which is available from the above address for a tax-free $20.00 donation (this includes not only a subscription to the Newsletter, but also discounts on their publications). The other is an international information exchange, published quarterly, on the subject of alternative work time, called "Work Times." A one year subscription is $50.00. NWW can also keep you informed of other organizations in the country devoted to job-sharing (they belong to a network called the National Job Sharing Network, and at this writing there are twenty-five such groups).

Levinson, Jay Conrad, *Earning Money Without a Job: The Economics of Freedom*. Holt, Rinehart, and Winston, 383 Madison Ave., New York, NY 10017. 1979. $4.95, paper. The first part of this book is the best, as Jay sets forth his idea of "modular economics"—putting together several small jobs, rather than one big one—and having plenty of time left over for leisure. (One in every 20 workers, currently, holds two or more jobs.)

Meier, Gretl, *Job-Sharing: A New Pattern for Quality of Work and Life*. W.E. Upjohn Institute for Employment Research, 300 S. Westnedge Ave., Kalamazoo, MI 49007. 1979. $4.50, paper.

Miller, Jeffrey M., *Innovations in Working Patterns*. The Communications Workers of America, 1925 K St. NW, Washington, DC 20036. 1978. A report of the U.S. Trade Union Seminar on Alternative Work Patterns in Europe, such as flexitime, elastic workweek, phased retirement, etc.

Robinson, David, *Alternative Work Patterns: Changing Approaches to Work Scheduling*. Work in America Institute, Inc., 700 White Plains Rd., Scarsdale, NY 10583. 1978, 1976. $5.00, paper. Discusses such patterns as flexitime, staggered work hours, job-sharing, permanent part-time, etc.—together with case studies.

Working Less But Enjoying It More: A Guide to Splitting or Sharing Your Job. New Ways to Work, 149 Ninth St., San Francisco, CA 94103, (415) 552-1000. A description of the

process involved in negotiating a shared job. $4.25.

Work is for People: Innovative Workplaces of the San Francisco Bay Area. New Ways to Work, 149 Ninth St., San Francisco, CA 94103, (415) 552-1000. Descriptions and discussions of workplaces experimental in process or product. 1978. $4.75.

Adjusting Work Time: Three New Models. New Ways to Work, 149 Ninth St., San Francisco, CA 94103, (415) 552-1000. Descriptions of three models of reduced work time: work sharing, job sharing, leave time. 1978. $3.50.

First National Directory on Part-Time and Flexitime Programs. National Council for Alternative Work Patterns, 1925 K St., NW, Suite 308A, Washington, DC 20036. 1978.

Babson, Steve, and Brigham, Nancy, *What's Happening to Our Jobs?* Popular Economics Press, Box 221, Somerville, MA 02143. 1976. $1.45.

Vocations for Social Change, *No Bosses Here: A Manual on Working Collectively.* VSX, Box 211, Essex Station, Boston, MA 02112. 1976. $3.00, paper. Deals with how to set up and run a collective. Detailed and practical.

See also Appendix C, Section VI, p. 301

3. VOCATIONAL OR CAREER PLANNING

Rockcastle, Madeline T., ed./author, *'Where to Start': An Annotated Career Planning Bibliography.* Cornell University Career Center, 14 East Ave., Ithaca, NY 14853. 1981-2, third ed. Paper.

Bloomfield, William M., *The Vocational Action Plan: A Workbook.* William Bloomfield and Associates, Inc., 90 Park St., Ste. 22, Brookline, MA 02146. 1982. Paper.

Borchard, David C., Kelly, John J., and Weaver, Nancy Pat K., *Your Career: Choices, Chances, Changes.* Kendall/Hunt Publishing Co., 2460 Kerper Blvd., Dubuque, IA 52001. 1982. Paper.

Gale, Barry and Linda, *Discover What You're Best At: The national career aptitude system and career directory.* Simon & Schuster, 1230 Avenue of the Americas, New York, NY 10020. 1982. $8.95, paper.

Hagberg, Janet, and Leider, Richard, *The Inventurers: Excursions in Life and Career Renewal.* Addison-Wesley Publishing Co., Jacob Way, Reading, MA 01867. 1982. $7.95, paper.

Tough, Allen, *Intentional Changes: A Fresh Approach to Helping People Change.* Follett Publishing Co./Dept. DM T82-39, 1010 W. Washington Blvd., Chicago, IL 60607. 1982. $17.95, hardcover.

Russell, P.A., and Vegso, K.A., *Come Alive! A Career and Life Planning Workbook.* Adult Resource Center, Continuing Education and Public Service, University of Akron, Akron, OH 44325. 1981. There are also six career and life planning videotapes that supplement this workbook. They may be ordered or previewed from: Great Plains National, Box 80669, Lincoln, NE 68501, or (in the state of Ohio) from: Ohio Educational Broadcasting Network, 2470 North Star Rd., Columbus, OH 43221.

Leider, Richard J., and Harding, James S., *Taking Stock: A daily self-management journal.* Taking Stock, Box 8709, Portland, OR 97208. 1981. $7.95 plus .50 postage, paper.

Healy, Charles, *Career Development: Counseling through the Life stages.* Allyn & Bacon, 470 Atlantic Ave., Boston, MA 02210. 1982. $19.95, hardcover.

Crites, John O., *Career Counseling: Models, Methods, and Materials.* McGraw-Hill, 1221 Avenue of the Americas, New York, NY 10020. 1981. $14.95, hardcover.

U.S. Dept. of Labor, Bureau of Labor Statistics, *Exploring Careers.* Supt. of Documents, Washington, DC 20402. $10.00.

Pilder, Richard J., and William F., *How to Find Your Life's Work*. Prentice-Hall, Englewood Cliffs, NJ 07632. 1981. $4.95, paper.

Deutsch, Arnold R., *The Complete Job Book*. Cornerstone Library, Inc., 1230 Avenue of the Americas, New York, NY 10020. 1980. $6.95, paper.

Miller, Donald B., *Careers '80/'81*. Vitality Associates, Box 154, Saratoga, CA 95070. 1980. $11.95, paper.

Morrisey, George, *Getting Your Act Together: Goal Setting for Fun, Health and Profit*. John Wiley & Sons Inc., 605 Third Ave., New York, NY 10158. 1980. $7.95, paper. Also available in audio-cassette.

Rinella, Richard J., and Robbins, Claire C., *Career Power! A Manual for Personal Career Advancement*. Amacom, 135 W. 50th St., New York, NY 10020. 1981. $14.95, hardcover.

Townley, John, *New Age Career Cycles: A Planetary Guide to the Patterns of Opportunity*. Destiny Books, 377 Park Ave. S., New York, NY 10016. 1980. $7.95, paper.

Guide for Occupational Exploration. Supt. of Documents, U.S. Govt. Printing Off., Washington, DC 20402. 1979. $11.00. Occupations organized by interest and job title.

Jelinek, Mariann, *Career Management for the Individual and the Organization*. St. Clair Press, 4 E. Huron St., Chicago, IL 60611. 1979. Paper.

Mitchell, Anita M; Jones, Brian G; and Krumboltz, John D., editors, *Social Learning and Career Decision Making*. The Carroll Press, 43 Squantum St., Cranston, RI 02920. 1979.

Mitchell, Joyce Slayton, *The Men's Career Book: Work and Life Planning For a New Age*. Bantam Books, Inc., 666 Fifth Ave., New York, NY 10019. 1979. $2.25, paper.

Tiedeman, David V., *Career Development: Designing Our Career Machines*. The Carroll Press, 43 Squantum St., Cranston, RI 02920. 1979. $9.95, paper. How to use computers to design a career-decision-and-development system.

Basso, Janice L.; Kendall, Nancy P.; and Miller, Donna S.M., *Creating a Canadian Career Information Centre*. University and College Placement Association, 43 Eglinton Ave. E., Suite 1003, Toronto, Ontario M4P 1A2. 1979.

Feldman, Beverly Neuer, *Jobs/Careers serving children and youth* (including Supplement: Appendix C and Index–inserted into the book, but separate). Till Press, Box 27816, Los Angeles, CA 90027. 1978. $9.95, paper. Groups the jobs and careers according to how much education the job-hunter has had. For all those who want to work with youth or children.

Kirn, Arthur G., and Kirn, Marie O'Donahoe, *Life Work Planning*. Fourth edition, McGraw-Hill Book Co., 1221 Avenue of the Americas, New York, NY 10020. 1978, 1975, 1972, 1971. $13.95, hardcover.

Schein, Edgar H., *Career Dynamics: matching individual and organizational needs*. Addison-Wesley, Jacob Way, Reading, MA 01867. 1978.

Shepard, Herbert A., *The Career Management System: Life Planning*. Management Decision Systems, Inc., Box 35, Darien, CT 06820. 1976. Cassettes and workbook.

Cameron, Clark T., *The Cameron Vocational Self-Evaluation and Guidance System*. Theta House, 301 Lyon St., San Francisco, CA 94117. 1975. Paper.

Ford, George A., and Lippitt, Gordon L., *Planning Your Future: A workbook for personal goal setting*. University Associates, Inc., 7596 Eads Ave., La Jolla, CA 92037. 1976, 1972.

McClure, Larry, *Career Education Survival Manual: A Guidebook for Career Educators and Their Friends*. Olympus Publishing Co., 1670 E. 13th S., Salt Lake City, UT 84105. 1975. An absolutely superb little handbook for everyone who wants to understand more about how to relate education to the world of work (and vice versa). Imaginatively laid out, and written by one of the experts in this field.

Hoyt, Kenneth, et al., *Career Education: What It Is and How to Do It*. Second edition. Olympus Publishing Co., 1670 E. 13th S., Salt Lake City, UT 84105. 1974. $6.95.

Cosgrave, Gerald, *Career Planning: Search for a Future.* Guidance Centre/Faculty of Education/University of Toronto. 1973. Available from Customer Service, Teacher's College Press, 1234 Amsterdam Ave., New York, NY 10027. $4.45; or from Consulting Psychologist's Press, 577 College Ave., Palo Alto, CA 94306. It relates to John L. Holland's six people-environments.

Hoppock, Robert, *Occupational Information: Where to Get It and How to Use It in Counseling and in Teaching.* Third edition. McGraw Hill, New York, NY. 1967. A pioneer in this field.

Super, Donald E., et al., *Career Development: Self-Concept Theory. Essays in Vocational Development.* College Board Publication Orders, Box 2815, Princeton, NJ 08540. 1963. $4.50, paper. Another pioneer in the field.

The books on individual fields or careers would fill a forty-foot bookshelf, but here are *some* of the books to be found in the bookstores currently. I have *not* included here books on such fields as Being An Executive, A Writer, A Craftsperson, A Government Employee, or Self-Employed Person, and these have their own separate sections later in this bibliography. Further, a section on resources for teachers is to be found in Appendix E, section 4.

Hopke, William E., ed., *The Encyclopedia of Careers and Vocational Guidance,* 4th rev. ed., Doubleday and Co., Inc., 245 Park Ave., New York, NY 10167. 1978. $49.95 (2 vol.), hardcover.

Rucker, T. Donald, *Pharmacy: Career Planning and Professional Opportunities.* Health Administration Press, University of Michigan, 1021 E. Huron St., Ann Arbor, MI 48109. 1981. $24.00, paper.

Katz, Judith A., *The Business of Show Business.* Harper & Row, 10 E. 53rd St., New York, NY 10022. 1981. $4.95, paper.

Mainstream Access, Inc., *The Data Processing/Information Technology Job Finder.* Prentice-Hall, Inc., Englewood Cliffs, NJ 07632. 1981. $5.95, paper.

Mainstream Access, Inc., *The Public Relations Job Finder.* Prentice-Hall, Inc., Englewood Cliffs, NJ 07632. 1981. $6.95, paper.

Rosenthal, Steven M., *How To Enter the Field of Human Resource and Organizational Development,* Part I. O.D. Network, 1011 Park Ave., Plainfield, NJ 07060. 1981. Paper.

Jaques Cattell Press, ed. *Energy Research Programs.* R.R. Bowker Co., 1180 Avenue of the Americas, New York, NY 10036. 1981. $75.00, hardcover.

Ericson, Kay, *The Solar Jobs Book: How To Take Part in the New Movement toward Energy Self-Sufficiency.* Brick House Publishing Co., 34 Essex St., Andover, MA 01810. 1980. $7.95, paper.

Miller, Saul, *After Law School: Finding a Job in a Tight Market.* 1978. $6.95, paper. Little, Brown and Co., 34 Beacon St., Boston, MA 02106.

4. GENERAL BOOKS ON JOB-HUNTING

At the United Nations, when Swahili is being spoken, most people from other nations do not understand—until, over the earphones, the speech is translated into their own language. So, with job-hunting. Many do not understand the language of *Parachute.* Yet the same thoughts, spoken in another's style of writing, say Howard Figler's or Tom Jackson's, may suddenly hit home to those readers. There are over 20,000,000 different job hunters out there, in an average year. No one book will ever be understood by them all. Hence, we will always need many different books on job-hunting; and the more different 'styles' or 'languages,' the better. This section of the bibliography deals with job-hunting books written for a general readership. The next fourteen sections deal with job-hunting books written for specific kinds of job-hunters.

Every book listed in these twenty-four sections of the bibliography has something valuable in it. But in some of the books it's like panning for gold. Minutes, hours or even days may go by, without your finding more than a few nuggets. Others (mercifully) are like a miner striking a rich vein of ore. You will see which is which. I strongly advise *browsing* in your library or some laid-back bookstore, before buying. Whatever you do, don't believe the book jackets or covers. Sometimes the most creative writing in the whole book is on that jacket or cover.

Karmos, Joe and Ann, Stafford, Emily, and Altekruse, Michael, *Help for Job Hunters*. University Press of America, Box 19101, Washington, DC 20036. 1982. $7.95, paper.

Kravette, Steve, *Get a Job in 60 Seconds*. Para Research, Inc., Whistlestop Mall, Rockport, MA 01966. 1982. $5.95, paper.

Munch, Glenn R., *Getting It Together! The practical job search guide*. General Methods Enterprises, 1763 White Oak Ave., Baltimore, MD 21234. 1982. $6, postpaid.

Straub, Joseph T., *The Job Hunt: How to Compete & Win*. Prentice-Hall, Inc., Englewood Cliffs, NJ 07632. 1981. $4.95, paper.

Half, Robert, *The Robert Half Way to Get Hired in Today's Job Market*. Rawson, Wade Publishers, Inc., 630 Third Ave., 10017 New York, NY 10017. 1981. $10.95, hardcover.

Martin, Phyllis, *Introduction to the Job-Hunt Success Kit*. Center for Career Development, 11385 Landon Lane, Cincinnati, OH 45246. 1981. Paper.

Martin, Phyllis, *How to Help the Job-Seeker*. Center for Career Development, 11385 Landon Lane, Cincinnati, OH 45246. 1981. $4.00, paper.

Martin, Phyllis, *Job-Hunt Success Kit, Part I: Action Book*. Center for Career Development, 11385 Landon Lane, Cincinnati, OH 45246. 1981. Paper.

Martin, Phyllis, *Sharpening Your Image*. Center for Career Development, 11385 Landon Lane, Cincinnati, OH 45246. 1981. Paper.

Petit, Ron E., *The Career Connection: Keys to employment*. Professional Development Services, Box 750, Harrisonburg, VA 22801. 1981. Paper.

Thomas, Martha, *Guide to Outdoor Careers*. Stackpole Books, Cameron & Kelker Streets, Box 1831, Harrisburg, PA 17105. 1981. $14.95, hardcover.

Van Roden, Albert C., and Bachhuber, Thomas D., *You're Hired! The Best Way to Find and Land a More Satisfying Job*. Liberty Publishing Co., Inc., 50 Scott Adam Rd., Cockeysville, MD 21030. 1981. $2.95, paper.

Feingold, S. Norman, and Winkler, Glenda, *Nine Hundred Thousand Plus Jobs Annually: Published Sources of Employment Listings*. Garrett Park Press, Garrett Park, MD 20766. Cites periodicals which list job announcements. 1982. $9.95, paper.

Martin, Phyllis, *Martin's Magic Formula for Getting the Right Job*. St. Martin's Press, 175 Fifth Ave., New York, NY 10010. 1981. $5.95, paper.

Billhartz, Celeste, *The Complete Book of Job Hunting, Finding, Changing*. Rainbow Collection, Box 75, Akron, OH 44309. 1980. $7.95, paper.

Jackson, Tom, and Mayleas, Davidyne, *The Hidden Job Market for the Eighties*. Quadrangle/The New York Times Book Co., 3 Park Ave., New York, NY 10016. 1981. $9.95, paper.

Job Information and Seeking Training Program Instructor's Guide and Job Seekers Workbook. JIST, 1001 W. 10th St., Indianapolis, IN 46202. 1980. Paper.

Komar, John J., *The Great Escape From Your Dead-End Job*. New Century Publishers Inc., 275 Old New Brunswick Rd., Piscataway, NJ 08854. 1980. $4.95, paper.

Moore, Charles G., *The Career Game*. Ballantine Books, 201 E. 50th St., New York, NY 10022. 1976. $5.95, paper. Written by an economist, from an economist's point of view. Excellent section on questions to ask during informational interviewing.

5. JOB-HUNTING RESOURCES ESPECIALLY FOR HIGH SCHOOL STUDENTS

Douglas, Martha C., *Go For It: How to Get Your First Good Job.* Ten Speed Press, Box 7123, Berkeley, CA 94707. 1983. $5.95, paper. Based on Ms. Douglas' experience as coordinator of an industry training program for teenagers, at the *Contra Costa Times* newspaper in Walnut Creek, California.

Nadler, Burton Jay, *Arming Yourself for a Part-time or Summer Job.* Olympus Publishing Co., 1670 E. 13th S., Salt Lake City, UT 84105. 1982. Paper.

Hardigree, Peggy, *Working Outside: A Career and Self-Employment Handbook.* Harmony Books, A Division of Crown Publishers, Inc., One Park Ave., New York, NY 10016. 1980. $7.95, paper.

O'Brien, Barbara, editor, *Summer Employment Directory of the United States.* Writer's Digest Books, 9933 Alliance Rd., Cincinnati, OH 45242. This book comes out each year. It lists 50,000 summer job openings at resorts, campuses, amusement parks, hotels, conferences and training centers, ranches, restaurants, national parks, etc. 1000 places, in all.

Woodworth, D.J., ed., *Overseas Summer Jobs 1983: Where the jobs are and how to get them.* Writer's Digest Books, 9933 Alliance Rd., Cincinnati, OH 45242. $7.95, paper.

Shedd, Charlie, ed., *You Are Somebody Special.* McGraw-Hill Book Co., 1221 Avenue of the Americas, New York, NY 10020. Chapters are written by various authors including Bill Cosby, Irene Kassorla, Rick Little (who created the idea for the book), Eugene Nida, and yours truly, among others. 1978. $2.25, paper. Written particularly for seniors in high school.

Mitchell, Joyce Slayton, *The Work Book—A Guide to Skilled Jobs.* Bantam Books, Inc., 666 Fifth Ave., New York, NY 10103. 1978. $2.25, paper. Skilled jobs, by Joyce's definition, require 2 weeks to 2 years of schooling or training, beyond high school. This book is largely based on the *Occupational Outlook Handbook*, and reviews in the *Vocational Guidance Quarterly*. Interesting chapter on "work talk—a new language" for the graduating high school student.

Career World—The Continuing Guide to Careers (a periodical), Joyce Lain Kennedy, Executive Editor. From $3.25 up, per subscription. Curriculum Innovations, Inc., 501 Lake Forest Ave., Highwood, IL 60040.

Garrison, Clifford B., et al., *Finding a job you feel good about.* Argus Communications, 7440 Natchez Ave., Niles, IL 60648. 1977. $2.50, paper. Good for high school students, especially.

Carkhuff, Robert, *The Art of Developing a Career.* Human Resource Development Press, Box 863, Dept. M-18, Amherst, MA 01002. 1974. $6.95 for students' guide; $9.95 for helper's guide. For grades 10–16.

6. FOR COLLEGE STUDENTS

Calano, James, and Salzman, Jeff, *Real World 101: What college never taught you about the new professionalism.* New View Press, 5370 Manhattan Circle, Suite 202, Boulder, CO 80303. 1982. $11.95, hardcover.

Goulet, Theresa, *Sell Yourself! The career handbook for Canadian university students and prospective students.* Atgood Publications, Ltd., 401 Varsity Estates Bay NW, Calgary, Alberta, Canada T3B 2W7. 1982. $9.95, paper.

Wallace, Wayne, et al., *For Your Action: A practical job search guide for the liberal arts student.* Arts and Sciences Placement Office, Indiana University, 326 N. Jordan, Bloomington, IN 47405. Paper.

Munschauer, John L., *Jobs for English Majors and Other Smart People.* Peterson's Guides, Inc., Box 2123, Princeton, NJ 08540. 1981. $6.95, paper.

Cook, William A., and Gonyea, James C., *Putting Liberal Arts to Work.* New England Center for Career Development, Box 293, Hooksett, NH 03106. 1981. Paper.

Kingstone, Brett, *The Student Entrepreneur's Guide.* Ten Speed Press, Box 7123, Berkeley, CA 94707. 1981. $4.95, paper. What college students are able to do as entrepreneurs, while still in college, has always staggered my imagination. One of them tells how it's done.

Schmidt, Peggy J., *Making It On Your First Job, When You're Young, Inexperienced, and Ambitious.* Avon Books, 959 Eighth Ave., New York, NY 10019. 1981. $2.95, paper.

Feingold, S. Norman, *Counseling for Careers in the 1980's.* Garrett Park Press, Garrett Park, MD 20766. 1979. $6.95, paper.

McBurney, William J., *Where The Jobs Are 1982.* Chilton Book Co., Chilton Way, Radnor, PA 19089. 1981. $6.95, paper.

Figler, Howard E., *Path: A Career Workbook for Liberal Arts Students.* The Carroll Press Publishers, Box 8113, Cranston, RI 02920. 1979, 1975. Second edition, completely revised. Good stuff.

Morgan, Richard L., *Leaving the Formation: A Career Planning Workbook for Community College Students.* Addison-Wesley, General Books Division, Jacob Way, Reading, MA 01867. 1979. Paper.

Thain, Richard J., *The Managers: Career Alternatives For The College Educated.* The College Placement Council, Inc., Box 2263, Bethlehem, PA 18001. $4.95, paper.

Mitchell, Joyce Slayton, *Stopout! Working Ways To Learn.* Avon Books, 959 Eighth Ave., New York, NY 10019. 1978. Using learning in order to work, using working in order to learn. $2.95, paper.

Fox, Marcia R., *Put Your Degree to Work: A Career Planning and Job Hunting Guide for the New Professional.* W.W. Norton Co., 500 Fifth Ave., New York, NY 10036. 1979. Advice for the new professional with a graduate degree. $4.95, paper.

Shingleton, John, and Bao, Robert, *College to Career: Finding Yourself in the Job Market.* McGraw-Hill Book Co., 1221 Avenue of the Americas, New York, NY 10020. 1977. $5.95, paper.

Malnig, Lawrence, and Morrow, Sandra L., *What Can I Do With A Major In...?* Garrett Park Press, Garrett Park, MD 20766. 1975. $8.95, prepaid; paper. Tells you all the career paths a major can branch out into, based on the experience of graduates at one college, at least.

Loughary, John W., and Ripley, Theresa M., *This Isn't Quite What I Had in Mind: A Career Planning Program for College Students.* United Learning Corporation, 3255 Olive St., Eugene, OR 97405. 1974. Very entertaining.

Our Canadian readers will want to know that their University and College Placement Association (43 Eglinton Ave. E., Suite 1003, Toronto, Ontario, M4P 1A2) puts out a number of publications for those related to the college scene. These include:

McClure, Ross M., *Destiny: Career Planning Manual.* 1980. Paper.

Gartley, Wayne, ed., *Your Future After High School.* 1980. Paper.

________, ed., *1980-1981 Annuaire D'Orientation Professionnelle.* Association de placement universitaire et collegial, 1980. Paper.

Carney, T.F., *Teaching Effective Letter Writing.* 1980. Paper.

________, *Teaching Effective Resume Writing.* 1980. Paper.

University of Toronto Career Counselling and Placement Centre, *Guide to Resume Writing.* 1978. Paper.

Dunlop, Elizabeth, et al., *Career Opportunities for Liberal Arts Graduates.* 1979. Paper.

Books on summer jobs are listed in the previous section.

7. FOR WOMEN

Now, just a (perhaps unnecessary) word of common sense—uncommon common sense, sad to say—about this whole business of job-hunting publications for women. There is a difference between *form* and *content*. In these days of liberated consciousness (or conscious liberation?) there is a great preoccupation with *form*: i.e., is the book written by a woman, or does it at least use non-sexist language? But let us not forget *content*, please. A book that does little more than outline the old numbers game (see chapter 2) is not going to do you much good, no matter how superb (i.e., non-sexist) its form may be. On the other hand, a book with helpful *content* (i.e., the creative minority's prescription) is going to help you, no matter how chauvinistic its language might be (just shut your eyes, and grit your teeth). The best of all possible worlds, of course, is to have both: a book whose form *and* content are both superb: that's the ideal women's book. But don't get hypnotized just by *form*, please.

Triere, Lynette, with Peacock, Richard, *Learning to Leave*. Contemporary Books, 180 N. Michigan Ave., Chicago, IL 60601. 1982. $15.95, hardcover. For any woman contemplating separation or divorce.

Phillips, Carole, *The Money Workbook for Women: A Step-by-Step Guide to Managing Your Personal Finances*. Arbor House Publishing, 235 E. 45th St., New York, NY 10017. 1982. $5.95, paper.

Buskirk, Richard H., and Miles, Beverly, *Beating Men at Their Own Game*. McGraw-Hill, Inc., 1221 Avenue of the Americas, New York, NY 10020. 1981. $5.95, paper.

Butler, Pamela E., *Self-Assertion for Women*. Harper & Row, 10 E. 53rd St., New York, NY 10022. 1981. $6.95, paper.

Goldfein, Donna, *Every Woman's Guide to Getting Ready for the Right Career*. Celestial Arts, 231 Adrian Rd., Millbrae, CA 94030. 1981. $5.95, paper.

Shields, Laurie, *Displaced Homemakers: Organizing for a New Life*. McGraw-Hill Book Co., 1221 Avenue of the Americas, New York, NY 10020. 1980. $5.95, paper.

Berne, Ph.D., Patricia; Dubin, Judy; and Muchnick, Sherri, *You've Got A Great Past Ahead of You; How Women Can Expand Their Work Options*. Bobbs-Merrill Co., Four W. 58th St., New York, NY 10019. 1980. $10.95, hardcover.

Burack, Elmer H.; Albrecht, Maryann; and Seitler, Helene, *Growing: A Woman's Guide to Career Satisfaction*. Lifetime Learning Publications, 10 Davis Dr., Belmont, CA 94002. 1980. $6.95, paper.

Catalyst, *What to Do with the Rest of Your Life: the Catalyst Career Guide for Women in the '80s*. Simon and Schuster, 1230 Avenue of the Americas, New York, NY 10020. 1980. $16.95, hardcover.

General Services Admin., *Women-Owned Business Directory 1980—Iowa, Kansas, Missouri, Nebraska*. General Services Admin., Region 6, 1500 E. Bannister Rd., Kansas City, MO 64131. 1980. Paper.

Kleiman, Carol, *Women's Networks*. Harper & Row, Publishers, Inc., 10 E. 53 St., New York, NY 10022. 1980. $5.95, paper.

Landau, Suzanne, and Bailey, Geoffrey, *The Landau Strategy: How Working Women Win Top Jobs*. Playboy Paperbacks, 1633 Broadway, New York, NY 10019. 1981. $2.50, paper.

Lee, Nancy, *Targeting the Top: Everything a Woman Needs to Know to Develop a Successful Career in Business, Year after Year*. Doubleday and Co., Inc., 245 Park Ave., New York, NY 10167. 1980. $11.95, hardcover.

Mouat, Lucia, *Back to Business: A Woman's Guide to Reentering The Job Market*. Signet/New American Library, Inc., 1633 Broadway, New York, NY 10019. 1980. $1.95, paper.

Welch, Mary Scott, *Networking*. Harcourt Brace Jovanovich, Inc., 757 Third Ave., New York, NY 10017. 1980. $9.95, hardcover.

Business & Professional Women's Foundation, *Where The Jobs Are: An Annotated Selected Bibliography*. B&PWF, 2012 Massachusetts Ave. NW, Washington, DC 20036. 1979. This foundation publishes a number of other booklets which may be of interest to women job-hunters or career-changers, including *Financial Aid: Where to Get It, How to Use It* (1978); *The Status of Clerical Workers* (1979); and some research not yet published. The foundation also runs workshops, conferences and seminars on career planning, at various places around the country, from time to time. If you are interested, you can ask them about these, when you write.

Calvert, Jr., Robert, *Affirmative Action: A Comprehensive Manual*. Garrett Park Press, Garrett Park, MD 20766. $14.00, prepaid. Written for employers, but useful to job-hunting women (and minorities) as well.

Lederer, Muriel, *Blue-Collar Jobs For Women.* A Sunrise Book. E.P. Dutton, Two Park Ave., New York, NY 10016. 1979. $7.95, paper.

Farley, Jennie, *Affirmative Action and the Woman Worker: Guidelines for Personnel Management.* Amacom, 135 W. 50th St., New York, NY 10020. 1979. $14.95, hardcover.

King, David, and Levine, Karen, *The Best Way in the World for a Woman to Make Money.* Warner Books, Box 690, New York, NY 10019. 1979. $2.95, paper.

Mitchell, Joyce Slayton, *I Can Be Anything: Careers and Colleges for Young Women.* Bantam Books, Inc., 666 Fifth Ave., New York, NY 10103. 1978. $2.25, paper.

Harragan, Betty Lehan, *Games Mother Never Taught You: Corporate Gamesmanship for Women.* Warner Books, Inc., 75 Rockefeller Plaza, New York, NY 10019. 1978, 1977. $2.50, paper. Detailing corporate politics as practiced by males, and how upwardly-mobile female executives can map their own game plan.

Trahey, Jane, *Jane Trahey on Women & Power.* Avon Books, 959 Eighth Ave., New York, NY 10019. 1978, 1977. $2.25, paper. A book about who's got power, and how women can get power.

Directory of Career Resources for Women. Ready Reference Press, Box 5169, Santa Monica, CA 90405. $37.50.

Doss, Martha Merrill, ed., *The Directory of Special Opportunities for Women.* Garrett Park Press, Garrett Park, MD 20766. $18.95. Directory of educational opportunities, career information, networks and peer counseling.

Scholz, Nelle Tumlin; Prince, Judith Sosebee; and Miller, Gordon Porter, *How To Decide, A Workbook for Women.* Avon Books, 959 Eighth Ave., New York, NY 10019. 1978, 1975. $4.95, paper. Where are you as a woman, who are you, what do you need to know, and how do you take action?

Ekstrom, Ruth B.; Harris, Abigail M.; and Lockheed, Marlaine E., *How To Get College Credit for What You Have Learned As A Homemaker and Volunteer.* Educational Testing Service, Princeton, NJ 08540. 1977. Even for those not interested in college credit, but only in assessing the skills they picked up or sharpened as a volunteer or homemaker, this is an excellent resource. Classifies the skills under the various roles: administrator/manager, financial manager, personnel manager, trainer, advocate/change agent, public relations/communicator, problem surveyor, researcher, fund raiser, counselor, youth group leader, group leader for a serving organization, museum staff assistant (docent), tutor/teacher's aide, manager of home finances, home nutritionist, home child caretaker, home designer and maintainer, home clothing and textile specialist, and home horticulturist. *Very* helpful book, with accompanying aids.

A Guide for Affirmative Action. Equal Employment Opportunity in State and Local Governments. U.S. Office of Personnel Management (formerly the Civil Service Commission), Washington, DC. They also publish a wealth of other material on Equal Opportunity for those who want to pursue the legal route, *while at the same time* using the principles in this book as their alternative route. (Court cases in some places are alleged to have a backlog equivalent to a two-year waiting period, and you don't want to wait *that* long for a job, do you?) Materials available from: U.S. Office of Personnel Management, Bureau of Intergovernmental Personnel Programs, Washington, DC 20415.

Books to help women with the world of work, appear faster than one can record them. Browse your local bookstore to see the full range of what's available, please.

8. FOR COUPLES

With more and more married women in the work-force, a body of literature is beginning to appear, and grow, concerning the problem of Both Partners Working:

Greiff, Barrie S., and Munter, Preston K., *Tradeoffs: Executive, Family, and Organizational Life*. New American Library, 1633 Broadway, New York, NY 10019. 1981. $3.50, paper.

Irish, Richard K., *How To Live Separately Together: A Guide for Working Couples*. Doubleday and Co., Inc., 245 Park Ave., New York, NY 10167. 1981. $11.95, hardcover.

Bird, Caroline, *The Two-Paycheck Marriage*. Pocket Books, 1230 Avenue of the Americas, New York, NY 10020. 1979. $2.75, paper.

Hall, Francine S., and Hall, Douglas T., *The Two-Career Couple*. Addison-Wesley, Jacob Way, Reading, MA 01867. 1979. $5.95, paper.

9. FOR MINORITIES

The Black Resource Guide. Black Resource Guide, Inc., 501 Oneida Pl., NW, Ste. 500, Washington, DC 20011. $10.00. A comprehensive listing of Black resources in the U.S.

Trower-Subira, *Black Folks' Guide to Making Big Money in America*. Very Serious Business Enterprises, Box 356, Newark, NJ 07101. 1980. $11.00, hardcover.

Douglas, Denise, *Career Planning for Chicano/Latino Students*. Spanish Career Materials Development, San Jose City College, 2100 Moorpark Ave., San Jose, CA 95128. Paper.

Johnson, Willis L., ed., *Directory of Special Programs for Minority Group Members: Career Information Services, Employment Skills Banks, Financial Aid Services*—Third Edition. Garrett Park Press, Garrett Park, MD 20766. 1980. $19.00, paper.

Wallace, Phyllis, with Datcher, Linda, and Malveaux, Julianne, *Black Women in the Labor Force*. The MIT Press, 28 Carleton St., Cambridge, MA 02142. 1980. $16.00, postpaid.

Wiseberg, Laurie S., and Scoble, Harry M., eds., *North American Human Rights Directory*. Garrett Park Press, Garrett Park, MD 20766. 1980. Prepaid, $11.00; billed, $12.00, paper.

Cole, Katherine W., ed., *Minority Organizations: A National Directory*. Garrett Park Press, Garrett Park, MD 20766. 1978. $16.00, paper. An annotated directory of 2700 Black, Hispanic, Native, and Asian American organizations.

Directory of Career Resources for Minorities, First Edition. Ready Reference Press, Box 5169, Santa Monica, CA 90405. $37.50.

Financial Aid for Minority Students in: Allied Health, Business, Education, Engineering, Law, Mass Communications, Medicine, or Science. $3.00 per booklet, or $20.00 for all eight. Available from Garrett Park Press, Garrett Park, MD 20766.

"Career Planning Needs of Unemployed Minority Persons," Special Issue of the *Journal of Employment Counseling*, Vol. 15, No. 4, December 1978. $2.50 per copy, from Publication Sales, American Personnel & Guidance Assn., 5203 Leesburg Pike, Falls Church, VA 22041.

10. FOR HANDICAPPED JOB-HUNTERS, INCLUDING EX-OFFENDERS

Rabby, Rami, *Locating, Recruiting, and Hiring the Disabled*. Pilot Books, 347 Fifth Ave., New York, NY 10016. 1981. $3.95, paper. Includes over 500 sources of information covering referral agencies, media lists and other points of contact for employers.

Eisenberg, Myron G.; Griggins, Cynthia; and Duval, Richard J., ed., *Disabled People as Second-Class Citizens*. Springer Publishing Co., 200 Park Ave. S., New York, NY 10003. 1982. $26.95, hardcover.

Hahn, Andrew, and Friedman, Barry, *The Effectiveness of Two Job Search Assistance Programs for Disadvantaged Youth.* Center for Employment & Income Studies, Heller Graduate School, Brandeis University, Waltham, MA 02254. 1981. Paper.

Bruck, Dr. Lilly, Producer, *The Assertive Jobseeker: A Telecommunications Conference of nationally prominent experts.* In Touch Networks, 322 W. 48th St., New York, NY 10036. A three-cassette series, with speakers on such subjects as job-hunting and assertiveness, including *Parachute's* author. $9.00 per set.

Root, Meganne, *Helping Offenders Find Meaningful Employment.* PROJECT TALENTS, Wilmington College, Wilmington, Ohio 45177. 1981. Paper.

Office of Human Development Services, Admin. on Developmental Disabilities, *Leisure Time Activities: A Resource Manual for the Developmentally Disabled.* Indices, Inc., 5827 Columbia Pike, Falls Church, VA 22041. 1980.

Mitchell, Joyce Slayton, with a special section by Wallach, Ellen J., *See Me More Clearly.* Harcourt Brace Jovanovich, Inc., 757 Third Ave., New York, NY 10017. 1980. $8.95, hardcover. Particularly for handicapped youth.

Benjamin, Libby, and Walz, Garry R., eds., *Counseling Exceptional People.* Publications, ERIC/CAPS, 2108 School of Education, University of Michigan, Ann Arbor, MI 48109. 1980. $8.50.

Cook, Paul F.; Dahl, Peter R.; and Gale, Margaret Ann, *Vocational Opportunities: Vocational Training and Placement of the Severely Handicapped.* The American Institutes for Research in the Behavioral Sciences. Published by: Olympus Publishing Co., 1670 E. 13th S., Salt Lake City, UT 84105. 1978. $7.95, paper. *Sensational* book. Lists barriers (such as "low self-esteem," "impaired ability to read," "lack of independent living skills," etc.) then occupational clusters/divisions, jobs held by handicapped workers, and which handicaps are able to encompass particular tasks/jobs in each division.

Appleby, Judith A., et al., *Training Programs and Placement Services: Vocational Training and Placement of the Severely Handicapped.* The American Institutes for Research in the Behavioral Sciences. Published by: Olympus Publishing Co., 1670 E. 13th S., Salt Lake City, UT 84105. 1978. $16.95, hardcover. Lists, by region/state *effective* programs for helping the handicapped—152 in all. Describes each facility/program in detail. Very helpful.

Dahl, Peter R.; Appleby, Judith A.; and Lipe, Dewey, *Mainstreaming Guidebook for Vocational Educators: Teaching the Handicapped.* The American Institutes for Research in the Behavioral Sciences. Published by: Olympus Publishing Co., 1670 E. 13th S., Salt Lake City, UT 84105. 1978. $16.95, hardcover. Designed for counselors/teachers helping the handicapped—whether it be developing positive attitudes, modifying curricula, placing handicapped students in jobs, or whatever. Very useful, as are the other two books in this series, previously mentioned.

Bruck, Lilly, *Access: The Guide to A Better Life for Disabled Americans.* David Obst Books, Random House, Inc., 201 E. 50th St., New York, NY 10022. 1978. $5.95, paper. Deals with jobs, health-care, travel, shopping without leaving home, special products, special technologies, etc. as these relate to disabled Americans. *Very* thorough.

"The So-Called 'Handicapped' Job-Hunter: Strategies for Helping Him or Her in Today's Job-Market," the November-December 1978 issue of the *Newsletter about life/work planning.* Single copies free if you send a self-addressed, stamped business envelope to: Newsletter, National Career Development Project, Box 379, Walnut Creek, CA 94596.

American Coalition of Citizens with Disabilities: Has a new program, designed to help *employers* who are looking for qualified disabled applicants for various jobs. ACCD gives assistance regarding employment, recruitment, interviewing, awareness training, architectural accessibility, etc. Write: Ted Brosnan, ACCD, 1346 Connecticut Ave. NW, No. 817, Washington, DC 20036.

11. FOR EXECUTIVES AND THOSE INTERESTED IN THE BUSINESS WORLD

Kaplan, Glenn, *The Big Time: How Success Really Works In 14 Top Business Careers.* Congdon & Weed, 298 Fifth Ave., New York, NY 10001. 1982. $16.95, hardcover.

Herzberg, Frederick, *The Managerial Choice: To be efficient and to be human.* Olympus Publishing Company, 1670 E. 13th S., Salt Lake City, UT 84105. 1982. $19.95, hardcover. By one of the pioneers in the whole field of jobs and motivation.

Haldane, Bernard, *Bernard Haldane's Career Satisfaction and Success: How to know and manage your strengths.* Revised and enlarged. Amacom, 135 W. 50th St., New York, NY 10020. $12.95, hardcover. By one of the pioneers in the creative job-hunting process.

Wood, Jr., Orrin G., *Your Hidden Assets: The Key to Getting Executive Jobs.* Dow Jones-Irwin, 1818 Ridge Rd., Homewood, IL 60430. 1981. $15.95, hardcover.

Levinson, Harry, with the assistance of Lang, Cynthia, *Executive.* Harvard University Press, 79 Garden St., Cambridge, MA 02138. 1981. $18.50, hardcover.

Campbell, David, *If I'm in Charge Here Why is Everybody Laughing?* Argus Communications, One DLM Pk., Allen, TX 75002. 1980. $2.50, paper.

Ferguson, Stewart, and Ferguson, Sherry Devereaux, *Intercom: Readings in Organizational Communication.* Hayden Book Co., Inc., 50 Essex St., Rochelle Park, NJ 07662. 1980. $13.95, hardcover.

Garry, William, et al., eds., *A Checklist for Technical Skills & Other Training.* American Society for Training and Development, Suite 305, 600 Maryland Ave. SW, Washington DC 20024.

Boll, Carl R., *Executive Jobs Unlimited.* Updated edition. Macmillan Publishing Co., Inc., 866 Third Ave., New York, NY 10022. 1979, 1965. $8.95, hardcover. The classic in the executive job-hunting field.

Rust, H. Lee, *Jobsearch: A Complete Guide to Successful Job Changing.* Amacom. A guide for the experienced manager or professional on self-marketing. 1979. $12.95.

Cohen, Barbara, S., *Career Development in Industry: A Study of Selected Programs and Recommendations for Program Planning.* Educational Testing Service, Princeton, NJ 08540. 1978. Discusses the programs in twenty-four corporations.

Jameson, Robert J., *The Professional Job Changing System: World's Fastest Way to Get a Better Job.* 1978 edition. Performance Dynamics, 300 Lanidex Plaza, Parsippany, NJ 07054. $9.95, hardcover.

Kanter, Rosabeth Moss, *Men and Women of the Corporation.* Basic Books, Inc., Publishers, New York, NY. 1977. $12.00, hardcover. A thoroughgoing study of how a corporation works, and how it affects the lives of the women and men in it.

Drucker, Peter, *Management: Tasks, Responsibilities, Practices.* Harper & Row, Publishers, 10 E. 53rd St., New York, NY 10022. 1973. $15.00. Should be absolutely required reading for anyone contemplating entering, changing to, or becoming a professional within the business world, or any organization.

Townsend, Robert, *Up the Organization: How to Stop the Corporation from Stifling People and Strangling Profits.* Alfred A. Knopf, New York, NY. 1970. Classic in the field.

Peter, Laurence F., and Hull, Raymond, *The Peter Principle: Why Things Always Go Wrong.* William Morrow & Co., Inc., New York, NY. 1969. $4.95, hardback. Another classic.

12. ON YOUR OWN: SELF-EMPLOYMENT, PART-TIME WORK

Long, Charles, *How to Survive Without a Salary.* Sterling Publishing, Inc., Two Park Ave., New York, NY 10016. 1981. $6.95, paper.

Lesko, Matthew, *Getting Yours: The complete guide to government money.* Penguin Books, 625 Madison Ave., New York, NY 10022. 1982. $5.95, paper.

DeBono, Edward, *Opportunities: A Handbook of Business Opportunity Search*. Penguin Books, 625 Madison Ave., New York, NY 10022. 1981. $3.95, paper.

Howard, Alice and Alfred, *Turn Your Kitchen into a GOLD MINE*. Stellar Books, Harper & Row, Publishers, 10 E. 53rd St., New York, NY 10022. 1981. $12.95, hardcover.

Kelley, Robert E., *Consulting: The Complete Guide to a Profitable Career*. Charles Scribner's Sons, 597 Fifth Ave., New York, NY 10017. 1981. $15.95, paper.

Revel, Chase, *184 Businesses Anyone Can Start And Make A Lot Of Money*. Bantam Books, Inc., 666 Fifth Ave., New York, NY 10103. 1981. $6.95, paper.

Schepps, Solomon J., ed., *The Concise Guide to Patents: Trademarks and Copyrights*. Bell Publishing Co., A Division of Crown Publishers, Inc., One Park Ave., New York, NY 10016. 1980. $2.98, hardcover.

Bass, Jack A., *How To Send Your Money Out To Work*. Warren Court Investments, Inc., 34 Carlton St., Winnipeg, Manitoba, R3C 1N9. 1979. $10.00, paper.

Holt, Nancy; Shuchat, Jo; and Regal, Mary Lewis, *Minding Your Own Small Business: An Introductory Curriculum for Small Business Management, Volumes I and II*. Stock #017-080-02002-05. For sale by the Supt. of Documents, U.S. Govt. Printing Off., Washington, DC 20402. 1979. Looseleaf.

Levinson, Jay Conrad, *Earning Money Without A Job: The Economics of Freedom*. Holt, Rinehart and Winston, 383 Madison Ave., New York, NY 10017. 1979.

Rosenthal, Ed, and Lichty, Ron, *132 Ways To Earn A Living Without Working (For Someone Else)*. St. Martin's Press, 175 Fifth Ave., New York, NY 10010. 1978. $5.95, paper.

Hallock, Robert Lay, *Inventing for Fun and Profit*. Harmony Books, A Division of Crown Publishers, Inc., One Park Ave., New York, NY 10016. 1978. $3.95, paper.

Clark, Leta W., *How To Open Your Own Shop or Gallery*. St. Martin's Press, 175 Fifth Ave., New York, NY 10010. 1978. $8.95, hardcover.

Lefferts, Robert, *Getting A Grant: How To Write Successful Grant Proposals*. Prentice-Hall, Inc., Englewood Cliffs, NJ 07632. 1978. $4.95, paper.

Baranov, Alvin B., *Incorporation Made Easy. Form Your Own Corporation With a Minimum of Expense*. Legal Publications, Inc., Box 3723, Van Nuys, CA 91407. 1978. $8.50, paper.

Mancuso, Anthony, *How To Form Your Own California Corporation*. Nolo Press, Box 544, Occidental, CA 95465. 1977. $9.95.

Bennett, Vivo, and Clagett, Cricket, *1001 Ways To Be Your Own Boss: A Unique Guide to Money-Making Enterprises for Financial Independence*. Prentice-Hall, Inc., Englewood Cliffs, NJ 07632. 1976. $5.95, paper.

Hoge, Cecil C., Sr., *Mail Order Moonlighting*. Ten Speed Press, Box 7123, Berkeley, CA 94707. 1976. $7.95, paper.

Nicholas, Ted, *How to Form Your Own Corporation Without a Lawyer for Under $50.00. Complete with Tear-out Forms, Certificate of Incorporation, Minutes, By-Laws*. Enterprise Publishing Co., Inc., 1000 Oakfield Lane, Wilmington, DE 19810. 1973. $7.95 plus $.45 postage and handling.

See also Section 2, p. 248, Alternative Patterns of Work

13. MAKING YOUR LIVING BY WRITING AND GETTING PUBLISHED

I used to live in an apartment-complex, and as I walked through the courtyard each day, I could hear typewriters going incessantly, out of every open window. They couldn't *all* be part-time secretaries, working at home. Obviously, there are a lot of budding authors and authoresses in the land. For them, some helps:

Appelbaum, Judith, and Evans, Nancy, *How to Get Happily Published: A Complete and Candid Guide*. New American Library, 1633 Broadway, New York, NY 10019. 1978. $6.95, paper.

Schemenaur, P.J., and Brady, John, eds., *Writer's Market: Where to Sell What You Write*. Writer's Digest Books, 9933 Alliance Rd., Cincinnati, OH 45242. Hardcover. Issued annually.

Mainstream Access, Inc., *The Publishing Job Finder*. Prentice-Hall, Englewood Cliffs, NJ 07632. 1981. $7.95, paper.

Mathieu, Aron, *The Book Market: How to Write, Publish and Market Your Book*. Andover Press, Inc., 516 W. 34th St., New York, NY 10001. 1981. $19.95, hardcover.

Fulton, Len, and Ferber, Ellen, *The Directory of Small Magazine Press Editors and Publishers*, 11th edition. Dustbooks, Box 100, Paradise, CA 95969. 1980. $9.95, paper.

Directory of Publishing Opportunities in Journals and Periodicals, Fourth edition. Marquis Academic Media, 200 E. Ohio St., Chicago, IL 60611. 1979. $44.50. (See your library, *please!*)

Polking, Kirk, and Meranus, Leonard S., eds., *Law and the Writer*. Writer's Digest Books, 9933 Alliance Rd., Cincinnati, OH 45242. 1978. $9.95, hardcover. Deals with such *minor* matters as: libel, invasion of privacy suits, the new copyright law, your first book contract, subsidiary rights, how to get paid if a publisher defaults, federal taxes and the writer, etc.

Greenfeld, Howard, *Books: From Writer to Reader*. Crown Publishers, Inc., One Park Ave., New York, NY 10016. 1976. $4.95, paper. Describes the role of the literary agent, publishing house, editor, illustrator, copy editor, designer, production supervisor, compositor, proofreader, indexer, printer, binder, etc. Fascinating. See your library if your bookstore doesn't have it.

14. ARTS AND CRAFTS, SELLING

If your creativity is not out of the left-hemisphere of your brain (words, words, words), but out of the right-hemisphere (pictures, art, crafts, and so forth), there are books for you, too; the first three are issued annually:

Lapin, Lynne, ed., *Artist's Market*. Writer's Digest Books, 9933 Alliance Rd., Cincinnati, OH 45242.

_________, ed., *Craftworker's Market*. Writer's Digest Books, 9933 Alliance Rd., Cincinnati, OH 45242.

Brohaugh, William, *Songwriter's Market*. Writer's Digest Books, 9933 Alliance Rd., Cincinnati, OH 45242.

Chung, Eve Z., *Is There Life After Art School?* Eve Zweben Chung, 2435 Seventh St., Berkeley, CA 94710. 1979. $7.95, postpaid.

Connaughton, Howard W., *Craftsmen in Business: A Guide to Financial Management & Taxes*. Revised edition. American Crafts Council, 22 W. 55th St., New York, NY 10019. 1979. $6.50. Concise and useful.

Davidson, Marion, and Blue, Martha, *Making It Legal: A Law Primer for the Craftmaker, Visual Artist, and Writer*. McGraw-Hill Paperbacks, 1221 Avenue of the Americas, New York, NY 10020. 1979. $8.95, paper.

Dooling, D.M., ed., *A Way of Working*. Anchor Books, Doubleday, Garden City, NY. 1979. $3.50, paper. Looking at craftsmanship from a philosophical point of view.

Berlye, Milton K., *How To Sell Your Artwork: A Complete Guide For Commercial and Fine Artists*. Prentice-Hall, Inc., Englewood Cliffs, NJ 07632. 1978. $7.95, paper.

Money Business: Grants and Awards for Creative Artists. The Artists Foundation, Inc., 100 Boylston St., Boston, MA 02116. 1978. $7.00, paper.

Cochrane, Diane, *This Business of Art*. Watson-Guptill Publications, A Division of Billboard Publications, Inc., 1515 Broadway, New York, NY 10036. 1978. $12.50, hardcover. Deals with copyrighting your creation, contracts with dealers, insurance, selling, renting, exhibiting, commissions, consignment, dealing with museums, cooperative galleries, income taxes, etc. Written by the editor of *American Artist Business Letter*.

Goodman, Calvin J. and Florence J., eds., *Art Marketing Handbook*. Published by: gee tee bee, 11901 Sunset Blvd., 102, Los Angeles, CA 90049. 1978. Deals with planning, sales, promotion, sales aids, pricing, marketing works of art. Calvin also appears in the aforementioned *American Artist Business Letter*—and other places.

15. GETTING A GOVERNMENT JOB

Federal Research Service, Inc., *Federal Career Opportunities*. Federal Research Service, Inc., 370 Maple Ave. W., Box 1059-PC, Vienna, VA 22180 (703) 281-0200. Biweekly 64-page magazine. $28 for six issues. Up-to-date listing of available federal jobs plus application instructions.

Waelde, David E., *How to Get a Federal Job and Advance*. Fourth edition. Federal Research Service, Inc., 370 Maple Ave. W., Box 1059-PC, Vienna, VA 22180 (703) 281-0200. 1981. $10.00 includes postage and handling. Unravels the maze of the federal employment and promotion processes. Includes discount coupon for current federal vacancy listing.

Zehring, John William, *Careers in State and Local Government*. Garrett Park Press, Garrett Park, MD 20766. 1980. Prepaid, $9.95 per copy; billed, $10.95.

Rashad, Hohari M., *Federal Job-Hunting Simplified*. James H. McFadden Publications, Box 56252, Washington, DC 20011. 1979. $2.95, plus $.50 postage and handling.

Moore, Donna J., *Take Charge of Your Own Career*. Donna J. Moore, Box 723, Baidbridge Island, WA 98110. 1979. $6.95, paper, plus $.80 for postage and handling. A guide for federal employees, or would-be federal employees.

Hawkins, James E., *The Uncle Sam Connection: An Insider's Guide to Federal Employment, Revised and Updated*. Follett Publishing Co., Attn: T.K. Washburn, 1010 W. Washington Blvd., Chicago, IL 60607. 1978. $4.95, paper. The author, at one time Deputy Assistant Secretary in the Department of Commerce, knows the federal hiring system inside and out. A helpful book, for those seeking a government job.

And, for those of you who are or were working for the government, and grew tired of it, there is of course a book, also:

Krannich, Ronald L., *Moving Out of Government: A guide to surviving and prospering in the 1980's*. Impact Publications, 4212 Gadwall Pl., Virginia Beach, VA 23462. 1982. Paper.

16. VOLUNTEER OPPORTUNITIES, INTERNSHIPS AND ORGANIZATIONS DEALING WITH SOCIAL CHANGE

I CAN Volunteer Development Workbook. National Center for Citizen Involvement's Volunteer Readership Service, Box 1807, Boulder, CO 80306. $3.50. There is also an *I CAN Advisor's Manual* ($1.55) and *I CAN Administrative Guidelines* ($2.40), for those wishing to help recruit or train volunteers. The I CAN program, which helps volunteers identify the basic skills they are using in their volunteer work, was developed by the Council of National Organizations for Adult Education, and by the I CAN Interagency Collaboration for Volunteer Development (which included such organizations as the American Red Cross, the Girl Scouts of the U.S.A., the YWCA, the YMCA, the Junior Leagues, and the National Council of Jewish Women).

Hughes, Kathleen, ed., *Good Works: A Guide to Social Change Careers.* Center for Study of Responsive Law, Box 19367, Washington, DC 20036. 1982. Paper.

Ali, Kamil, and Stanton, Timothy, *The Experience Hand: A student manual for making the most of an internship.* Carroll Press Publishers, 43-D Squantum St., Cranston, RI 02920. 1982. $5.95, paper.

Free Spirit, Box 279, Riverdale, NY 10471, is called 'a free directory to New York and beyond for people who are reaching out.' Published three times yearly. Information on such subjects as healing, holistic health, personal growth, and counseling.

Mann, Debra L., ed., *Directory of Washington Internships.* National Society for Internships and Experiential Education, 1735 Eye St. NW, Ste. 601, Washington, DC 20006. Updated yearly. $7.00, paper.

McRobie, George, *Small Is Possible.* Harper & Row, 10 E. 53rd St., New York, NY 10022. 1981. $5.95, paper.

Alternative Access Directory. Catalyst Press, Box 462, Kentfield, CA 94904. 1980. $5.95, paper.

Polking, Kirk, and Cannon, Colleen, eds., *1981 Internships: 1,500 On-The-Job Training Opportunities.* Writer's Digest Books, 9933 Alliance Rd., Cincinnati, OH 45242. 1981. $7.95, paper.

The San Francisco Bay Area People's Yellow Pages, Box 31291, San Francisco, CA 94131. $5.95, paper. Alternative services catalog.

Brennan, David, ed., et al., *Boston People's Yellow Pages.* Vocations for Social Change, Box 211, Essex Station, Boston, MA 02112. 1980. $4.95, paper.

Gartner, Alan, and Riessman, Frank, *Help: A Working Guide to Self-Help Groups.* New Viewpoints/Vision Books, A Division of Franklin Watts, 730 Fifth Ave., New York, NY 10019. 1980. $9.95, paper.

Edited by: *Communities, Journal of Cooperative Living; A Guide to Cooperative Alternatives.* Community Publications Cooperative, Box 426, Louisa, VA 23093. 1979. $5.95, paper.

Invest Yourself, published by LAOS/ASF. Order from: Invest Yourself, Circulation Dept., 418 Peltoma Rd., Haddonfield, NJ 08033. $2.25, first class mail. Check payable to Invest Yourself *must* accompany order. Lists 26,000 openings.

Additional resources are to be found in Appendix E, the section entitled "What Can I Do If I Am Interested In Doing Something That is Not Your Normal Occupation, But Maybe Something That Contributes Toward Changing Our Country or Society?" See also p. 109 in Chapter Five.

17. MID-LIFE OR SECOND CAREERS, ON TO RETIREMENT

Downs, Hugh, and Roll, Richard J., *The Best Years Book: How to plan for fulfillment, security, and happiness in the retirement years.* Delacorte Press, 1 Dag Hammarskjold Plaza, New York, NY 10017. 1981. $14.95, hardcover.

Sheehy, Gail, *Pathfinders.* William Morrow, 105 Madison Ave., New York, NY 10016. 1981. $15.95, hardcover.

Action for Independent Maturity, *Looking Ahead: How to Plan Your Successful Retirement.* American Association of Retired Persons, 1909 K St. NW, Washington, DC 20049. 1980. Paper.

Aslanian,Carol B., and Schmelter, Harvey B., *Adult Access to Education and New Careers: A Handbook for Action.* College Entrance Examination Board, Box 2815, Princeton, NJ 08541. 1980. $9.75, paper.

Bailyn, Lotte, with Schein, Edgar H., *Living with Technology: Issues at Mid-Career.* The MIT Press, 28 Carleton St., Cambridge, MA 02142. 1980. $16.00, postpaid.

Brill, Peter, and Hayes, John P., *Taming Your Turmoil: Managing the Transitions of Adult Life.* Prentice-Hall, General Book Marketing, Englewood Cliffs, NJ 07632. 1981. $6.95, paper.

Odell, Louise Minter and Odell, Charles E., Sr., *You and the Senior Boom: New Challenges and Opportunities for All.* Exposition Press, Inc., 900 S. Oyster Bay Rd., Hicksville, NY 11801. 1980. $12.50, hardback.

U.S. Dept. of Health, Education, and Welfare, *Income and Resources of the Aged.* Superintendent of Documents, U.S. Govt. Printing Office, Washington, DC 20402. 1980. Paper.

Weaver, Peter, *Strategies for the Second Half of Life.* Franklin Watts, 730 Fifth Ave., New York, NY 10019. 1980. $12.95, hardcover.

Gould, Roger L., *Transformations, Growth and Change in Adult Life.* Simon and Schuster, 1230 Avenue of the Americas, New York, NY 10020. 1978. $9.95, hardcover. The developmental stages theory of life again, this time as a consequence of a study of almost a thousand subjects. Thesis: most problems of adult crisis and change are age related.

Levinson, Daniel J., with Darrow, Charlotte N.; Klein, Edward B.; Levinson, Maria H.; and McKee, Braxton, *The Seasons of a Man's Life.* Alfred A. Knopf, Inc., 201 E. 50th St., New York, NY 10022. 1978. $10.95, hardcover. The theory of developmental periods or stages, based on long-term interviewing of forty selected men.

Vaillant, George E., *Adaptation to Life.* Little, Brown and Co., 34 Beacon St., Boston, MA 02106. 1977. $9.95, hardcover. A longitudinal (long-range) study of 268 subjects, in order to find out how—over forty years—these people coped, and how they found (or did not find) happiness. Adaptive mechanisms—methods of coping—are illustrated over various periods or stages.

Sheehy, Gail, *Passages, Predictable Crises of Adult Life.* Bantam Books, Inc., 666 Fifth Ave., New York, NY 10019. 1977, 1976. $2.50, paper. Gail acknowledges "a primary professional debt" to the three authors above.

Durkin, Jon, "Mid-Life Career Changes." Johnson O'Connor Research Foundation, Human Engineering Laboratory, 701 Sutter St., San Francisco, CA 94109.

Robbins, Paula I., *Successful Midlife Career Change: Self-Understanding and Strategies for Action.* Amacom, 135 W. 50th St., New York, NY 10020. 1978. $12.95, hardcover. Very up-to-date, very thorough, very helpful. Probably the best book dealing with this problem.

18. RESOURCES WRITTEN FROM A CHRISTIAN PERSPECTIVE, OR DIRECTED AT CLERGY

Martin, Rev. Richard K., *New Parish/New Cure: A job search guide for Episcopal Clergy.* Available from the author, 14 Clark St., Belmont, MA 02178. 1982. $4.75, paper.

Malcomson, William L., ed., *How to Survive in the Ministry.* Judson Press, Valley Forge, PA 19481. 1982. $5.95, paper.

Eternity Magazine, Doors '82: "A Guide to Educational and Employment Opportunities for Christian Students." Doors '82, 1716 Spruce St., Philadelphia, PA 19103. Periodical.

Farnsworth, Kirk, and Lawhead, Wendell, *Life Planning.* InterVarsity Press, 5206 Main St., Downers Grove, IL 60515. 1981. $6.95, paper.

Ballenger, Sharon M., Respond, Volume 6: *Resources for Senior Highs in the Church.* Judson Press, Valley Forge, PA 19481. 1980. $7.95, paper.

Ghezzi, Burt, *Striking Back at Unemployment:* New Covenant Magazine, October 1980 issue. New Covenant, 840 Airport Blvd., Box 8617, Ann Arbor, MI 48107. $.75, periodical.

Olson, Richard P., *Mid-Life: A Time to Discover, A Time to Decide: A Christian Perspective on Middle Age.* Judson Press, Valley Forge, PA 19481. 1980. $5.95, paper.

Zehring, John William, *Making Your Life Count.* Judson Press, Valley Forge, PA 19481. 1980. $3.95, paper.

Rightor, Henry H., *An Introduction to the Job Search.* Virginia Theological Seminary, Alexandria, VA. 1980. Paper. Written for seminary graduates.

Rightor, Henry, *Pastoral Counseling in Work Crises.* Judson Press, Valley Forge, PA 19481. 1979. $2.95, paper.

Moran, Pamela J., *Seek and You Will Find: A Practical Job Hunting Guide.* The Word of God, Box 7087, Ann Arbor, MI 48107. 1978. A job-seeking handbook for Christians.

Harris, John C., *The Minister Looks for a Job, Finding Work as a Parish Minister.* From: The Alban Institute, Inc., Mount St. Alban, Washington, DC 20016. 1974. $1.50.

19. THE NATURE OF YOUR BRAIN, AND HOW TO STIMULATE CREATIVITY, AND DECISION-MAKING

Our whole vocational system is oriented toward people with verbal skills, rather than intuitive; and toward achievement, rather than relationship goals. Those wishing to correct this imbalance, in themselves or in those they are trying to help, will find it extremely helpful to know more about the brain, how it is divided, and how it works. So constant are the new findings in this field, that one almost needs a newsletter to keep up. Fortunately, there are two such, which for those who can afford them, admirably serve that purpose:

Brain and Strategy. Publisher: Sherry Ann Lynch. Editor: Dudley Lynch. Brain Technologies Corporation, 827 Westwood Dr., Richardson, TX 75080. Published ten times yearly. $29.00, annually.

Brain/Mind Bulletin. Marilyn Ferguson, editor. Interface Press, Box 42247, Los Angeles, CA 90042. Published every three weeks; $15.00/year.

Following are some books that I think are very helpful, though most books in the very nature of things lag behind newsletters, in their up-to-dateness:

Hunt, Morton, *The Human Difference: What a new science is discovering about the way the mind works.* Simon & Schuster, 1230 Avenue of the Americas, New York, NY 10020. 1982. $14.95, hardcover.

Jastrow, Robert. *The Enchanted Loom: The Universe Within.* Simon and Schuster, 1230 Avenue of the Americas, New York, NY 10020. 1981. $17.95, hardcover.

Gregory, Richard L., *Mind in Science.* The Press Syndicate/University of Cambridge, 32 E. 57th St., New York, NY 10022. 1981. Hardcover.

Pietsch, Paul, *Shuffle-Brain: The Search for the Holographic Mind.* Houghton Mifflin, Two Park St., Boston, MA 02107. 1981. $10.95, hardcover.

Springer, Sally P., and Deutsch, Georg, *Left Brain, Right Brain.* W.H. Freeman and Co., 660 Market St., San Francisco, CA 94104. 1981. $15.95, hardcover; $7.95, paper.

Taylor, Gordon Rattray, *The Natural History of the Mind.* Penguin Books, 625 Madison Ave., New York, NY 10022. 1981. $4.95, paper.

Turner, Charles Hampden, *Maps of the Mind.* Macmillan Publishing Co., Inc., 866 Third Ave., New York, NY 10022. 1981. $14.95.

Anderson, Barry F., *The Complete Thinker.* Prentice-Hall, Englewood Cliffs, NJ 07632. 1980. $4.95, paper.

Ferguson, Marilyn, *The Aquarian Conspiracy: Personal and Social Transformation in the 1980's.* J.P. Tarcher, Inc., 9110 Sunset Blvd., Los Angeles, CA 90069. 1981. $15.00, hardcover.

LeBoeuf, Michael, *Imagineering: How to Profit From Your Creative Powers.* McGraw-Hill Book Co., 1221 Avenue of the Americas, New York, NY 10020. 1980. $9.95, hardcover.

Scientific American, *Mind and Behavior.* W.H. Freeman and Co., 660 Market St., San Francisco, CA 94104. 1980. $9.95, paper.

Montagu, Ashley, and Matson, Floyd, *The Human Connection.* McGraw-Hill Paperbacks, 1221 Avenue of the Americas, New York, NY 10020. 1979. $4.95, paper.

Russell, Peter, *The Brain Book.* Hawthorne Books, Inc., 260 Madison Ave., New York, NY 10016. 1979. $12.95, hardcover.

Edwards, Betty, *Drawing on the Right Side of the Brain: A Course in Enhancing Creativity and Artistic Confidence.* J.P. Tarcher, Inc., 9110 Sunset Blvd., Los Angeles, CA 90069. 1979. $8.95, paper. Absolutely top-notch. On the surface, a book about drawing. Actually, a book about creativity in all its facets. Splendid.

Weinhold, Barry, and Andersen, Gail, *Threads: Unraveling the Mysteries of Adult Life.* Richard Marek Publishers, 200 Madison Ave., New York, NY 10016. 1979. $9.95, paper.

de Kay, James T., *The Left-Hander.* M. Evans and Co., Inc., 216 E. 49th St., New York, NY 10017. 1979. $3.95, paper.

Asimov, Isaac, *The Human Brain: Its Capacities and Functions.* New American Library, 1633 Broadway, New York, NY 10019. 1965. $2.25, paper.

20. TUNING UP YOUR BRAIN, AND INCREASING YOUR POWERS: EXERCISES, IMAGES AND FANTASY

Casewit, Curtis W., *The Diary: A Complete Guide to Journal Writing.* Argus Communications, One DLM Park, Allen, TX 75002. 1981. $2.95, paper.

Albrecht, Karl. *Learn to Improve Your Thinking Skills.* Prentice-Hall, Englewood Cliffs, NJ 07632. 1980. $6.95, paper.

Daitzman, Reid J., *Mental Jogging.* Richard Marek Publishers, 200 Madison Ave., New York, NY 10016. 1980. $7.95, paper.

Houston, Jean, *Life-Force: The Psycho-Historical Recovery of the Self.* Delacorte Press, One Dag Hammarskjold Plaza, New York, NY 10017. 1980. $12.95, hardcover. This is a bridge between the brain/mind literature and the work done by journal-keeping (e.g., Progoff).

Progoff, Ira, *The Practice of Process Meditation.* Dialogue House, 80 E. 11th St., New York, NY 10003. 1980. $12.95, hardcover.

Bry, Adelaide, with Bair, Marjorie, *Visualization: Directing the Movies of Your Mind.* Harper & Row, 10 E. 53rd St., New York, NY 10022. 1978. $3.95, paper.

Gawain, Shakti, *Creative Visualization.* Whatever Publishing, 158 E. Blithedale #4, Mill Valley, CA 94941. 1978. $5.95, paper.

Masters, Robert, and Houston, Jean, *Listening to the Body: The Psychophysical Way to Health and Awareness.* Delacorte Press, 245 E. 47th St., New York, NY 10017. Effects of mental images and habits on body and physical functioning. 1978.

Rainer, Tristine, *The New Diary.* J.P. Tarcher, Inc., 9110 Sunset Blvd., Los Angeles, CA 90069. 1978. $9.95. Ideas for stimulating creativity in writing about the present as well as delving into the past.

Harvey, Bill, *Mind Magic.* Ourobourus Institute, Sundown Press, Box 6, Sundown, NY 12782. 1978. $7.95, paper.

Baldwin, Christina, *One to One: Self-Understanding Through Journal Writing.* M. Evans & Co. 1977.

Campbell, David, *Take the road to creativity and get off your dead end.* Argus Communications, One DLM Park, Allen TX 75002. 1977. $2.60. Simple, inventive, and helpful.

Arieti, Silvano, *Creativity: The Magic Synthesis.* Basic Books, 10 E. 53 St., New York, NY 10022. 1976. $6.95, paper.

Buzan, Tony, *Use Both Sides of Your Brain.* E.P. Dutton & Co., Inc., Two Park Ave., New York, NY 10016. 1974. $4.95. Excellent resource.

Masters, Robert, and Houston, Jean, *Mind Games: The Guide to Inner Space.* Dell Publishing Co., One Dag Hammarskjold Plaza, New York, NY 10017. Experiences in brain/mind relationships, left/right functions. 1972.

21. ANALYSIS OF SKILLS

Pearson, Henry G., *Your Hidden Skills: Clues to Careers and Future Pursuits.* Mowry Press, Box 405, Wayland, MA 01778. 1981, paper.

Myers, Isabel Briggs and Peter, *Gifts Differing.* Consulting Psychologists Press, Inc., 577 College Ave., Palo Alto, CA 94306. 1980. $12.00, paper. Related to the increasingly-popular Myers-Briggs Test.

Figler, Howard E., *The Complete Job Search Handbook: Presenting the Skills You Need to Get Any Job, and Have a Good Time Doing It.* Holt, Rinehart and Winston, 383 Madison Ave., New York, NY 10017. 1979. $5.95, paper. Deals with the skills actually used in the job-hunt process itself.

McCormick, Ernest J., *Job Analysis: Methods and Applications.* Amacom, 135 W. 50th St., New York NY 10020. 1979. $25.95, hardcover.

Ontario Society for Training and Development, *Competency Analysis for Trainers: A Personal Planning Guide.* OSTD, Box 537, Postal Station K, Toronto, Ontario M4P 2G9 Canada. 1979. Paper.

Scheele, Adele, *Skills For Success: A Guide to the Top for Men and Women.* Ballantine Books, 201 E. 50th St., New York, NY 10022. 1979. $2.95, paper.

Brickell, Henry M., and Paul, Regina H., *Minimum Competencies and Transferable Skills: What Can Be Learned from the Two Movements.* The National Center for Research in Vocational Education, Ohio State University, 1960 Kenny Rd., Columbus, OH 43210. 1978. Paper.

Sjogren, Douglas, *Occupationally-Transferable Skills and Characteristics: Review of Literature and Research.* The Center for Vocational Education, Ohio State University, 1960 Kenny Rd., Columbus, OH 43210. 1977.

Miguel, Richard J., *Developing Skills for Occupational Transferability; Insights Gained from Current Practice.* The Center for Vocational Education, Ohio State University, 1960 Kenny Rd., Columbus, OH 43210. 1977.

Fine, Sidney A., *Functional Job Analysis Scales: A Desk Aid.* Methods for Manpower Analysis, No. 5. April 1973.

________, and Wiley, Wretha W., *An Introduction to Functional Job Analysis: A Scaling of Selected Tasks from the Social Welfare Field.* Methods for Manpower Analysis, No. 4. September 1971.

________, *A Systems Approach to New Careers: Two Papers.* Methods for Manpower Analysis, No. 3. November 1969.

________, *Guidelines for the Design of New Careers.* September 1967.

The W.E. Upjohn Institute for Employment Research's *Studies on Functional Job Analysis and Career Design.*

The above pamphlets are available from The W.E. Upjohn Institute for Employment Research, 300 S. Westnedge Ave., Kalamazoo, MI 49007.

Fine, Sidney A., *Nature of Skill: Implication for Education and Training.* 1870 Wyoming Ave. NW, Washington, DC 20009. A superb summary of some recent thinking from the father of skills analysis in the Dictionary of Occupational Titles.

22. INTERVIEWING SKILLS, RESUMES, ETC.

Biegeleisen, J.I., *Job Resumes: How to write them, how to present them, preparing for interviews.* Grosset & Dunlap, 51 Madison Ave., New York, NY 10010. 1982, revised. $4.95, paper. A classic in the field.

Krannich, Ronald L., and Banis, William J., *High Impact Resumes and Letters.* Progressive Concepts Inc., 2541 Lakewood Lane, Chesapeake, VA 23321. 1982. $7.95, paper.

Rogers, Edward J., *Getting Hired: Everything you need to know about resumes, interviews, and job-hunting strategies.* Prentice-Hall, Englewood Cliffs, NJ 07632. $14.95, hardcover.

Williams, Eugene, *Getting the Job You Want With the Audiovisual Portfolio.* Comptex Associates, Inc., Box 6745, Washington, DC 20020. 1982. $12.95, paper. Manual for job-seekers and career changers in professions other than teaching.

Martin, Phyllis, *The Job Interview: The job-hunt success kit.* Center for Career Development, 11385 Landon Lane, Cincinnati, OH 45246. 1981. Paper.

The Catalyst Staff, *Marketing Yourself: The Catalyst Guide to Successful Resumes and Interviews.* Bantam Books, 666 Fifth Ave., New York, NY 10103. 1981. $3.50, paper.

Meyer, John L., and Donaho, Melvin W., *Get the Right Person for the Job.* Prentice-Hall, Inc., Englewood Cliffs, NJ 07632. 1979. $7.50, paper.

Medley, H. Anthony, *Sweaty Palms: The Neglected Art of Being Interviewed.* Lifetime Learning Publications, 10 Davis Dr., Belmont, CA 94002. 1978. $4.95, paper. Very helpful.

23. SURVIVING ON THE JOB, SURVIVING 'BURNOUT', AND/OR GETTING PROMOTED

There is not enough said, generally, in job-hunting books about surviving after you get the job. The enemy is both within, and without. From within, the now-familiar problem of burnout (See Appendix D, p. 303). From without, various adversaries—both animate and inanimate. Marilyn Moats Kennedy, a former student of mine, has written the best overall book on this subject. Other resources follow.

Kennedy, Marilyn Moats, *Office Politics: Seizing Power, Wielding Clout.* Warner Books, 75 Rockefeller Plaza, New York, NY 10019. 1981. $2.95, paper.

Kennedy, Marilyn Moats, *Career Knockouts: How to Battle Back.* New Century Publishers, Inc., 275 Old New Brunswick Rd., Piscataway, NJ 08854. 1980. $10.95, hardcover.

Veninga, Robert L., and Spradley, James P., *The Work-Stress Connection: How to cope with job burnout.* Little, Brown & Co., 34 Beacon St., Boston, MA 02106. 1981. $12.95, hardcover.

Waitley, Denis, *Helping people live more effective lives.* Advanced Learning Corporation, 10800 Lyndale Ave., Minneapolis, MN 55420. Looseleaf binder, tape.

Blue Cross/Blue Shield of North Carolina, *Employee Development Planning.* Training and Development Department, Blue Cross/Blue Shield, Box 2291, Durham, NC 27702. Paper.

Behn, Robert D., and Vaupel, James W., *Quick Analysis for Busy Decision Makers.* Basic Books, Inc., 10 E. 53rd St., New York, NY 10022. 1982. $18.95, hardcover. Outlines various decision-making strategies.

Edelwich, Jerry, with Brodsky, Archie, *Burn-Out: Stages of Disillusionment in the Helping Professions.* Human Sciences Press, 72 Fifth Ave., New York, NY 10011. 1980. $19.95, hardcover.

Freudenberger, Dr. Herbert J., with Richelson, Geraldine, *Burn-Out: How to Beat the High Cost of Success.* 1981. $3.95, paper.

Kantner, Rosabeth Moss, and Stein, Barry A., *A Tale of O: On Being Different in an Organization.* Harper & Row, 10 E. 53rd St., New York, NY 10022. 1980. $4.95, paper.

Potter, Beverly A., *Beating Job Burnout: Overcome Job Frustration, Renew Your Enthusiasm for Work.* Harbor Publishing Co., San Francisco, CA. 1980. $11.95, hardcover.

Vash, Carolyn L., *The Burn-Out Administrator.* Springer Publishing Co., Inc., 200 Park Ave. S., New York, NY 10003. 1979. $10.95, hardcover.

You will also find some *very* helpful words on this subject in *Where Do I Go From Here With My Life?* (Ten Speed Press, Box 7123, Berkeley, CA 94707, 1974), pages 241–245 ("Understanding the Nature of the World of Work"), and 150–160 ("How to Survive After You Get the Job").

24. CONCERNING BEING FIRED, REJECTED, RIFFED OR LAID-OFF

May, John, *The RIF Survival Handbook: How to manage your money if you're unemployed.* Tilden Press, 1737 DeSales St. NW, Suite 300, Washington, DC 20036. $4.95, plus $1.00 postage.

In recent times, definitions of eligibility for unemployment benefits have been dramatically narrowed, so any book on this subject becomes questionably dated; nonetheless, there are two you may find in bookstores or libraries, that give you some clues at least:

Honigsberg, Peter Jan, *The Unemployment Benefits Handbook.* Addison-Wesley Publishing Co., Jacob Way, Reading, MA 01867. 1981. $5.95, paper.

Avrutis, Raymond, *How to Collect Unemployment Benefits.* Schocken Books, 200 Madison Ave., New York, NY 10016. 1975. $1.25, paper.

White, John, *Rejection.* Addison-Wesley Publishing Co., Reading, MA. 1982. $5.95, paper. A humorous/serious helpful reader on the omnipresence of rejection in human life, which both the Greatest and the Least have had to deal with. Helps to put *our* rejection in perspective.

Martin, Phyllis, *How to Handle Rejection.* Center for Career Development, 11385 Landon Lane, Cincinnati, OH 45246. $3.00, paper.

Simon, Sidney B., *Negative Criticism: And what to do about it.* Argus Communications, One DLM Park, Allen, TX 75002. 1978. $2.75, paper.

Peskin, Dean B., *A Job Loss Survival Manual.* Amacom, 135 W. 50th St., New York, NY 10020. 1981. $5.95, paper.

Cowle, Jerry, *How To Survive Getting Fired—And Win!* Follett Publishing Co., 1010 W. Washington Blvd., Chicago, IL 60607. 1979. $9.95, hardcover.

Irish, Richard K., *If Things Don't Improve Soon I May Ask You to Fire Me: The Management Book for Everyone Who Works.* Anchor Press/Doubleday, Garden City, NY. 1975. $7.95, hardcover.

Two are better than one;
for if they fall,
the one will lift up his fellow;

but woe to him that is alone when he falleth,
and hath not another to lift him up.

Ecclesiastes

Appendix C

Resources Guide:

Professional Help

REQUIRED READING:
If You're Thinking of Hiring A Career Counselor To Help You

Okay, you're back here in this section either because you're just curious to know what it says, or because you're ready to admit you've just got to hire *somebody* to help you, with all this.

And you've decided you've got to find somebody to help you because either:

a) you *tried* doing the exercises in the book, and you just aren't getting anywhere; or

b) you've read the book—sections of it anyway—and without even trying the exercises, you know yourself well enough to know you need someone who will explain it all to you, step by step. You're an "ear" person, more than an "eye" person, and you do better when a human being is explaining something to you, than when you're trying to read it for yourself; OR

c) you've not read the book, nor tried any of the exercises, but you *have* counted the number of pages in the book, and the very thickness of it all was so intimidating, that you've decided to toss in the towel before you even begin. ("Help!")

You've turned to this section because you figure that back here must be some sort of "authorized list" of names: people who understand this whole job-hunting process thoroughly, know how to do all the exercises in this book, have been through some kind of careful credentialing process, and received the Parachute Seal of Approval.

Ah, dear reader, how I wish it were so. But, unhappily, there is no such list. First of all, while I do train people once a year, I haven't trained all that many, over the years. Moreover, I can't guarantee that simply because they've been through my hands, they truly understand. So, publishing a list of their names wouldn't give you the information you want.

Secondly, there are lots of people "out there" who understand the whole job-hunting process thoroughly and well, even though they've never been trained by me and may not even (necessarily) have read this book. In most cases, of course, I've never met them, and consequently I don't know who they are or where they are. I simply know *that* they are.

What this all adds up to, you've already guessed. Hunting for a decent person or place to help you is just like hunting for a job. You've got to do your own research, and your own informational interviewing, in your own area. Getting somebody else's opinion, in effect letting them do your research for you, isn't very effective. First of all, their information is often somewhat outdated, and therefore questionable. Maybe the counselor or place they're telling you about is one they ran into a year ago. The counselor was excellent, at that time. But since then (unbeknownst to your friend) that counselor has been through a really rough time, personally: divorce, burnout, overwhelming fatigue—the works. It's affected their counseling, to say the least; they're no longer functioning at the top level they were a year ago. Your friend's recommendation is outdated—at least for the present. And, of course, it can be just the other way around. Your friend tells you someone is terrible, as a counselor, because when your friend ran into them, two or three years ago, it was true. But, that counselor has had dozens and dozens of clients since then, and learned a lot (most career counselors are trained by their clients, you know). That counselor is now very good. Your friend's "dis-recommendation" is now outdated.

Secondly, the three things you absolutely want from anyone you're paying good money to, are:

a) a firm grasp of the whole job-hunting process, at its most creative and effective level;

b) the ability to communicate that information lucidly and clearly to others;

c) rapport with you.

This last is a very difficult thing to pin down. Maybe this counselor is simply wonderful on the first two counts, but he reminds you of your Uncle Harry. You've always *hated* your Uncle Harry. No go. But how could anyone have known that, except you?

I repeat: no one can do this informational interviewing about which job counselor is best, except you. Because the real question is not "Who is best?" but "Who is best for you?" Those last two words change everything.

What I want to do for you is:

1. Give you a brief crash course about this whole field of career counseling.

2. Tell you where to find some names with which *to start* your search for "who is best for you."

3. Give you some questions, that will help you separate the sheep from the goats, and make an intelligent decision.

Okay, here we go:

1. A CRASH COURSE ABOUT THIS WHOLE FIELD OF CAREER COUNSELING

In the whole big field of The Job Hunt, all professional help divides (one regrets to say) into the following three categories, so far as the job-hunter is concerned:

1. Professionals who are sincere and skilled.
2. Professionals who are sincere but inept.
3. Professionals who are insincere and inept.

The problem we all face when we decide to seek help with our job-hunt, is: which is which. Or, who is who. We want a career counselor who falls into category No. 1; if he or she falls into the other two categories, which of the other two they fall into is really irrelevant: ineptness is ineptness, whether it is sincere or not.

The various clues which may at first occur to us, for identifying good career counselors, are upon more serious examination not terribly fruitful. Let us tick off some of them, and see why:

⋆ Clue No. 1: Perhaps we can tell who is sincere and skilled, by the name of the specialist or their agency. Difficulty: names vary greatly from one operation to another, even when the operations are similar. Among the names which some counselors or agencies bear, you will find: executive career counselors, executive career consultants, career management teams, vocational psychologists, executive consulting counselors, career guidance counselors, executive advisors, executive development specialists, executive job counselors, manpower experts, career advisors, employment specialists, executive recruitment consultants, professional career counselors, management consultants, placement specialists, executive search specialists, vocational counselors, life/work planners, etc. If, tomorrow, some legitimate counselor who is sincere and skilled takes on a new name, the day after that some counselor who is insincere and inept will copy the name directly. What it all comes down to, is this: Wolves need sheep's clothing. Names are sheep's clothing. Trouble is, hidden in there are some genuinely helpful people. We need another clue.

⋆ Clue No. 2: Perhaps we can tell who is sincere and skilled by reading everything that the agency or counselor has written. Difficulty: both good and bad counselors know the areas where the job-hunter feels exceedingly vulnerable. Consequently, there are "turn on" words which occur in almost everybody's advertisements, brochures, and books: we will give you help, say they, with evaluating your career history, in-depth analysis of your background, establishment of your job objective, in-depth analysis of your capabilities, writing an effective resume, names of companies, preparing the covering letter, background materials on companies, interviewing techniques, salary negotiations, filling out forms, answering ads, aptitude tests, special problems—unemployment, age, too broad a background, too narrow a background, too many job changes, too few job changes, poor references, etc. We will, say they, open doors for you, tell you which companies are

hiring, and so forth. Both the counselors who are skilled and those who are inept will never get anyone in their doors if they don't mention the areas that have put the job-hunter in Desperation City. So how they describe their services (real or alleged) doesn't separate the sheep from the goats, unfortunately. Next clue?

★ Clue No. 3: Perhaps we can tell who is sincere and skilled by the fee they charge? I mean, they wouldn't charge a high fee, would they, if they weren't skilled? Difficulty: as insiders say, low fees may mean well-intentioned but amateurish help. However, the reverse of this is *not* true. As we have already mentioned, the vacuum created by the chaotic condition of our job-hunting process has attracted both competent people *and* people who are determined to prey upon the acute state of anxiety that job-hunters are often in. And when the latter say "Let us prey" they *really* prey. And they *thrive*. They can charge anywhere between $2,000 and $10,000 (it's solely dependent on your previous salary) *up front*, before they've given you *any* services or help at all. And if you are later dissatisfied, your chances of getting your money back are remote, indeed—no matter what the contract said. (They've fashioned every legal loophole in the book, in order to keep your money.) P.T. Barnum knew what he was talking about.[1] Next.

★ Clue No. 4: Perhaps we can tell which professionals are both sincere and skilled, by talking to satisfied clients—or asking our friends to tell us who was helpful to them. If you stop to think about it, you will realize this most crucial truth: *all your friends can possibly speak to you about is the particular counselor or counselors that they worked with, at that agency, in that particular city.* Should you go to the same place, and get a different counselor, you might have a very different experience. One bad counselor in an agency that has say, six good ones, can cost you much money, time, and self-esteem, if *you* get that bad one as *your* counselor. The six good ones might as well be in Timbuktu, for all the good they'll do you. So should any of your friends offer (or should you solicit from them) advice about a place they went to, be sure to find out the counselor (or counselors) they worked with, there, *by name* so you will know who to ask for, if you decide to investigate or follow their lead.

Before we leave this clue, let us also observe that while most professional career counselors will show you letters from satisfied customers, or even give you (in some cases) their names to check out, it is impossible to find out what percentage of their total clientele these satisfied persons represent: 100%? 10? 1? .1? a fluke? If you want a clue, you may make what you will out of the fact that the top officers of the largest executive counseling firm, which allegedly did over 50% of the business in the industry before it declared bankruptcy in the fall of 1974, (namely, Frederick Chusid & Co.) gave testimony during a civil suit in a New York Federal district court which indicated that only three or four out of every ten clients had been successful in getting a new job, during a previous six-month period. More recently, another prominent executive counseling firm was reported by the Attorney

1. A sucker is born every minute. Or as the post office has updated it: "A sucker is shorn every minute."

General's Office of New York City to have placed only 38 out of 55 clients.[1] Are these figures average for the industry? Better than average? Worse? Nobody knows.

In any event, virtually no career counselor or career counseling firm will EVER show you letters from DISsatisfied clients. Were you to be given access to such letters (the files of many Better Business Bureaus, the Consumer Fraud division of your state or city Attorney-General's office, not to mention the Federal Trade Commission, are loaded with such letters) you would find the complaints have certain recurrent themes: the career counseling firm being complained about, they say, did not do what they *verbally* promised to do, have the exclusive lists of job openings they claimed to have, nor the access to executive suites they claimed to have, nor the success rate they claimed, nor did they give the amount of time to the client they *verbally* promised in advance (sometimes it turned out to be as few as six hours). 'Job campaigns' for the clients were slow to start, usually not until the full advance fee was paid, promised lists were slow in being provided and often were outdated and full of errors, the friendly 'intake counselor' was actually a salesperson, and is never seen again once the contract is signed, the actual counselor was often difficult (or impossible) to get ahold of after a certain period of time (sometimes coinciding with the final payment by the client of the advance fee), the 'plan' was often no news at all to the client, the promised contact with employers on the client's behalf was not forthcoming, phone calls or letters of complaint were ignored, and the fee was not refunded in whole or in part, when the client was dissatisfied, despite implicit (or explicit) promises to the contrary. Whew!

Well, that's enough of a crash course on career counseling, and the pitfalls that await the unwary or the innocent. If you are dying to know more, and your local library has back files of magazines and newspapers (on microfiche, or otherwise), you can look up:

"Career-Counseling Industry Accused of Misrepresentation," *New York Times*, Sept. 30, 1982, p. C1.

"Consumer Law: Career Counselors and Employment Agencies" by Reed Brody, *New York Law Journal*, Feb. 26, 1982, p. 1. Reed is one of the leading experts in the country on career counseling malpractices. He is Assistant Attorney General of the State of New York (Department of Law, Two World Trade Center, New York, NY 10047).

"Career Counselors: Will They Lead You Down The Primrose Path?" by Lee Guthrie. *Savvy Magazine*, Dec., 1981, p. 60ff.

"Franklin Career Search Is Accused of Fraud In New York State Suit," *Wall Street Journal*, Jan. 29, 1981, p. 50.

"Job Counseling Firms Under Fire For Promising Much, Giving Little," *Wall Street Journal*, Jan. 27, 1981, p. 33.

---

1. "Career Counselors: Will They Lead You Down The Primrose Path?" by Lee Guthrie, in the December 1981 issue of *Savvy Magazine*, p. 60 ff.

2. WHERE TO FIND SOME NAMES TO START YOUR SEARCH FOR WHO IS BEST FOR YOU

You start, of course, by asking everyone you know—family, friends, and people you've just met—if they know any really helpful career counselors.

You supplement this by looking in the Yellow Pages of your local telephone book. Possible headings to check out (they vary from phone book to phone book) are: vocational counselors, executive career counselors, career counselors, job counseling, guidance counselors, career consultants, employment counselors. Also any cross references that these lead you to.

I am printing in this Appendix a Sampler (only) of some of the kinds of places to be found around the country, including a number of private counselors who aren't very easy to stumble across. This is not a complete directory of anything. Countless good people, agencies and places exist, which will not be found in this Sampler. Also, countless bad people, places and agencies. To list all such, would require an encyclopedia.

The listing of an organization, agency or person in this directory is NOT a recommendation or endorsement of that organization agency or person. You MUST do your own comparison shopping, and ask some sharp questions. If you don't comparison shop, you will deserve whatever you get (or don't get).

Places fold, almost weekly in this field. Places move. The staff changes. Their phone numbers and hours change. There is *no way* this Sampler can stay up-to-date and accurate, for more than about two days. I apologize for any information or listing that proves to be inaccurate. You could be of great service by dropping us a line, if you find a place is no longer in existence, or impossible to get a hold of, or is—in your opinion—totally unhelpful. (Box 379, Walnut Creek, CA 94597)

3. SOME QUESTIONS, BY MEANS OF WHICH YOU MAY BE ABLE TO SEPARATE THE SHEEP FROM THE GOATS

Choose, from your friends' recommendations, from the phone book, from the Sampler attached hereto, at least THREE PLACES OR COUNSELORS.

VISIT IN PERSON EACH OF THE THREE PLACES YOU HAVE CHOSEN. These are exploratory visits only. Leave your wallet and your checkbook home, please! You are only comparison shopping at this point, not decision reaching!!

Make this unmistakably clear, when you are setting up the appointment for the interview.

You will need a notebook. In this notebook, *before* you go to see each career counselor (or firm), you will need to write out the following questions. And, as you ask the questions at each place, take time to write down some notes (or direct quotes) of their answers. DON'T trust your memory.

You may prefer to make four columns across your notebook, so that it will be easier to compare the places, after you have visited all three:

MY SEARCH FOR A GOOD CAREER COUNSELOR

Questions	Answer from Counselor #1	Answer from Counselor #2	Answer from Counselor #3
1. What is their program?			
2. Who will be doing it?			
3. Guarantee?			
4. Who is the actual counselor?			

At each place, with each counselor, ask every one of these questions—omitting none.

- *What is their program?* When all their gimmicks are set aside (and some have great ones, like rehearsing for interviews on closed circuit TV, or using video-tape or cassettes to record your skills or your resume, etc.) what are they offering: is it basically "the numbers game," *or* is it basically some variation of the creative minority's prescription?

- *Who will be doing it?* Do you get the feeling that you must do most of it, with their basically assuming the role of coach? (if so, three cheers); or do you get the feeling that everything (including decision making about what you do, where you do it, etc.) will be done for you (if so, three warning bells should go off in your head)?

- *What guarantee is there that it will work?* If they make it clear that they have had a good success rate, but if you fail to work hard at the whole process, then there is no guarantee you are going to find a job, give them three stars. On the other hand, if they practically guarantee you a job, and say they have never had a client that failed to find a job, no matter what, *watch out.* Pulmotor job-counseling is very suspect; lifeless bodies make poor employees.

• *Are you face-to-face, and talking, with the actual persons who will be working with you, should you decide to become a client?* It might help you to be aware that some job-hunting or career counseling firms have professional salesmen who introduce you to the company, convince you of their 100% integrity and charm, secure your decision, get you to sign the contract—and then you never see them again. You work with someone entirely different (or a whole team). *Ask the person you are talking to, if they are the one (and the only one) you will be working with, should you eventually decide to become a client.* If they say No, ask to meet those who would be actually working with you—even if it's a whole battery of people. When you actually meet them, there are three considerations you should weigh:

(1) *Do you like the counselor?* Bad vibes can cause great difficulties, even if this person is extremely competent. Don't dismiss this factor!

(2) *How long has this counselor been doing this?* Ask them! And what training did they have for it? (Legitimate questions; if they get huffy, politely thank them for their time, and take your leave gently *but firmly.*) Some agencies hire former clients as new staff. Such new staff are sometimes given only "on the job training." Since you're paying for Expertise already acquired, you have a *right* to ask about this before making up your mind. Incidentally, beware of such phrases as "I've had eighteen years experience in the business and career counseling world." What that may mean is: seventeen and a half years as a fertilizer salesman, and one half year doing career counseling. Persist. "How long have you been doing formal career counseling, as you are now?"

(3) *How much time will they give you?* As a minimum? As a maximum? (There's got to be a maximum, no matter what they may at first claim. Every career counselor runs into extremely dependent types as clients, who would be there all day every day if the counselor or the firm didn't have some policy about time limits. *Press* to find out what it is, just so you'll know.) Over how long a period can you use their services? And, *will they put this in writing?* (That's the question that separates the men from the boys, and the women from the girls).

• *What is the cost of their services? Is it paid hourly, as you go along, or must it all be paid "up front" before you even start?* You will discover that there are some career counselors or agencies that charge you an hourly rate, just as a therapist might. The fee normally ranges between $35–$75 an hour. Each time you keep an appointment, you pay them at the end of that hour (or hours) for their help. There is no written contract. You signed nothing. You can stop seeing them at any time, if you feel you are not getting the help you wish. Obviously, this sort of arrangement is very much to the advantage of the job-hunter. *However,* you will also discover that there are some career counselors or agencies that, by contrast, have a policy of requiring you to pay for the entire "program" before you start, —or shortly after you start. There is *always* a written contract. You *must* sign it. (If you are married, your spouse will usually be invited to come in, before the contract is signed; you may suspect this is to help "sell" them on the idea of the contract, so they then can sell you. You may be right.) The fee normally ranges between $600–$8,000.

The contract sometimes allows it to be paid in installments, but you *are* obligated to pay it, one way or the other. You are sometimes *verbally* told that you can get your money back, or a portion of it, at any time, should you be dissatisfied with the career counselor's services. This is often *not* in the written contract. (Verbal promises, without witnesses, are difficult if not impossible to enforce. The written contract takes precedence.) Sometimes the written contract will provide for a partial refund, up to a certain cut-off point in the program. (There is *always* a cut-off point; and many times it is calculated by the counselor or agency in a manner other than the way *you* are calculating it. Consequently you are beyond the cut-off point, and the possibility of any refund, before you know it. Or, you reach the cut-off point and allow it to pass because you are, up to that point, satisfied with their services, and you have been led to believe there is much more to come. Only, there isn't. Once the cut-off point is passed, the career counselor's time becomes harder and harder to get.)

Clearly this second financial arrangement (as opposed to the hourly) is to the advantage of the career counselor or agency, more than it is to the advantage of the job-hunter. There's nothing inherently meritorious about paying someone a whole lot of money before he (or she) has performed any of the services they say they are going to perform. Except that once you've parted with that much cash, you *will* work extra hard at doing whatever you are asked to do, in order to make such an investment in yourself (as it were) pay off. If you are a person who is normally tempted to dilly-dally, this *will* keep your nose to the grindstone. On the other hand, if you should become increasingly dissatisfied with the counseling or "program" as it progresses, you may be "out" a lot of dough. With no legal recourse.

It would be lovely if one could make a simple equation, such as "career counselors who charge by the hour are good guys, while career counselors who ask you to pay it all up front are bad guys." Unhappily, this isn't true. There are some simply awful career counselors who charge by the hour; and there are some very helpful career counselors who ask you to pay up front, before their program begins.

Generally speaking, the type of financial arrangement you go for, will depend on your personal preference for being safe or taking a gamble. And it will depend also—let us not forget this—on the size of your bank account. *Don't pay any fee, in any case, that you can't afford to lose.*

While you are still doing your information gathering on the three places, find out which of these two financial arrangements the counselor or agency requires. If a contract will be involved, should you later choose this particular place, ask for a copy of it, take it home, and show it to a good lawyer. Think *hard* about which of the two financial arrangement *you* feel most comfortable with. Then let that be one of the factors, but not the only factor, that helps you decide which career counselor to choose.

Having gotten the information *you* want, and therefore having accomplished *your* purpose for this particular visit, you politely thank them for their time and trouble, and depart. You then go on to two other places, and ask the very same questions, please! There ought to be no charges involved for such comparison-shopping visits as this, and if they subsequently bill you, inquire politely whether or not a mistake has been made by their accounting department (good thinking). If they persist in billing you, pay a visit to your local friendly Better Business Bureau, and lodge a nice unfriendly complaint against the firm in question. You'd be surprised at how many firms experience *instant repentance* when the Better Business Bureau phones them. They don't want a complaint on their BBB record.

BACK HOME NOW, after visiting the three places you chose for your comparison shopping, you have to decide: a) whether you want none of the three, or b) one of the three and if so, which one.

Look over your notes on all three places. Compare those places. Time for thought, maybe using some others as a sounding board: business friend, consultant friend, placement center, buddy, mate, or anyone whose judgment you trust.

Remember, you don't have to choose *any* of the three counselors. If you didn't really care for any of them, listen to your intuition. Choose three new counselors, dust off the notebook, and go out again. It may take a few more hours to find what you want. But, remember: the wallet or purse you will be saving is your own.

A Sampler

I. PLACES WHICH COUNSEL ANYONE

Since this Sampler has gotten larger and longer each year, I have this year begun listing the remainder of the "Help for Anyone" names by the state they are in. You are hereby advised that some of these counseling places have particular ways in which they do what they do: some prefer to work with individuals, some do mostly group counseling, some do both. Some of these places are experts in particular areas, such as Burnout, Outplacement, Interviewing, Resumes and all that good stuff. And some of these places offer services not only to individuals, but also to organizations and groups—workshops, speaking, in-house programs, etc. But many change so rapidly in their specialties, offerings, and even in their very existence, that it is better you phone the ones in your area to ask what they do, than that this Sampler should any longer try to do that.

ALABAMA

The Key—Center for Creative Living and Spiritual Growth, 219 Grove Ave. NW, Huntsville, AL 35801, 205-539-0641. Rev. Luther Kramer, Director. John Haley, Staff Associate.

ALASKA

Alaska Life/Work Planning Center, 600 University Ave., Ste. 100 E., Fairbanks, AK 99707, 907-479-8160. John F. Reeves, Consultant/Trainer.

ARIZONA

Southwest Institute of Life Management, Theodore Donald Risch, Director, 2500 N. Pantano Rd., Ste. 120, Tucson, AZ 85715, 602-296-4764.

CALIFORNIA

Alumnae Resources, 965 Mission St., Rm. 514, San Francisco, CA 94103, 415-546-7220.

Aware Advisory Center, YWCA, Second Floor, 2019 14th St. (near Pico Blvd.), Santa Monica, CA 90405, 213-392-1303.

Branham & Associates, 2117 E. Brentford Ave., Orange, CA 92667, 714-637-4694.

Career Alternatives, 3443 Camino Del Rio S., Ste. 212, San Diego, CA 92103, 619-283-2291.

Career Development Institute, 690 Market St., Ste. 404, San Francisco, CA 94104, 415-982-2636.

Career Dimensions, 1231 W. Robinhood Dr., Ste. D-1, Stockton, CA 95207, 209-957-3685. Fran Abbott.

Constructive Leisure, Patsy B. Edwards, 511 N. La Cienega Blvd., Los Angeles, CA 90048, 213-652-7389.

Criket Consultants, Box 323, Rancho Cordova, CA 95670, 916-363-4545.

DeLara and Associates, Fidelity Savings Building, 1990 N. California Blvd., Ste. 830, Walnut Creek, CA 94598, 415-932-7015. Joy DeLara, Director.

Experience Unlimited, Mr. Herman L. Leopold, Coordinator, Employment Development Department, 1225 4th Avenue, Oakland, CA 94606, 415-464-1259/464-0659.

Life/Career Development, 4035 El Macero Dr., Davis, CA 95616, 916-756-8637. Russell A. Bruch, Director, Career consultant.

Management Development International, 5130 Gilchrist Rd., Sebastopol, CA 95472, 707-795-3087. Thomas Scott, Principal Associate.

National University Career Center, 4007 Camino Del Rio S., San Diego, CA 92108, 619-563-7250.

ProTalents, Inc., 1299 Newell Hill Pl., Ste. 201, Walnut Creek, CA 94596, 415-945-2006.

Fran Schwartz, 13219 Dobbins Pl., Los Angeles, CA 90049, 213-451-2755/778-1772.

Fran Wallace, 1431 Beach Park Blvd., Ste. 216, Foster City, CA 94404, 415-571-7874.

Withers, Wendy C., LCSW, Center for Evaluation and Service, Ste. #107, 2020 N. Broadway, Walnut Creek, CA 94596, 415-930-6454.

Joanne Young, Box 19273, Irvine, CA 92714, 714-552-7384.

COLORADO

Colorado Growth Center, Inc., 965 Humboldt St., Ste. 105, Denver, CO 80218, 303-831-9578. Arthur F. Smith, Jr., Counselor.

Samuel Kirk and Associates, Central Office, 1418 S. Race, Denver, CO 80210, 303-722-0717.

CONNECTICUT

Career Evaluation Services, 998 Farmington Ave., W. Hartford, CT 06107, 203-236-2914.

The Counseling Service of the Metropolitan Hartford YMCA, Inc., 160 Jewell St., Third Floor, Hartford, CT 06103, 203-522-4183.

People Management Inc., 10 Station St., King's Head Row, Simsbury CT 06070, 203-651-3581. Arthur F. Miller, Jr., President.

DISTRICT OF COLUMBIA

Georgetown University, School for Summer and Continuing Education, 36th and N. Sts. NW, Washington, DC 20057, 202-625-3003.

FLORIDA

Center for Career Transition, Continuing Education Building, University of Florida, 2102 W. University Ave., Gainesville, FL 32603.

Ellen O. Jonassen, Ph.D., 1105 S. Fort Harrison Ave., Clearwater, FL 33516, 813-441-2629/585-6133.

Life Designs, Inc., Life/Work Planning Consultants, 7400 SW 57 Court, S. Miami, FL 33143, 305-665-3212.

Shea Yablonsky Associates, Inc., 2626 W. Oakland Park Blvd., Ste. 213, Fort Lauderdale, FL 33311, 305-486-1800.

GEORGIA

Charles W. Cates, Ph.D., Life Work Associates, Box 52, Decatur, GA 30030, 404-373-0336.

Judith L. Cole, M.Ed., Lenox Towers, 3390 Peachtree Rd., Atlanta, GA 30327, 404-233-0946.

IDAHO

Life/Work Planning Services, 1955 Wilmington Dr., Boise, ID 83704, 208-375-0742. Janet Atkinson Lawrence, M.Ed.

ILLINOIS

Career Potential, 1318 E. State St., Rockford, IL 61107, 815-962-7666. Linda Ream and Mary-Stuart Carruthers.

The Disier Group, Institute of Applied Academics, Career Advancement Center, 625 N. Michigan Ave., Ste. 500, Chicago, IL 60611, 312-944-0990. (Formerly Institute of Applied Academics...)

The Employment Consulting Group, North Shore Unitarian Church, 2100 Half Day Rd. (12700 West Highway 22), Deerfield, IL 60015, 312-234-2460.

National Office of Program Development, Inc., 103 S. Washington, Bening Square, Ste. 202, Carbondale, IL 62901, 618-529-1910; 220 S. State, Consumers Building, Ste. 1308, Chicago, IL 60604, 312-987-1171.

Occupational Consultants, Paul J. Reibman, 1030 Indian Rd., Glenview, IL 60025, 312-729-2117.

MARYLAND

Careerscope, Harriet Tubman Center, 8045 Route 32, Columbia, MD 21044, 301-531-6655.

Womanscope, 222 Long Reach Village Center, Columbia, MD 21045, 301-997-2916.

MASSACHUSETTS

Career Change Consultant, Jane Hynes, 51 Highland St., W. Newton, MA 02165, 617-369-1686.

Career Development Consultant, Ellen J. Wallach, 8 Sherburne Rd., Lexington, MA 02173, 617-862-0997.

Changes, Carl Schneider, 7 Woodbridge St., Cambridge, MA 02140, 617-876-5085.

Communication Resources, 75 Parker Rd., Wellesley, MA 02181, 617-237-3599. John C. Zacharis, Counselor.

New England Career Center, 70 Chase St., Newton Centre, MA 02159. Barton M. Lloyd, Associate Director.

MICHIGAN

Career Planning Services, 2777 Colony Rd., Ann Arbor, MI 48104, 313-973-9286. Catherine Schwarz.

Lifework Options, 1609 E. Kalamazoo St., Lansing, MI 48912, 517-374-8896. Dolores Wood, Career Consultant.

MINNESOTA

Human Renewal Center, 2720 W. 43rd St., Minneapolis, MN 55410, 612-925-0330. Richard Leider and Janet Hagberg, Directors.

MISSOURI

Career Planning and Placement Center, Adult Evening Program, 110 Noyes Hall, University of Missouri, Columbia, MO 65201, 314-882-6803.

NEW JERSEY

Walter Goldschlager & Associates, 8D Appletree Lane, Old Bridge, NJ 08857, 201-679-8086.

NEW YORK

The John C. Crystal Center, 111 E. 31st St., New York, NY 10016. Phone 212-889-8500. Our good friend, John Crystal, devotes himself exclusively to the work of the Crystal Center, of which he is Chairman (Nella G. Barkley is president).

NORTH CAROLINA

Thomas S. Baldwin, Ph.D., Licensed Practicing Psychologist, 87 S. Elliott Rd., Ste. 200, Chapel Hill, NC 27514, 919-929-0496.

OHIO

Career Resources, Third National Bank Building, 32 N. Main St., Ste. 1245, Dayton, OH 45402, 513-223-8000.

The University of Akron, Adult Resource Center, Akron, OH 44325, 216-375-7448.

WIS, 6874 Hayhurst St., Worthington, OH 43085, 614-888-3709. Marion E. Rucker, Ph.D.

OREGON

Sylvan Psychological and Counseling Services, 215 Skyline Bldg., 2041 SW 58th Ave., Portland, OR 97221, 503-292-9867. Joseph A. Dubay, Career Counselor and Consultant.

PENNSYLVANIA

Career Focus Counseling Service, Inc., 311 Pinevue Dr., Monroeville, PA 15146, 412-372-4564. Mike and Betty Fonfara, Counselors.

Center For the Study of Adult Development, affiliated with Dept. of Psychiatry, University of Pennsylvania, Ste. 260, 3401 Market St., Philadelphia, PA 19104, 215-662-4080.

LaRoche College Career Center, 9000 Babcock Blvd., Pittsburgh, PA 15237, 412-367-9300, ext. 144, 145 & 146. Kris Rosenberg, Director.

Pennsburg Outreach Center, 643 Main St., Pennsburg, PA 18073, 215-679-5511. Sponsored by Montgomery County Community College, Blue Bell, PA 19422.

Pottstown Outreach Center, Walnut and Penn Sts., Pottstown, PA 19464, 215-323-1939. Sponsored by Montgomery County Community College, Blue Bell, PA 19422.

TENNESSEE

Career and Life Planning, 372 Reedwood Dr., Nashville, TN 37217, 615-367-1816. Marshall Cooper, M.Ed., Director.

Resume Resources, 400 21st Ave. S., Nashville, TN 37203, 615-327-0747. Jane C. Hardy, Career Development Consultant.

TEXAS

Adult Career Exploration Services (ACES), 300 E. Fifth St., Austin, TX 78768, 512-476-2716. ACES is an open-door community service provided by Austin Community College.

Austin Women's Center, 711 San Antonio, Austin, TX 78701, 512-472-3775.

Cochran Chapel United Methodist Church, Life/Work Planning Workshop, 9027 Midway Rd., Dallas, TX 75209. Rev. Wallace Chappell and Rev. Bill Johnson.

Creative Careers, Jon Patrick Bourg. Box 16817, San Antonio, TX 78216-1517. 512-344-6672.

Life/Work Design, 3906 North Lamar Blvd., Ste. 202, Austin, TX 78756, 512-458-2807. Jeanne Quereau, M.A.

Donald McKinney, Ed.D, Director, Career Planning/Job Search Division, Leonard's Training Program, Inc., Box 5547, Arlington, TX 76011, 800-433-5032, or 214-261-3108.

Self Directions, 109 Lexington, Ste. 218, San Antonio, TX 78205, 512-220-1086. Nancy R. Lopez, Director.

VIRGINIA

Endependence Center of Northern Virginia, 2300 Ninth St. S., Ste. 212, Arlington, VA 22204, 703-979-8900.

Life Management Services, Inc., 6825 Redmond Drive, McLean, VA 22101, 703-356-2630. Hal and Marilyn Shook, President and Vice President.

Psychological Consultants, Inc., 6724 Patterson Ave., Richmond, VA 23226, 804-288-4125.

Swenholt Associates, Inc., 3414 Barger Dr., Falls Church, VA 22044, 702-256-2383. Frankie P. Swenholt, President.

WISCONSIN

David Swanson, Career Directions, 11621 W. Blue Mound Rd., Milwaukee, WI 53226, 414-259-0265.

Madison Campus Ministry, 731 State St., Madison, WI 53706, 608-257-1039.

WYOMING

University of Wyoming, Counseling Center, Box 3708, University Station, Laramie, WY 82071, 307-766-2187.

FOREIGN

Robert J. Bisdee & Associates, 22 Allenby Ave., Malvern East, Victoria, Australia 3145, 613-025-4716.

Walt Hopkins, Ph.D., is now based in London, England, where he directs Castle Consultants. Walt can be reached through his North American office at 19725 Shoreland Dr., Cleveland, OH 44116.

The previous places are listed at their own request. The listing here is *not* a recommendation of them necessarily. If you have a terrible experience with any of them, please let us know. Do remember to ask the proper questions, please, (page 279–81) before signing on. Otherwise, you may have only yourself to blame.

CAREER COUNSELOR CATALOGS

Enterprising souls are now putting together listings of counselors, agencies, resources and (sometimes) employers for individual cities or metropolitan areas. While such books, unless they are revised annually, are bound to become outdated rapidly (ah, how well I know) due to places moving, folding, or rising Phoenixlike from their own ashes in a different form and place, nonetheless these books offer at least a starting place if you are looking for help. These works have been brought to our attention, so far:

The Boston Job Bank, 1981
The Greater Chicago Job Bank, 1982
The Metropolitan New York Job Bank, 1982
The Southern California Job Bank, 1982
The Northern California Job Bank, 1982
The Texas Job Bank, 1982
The Pennsylvania Job Bank, 1982
The Washington Metropolitan Job Bank, 1983.

(All of the above publications were edited by Robert Lang Adams, and can be obtained in paperback from Bob Adams, Inc., 2945 Commonwealth Ave., Brighton, MA 02135, for $9.95 plus $1.00 postage, each.)

Lewis, Florence, *Help Wanted: A Guide to Career Counseling in the Bay Area*. Available from the author, JFK University, 12 Altarinda Rd., Orinda, CA 94563. $4.95, paper. It covers San Francisco, Marin County, the East Bay, and Santa Clara County.

O'Callaghan, Dorothy, *The Job Catalog: Where to find that creative job in Washington/ Baltimore in the private sector*, c/o Mail Order USA, Box 19083, Washington, DC 20036. 1982. $8.00, paper.

Levine, Renee, *How to Get a Job in Boston*. Resources, networks and tips on finding a job in you-can-guess-where. This is the third edition of this 90-page book/pamphlet. You can order it from: Vocations for Social Change, Box 211, Essex Station, Boston, MA 02112. $3.95, paper.

Albin, James R., *Bay Area Employment Agency and Executive Recruiter Directory*. James R. Albin, 431 Bridgeway, Sausalito, CA 94965. $9.95. (California residents add $.60 sales tax; BART counties, $.65.)

Donnis, Mary; Harms, Sally; Mullinack, Winifred; Saff, Joan; and Sampson, Diane, *The San Francisco Bay Area People's Yellow Pages*. People's Yellow Pages, Box 31291, San Francisco, CA 94131. 1981. $5.95, paper.

Raders, Sheri, *Portland Career Hunter's Guide, A Sourcebook of Local Resources for the Serious Career Planner and Job Hunter*. You can order it from: Victoria House, Publishers, 2218 NE Eighth Ave., Portland, OR 97212. 1977. $3.95, paper.

When we turn from counselors who help anyone, to counselors who work with specified populations, it is no longer sufficient to just give names and addresses. Since we are giving you more information in the rest of this Sampler, we are concommitantly increasing the likelihood of Glaring Error. If you discover such, please let us know at once, and we will make the appropriate changes in next year's revision. (Write: Box 379, Walnut Creek, CA 94597.)

II. GROUP-SUPPORT FOR THOSE WHO ARE UNEMPLOYED

Forty-Plus Clubs. Not a national organization, but a voluntary group of autonomous non-profit clubs, manned by members, paying no salaries, supported by initiation fees and monthly dues of members. Clubs now operating in New York City (Manhattan), Philadelphia, Washington, DC, Chicago, Milwaukee, Houston, Denver, Los Angeles, the Bay Area (Oakland) of California, and Hawaii. (See phone book for exact addresses.) *Normally only open to those who are forty years or older, unemployed, seeking employment, making an average of at least $12,000-$15,000 (this varies from one club to another) for the preceding five years, and able to pass a screening process.* Screening procedures of all these 'Forty-Plus' type groups may also vary, but usually they involve personal interview, checking out of business references, and informal meeting with representative active members. Process may take two to three weeks, in normal course. Insiders say it takes the average member about three months to find placement, and one (at least) alleges that about one-third leave without finding placement—or hang around for indefinite periods. Members must agree to give (typically) sixteen hours a week or two and one-half days to the club. Fees and dues vary from club to club.

NE-VEST (New England Volunteer Employment Services Team), 400 Totten Pond Rd., Waltham, MA 02154, (617) 890-7150. An organization of unemployed professionals who help themselves and each other to find jobs. Basic, Advanced and Career Planning Workshops, plus videotape workshops, and others for special interest groups: men over forty-five, women, etc. There are no fees; the only requirement is that for every hour you attend a workshop, you volunteer an hour of your time to NE-VEST. Orientation every Friday, 1–2 pm.

Talent Bank Associates, 475 Calkins Rd., Henrietta (near Rochester), NY 14467, (716) 334-9676. An organized form of the "Job-Hunters Anonymous" idea described on page 57. A non-profit organization comprised of unemployed persons of various professions and skills working together on a volunteer basis to find themselves meaningful, permanent employment. Free of charge.

The Employment Consulting Group, North Shore Unitarian Church, Deerfield, IL. Anne Bartenfeld-Barrows, Coordinator. A group process for the unemployed, involving use of *The Quick Job-Hunting Map*, job-goal definition, contact building, the interview process, and negotiation. Volunteer consultants help in the process. Small fee, after finding the job.

Career Planning and Placement Center, Adult Evening Program, 110 Noyes Hall, University of Missouri, Columbia, MO 65201, (314) 882-6803. Tuesday and Thursday, 5–9 pm. Open to the public. Free. Drop-in for research. Schedule individual appointment. Help with goal clarification, resumes, interviews, job-seeking strategies, training opportunities. Job-seeking group.

Experience Unlimited. An organization for unemployed professionals, based in California. Contact: Mr. Herman L. Leopold, Experience Unlimited Coordinator, Dept. of Human Resources Development, 1111 Jackson St., Room 1009, Oakland, CA 94607, (415) 464-1337.

Civic Center Volunteers. Marin County Personnel Office, Administration Bldg., Civic Center, San Rafael, CA 94903, (415) 499-6104. Placement in county jobs of volunteer re-entry women, career-experimenters and students wishing to gain experience. Volunteers sign a contract for each specific job, and receive supervision and evaluation. The purpose of this program is to give work experience in various jobs and provide a place to gain confidence in one's skills, new self-esteem, etc.

T-I-E (Together in Employment). Offered in the Seattle-Tacoma area. Five individualized group sessions over two weeks. $25.00 fee. Sponsored by the Episcopal Diocese of Olympia, the specially-trained volunteers (trained by Bernard Haldane) offer their programs through neighborhood churches. The seminars are however ecumenical, open to all. To register: (206) 325-4200. Dick French is chairman of TIE's advisory board.

III. HELP FOR COLLEGE STUDENTS OR GRADUATES

As we stated earlier (page 28), most of the colleges in this country—two-year or four-year—have some kind of Career Planning or Placement Office. Usually the office on a particular campus can be found under the above title, although sometimes it is "buried" in the Counseling Department, or in the Dean of Student Services Office. How helpful the Career Planning office is, on the particular campus you are attending, depends on the staffing, philosophy, and funding of that office—and this may vary from year to year (and even from season to season). So, go explore for yourself.

A directory of these offices is published, and is available for perusal in most Placement Offices. It is called the *Directory of Career Planning and Placement Offices*, and is published by the College Placement Council, Inc., Box 2263, Bethlehem, PA 18001. This directory is not a complete listing of all such offices in the country. The Career Planning and Placement Office (c/o Office of Counseling and Testing) at Western Nevada Community College, for example, has asked us to point out that they exist, even though they are not in this directory. (7000 Sullivan Lane, Reno, NV 89505, [702] 673-4666.)

Now, if you are not only a college graduate but also a hopeless romantic, you will have a vision of blissful cooperation existing between all of these placement offices across the country. So that if you are a graduate of an East Coast college, let us say, and subsequently you move to California, and want help with career planning, you should in theory be able to walk into the placement office on any California campus, and be helped by that office (a non-altruistic service based on the likelihood that a graduate of that California campus is, at the same moment, walking into the placement office of your East Coast college—and thus, to coin a phrase, "one hand is washing another"). Alas and alack, dear graduate, in most cases it doesn't work like that. You will be told, sometimes with genuine regret, that *by official policy*, this particular placement office on this particular campus is only allowed to aid its own students and alumni. One Slight Ray of Hope: on a number of campuses, there are career counselors who think this policy is absolutely asinine, so if you walk into the Career Planning office on that campus, *are lucky enough to get one of Those Counselors,* and you don't mention whether or not you went to that college—the counselor will never ask, and will proceed to help you just as though you were a real person.

This restriction (to their own students and graduates) is less likely to be found at Community Colleges than it is at four-year institutions. So, if you run into a dead end, try a Community College near you. For high school students considering college, there are various agencies that help, such as:

Educational Talent Search, Spanish Education Development Center, 1840 Kalorama Rd. NW, Washington, DC 20009, 202-462-8782. Funded by the Department of Education to provide minority and low-income individuals between the ages of 12 and 27 with academic and vocational counseling and information on career, post-secondary education, and financial aid opportunities.

IV. HELP FOR WOMEN

(MANY OF THESE ALSO SERVE MEN)

Resource centers for women are springing up all over the country, faster than we can record them. We are listing here *only a sampling* of same. If you have a favorite, not listed here, send us the pertinent information—in format similar to the next pages—and we'll list it in the next edition. (Don't, however, bother to send us college services which are available only to the students and alumnae of that college. We try not to list such places, since such a listing only frustrates non-alumnae. If, inadvertently, any such place already listed here is thus restricted, please let us know, and we'll gently remove it from the next edition.) Incidentally, the centers which are listed here will know (in all probability) what other centers or resources there are in your geographical area. Also, try your telephone book's yellow pages: "Women's Organizations and Services," or "Vocational Consultants."

In all of this you will remember won't you, our earlier description (page 275) of all career counseling professionals, as falling into one of three groups: (1) Sincere and skilled; (2) Sincere but inept; and (3) Insincere and inept? Well, dear friend, groups or organizations or centers which have been organized specifically to help women job-hunters or career-changers are not—by that act—made immune to the above distinctions. Think about it, before you agree to put your (vocational) life into somebody else's hands. Remember: the numbers game (chapter 2), even if it is expressed in beautifully non-sexist language, is still the numbers game.

RESOURCES FOR WOMEN

ALABAMA

Enterprise State Junior College, Women's Center, Career Development Center, Highway 84 E., Box 1300, Enterprise, AL 36330, 205-347-7881 or 5431. Monday–Friday, 8 am–4:30 pm.

University of Alabama, Career Planning and Placement, 1300 8th Avenue S., Bldg. 5, Rm. 110, Birmingham, AL 35294, 205-934-4324 or 4470. Monday–Friday, 8:30 am–5 pm.

ALASKA

University of Alaska, Anchorage Education Opportunity Center, 3211 Providence Ave., Library Bldg., Rm. 103, Anchorage, AK 99504, 907-263-1525. Monday–Friday, 8am–5 pm.

ARIZONA

University of Arizona, Student Counseling Service, Old Main, Tucson, AZ 85721, 602-626-2316. Monday–Friday, 8 am–noon and 1–5 pm; Tuesday and Wednesday, 5 pm–7 pm. Official college office. Restricted to students. Educational and career counseling, and personal and marital counseling, continuing education courses. No fees.

CALIFORNIA

Advocates for Women, 414 Mason St., 4th Fl., San Francisco, CA 94102, 415-391-4870. Monday–Friday, 8:30 am–4:30 pm; Tuesday, 8:30 am–9 pm. Independent nonprofit agency. Career counseling, job referral, placement. Offices also in Berkeley and Hayward.

Alumnae Resources, 965 Mission St., Ste. 514, San Francisco, CA 94103, 415-546-7220. Emphasis on Liberal Arts graduates. Offers workshops, seminars, individual counseling, and special events. Fees vary. Appointments necessary.

American River College, Student Services Bldg., 4700 College Oak Dr., Sacramento, CA 95841, 916-484-8391. Monday–Friday, 8 am–6 pm.

Career Design, An Affiliate of Ranny Riley & Assoc., Box 1552, San Francisco, CA 94101, 415-929-8161/929-8150. Offers a variety of intensive seminars and comprehensive workshops. Fees vary.

Career Planning Center/Business Action Center, 6022 W. Pico Blvd., Los Angeles, CA 90035, 213-273-6633. Monday–Friday, 8:30 am–5 pm. Independent, non-profit agency. Offers career planning information, assessment and training through seminars, workshops and individual consultation. Specific programs for re-entry women, women in non-traditional occupations, and teachers. Job referral and placement. Fees vary.

The Claremont Colleges, Special Academic Programs and Office for Continuing Education, Harper Hall 160, Claremont, CA 91711, 714-621-8000, ext. 8069. Monday–Friday, 9 am–5 pm. College sponsored office. Educational and career counseling, job referral, continuing education courses. Registration fee.

Crossroads Institute for Career Development, 2288 Fulton St., Berkeley, CA 94704, 415-848-0698. Monday–Friday, 9 am–5 pm.

Cypress College, Career Planning Center, 9200 Valley View St., Cypress, CA 90630, 714-826-2220, Ext. 221. Monday–Friday, 8 am–4:30 pm. Official college office. Educational and career counseling. No fees.

Information Advisory Service, UCLA Extension, 10995 Le Conte Ave., Rm. 114, Los Angeles, CA 90024, 213-206-8201. Monday–Friday, 9 am–5 pm. College sponsored office. Educational and career counseling, job referral information, continuing education courses. No fees.

Susan W. Miller, M.A., 360 N. Bedford, Ste. 312, Beverly Hills, CA 90210, 213-837-7768. Career Counselor, Educational Consultant, private practice. Career counseling for individuals using a structured, action-oriented approach.

Resource Center for Women, 445 Sherman Ave., Palo Alto, CA 94306, 415-324-1710. Monday–Friday, 9 am–5 pm; Thursday, 9 am–9 pm. Independent nonprofit agency. Educational and career counseling, adult education courses, job referral. Fees for workshops.

San Jose State University, Re-Entry Advisory Program, Old Cafeteria Bldg., San Jose, CA 95192, 408-277-2188. Monday–Friday, 9 am–5 pm; Wednesday, 9 am–7 pm. Official college program. Educational and career counseling, referral to other services. No fees.

Allyah Stein, M.F.C.C., Integrated Counseling Services—For Career and Personal Development, 50 Montell St., Oakland, CA 94611 and 141 Belvedere St., San Francisco, CA 94117, 415-848-5167. Offers a comprehensive program of career and personal counseling, with special programs for homemakers and others concerned with re-entry or career change. Fees on a sliding scale.

Caroline Voorsanger, Career Counselor for Women, 2000 Broadway, No. 1108, San Francisco, CA 94115, 415-567-0890. Career counseling, assistance with skill assessment and focusing.

West Los Angeles College, Career/Life Planning Center, 4800 Freshman Dr., Culver city, CA 90230, 213-836-7110, Ext. 355. Monday–Friday, 8 am–4:30 pm. Educational, personal and career counseling. No fees.

The Women's Opportunities Center, Univ. of California's Extension, 4211 Campus Drive, Irvine, CA 92716, 714-833-7128. Monday–Friday, 9 am–4 pm. College sponsored office. Educational and career counseling.

Women's World International, 400 N. Tustin, Ste. 410, Santa Ana, CA 92705, 714-547-7726. Assistance with interviewing techniques, communications skills, exploring career alternatives, and achieving a professional image.

Woman's Way, 1000 Sir Francis Drake Blvd., San Anselmo, CA 94960, 415-453-4490. Monday–Friday, 9 am–5 pm.

COLORADO

Women's Resource Agency, 2340 Robinson St., Ste. 216, Colorado Springs, CO 80904, 303-471-3170. Monday–Friday, 8 am–5 pm.

CONNECTICUT

Fairfield University, Fairfield Adult Career & Educational Services (FACES), North Benson Rd., Julie Hall, Fairfield, CT 06430, 203-255-5411. Monday–Friday, 9 am–4 pm.

Norwalk Community College, Counseling Center, 333 Wilson Ave., Norwalk, CT 06854, 203-853-2040. Monday–Thursday, 9 am–7:30 pm, Friday 9 am–4 pm.

Vocational and Academic Counseling for Adults (VOCA), 115 Berrian Road, Stamford, CT 06905, 203-329-1955. Monday–Friday, 9 am–5 pm; weekends and evenings by arrangement.

DELAWARE

University of Delaware, The Women's Center, State Office Bldg., 5th Floor, Wilmington, DE 19801, 302-571-2088. Monday–Friday, 8:15 am–2:15 pm. Official college office. Educational and career counseling, continuing education courses. No registration fee. Other fees vary.

DISTRICT OF COLUMBIA

George Washington University, Continuing Education for Women, 801 22nd St. NW, Ste. T409, Washington, DC 20052, 202-676-7036. Monday–Friday, 9 am–5 pm. College sponsored. Educational and career counseling, continuing education courses, job referral. Fees vary.

Wider Opportunities for Women, 1511 K St. NW, Washington, DC 20005, 202-638-3065. A national nonprofit organization. Maintains a national directory of women's employment programs, a national resource and advocacy network for women's employment organizations, training programs for low-income women, and a handbook (Working for You) to help employers who want to hire women in "nontraditional" jobs.

FLORIDA

Council for Continuing Education for Women of Central Florida, Inc., Valencia Community College, 190 S. Orange Ave., 1st Floor, Box 3028, Orlando, FL 32802, 305-423-4813. Monday–Friday, 9 am–5 pm. Independent nonprofit agency. Educational and career counseling, adult education courses, testing.

Face Learning Center, Inc., 12945 Seminole Blvd., Bldg. 2, Ste. 8, Largo, FL 33540, 813-586-1110/585-8155. Monday–Friday, 9 am–5 pm and by appointment.

The Center for the Continuing Education of Women, Miami-Dade Community College, 300 NE Second Ave., Miami FL 33132, 305-577-6840. Monday–Friday, 8:30 am–5 pm. College sponsored office. Educational and career counseling, limited job referral, continuing education courses. Fees vary.

Stetson University Counseling Center, Campus Box 1365, North Woodland Blvd., De Land, FL 32720, 904-734-4121, Ext. 215. Monday–Friday, 8:30 am–4:30 pm.

ILLINOIS

Applied Potential, Box 585, Highland Park, IL 60035, 312-234-2310. Monday–Friday, 9 am–5 pm; evenings and Saturdays by arrangement. Nonprofit educational corporation. Professional counselors. Educational, career and personal counseling. No registration fee. Other fees vary.

Harper College Community Counseling Center, Palatine, IL 60067, 312-397-3000. Monday–Thursday, 8:30 am–4:30 pm and 6–10 pm; Friday, 8:30 am–4:30 pm. College sponsored office. Educational and career counseling. No registration fee. Other fees vary.

Jean Davis, Career Counseling, 500 Davis Center, Ste. 600, Evanston, IL 60201, 312-492-1002. Offers career assessment/design, resume and marketing strategies, job interview preparation, individual consultation and workshops.

Moraine Valley Community College, Career/Life Planning and Counseling, 10900 S. 88th Ave., Palos Hills, IL 60465, 312-974-4300. Monday–Thursday, 9 am–9 pm; Friday, 9 am–5 pm. Official college office. Fees vary.

Northwestern Illinois Career Guidance Center, 1515 S. 4th St., Dekalb, IL 60115, 815-758-7431. Monday–Friday, 8 am–4 pm.

Southern Illinois University, General Studies Division, Office of Continuing Education, Campus Box 48, Edwardsville, IL 62026, 618-692-3210. Monday–Friday, 8 am–5 pm. Official college office. Educational and career counseling, continuing education courses. No fees.

Southern Illinois University, Women's Programs Office, Woody Hall, B-244/245, Carbondale, IL 62901, 618-453-3655. Monday–Friday, 8 am–5 pm. Individual advising, group discussions. No appointment needed.

Thornton Community College, Counseling Center, 15800 S. State Street, South Holland, IL 60473, 312-596-2000, Ext. 306. Monday–Thursday, 8 am–8:30 pm; Friday, 8 am–5 pm. Career Information Center.

University of Illinois Urbana-Champaign, Student Services Office for Married Students and Continuing Education for Women, 610 East John St., Champaign, IL 61820, 217-333-3137. Monday–Friday, 8 am–5 pm. Official college office. Educational and career counseling. No fees.

Women's Employment Counseling Center, 44 East Main, Champaign, IL 61820, 217-359-3800. Monday–Friday, 9 am–5 pm. Independent, nonprofit office. Educational and career counseling, job referral and placement. No fees.

INDIANA

Ball State University, Office of Information Services, Student Affairs, Muncie, IN 47306, 317-285-8282. Monday–Friday, 8 am–5 pm.

Continuing Education Center for Women, Indiana University/Purdue University at Indianapolis, 1317 W. Mich River, Indianapolis, IN 46223, 317-264-4784. Monday–Friday, 8 am–5 pm. Official college office. Educational and career counseling, continuing education courses. Fees vary.

Fort Wayne Women's Bureau, Inc., 203 W. Wayne St., Fort Wayne, IN 46802, 219-424-7977/426-0023. Peer counseling, Monday–Friday, 10 am–2 pm. Not-for-profit agency. Career counseling, job search skills training, job opportunity book.

Indiana University, Continuing Education for Women, Owen Hall 201, Bloomington, IN 47405, 812-335-0225. Monday–Friday, 8 am–5 pm. Official college office. Educational and career counseling, continuing education courses. Fees vary.

University Center for Women, Counseling and Academic Development Division, Purdue University, 2101 Coliseum Blvd. East, Fort Wayne, IN 46805, 219-482-5393. Monday–Friday, 8 am–noon, 1 pm–5 pm. College sponsored office. Educational and career counseling, continuing education courses, job referral. Fees vary.

Woman Alive!, YWCA, 229 Ogden St., Box 1121, Hammond, IN 46325, 219-933-7168. Wednesdays (or by appointment).

Women's Resource Center, YWCA, 802 N. Lafayette Boulevard, South Bend, IN 46601, 219-233-9491. Monday–Friday, 9 am–5 pm.

IOWA

Drake University, Community Career Planning Center for Women, 1158 27th St., Des Moines, IA 50311, 515-271-2916. Monday–Friday, 8 am–4:30 pm. Official college office. Educational and career counseling, continuing education courses. No fee for individual counseling. Fee for group sessions.

University Counseling Service, Iowa Memorial Union, University of Iowa, Iowa City, IA 52242, 319-353-4484. Monday–Friday, 8 am–5 pm. College sponsored office. Educational, vocational and personal counseling.

University of Iowa, Office of Career Planning and Placement, Iowa City, IA 52242, 319-353-3147. Monday–Friday, 8 am–5 pm. Official college office. Educational and career counseling, job referral, placement. Fee for job placement only.

KANSAS

University of Kansas, Adult Life Resource Center, Division of Continuing Education, 1246 Mississippi St., Annex A, Lawrence, KS 66045, 913-864-4794 or 800-532-6772 (toll free in Kansas). Monday–Friday, 8 am–noon and 1–5 pm. College sponsored. Educational and career counseling, continuing education, program for displaced homemakers. No registration fee. Other fees vary.

MARYLAND

Baltimore New Directions for Women, 2511 N. Charles St., Baltimore, MD 21218, 301-235-8800. Monday–Friday, 9 am–4:30 pm. Educational and career counseling, continuing education courses, job referral, placement. Information center.

College of Notre Dame of Maryland, Continuing Education Center, 4701 N. Charles St., Baltimore, MD 21210, 301-435-0100. Monday–Friday, 8:30 am–4:30 pm. College sponsored. Educational and career counseling, continuing education courses. Fees vary.

Goucher College, Goucher Center for Educational Resources, Towson, Baltimore, MD 21204, 301-337-6200. Monday–Friday, 9 am–4:30 pm. College sponsored. Counseling to women considering a return to school. Noncredit and credit courses for adults. Referrals for career and volunteer work.

MASSACHUSETTS

Career & Volunteer Advisory Service, Project Re-Entry, 14 Beacon St., Boston, MA 02108, 617-227-1762. Monday–Friday, 10 am–4 pm. Independent nonprofit agency. Career counseling, job information. Fee for consultation.

Continuum, Inc., 785 Centre St., Newton, MA 02158, 617-964-3322. Monday–Friday, 9 am–3:30 pm. A private, licensed school of career education. Internship programs for women changing, entering, or advancing careers. Career counseling for related spouses, and men and women of all ages. Vocational testing available. Fees vary.

Resources Center for Educational Opportunities, 19 Fort Hill St., Hingham, MA 02043, 617-749-7445. Monday–Friday, 9:30 am–11:30 am and by appointment. Branch action project of American Association of University Women.

Smith College, Career Development Office, Pierce Hall, Northampton, MA 01063, 413-584-2700. Monday–Friday, 8:30 am–4:30 pm. Official college office. Educational and career counseling. No fees.

Widening Opportunity Research Center, Middlesex Community College, Box T, Bedford, MA 01730, 617-275-8910, Ext. 291. Monday–Friday, 9 am–2 pm. College sponsored office. Educational and career counseling, continuing education courses. Fees vary.

Wider Opportunities for Women—Boston, 413 Commonwealth Ave., Boston, MA 02215, 617-437-1040. Monday, Thursday and Friday, 9 am–5 pm; Tuesday and Wednesday, 9 am–8 pm; Saturday, 10 am–2 pm. A private, nonprofit organization, serving career counseling to women on a self-help basis. A membership organization, charging a bi-annual fee, which entitles members thereafter to unlimited drop-in career counseling and use of job-listings. Also offers workshops.

Women's Educational & Industrial Union, Career Services, 356 Boylston St., Boston, MA 02116, 617-536-5651. Monday–Friday, 9 am–5 pm. Independent nonprofit agency. Career counseling, job referral and placement. No registration fee. Placement fees vary.

Why Not? Program, YWCA, 1 Salem Sq., Worcester, MA 01608, 617-791-3181. Monday–Friday, 9 am–5 pm; evenings by appointment. Fees vary.

MICHIGAN

Every Woman's Place, 1433 Clinton, Muskegon, MI 49442, 616-726-4493. Monday–Friday, 9 am–5 pm.

Michigan Technological University, Center for Continuing Education for Women, Rm. 301A Administration Bldg., Houghton, MI 49931, 906-487-2270. Monday–Friday, 8 am–5 pm. Official college office. Educational and career counseling, continuing education courses. No registration fee. Other fees vary.

Macomb County Community College, Community Resource Center, 14500 Twelve Mile Road, K-332, Warren, MI 48093, 313-445-7417. Monday–Friday, 8:30 am–5 pm.

Montcalm Community College, Student Services Office, Sidney, MI 48885, 517-328-2111. Monday–Friday, 8 am–5 pm; evenings by appointment. College sponsored office. Education and career counseling. No fees.

C.S. Mott Community College, Guidance Services and Counseling Division, 1401 East Court St., Flint, MI 48503, 313-762-0356. Monday–Thursday, 8 am–7 pm; Friday, 8 am–4:30 pm. Health counseling and vocational testing.

Northern Michigan University, Women's Center for Continuing Education, Marquette, MI 49855, 906-227-2101. Monday–Friday, 8:30 am–4:30 pm. Official college office. Educational and career counseling, job referral, continuing education courses. Fees vary.

Oakland University, Continuum Center for Adult Counseling and Leadership Training, Rochester, MI 48063, 313-377-3033. Monday–Friday, 8 am–5 pm. College affiliated. Personal, educational and career counseling, continuing education courses. Fees vary.

Schoolcraft College, Women's Resource Center, 18600 Haggerty Road, Livonia, MI 48152, 313-591-6400, Ext. 430. Monday–Friday, 9 am–3 pm. Continuing Education Community Services; Educational and career counseling courses, workshops, referral to other agencies, and peer counseling. For widowed, displaced homemakers and re-entry women and men. Fees for courses and workshops only.

University of Michigan, Center for Continuing Education of Women, 350 S. Thayer St., Ann Arbor, MI 48109, 313-764-6555.

Western Michigan University, Center for Women's Services, Kalamazoo, MI 49008, 616-383-6097. Monday–Friday, 8 am–5 pm. Official college office. Educational and career counseling. Fees vary.

Women's Center, University of Michigan-Dearborn, Office of Student Affairs, 4901 Evergreen Rd., Dearborn, MI 48128, 313-593-5147. Discussions and information about employment trends, study skills, childcare, re-entry, scholarships, career planning, social interactions, marriage and divorce, legal issues, rape prevention, and health care. Fees vary.

Women's Resource Center, 226 Bostwick NE, Grand Rapids, MI 49503, 616-456-8571. Monday and Wednesday, 9 am–8 pm; Tuesday and Thursday, 9 am–5 pm. Independent nonprofit agency. Educational and career counseling, job referral. Fees vary.

MINNESOTA

Minnesota Women's Center, University of Minnesota, 5 Eddy Hall, Minneapolis, MN 55455, 612-373-3850. Monday–Friday, 8 am–4:30 pm. Official college office. Informal advising and referral. No fees.

Southwest State University, Women's Resource Center, Marshall, MN 56258, 507-537-7160, September–May. Monday–Friday, 8 am–4:30 pm; evening schedule varies. Official college office. Educational and career counseling, job referral and placement, continuing education courses. Placement fee only.

Working Opportunities for Women, 2233 University Ave., Ste. 340, St. Paul, MN 55114, 612-647-9961. Monday–Friday, 8:30 am–5 pm. Monday, 6 pm–9 pm. Complete career planning services for women.

MISSISSIPPI

Mississippi State University, Placement and Career Information Center, Drawer P, Mississippi State, MS 39762, 601-325-3344. Monday–Friday, 8 am–5 pm.

MISSOURI

New Directions Center, 806 N. Providence Rd., Columbia, MO 65201, 314-443-2421. Monday–Friday, 9 am–4 pm. Career planning, education referral and job placement center for women. Workshops and individual career counseling.

University of Missouri, St. Louis, Continuing Education-Extension, 313 Education Office Bldg., 8001 Natural Bridge Rd., St. Louis, MO 63121, 314-553-5511. Monday–Friday, 8 am–5 pm. Official college office. Educational and career counseling, adult education courses, limited job referral. Fees vary.

The Women's Center, University of Missouri, Kansas City, 5204 Rockhill Rd., Kansas City, MO 64110, 816-276-1638. Monday–Friday, 8 am–5 pm. Official college office. Educational and career counseling, job referral, continuing education courses. No fees.

MONTANA

Focus on Women, 9 Hamilton Hall, Montana State University, Bozeman, MT 59717, 406-994-4541. Monday–Friday, 8 am–5 pm. Workshops, seminars. Fee varies.

Women's Resource Center, Non-traditional Job Counselor, University of Montana, Missoula, MT 59801, 406-453-6691. Monday–Friday, 8 am–5 pm. Non-traditional career counseling, and job referral. No fee.

Women in Transition, Missoula YWCA, 1130 W. Broadway, Missoula, MT 59801, 406-543-6691. Monday–Friday, 8 am–5 pm. Job counseling, career counseling, job referral, resume preparation. Works with displaced homemakers. No fee.

NEW JERSEY

Adult Service Center, 112 Main Rd., Montville, NJ 07045, 201-575-0855, 335-4420. Monday, Tuesday, Thursday, Friday, 9 am–1 pm; Wednesday, 7 pm–10 pm.

Bergen Community College, Division of Community Services, 400 Paramus Rd., Paramus, NJ 07652, 201-447-1940. Monday–Friday, 9 am–5 pm. College sponsored office. Educational and career counseling, adult education courses. No fees.

Caldwell College, Career Development Center, Caldwell, NJ 07006, 201-228-4424, Ext. 307. Monday–Friday, 8:30 am–4:30 pm. College sponsored office. Educational and career counseling, limited job referral. No fees.

College Counseling and Education Center, 369 Forest Ave., Paramus, NJ 07652, 201-265-7729. Monday–Saturday, 9 am–9 pm.

Douglass College, Douglass Advisory Services for Women, Rutgers Women's Center, 132 George St., New Brunswick, NJ 08903, 201-932-9603. Monday–Friday, 9 am–2 pm. Educational and career counseling. No fees.

Fairleigh Dickinson University, Center for Women, Madison Ave., Madison, NJ 07940, 201-377-4700, Ext. 320. Monday–Friday, 9 am–5 pm. Official college office, Educational and career counseling, continuing education courses, job referral and placement. No fees.

Eve Adult Advisory Services, Kean College of New Jersey, Administration Bldg., Union, NJ 07083, 201-527-2210. Monday–Friday, 9 am–4:30 pm. College sponsored. Educational and career counseling. No registration fee. Other fees vary.

Jersey City State College, The Women's Center, 94 Audubon, Jersey City, NJ 07305, 201-547-3189. Monday–Friday, 9 am–4:30 pm. Official college office. Educational and career counseling, continuing education courses. No fees.

Jewish Vocational Service, 111 Prospect St., East Orange, NJ 07017, 201-674-6330. Five days, thirty-seven hours. Independent, nonprofit office. Eduational and career counseling, job referral and placement. Fees vary.

Middlesex County College, Women's Career Information Center, Woodbridge Ave., West Hall Annex, Edison, NJ 08818, 201-548-6000, Ext. 411. Monday–Friday, 10 am–4 pm.

Montclair State College, Women's Center, Valley Rd., Upper Montclair, NJ 07043, 201-893-5106. Monday–Friday, 8:30 am–4:30 pm; evenings by appointment. College sponsored office. Educational and career counseling. No fees.

The Professional Roster, 171 Broadmead, Princeton, NJ 08609, 609-921-9561. Monday–Friday, 10 am–1 pm. Independent, nonprofit organization. Career counseling, job referral.

Reach, Inc., College of St. Elizabeth, O'Connor Hall, NJ 07961, 201-267-2530. Monday–Friday, 9:30 am–3 pm. Independent nonprofit office, Educational and career counseling, job referral. Fees vary.

NEW MEXICO

Young Women's Christian Association, Women's Resource Center, 316 Fourth St. SW, Albuquerque, NM 87102, 505-247-8841. Monday–Friday, 8 am–5 pm. Career counseling on a group basis. Classes, workshops, support groups, library. Fees on sliding scale: no one turned away for inability to pay.

NEW YORK

Academic Advisory Center for Adults, Turf Ave., Rye, NY 10580, 914-967-1653. Monday–Thursday, 9am–4 pm, some evenings.

Columbia University, Womanspace Career Options Program for Women, School of General Studies, Lewisohn Hall 211, New York, NY 10027, 212-280-2820. Monday, Thursday, Friday, 9 am–5 pm. Tuesday, Wednesday, 9 am–7 pm.

Counseling Women, 14 East 60th St., Rm. 702, New York, NY 10022, 212-486-9755. Monday–Friday, 9:30 am–7 pm. Individual and group counseling, workshops.

Hofstra University, Counseling Center, 240 Student Center, Hempstead, NY 11550, 516-560-6788. Monday–Friday, 9 am–5 pm; Monday, Thursday, 6–10 pm. Official college office. Educational and vocational counseling, testing, continuing education courses. Fees vary.

Human Relations Work-Study Center, New School for Social Research, 66 West 12th St., New York, NY 10011, 212-741-5684. Monday–Friday, 9 am–5 pm. Official college office. Educational counseling, continuing education courses. Special training for human services. Fees vary.

Kingsborough Community College, Office of Career Counseling and Placement, 2001 Oriental Blvd., Rm. C102, Brooklyn, NY 11235, 212-934-5115. Monday–Friday, 8 am–5 pm.

Janice La Rouche Assoc., Workshops for Women, 333 Central Park West, New York, NY 10025, 212-663-0970. Monday–Saturday, 9 am–6 pm. Independent private agency. Career strategies counseling. Assertiveness training. No registration fee. Other fees vary.

Mercy College, Career Counseling and Placement Office, 555 Broadway, Dobbs Ferry, NY 10522, 914-693-4500, Ext. 215. Monday–Friday, 9 am–5 pm. Evenings by appointment. Official college office. Career counseling. Fees vary.

More for Women, 1435 Lexington Ave., New York, NY 10028, 212-534-0852. Monday–Friday, 9 am–9 pm; Saturday, 9 am–4 pm. Independent private agency. Educational and career counseling, workshops. Fees vary.

New Options, 11 E. 80th St., New York, NY 10021, 212-535-1444. Monday–Friday, 9 am–5 pm. Evenings by appointment.

Orange County Community College, Office of Community Services, 115 South St., Middletown, NY 10940, 914-343-1121. Monday–Friday, 9 am–5 pm. Official college office. Educational counseling, continuing education courses. Fees vary.

Personnel Sciences Center, 341 Madison Ave., New York, NY 10017, 212-661-1870. Monday–Saturday, 9 am–5 pm. Independent private agency. Educational and career counseling. Fees vary.

Professional Skills Roster, 512 E. State St., Ithaca, NY 14850, 607-272-5533. Monday–Friday, 9:30 am–12:30 pm. Independent nonprofit agency. Job referral, limited educational and career counseling. No fees. Suggested donation.

Regional Learning Service Center of New York, 405 Oak St., Syracuse, NY 13203, 315-425-5252. Monday–Friday, 8:30 am–4:30 pm. Independent nonprofit agency. Educational and career counseling, education courses. Registration fees vary.

Ruth Shapiro Associates, Career Development and Self-Marketing Workshops, 200 E. 30th St., New York, NY 10016, 212-889-4284, 679-9858. Monday–Saturday, 9 am–5 pm. Evenings by appointment.

SUNY at Buffalo, Career Planning Office, 252 Capen Hall, Buffalo, NY 14260, 716-636-2231. Monday–Friday, 8:30 am–5 pm. Official college office. Educational and career counseling, job referral and placement. No fees.

SUNY at Stony Brook, Mid-Career Counseling Center, Social and Behavioral Services Bldg., Rm. N211, Stony Brook, NY 11794, 516-246-5000, Ext. 3304. Monday–Friday, 9 am–8 pm. Official college office. Educational and career counseling, continuing education courses. Fees vary.

Syracuse University/University College, Women's Center for Continuing Education, 610 E. Fayette St., Syracuse, NY 13202, 315-423-3294. Monday–Friday, 9 am–5 pm. College sponsored office. Educational and career counseling, continuing education courses. No fees.

Vistas for Women, YWCA, 515 North St., White Plains, NY 10605, 914-949-6227. Monday–Thursday, 9 am–5 pm.

Women's Career Center, Inc., 121 North Fitzhugh St., Rochester, NY 14614, 716-325-2274. Monday, Tuesday, Wednesday, Friday, 9 am–4 pm; Monday, Tuesday, 4:30 pm–8:30 pm.

NORTH CAROLINA

Duke University, Office of Continuing Education, 107 Bivins Bldg., Durham, NC 27708, 919-684-6259. Monday–Friday, 8:30 am–5 pm. Official college office. Educational and career counseling, continuing education courses, for men as well as women. Fees vary.

Fayetteville Family Life Center, Bordeaux Shopping Center, Fayetteville, NC 28304, 919-484-0176. Monday–Friday, 8:30 am–5 pm. Tuesdays and Thursdays in evening.

Salem College, Lifespan Center, Lehman Hall, Box 10548, Salem Station, Winston-Salem, NC 27108, 919-721-2807. Monday–Friday, 9 am–5 pm. College sponsored office. Lifespan planning, educational and vocational counseling. Fees vary.

OHIO

Baldwin-Wallace College, Experience CUE, Developmental Services, Administration Bldg. - No. 118, Berea, OH 44017, 216-826-2188. Monday–Friday, 8:30 am–5 pm; Tuesday and Thursday, 5:30 pm–9 pm.

Bowling Green State University, Center for Continued Learning, 194 S. Main St., Bowling Green, OH 43402, 419-372-0363. Monday–Friday, 9 am–5 pm.

Cleveland Jewish Vocational Service, 13878 Cedar Rd., University Heights, OH 44118, 216-321-1381. Monday–Friday, 8:30 am–5 pm; Thursday, 9 am–6:40 pm. Independent nonprofit agency. Educational and career counseling, job referral, placement.

Lifelong Learning/Women's Programs, Cuyahoga Community College, 2900 Community College Ave., Cleveland, OH 44115, 216-241-5966. Monday–Friday, 9 am–5 pm. Community service. College sponsored office. Individual educational and career counseling, no fee. Group series and programs, fees vary.

Ohio State University, Women's Programs, Division of Continuing Education, 210 Sullivant Hall, 1813 North High St., Columbus, OH 43210, 614-422-8860. Monday–Thursday, 8 am–7:30 pm; Friday, 8 am–5 pm; Saturday, 8 am–12 pm. Career services, continuing education for mature women. Individual counseling, no fee. Career planning courses, special programs and workshops, fees vary.

Pyramid, Inc., 1642 Cleveland Ave. NW, Canton, OH 44703, 216-453-3767. Monday–Friday, 8:30 am–4:30 pm.

Resource Women, The Untapped Resource, 1258 Euclid Ave., Ste. 204, Cleveland, OH 44115, 216-579-1414. For professional development of women with one year of college or more. By appointment only. Fees vary.

Wright State University, Women's Career Development Center, 140 East Monument Ave., Dayton, OH 45402, 513-223-6041. Monday–Friday, 8:30 am–5 pm.

University of Akron, Adult Resource Center, Akron, OH 44325, 216-375-7448. Monday–Friday, 8 am–5 pm. Educational and career counseling, adult education courses, job referral, placement. No registration fee.

OREGON

Women's Programs, Division of Continuing Education, Oregon State System of Higher Education, 1633 SW Park Ave., (mail) Box 1491, Portland, OR 97207, 503-448-2219. Monday–Friday, 8:30 am–4:30 pm. Official college office. Educational and career counseling, continuing education courses. No registration fee. Other fees vary.

PENNSYLVANIA

Career Resource Center, Harcum Junior College, Morris and Montgomery Aves., Bryn Mawr, PA 19010, 215-525-4100, Ext. 268. Monday–Friday, 9 am–5 pm. Career counseling, job referral and placement.

Cedar Crest College, Career Planning Office and Women's Center, Allentown, PA 18104, 215-437-4471. Monday–Friday, 8:30 am–4:30 pm. Official college office and community center. Educational and career counseling, continuing education courses, job referral, alumnae placement. No fees for alumnae; other fees vary.

Indiana University of Pennsylvania, Transition Center, Uhler Hall, Indiana, PA 15705, 412-357-2227, Ext. 18. Monday–Friday, 8:30 am–4:30 pm. Educational counseling, workshops, continuing education. No fees.

Institute of Awareness, 401 S. Broad St., Philadelphia, PA 19147, 215-545-4400. Monday–Friday, 9 am–5 pm. Independent and nonprofit agency. Adult education courses, special workshops, training programs. Fees vary.

Job Advisory Service, 300 S. Craig St., Pittsburgh, PA 15213, 412-621-0940. Monday–Friday, 9 am–4:30 pm; Saturday, 9 am–1 pm. Independent nonprofit office. Job counseling and referral, workshops. Fees.

Lehigh County Community College, Alternatives for Women, 2370 Main St., Schnecksville, PA 18078, 215-799-2121, Ext. 177. Sponsored by college community service office. Workshops. Fees vary.

Options, Inc., 8419 Germantown Ave., Philadelphia, PA 19118, 215-799-2121; 1220 Sansom St., Philadelphia, PA 19107, 205-627-4747. Monday–Friday, 9 am–5 pm. Independent nonprofit agency. Individual career counseling, day and evening hours by appointment. Career development workshops for employed women. Consult on Affirmative Action and Career Development for Business. Fees vary. Free weekly orientations.

Temple University, Career Services, Mitten Hall, Philadelphia, PA 19122; or 1619 Walnut St., Philadelphia, PA, 215-787-1503. Monday–Friday, 9 am–5 pm. College sponsored offices: 215-787-7981. No registration fee.

University of Pennsylvania, Resources for Women, 3601 Locust Walk / C8, Philadelphia, PA 19104, 215-898-5537. Monday–Thursday, 9:30 am–12:30 pm. University sponsored, continuing supportive career services, career and resume counseling, workshops, job referral and placement. Fees vary.

Villa Maria College, Counseling Services for Women, 2551 West Lake Rd., Erie, PA 16505, 814-838-1966. Monday–Friday, 9 am–4 pm. Official college office. Educational and career counseling, job referral, placement, adult education courses. No fees.

Wilson College, Office of Career Services, Chambersburg, PA 17201, 717-264-4141. Monday–Friday, 8 am–5 pm. Official college office. Educational and career counseling, job referral and placement. No fees.

SOUTH CAROLINA

Converse College, Women's Center, Spartanburg, SC 29301, 803-585-6421, Ext. 340. Monday–Friday, 8 am–5 pm. Free to students and alumnae.

Greenville Technical College, Center for Continuing Education for Women, Greenville, SC 29606, 803-242-3170. Monday–Thursday, 8 am–8:30 pm; Friday, 8 am–4:30 pm.

TENNESSEE

YWCA of Nashville, Career/Life Planning Center, 1608 Woodmont Blvd., Nashville, TN 37215, 615-385-3952. Monday–Saturday, 8 am–12 noon.

TEXAS

Amarillo College, Women's Programs, Box 447, Amarillo, TX 79178, 806-376-5111, Ext. 2683. Monday–Friday, 8 am–5 pm.

Brookhaven College, Brookhaven College Counseling Center, 3939 Valley View Lane, Farmers Branch, TX 75234, 214-620-4830. Monday–Thursday, 8 am–8 pm; Friday, 8 am–5 pm.

Vocational Guidance Service, Inc., 2525 San Jacinto, Houston, TX 77002, 713-659-1800. Monday–Thursday, 8:30 am–7 pm; Friday, 8:30 am–5 pm. Nonprofit organization. Educational and career counseling, job referral and placement. Fees based on sliding scale.

Women's Counseling Service, 1950 W. Gray, Ste. 1, Houston, TX 77019, 713-521-9391. Career development. Individual vocational, divorce adjustment and educational counseling.

UTAH

The Phoenix Institute, 383 S. 600 E., Salt Lake City, UT 84102, 801-532-5080. Monday–Friday, 8 am–8 pm. Saturdays by appointment.

Women's Resource Center, 293 Union Bldg., University of Utah, Salt Lake City, UT 84112, 801-581-8030. Monday–Friday, 8 am–5 pm. Evening groups. Conferences, discussion programs, groups, personal and career counseling and referral information open to the community.

VIRGINIA

Educational Opportunity Center, 3830 Virginia Beach Blvd., Virginia Beach, VA 23452, 804-463-4810. Monday–Friday, 8 am–4:30 pm. Nonprofit agency. Educational, career, and financial aid counseling. No fees.

Hollins College, Career Counseling Center, Rose Hill House, Hollins College, VA 24020, 703-362-6364. Monday–Friday, 9 am–4:30 pm.

Mary Baldwin College, Career & Personal Counseling Center, Staunton, VA 24401, 703-885-0811, Ext. 276. Monday–Friday, 9 am–5 pm. College affiliated office. Educational and career counseling. Fees vary.

University of Richmond, Women's Resource Center, University College, VA 23173, 804-285-6319. Call for appointment.

Virginia Commonwealth University, Evening College, 901 W. Franklin St., Richmond, VA 23284, 804-257-0200. Monday–Saturday, 9 am–1 pm. Official university office. Educational counseling, referral to university career and personal counseling services, continuing education courses.

WASHINGTON

Individual Development Center, Inc. (I.D. Center), Career and Life Planning, 1020 E. John St., Seattle, WA 98102, 206-329-0600. Monday–Friday, 9 am–4 pm. Evening counseling and appointments. Independent private agency. Career and life decision counseling, career development workshops for company and government agency employees, awareness seminars for managers and supervisors of women employees. Partial scholarships available.

University of Washington, Office of Career Planning, Continuing Education DW-25, Seattle, WA 98195, 206-543-4262. Monday–Friday, 9 am–4 pm. Individual counseling by appointment; evening and Saturday groups and workshops. University sponsored office. Educational and career counseling and testing, career assessment groups, career change workshops. Fees vary.

WEST VIRGINIA

West Virginia University, Placement Service, Mountain Lair, Morgantown, WV 26506, 304-293-2221. Monday–Thursday, 8 am–8 pm; Friday, 8 am–5 pm. Official college office. Restricted to alumnae. Educational and career counseling, job referral. Registration fee.

WISCONSIN

Skilled jobs for Women, Inc., 2095 Winnebago St., Madison, WI 53704, 608-244-5181. Monday–Friday, 8:30 am–6 pm. Evening and weekend appointments arranged.

Waukesha County Technical Institute, Women's Development Center, 800 Main St., Pewaukee, WI 53072, 414-548-5400. Career and vocational counseling; free seminars and workshops on decision making, coping, career planning and job seeking skills. Special emphasis on nontraditional employment. All services free. Appointments and reservations advised. All services open to men also.

WYOMING

University of Wyoming, Placement Service, Box 3195, University Station, Laramie, WY 82071, 307-766-2398. Monday–Friday, 8 am–5 pm. Official college office, restricted to students and alumnae. Educational and career consulting, job referral. No fees.

V. HELP FOR CLERGY & RELIGIOUS

Probably no profession has developed, or had developed for it, so many resources to aid in career assessment as has the clerical profession. Nonetheless, the warning sounded at the introduction to the last section (IV. Help for Women) should be read at this point, for it applies with equal force to this section of resources. Where you run into a clerical counselor who is sincere but inept, you will probably discover that the ineptness consists in an inadequate understanding of the distinction between career *assessment*—roughly comparable to taking a snapshot of people as they are in one frozen moment of time—vs. career *development*—which is roughly comparable to teaching people how to take their own motion pictures of themselves, from here on out.

Having issued this caution, however, we must go on to add that at some of these centers, listed below, are some simply excellent counselors who fully understand this distinction, and are well trained in that empowering of the client which is what career *development* is all about. If you ask the right question before you sign on the dotted line (p. 279–81), you should be readily able to identify them.

THE OFFICIAL INTERDENOMINATIONAL CAREER DEVELOPMENT CENTERS

The Career and Personal Counseling Service
St. Andrews Presbyterian College, Laurinburg, NC 29352
919-276-3162
Also at: 725 Providence Rd.
Charlotte, NC 28207
704-376-4086
Alfred E. Thomas, Director

The Career & Personal Counseling Center
Eckerd College
St. Petersburg, FL 33733
813-867-1166, Ext. 356
John R. Sims, Director

American Baptist Center for the Ministry
7804 Capwell Dr.
Oakland, CA 94621
415-635-4246
John R. Langraf, Director-Counselor

Clergy Career Support System
3501 Campbell
Kansas City, MO 64109
816-931-2516
Eugene E. Timmons, Director

Lancaster Career Development Center
561 College Ave.
Lancaster, PA 17603
717-397-7451
L. Guy Mehl, Director

North Central Career Development Center
3000 Fifth St. NW
New Brighton, MN 55112
612-636-5120
Dr. John Davis, Director

Northeast Career Development Center
291 Witherspoon St.
Princeton, NJ 08540
609-924-4814
Robert G. Foulkes, Director

Career Development Center of the Southeast
531 Kirk Rd.
Decatur, GA 30030
Robert M. Urie, Director
404-371-0336

Midwest Career Development Center, 2501 North Star Rd., Ste. 200
Columbus, OH 43221
614-486-0469
Frank C. Williams, Director

Mid-South Career Development Center
Box 120815, Acklen Sta.
Nashville, TE 37212
615-327-9572
W. Scott Root, Director

Midwest Career Development Center
Box 249
Westchester, IL 60153
312-343-6268
Ronald Brushwyler, Associate Director

Southwest Career Development Center
Box 5923
Arlington, TX 76011
817-265-5541
William M. Gould, Jr., Director-Counselor

Center for Career Development and Ministry
70 Chase Street
Newton Centre, MA 02159
617-969-7750
Barton M. Lloyd, Associate Director
Harold D. Moore, Director

The centers listed above are all accredited and coordinated by the Career Development Council, Room 760, 475 Riverside Dr., New York, NY 10027. Some of them are accepting directors of Christian Education, ministers of music, and others in addition to clergy; some centers are open to all and not merely to church-related clients; some are open to high school students, as well as to adults.

ALSO DOING WORK IN THIS FIELD:

Career and Personal Counseling Center, 1904 Mt. Vernon St., Waynesboro, VA 22980, 703-943-9997. Lillian Pennell, Director.

The Episcopal Office of Pastoral Development, 116 Alhambra Circle, Ste. 210, Coral Gables, FL 33134. The Rt. Rev. David E. Richards.

Bernard Haldane, 154 Lombard St., #50, San Francisco, CA 94111, 415-434-3424. One of the pioneers in the clergy career management and assessment field, Bernard works through seminars and in training of volunteers to do job-finding counseling.

VI. PLACES HELPING PEOPLE WHO WANT FLEXIBLE WORK-TIME OPTIONS

Work/Life Options
5004 W. Tierra Buena
Glendale, AZ 85306
602-938-2351

New Ways to Work
149 Ninth St.
San Francisco, CA 94103
415-552-1000.

Flexible Career Associates
Box 6701
Santa Barbara, CA 93111
805-687-2572

Innovative Career Options
School of Business–Box 13
Metropolitan State College
1006 Eleventh St.
Denver, CO 80204
303-629-3245

Family and Career Together (FACT)
Box 486
W. Hartford, CT 06107
203-521-1603

Association of Part-Time Professionals
Atlanta Chapter
c/o Debbie Weil
77 28th St. NW
Atlanta, GA 30309
404-351-6637

Flexible Careers
37 S. Wabash
Chicago, IL 60603
312-236-6028

Division of Women's Programs
Alternative Working Arrangements Project
27000 University Ave.
Drake University
Des Moines, IA 50311
515-271-2181

Work Options for Women
1358 N. Waco
Wichita, KS 67203
316-264-6604

Work Options Limited
645 Boylston St.
Boston, MA 02116
617-247-3600

Nancy Viehmann
Pier Rd., Box 78
Cape Porpoise, ME 04014
207-967-3462

Lansing Women's Bureau
Human Resources Dept.
City of Lansing
119 N. Washington Sq.
Lansing, MI 48933
517-317-2115

Adult Career Exploration Center
Counseling Center–Memorial Hall
Glassboro State College
Glassboro, NJ 08028
609-445-5378

Work Time Alternatives
Box 7514
Albuquerque, NM 87194
505-848-9044

Workshare
311 E. 50th St.
New York, NY 10022
212-832-7061

Flexible Ways to Work
c/o YWCA
1111 SW Tenth Ave.
Portland, OR 97205
503-241-0537

Center for Flexible Employment
3060 Bristol Road
Box 404
Bensalem, PA 19020
215-757-3328

Phoenix Institute
383 S. 600 E.
Salt Lake City, UT 84102
801-532-5080

Association of Part-Time Professionals
Box 3632
Alexandria, VA 22302
202-370-6206

Focus
509 Tenth Ave. E.
Seattle, WA 98102
206-329-7918

Appendix D

When More Than Career Counseling Is Needed: BURNOUT

The symptoms have been thoroughly described in the literature. You used to go to work with a lot of energy, and now you practically drag yourself there. You used to be thrilled with the job, and now it tastes like cotton in your mouth. The challenges used to add zest to your life, but now they seem only to be endlessly wearing you down. You used to enjoy the clients or people you worked with, and now you rather dread seeing them. You feel in dreadful need of a vacation—say for two or three years. You feel an immobilization in your spiritual life, and an increasing unpredictability in your emotional life. Your feeling of self-confidence is very low, your ability to make necessary changes is in some kind of frozen state—and you wonder what on earth is happening to you.

Burnout—that's what. You have been worn down—by the world, by life, and by your job. It may be elementary burnout—in which case a good rest may be sufficient; it may be intermediate burnout—in which case a good career transition, using all the resources at your disposal, may be just what the doctor ordered. Read and use this book, engage a career counselor if you need one, and get at it.

Sometimes, however, it may be advanced burnout. Usually this occurs when the problems in your contemporary life—a bad job, broken marriage, or whatever—tap into and resurrect old problems undealt with. Not unlike drilling down into the earth and suddenly tapping into the molten lava reservoir of some slumbering volcano.

Career transition often occurs because of burnout. That is to say, you find the idea of career transition looking more and more appealing—just because you already are "in burnout" due to too much constant exposure to people pressures, or whatever. What is not so commonly realized is that career transition itself can precipitate burnout. You leave a job with good feelings, go into career transition with good feelings, and whamo! all of a sudden it hits you. Immobilization, inability to get going, and a sense of bafflement on your part, as to what is happening to you.

Transition burnout is the answer. In a study done some ten years ago, and reported in *The American Journal of Psychiatry,* McNeil and Giffen discovered that when military people made the transition to civilian life, emotionally the transition took them about five years. If the individual saw the transition coming, symptoms would begin to appear as early as two years before his or her discharge date, and *could* continue for up to three years afterward. The symptoms included: reduced efficiency, psychosomatic symptoms (chest or intestinal), loss of energy, loss of interest, loss of confidence, and sometimes a singular incident of unusual (for that individual) conduct. These, however, are the symptoms commonly attributed to burnout, and that is why I call the phenomenon or experience: transition burnout. Burnout caused by the transition itself.

Its existence is hardly surprising news. A man named Anton Boisen reported some forty-five years ago (in *The Exploration of the Inner World: A Study of Mental Disorder and Religious Experience,* University of Pennsylvania Press, 1971, 1936) his conviction that transition, in its broadest view, has three essential phases to it: (1) the abandonment of the old center around which that life once revolved; (2) a feeling of lostness and self-distress in the middle period, followed by; (3) the finding of a new center around which that life chooses to revolve thereafter, with ensuing peacefulness and sense of purpose once again. The middle period, which is precisely what most people mean by "transition," Boisen called "the disorganization of the person's world." "The body," he said, "is strong, and the brain in good working order... [But] something has happened which has upset the foundations upon which his ordinary reasoning is based."

If your are facing the job-hunt or career-change, and you are feeling this kind of immobilization and inability to get going, it *may be* that you will profit greatly from some personal counseling, rather than just career counseling. Heaven knows, there are a number of therapists who will tell you so, and urge this solution upon you.

I would like to recommend, however, that before you blindly rush into three years of therapy just because you are having difficulty with a career transition, you adopt the following three-point program:

FIRST, try reading this book and getting at the job-hunt/career-change on your own, doing the exercises you think will be most helpful, and particularly the Quick Job-Hunting Map in Appendix A.

SECOND, if this proves to be more than you can cope with, try seeking a good career counselor, using the resources in the previous appendix. The operative word in the previous sentence, incidentally, is "good." If you momentarily fall into the hands of a poor one, try again, and again if necessary, until you find a good one. See if that solves the problem.

THIRD, only if you've tried the above two steps, and are still immobilized and unable to get going, should you try a therapist of your own persuasion (see the following directory, for the range of possibilities). Do remember that you are not going to the therapist simply to get you out of burnout, or out of the disorganization of your personal world. You are going to her or him in order to get help in moving on to the third phase of transition that Boisen talked about: the reorganization of your life around a new center. In other words you are going to a therapist for help with your personal growth, to aid you in getting on to the next station in your life.

The range of possibilities or options, should you decide on some form of therapy, is quite staggering. But, basically, all therapies divide into three classifications: INSTRUCTION, or EXPLORATION, or PSYCHOTHERAPY. Now, let us look at each of these in turn, to see what *your* options are. In general, they will depend on where you live. If you're in a midwestern town, say, with a population of 200 people, and not a therapist in sight, INSTRUCTION is more likely to be your preferred option—via

Books explaining different people's views of Burnout may be found in the bibliography in Appendix B, section 23 (p. 270).

books or a trip to a nearby learning place, on a one-shot basis. On the other hand, if you are in a large urban center, you have more room to choose from among a number of possibilities.

• PROFESSIONAL HELP (FOR A FEE) BY MEANS OF A LIMITED COURSE OF INSTRUCTION:

1. Local college or university: cf. courses in the psychology department, and adult education.
2. Free universities (informal experimental colleges) have grown to life in a number of communities across the country, and it you know of one, it may be worth investigating to see if they have instructional types of personal growth seminars. Example: Entropy, 1914 Polk St., Ste. 205, San Francisco, CA 94109.
3. Many of the growth centers (see below, under *Exploration*) also have lectures, seminars, etc., which offer help by means of instruction; and, some—like Dialogue House—have produced books or other materials to instruct the isolated and others.

A further printed resource:

Bridges, William, *Transitions: Making Sense of Life's Changes.* Addison-Wesley, Reading, MA. 1980. $5.95, paper.

• PROFESSIONAL HELP WITH PERSONAL GROWTH BY MEANS OF SHORT-TERM EXPLORATION:

This covers a wide range of techniques designed to produce new awareness and/or change in the self, in one's relations to others, and in one's relation to God. In general, they are explorations of new experiences which then become (hopefully) challenges to all of the rest of one's experiences, day by day. Techniques include *gestalt therapy, neuro-linguistic programming, body awareness therapy, hypno-therapy, bioenergetics, transactional analysis, logo-therapy, reality therapy, journal or diary keeping* (see Section 20, in the bibliography in the preceding Appendix (p. 268). These techniques are largely group techniques, for use by and in groups.

The Association for Humanistic Psychology, 325 Ninth St., San Francisco, CA 94103. AHP produces a list of Growth Centers with corrections and updatings in its *AHP Newsletter*. Includes other countries' centers, as well as this one's. You can order both the list and the *Newsletter* from the Association, at the address above. You can then find the center, or centers, nearest you, and ask them for their catalog and/or schedule of events.

NTL Institute for Applied Behavioral Science, Box 9155, Rosslyn Sta., VA 22209. As of 1967, an independent non-profit corporation associated with the National Educational Association. It certifies competency of leaders; an inquiry to the Institute may secure names of competent leaders in your area of the country, who (likely as not) offer various events. Ask for their list of publications, also.

Dialogue House, 80 E. 11th St., New York, NY 10003, conducts some 400 Intensive Journal workshops throughout the country, under the local auspices of churches, retreat centers and mental health centers, helping individuals to do personal growth through exploration of themselves in a self-directed journal. Those wishing to know more about such exploration, can write directly to Dialogue House for their schedule. You may also want to read their founder's book: *At A Journal Workshop,* by Ira Progoff.

Obtainable directly from Dialogue House, $7.95, paper, plus $1 postage. In addition, you may want to order a more recent companion volume, *The Practice of Process Meditation*, also available from Dialogue House. $12.95.

- **PROFESSIONAL HELP WITH PERSONAL GROWTH BY MEANS OF LONG-TERM PSYCHOTHERAPY:**

First of all, it helps here—as earlier—to know what all your options are. You may know of someone who was in distress, went to a particular kind of therapist, and found a lot of help; consequently you may be tempted to run, not walk, to that particular therapist. Well and good. But, if you have a little patience, and are willing to do a little reading, you may discover there is another kind of therapy that would be much more to your liking. Your friend, for example, may have been highly verbal, and so may have profited from a form of therapy that was largely verbal. You, on the other hand, may find the body is the place where you feel all your tension, and may prefer the use of your body in general (let us say you're an exercise enthusiast and diet addict)—in which case a body-movement person may be much more appropriate for you. So, a little reading, to acquaint you with the possibilities, couldn't hurt—for starters.

A book which summarizes the various options—the different sorts of therapies that are available—is Ehrenberg, Otto and Miriam, *The Psychotherapy Maze: A Consumer's Guide to the Ins and Outs of Therapy*. Holt Paperback. 1977. $3.95. If your bookstore doesn't have it, try your local library.

There is also Mishara, Brian, and Patterson, Robert, *Consumer's Guide to Mental Health*. Times Books. 1977. In addition to how to rate your therapist, it includes specific data on the various modalities of therapy. Highly recommended! There is, alternatively: Adams, Sallie and Orgel, Michael, *Through the Mental Health Maze: A Consumer's Guide to Finding a Psychotherapist*. Health Research Group, 2000 P St. NW, Washington, DC 20036. 1975. $2.50 (prepaid). And: Wiener, Daniel N., *A Consumer's Guide to Psychotherapy*. Hawthorn. 1975, rev. ed. $4.95, paper.

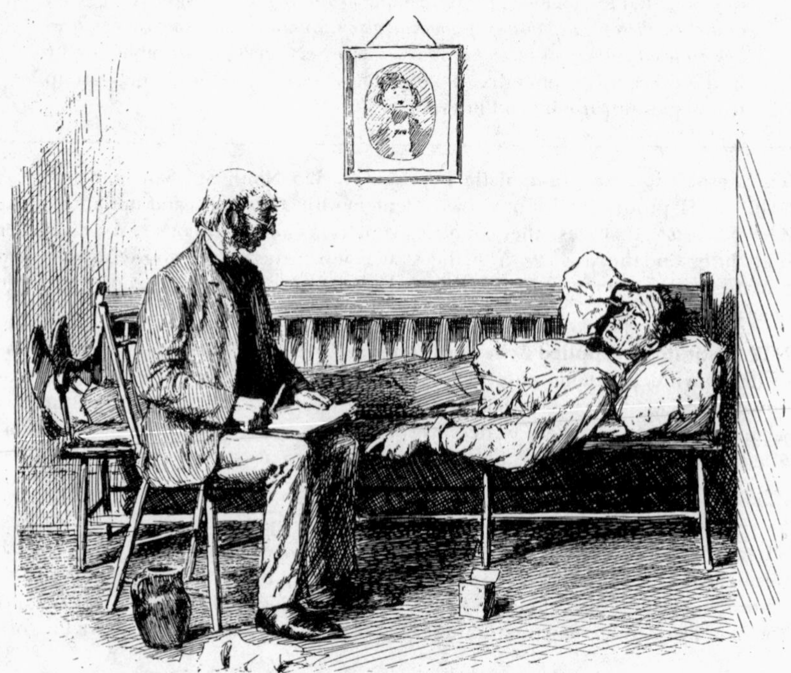

Once you've decided on what kind of therapy you're looking for, how do you go about locating a good (underline that twice) good therapist? Well, there are several ways:

1. Try your friends. Tell them the kind of person you're looking for. See if they have themselves experienced or known someone who is good. If the answer is negative, kindly ask them to ask around among *their* friends. Other places to try:

2. *The Directory of Counseling Services* lists accredited places which offer psychotherapy. You can obtain it from International Assn. of Counseling Services, Inc., Two Skyline Pl., Ste. 400, 5203 Leesburg Pike, Falls Church, VA 22041. $6.

3. The Psychology Department of your local college or university may be able to suggest places or persons which offer psychotherapy.

4. Consult also your local physician for referral suggestions, and/or your local or state psychiatric association, psychologists' association, and psychoanalytic institute (see "Professional Organizations" in your telephone book's yellow pages), for recommendations or lists of accredited personnel. See also your community mental health association or center.

If you decide to consult a psychologist, psychiatrist, psychotherapist, analyst, psychoanalyst, or whatever, here are a few suggestions or guiding principles for choosing one:

1. If you can manage it, get the names of three therapists.

2. We recommend you go see each one for a one-hour exploratory visit. You will almost certainly have to pay the going rates for this hour, with each therapist. It's *well* worth it.

3. Guidelines in evaluating therapists: a) Do you like them? (Lack of rapport can kill therapy.) b) How much personal therapy have they had? (You have a right to ask. An answer in terms of years doesn't count; hours does. Like, 200–300, or more.) c) Do you feel they are real people? (If they come across as pasteboard, maybe that's their ideal for you, too.) d) Do they assiduously avoid giving you advice? Hope so. (You need someone living their life out through you like you need a hole in the head.) Beware of the therapist who gives lots and lots of advice. (Like this!) On the other hand, give them three stars if they come across as clarifiers, primarily.

4. After you have weighed your impressions of all three, choose one. Give serious consideration to committing yourself to say, six-eight sessions with this therapist, after which each of you will evaluate whether or not to continue. That way, if you chose badly, you can terminate it gracefully; if you chose wisely, you have an impetus to begin working immediately.

5. If you have done the exercises in this book, you may have an idea of what goals you have for your own personal therapy: things you want to work on, hangups you want to get rid of, etc. Part of your arrangement with your therapist should be to clarify why you want therapy, so that you will have goals by which to measure progress. With this one proviso: you should feel free to revise these goals, if you want to, as therapy progresses. But therapy without any definition of what you are working toward *can be deadly. Or innocuous*—the way in which lonely people simply *purchase* friendship.

6. If after eight weeks, or whenever, you conclude this isn't helpful, shake hands, part—amiably but firmly—and go seek another. Give up on that first therapist of yours, but *not* on therapy itself, until you get what you want. Persistence is the key. That was the whole point of Jacob wrestling with the angel, in the Old Testament. His words to that dark figure of the night, should be yours to your therapy: "I will not let you go until you bless me."

All men dream... but not equally. They who dream by night in the dusty recesses of their minds wake in the day to find that it is vanity; but the dreamers of the day are dangerous men, for they act their dream with open eyes, to make it possible.

T. E. LAWRENCE

Appendix E

Where The Best Jobs Are

Well, you're browsing in the bookstore, and you see the above title, so you turn immediately to this section, right? And you're waiting for the hot scoop about just what sections of the country have the best job market, and just what jobs employers are so anxious to have filled, that they will promise you practically *any*thing. Your object: to avoid the job-hunt almost altogether, if possible, by going for those jobs where the competition is so trivial, that you can practically walk in off the street and be hired—at *your* price.

Okay, I'll tell you what the popular wisdom is, among job experts these days, and then I'll tell you what I think is wrong with that wisdom. The popular wisdom is that the ten fastest growing places—geography-wise, and hence job-wise, are (in order): Fort Lauderdale, Tucson, Houston, Phoenix, Austin, San Diego, Oxnard (California), Columbia (South Carolina), Tampa, and Albuquerque. In other words, with few exceptions, the Sunbelt.

The jobs which are going to have the greatest demand from employers are: computer technology, especially computer programmers; data processing (another way of saying the same thing), especially in software; robotics, dealing especially with the use of robots in industry; productivity experts; genetic engineering or bio-engineering; machine-tool workers; tool-and-die workers; and—surprise—secretaries (a vanishing breed in some sections of the country).

The biggest changes forecast for the coming decade are (1) those connected with the computerizing of small businesses (and large) as we move more and more rapidly toward "the electronic society;" (2) the growth in home offices—linked by computer to a central work office; (3) the growth in consequent "employment by contract"—with home-officed persons contracting their services perhaps to more than one company; (4) the growth of self-employment comprised of several contract jobs rather than just one—with some individuals holding down not two jobs but three, four, or five part-time jobs, all of which together add up to one full-time job; (5) the growth of totally new industries based on research and development currently being done in the energy field; and (6) the growth of hospices, home medical care, and other alternatives to hospitals. Workers looking ahead at these changes, and moving into these fields before they surge, will probably find the greatest opportunities—according to popular wisdom.

Now if something on the above list immediately piques your interest, and sends off rockets in your head and heart, wonderful! But if, on the other hand, your response in your gut is: "None of the above," what can we say to you? (Here's where the criticism of the popular wisdom begins.)

Well, first of all, the forecasts of job-experts are often wrong. We can begin with that. And boy, have they been wrong! Back in 1970, few if any 'experts' saw the energy crisis coming, with all its consequent effects upon the job-market. They have been just as in error over trends they thought were coming, but which never materialized.

Secondly, new trends and new jobs are the "glamor" parts of the world of work; but these depend upon the less glamorous sections of the world of work for their survival and growth. What St. Paul said in another connection is equally applicable here: "There are many members, but one body. And the eye cannot say to the hand, 'I have no need of you'; or again the head to the feet, 'I have no need of you.' On the contrary, it is much truer that the members of the body which seem to be weaker are necessary." (I Corinthians 12:20–22) All the talk about the glamor trends in the world of work during the 1980's should not obscure the fact that we still need good auto mechanics to fix our cars, and good doctors to assist us in maintaining our body's health, and good mailpersons to get our bills to us.[1]

Thirdly, by the time forecasts get published, and by the time you prepare for the specialty of interest, there often is a lot more competition for that sort of job than you

had been led to believe there would be. So, you're not delivered from the need to compete, any more than you would be for some of the less glamorous jobs. Your chance of beating the competition will depend upon four factors (to repeat the main substance of this book):

a) If you are determined to keep at it, making job-hunting a full-time job, and enlisting other job-hunters to do their hunt with you, you will vastly increase your chances of beating out the competition;

b) If you know what your best skills are, and which of those you most enjoy using, you will greatly increase your chances over the competition;

c) If you know exactly what industry and in what kind of place you most want to use those skills, you will greatly increase your chances of getting the job; and

---

1. Incidentally, the government puts out each month a list of occupations most in demand that month (that they *know of*). It's called *Occupations in Demand*. It's Bulletin #533J, and you can order it from the Supt. of Documents, U.S. Govt. Printing Off., Washington, DC 20402.

d) If you know how to identify the places which have such jobs, and how to approach places whether or not they have a vacancy, you will greatly increase your chances of getting the job; and...

You will want to remember, most of all, that generally speaking—in good times or bad—our economy tends to create one to two million *new* positions each year. That means two things. There are always jobs out there for the job-hunters who are on their toes. AND, one to two million is an awful lot to choose from. The choices are wide and vast. YOU have got to look at a job basically as though you were a plant or flower. In what climate and in what soil will you thrive best?—that is the question. If being a computer programmer is attractive to you, that's an answer. But only part of the answer. *Where* do you want to be a computer programmer? is the rest of the answer. In other words: where is the soil that the-kind-of-plant-you-are will best thrive in?

If being a computer programmer is not the answer for you, then you are back to the environment question: do you thrive best in the plains, the mountains or the desert? Are you rose, wildflower, or cactus? A wildflower will perish in the desert; a cactus will die in the mountains. You must find your appropriate environment. A job is an environment.

That's what this book, in your hands, is all about. Exercises, self-examination questions to help you figure out not where the best jobs are, but where the best job is FOR YOU.

INFORMATION ABOUT PARTICULAR FIELDS OR JOBS

Readers often write us, asking why we do not have information about their particular field of interest (such as: travel agencies, sales, nursing, computer programming, hotel/motel management, tourism, medicine, acting, singing, etc., etc.). Obviously they haven't read this book all the way through (they browsed, maybe, skimmed, certainly, but really digested it, nein). If they HAD read the whole book, they would know that:

a) We believe there are too many occupations out there, for any one book—or even an encyclopedia—to contain detailed information about.

b) We believe that in the case of the "obvious" occupations, information changes so rapidly, that it is out of date almost before it is put into print.

c) We believe there are vast regional differences with respect to occupations, and also vast industry differences within regions.

d) We therefore believe that the very best person to gather current, correct information about the field that interests you is YOU. And it is our job, not to have that information, but to tell you where to find it and how to find it for yourself. That's the whole purpose of chapter 6, dealing with Informational Interviewing.

e) We have an extensive bibliography in Appendix B, to help you get started in certain key fields. You will note, by looking there, that we have listed books dealing with being an executive or manager; with being a writer; a craftsperson; a government employee; a self-employed person; as well as books dealing with the subject of being in show business, data processing, public relations, human resources, and organizational development. (See pages 261 to 264.) Browsing in your local library or some large local bookstore may turn up titles dealing with other fields as well. So, it may be there is a book that can get you started. Even so, you are going to have to do your own research—what we call Informational Interviewing, in the end. There is no refuge from it. The job-hunt is, above all else, an information search. It would be nice if someone had already done that searching for you; maybe. But it's even nicer if you do it for yourself. It builds up, in you, all the skills you will truly need after you are in the job—whatever that job may be.

LETTERS, WE GET LETTERS

Over the years, our mail has consistently inquired about certain key problems or areas facing the career changer. These are:

(1) should I go back to school?
(2) what can I do if I am interested in doing something that is not your normal occupation, but maybe something that contributes toward changing our country or our society?
(3) what can I do if I want to create a job no-one has ever heard of, or otherwise go the route of self-employment?
(4) what do I do if I want to work in the education field, but there are no jobs for teachers in the local schools or colleges?
(5) what do I do if I want to get a government job?
(6) what do I need to know if I want to get into the business world?
(7) what do I do if I decide I want to work overseas?

Since we know that these are key concerns for many of our readers, we have included some notes about each of these. *However, these notes are intended as mere primers for your own research (pump). Most of the research you are still going to have to do for yourself.*

---

1. Should I go back to school?

Well, it depends. Not necessarily. There are five reasons why people go back to school:

1. To learn more about the world in which we are called to do our work; e.g., *astronomy, history, geography, anthropology,* etc.

2. To pick up additional skills for the work we are presently doing full-time, or for the work we intend to move into; e.g., *psychology, computer programming,* etc.

3. To pick up a degree in our present or future field; e.g., *business administration.*

4. To broaden the horizons of our mind; e.g., *some authorities (probably math teachers) maintain that mathematics is a means of making the mind more elastic and receptive to change.*

5. To postpone decision, and create a never-never land between one's past and any future career.

If you want to go back for the third reason, dear friend, please be very sure you have done the exercises in chapter 5, in detail, because you can take some course that will be, in retrospect, a waste of time—in terms of your priority goals and skills.

Read the books on this subject that have appeared in recent years (e.g., Berg, Ivar, *Education and Jobs: The Great Training Robbery,* The Center for Urban Education, Dept. NM, 105 Madison Ave., New York, NY 10016. $7.50.) *if your only reason for going back is to get a degree. ("That ol' black magic.")*

Confirmation of the futility of degrees is found in a study done some ten years ago by a researcher named Richardson, of 367 Air Force officers who got full-time secular jobs. They agreed that more or "higher" *education credentials were asked of them in order to get hired, than were necessary for the actual performance of the job.* You can get around this in many, many occupations, if you faithfully follow all of chapters 6 and 7.

If you don't care about a degree, but *you just want to gain some knowledge,* three good introductory volumes to help you choose the *method* of learning are: Gross, Ronald, *The Independent Scholar's Handbook: How to Turn Your Interest in Any Subject Into Expertise.* Addison-Wesley, Jacob Way, Reading, MA 01867. 1982. $8.95, paper. And: Gross, Ronald, ed., *Invitation to Lifelong Learning.* Follett Publishing Co./Dept. DM T82-40, 1010 W. Washington Blvd., Chicago, IL 60607. $18.95, hardcover. And another earlier book by Ron: *The Lifelong Learner* ($8.95, hardcover), which you can order from Simon and Schuster, 1230 Avenue of the Americas, New York, NY 10020. See especially pages 88–89 and following, for an overview of your options. Among the possibilities, there are:

1. *Seminars, workshops, etc.* Get your hands on *The Weekend Education Source Book* by Wilbur Cross. $6.95, paper. You can order it from Harper & Row, 10 E. 53rd St., New York, NY 10022. Lists various types of organizations (with addresses) that offer seminars or workshops.

2. *Independent study at home: guided by others.* Get your hands on *Guide to Independent Study Through Correspondence Instruction,* published by National University Extension Association; you can order it from: Petersen's Guides, 228 Alexander St., Princeton, NJ 08540. $2, plus $1 for postage and handling. Or: you may want *Directory of Accredited Private Home Study Schools,* from National Home Study Council, 1601 18th St. NW, Washington, DC 20009.

3. *Independent study at home: guided by yourself.* If you want to do it the traditional way, i.e., by reading a bunch of books in a particular subject, but you don't know which books to choose, you'll want to consult *College On Your Own: How You Can Get a College Education at Home* by Gail Thain Parker and Gene R. Hawes ($6.95, paper), in your library, or ordered directly from Bantam Books, Inc., 666 Fifth Ave., New York, NY 10019. It lists various subjects, and then the recommended books in that field.

Or, if you prefer to listen, rather than to read, try learning by means of cassettes. This is an extremely popular way to learn.

4. *Study with others at a community college, college extension division, university, etc.* In case you don't know, *The Education Directory, Part 3 (Higher Education)* will tell you which schools of this nature are near you (or near the area where you would like to go and live). Consult the directory at your local library. See also: Hapunski, William C., and McCabe, Charles E., *Back to School: The College Guide for Adults.* Peterson's Guides, Dept. 2601, Box 2123, Princeton, NJ 08540.

5. *Study with others, but not in a traditional-type college.* A list of such places can be found in: Blaze, Wayne, et al., *Guide to Alternative Colleges and Universities.* Garrett Park Press, Garrett Park, MD 20766. $5.25, prepaid; or Bear, Ph.D., John, *How to Get the Degree You Want: Bear's Guide to Non-Traditional College Degrees.* Ten Speed Press, Box 7123, Berkeley, CA 94707. 1982. $9.95.

You should also know that many communities or geographical areas have regional clearinghouses of information about educational opportunities. I am thinking of such places as the Educational Information and Referral Service which Atlanta, Georgia, has (3393 Peachtree Rd. NE, [404] 233-7497). For other places, in your area, read pages 78-83 in *The Three Boxes of Life,* or consult the National Center for Educational Brokering.

As for financing your learning times, there are three possible ways to get finances: a) Consult your university or college office to see what resources they have for aiding people in financial binds (like you); b) Consult your local service clubs (in town) to see if they have or know of, similar kinds of aid: scholarships or whatever; c) Get your hands on: *Catalog of Federal Domestic Assistance,* Supt. of Documents, U.S. Govt. Printing Off., Washington, DC 20402. $7.

You can also get financed, by various ingenious methods, on your own. One cleric, for example, wrote to all the clergy whom he knew in large parishes, and asked for gifts from their *discretionary funds or other special funds.* He secured enough money to cover his whole study program.

Now, for some other matters. If you are determined to get a degree, consider whether or not you could pass equivalency examinations for the knowledge or experience you've already acquired out of life. Write to The College Entrance Examination Board, Box 592, Princeton, NJ 08540 or Box 1025, Berkeley, CA 94701, and ask them for details of their College-Level Examination Program.

If it's a Master's or Doctorate you're determined upon, do a little Informational Interviewing first—with those who already have such a degree, and are out earning a living—to find out what good they feel it did them. I urged this recently upon a woman who wanted one of the current glamor master's degrees; she interviewed people in business who already had that degree, and they told her exactly how useful or useless it was to them. As a consequence, she decided not to enroll in the program. So, if you're thinking about a particular degree, go and do thou likewise, before enrolling.

If you're not determined to get a degree, but would simply like to learn more about a particular field, please consider Internships. There are directories of the possibilities, which your local library should have—for example: *Directory of Internships, Work Experience Programs, and On-The-Job Training Opportunities.* $45. *The First Supplement to the Directory.* $37.50. Ready Reference Press, Box 5169, Santa Monica, CA 90405.

And if you want to learn, but are determined it shouldn't be in the U.S., but rather in some far-off exotic land, get your hands on: *International Education: A Directory of Resource Materials on Comparative Education and Study in Another Country* by Lily von Klemperer. (Garrett Park Press, Garrett Park, MD 20766. $5.95, if payment is enclosed with order.)

---

2. What can I do if I am interested in doing something that is not your normal occupation, but maybe something that contributes toward changing our society?

In the field of social change careers, there are the obvious old-time occupations, such as social work, case work, public service careers and human service occupations. About which, more later on in these notes.

The newer occupations in this arena are called social change careers or vocations.

Now, for those interested more particularly in *working for social change,* your first and most helpful resource has got to be Vocations for Social Change, at Box 211, Essex Sta., Boston, MA 02112. It produces a number of extremely helpful publications, including *Boston People's Yellow Pages* ($4.95).

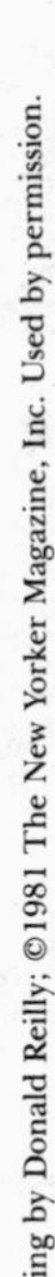

"I'm hoping to find something in a meaningful, humanist, outreach kind of bag, with flexible hours, non-sexist bosses, and fabulous fringes."

There is also: *Good Works: A Guide to Social Change Careers,* edited by Karen Aptakin, with a preface by Ralph Nader. It's produced by Nader's organization, The Center for Study of Responsive Law, Box 19367, Washington, DC 20036, and a check payable to the Center, in the amount of $22.50, must accompany your order.

If it's Christian opportunities for service that you're interested in, you'll want to know about Intercristo, 19303 Fremont Ave. N., Seattle, WA 98133. They have a job-matching system they call "Intermatch." You can call 800-426-1342 for information.

If you are interested in social change *personally*—that is to say, you are interested in exploring Alternatives not merely in your choice of Work, but also in your lifestyle, choice of technologies, use of resources, etc., there are—as you may be aware from visiting any "Alternative Bookstore" or "Headshop"—a whole library of helpful books and catalogs to help you out. A comparatively new one is *Rainbook: Resources for Appropriate Technology,* published by a group of people in Portland, Oregon, who have been experimenting with "living better with less," for some years now. It costs $7.95, paper, and is available from RAIN, 2270 NW Irving, Portland, OR 97210, 503-227-5110. They also publish a magazine called *Rain,* which updates the book.

But if it's more specifically in the area of your work, that you are interested in social change, there are resources to help you do your research *before* you come down to that more immediate decision as to which places interest you the most. One such resource is *Profiles of Involvement* (Human Resources Corp. Philadelphia. 1972. $50.) which describes and evaluates the social involvement of corporations, organizations, government agencies, banks, non-profit organizations, etc. Very helpful to anyone doing research on the social involvement of potential employers. See your local library.

There is also *Open The Books: How To Research A Corporation.* Available from: The Midwest Academy, 600 W. Fullerton, Chicago IL 60614. 1974. How to research a multinational corporation, banks, insurance companies, mutual funds, foundations, churches, universities, real estate companies, subsidiaries, cab companies, etc. Very thorough and helpful.

Then, there is the *Corporate Action Guide* published by the Corporate Action Project, 1500 Farragut St. NW, Washington, DC 20011 (1974) which is an information guide about corporate power and how it works. ($2.95, with postage.)

Finally, there is: *What's Happening To Our Jobs?* by Steve Babson and Nancy Bingham, published by Popular Economics Press, Box 221, Somerville, MA 02143. 1976. $1.45, paper. An anti-establishment radical analysis of the job-market in toto.

You will find additional resources in section 16 of Appendix B in this book, which lists other kinds of places trying to help our society become a better place. Look there to see what sorts of places really grab you—then go research them at length to see what sorts of skills they need. Maybe that will match up with the skills you *have*.

Now, back to the more traditional old-time careers in this arena, called "public service careers."

Public service careers may be with *government* (federal, state, or local), with *non-profit organizations,* with *agencies* (independent of state or local government, but often cooperating with them) or with *colleges* (particularly community colleges), etc.

Public service careers include such varied occupations as *Community Services Officer* at a community college, *recreation educator, city planner, social service technician* (working with any or all agencies that deliver social services), *welfare administration, gerontology specialist* (for further information, contact—among others—your State Commission on Aging), etc.

Other public service careers: *Workers with the handicapped, public health officials* (see your State Department of Public Health, or the Chief Medical Doctor at the county Public Health Agency—the Doctor often being the best informed person about *opportunities), officials dealing with the foster parent program for mentally retarded persons, workers in the child welfare program,* and so forth.

If you are interested in this general field of social service, you ought to do extensive research, including talking with national associations in the fields that interest you, state departments, county, city. And do not forget college people. They have a whole bag of positions, themselves, such as: *Division Director in Human Service Careers, Director of the Department of Human Services* (write Vermont College's Department of Behavioral Science, Montpelier, VT, for further information).

Potential employers for social or public service occupations include social welfare agencies, public health department, correctional institutions, government offices, economic opportunity offices, hospitals, rest homes, schools, parks and recreation agencies, etc.

As a research aid, there is *Human Service Organizations: A Book of Readings,* University of Michigan Press, 615 E. University, Ann Arbor, MI 48106. $7.95, paper. Deals with an analysis of the structure of schools, employment agencies, mental health clinics, correctional institutions, welfare agencies and hospitals. If you're thinking about going to work in one of these human service organizations, this could help your research.

For those interested in working in state and local government, a most helpful resource is the Western Governmental Research Association, 109 Moses Hall, University of California, Berkeley, CA 94720. They have monthly compilations of employment opportunities in *The Jobfinder,* as well as much other helpful material. They are trying to attract people with integrity into local government.

Do not overlook the fact that it is very possible to create your own job. For example, in California, before Proposition 13 hit, the state used to collect an override tax of five cents per person, which was designated for the one or more community colleges that were in each particular county, *to be used for community services.* Many of the one hundred community colleges in that state could therefore at that time be approached by career changers who could sell themselves for the job of Community Services Officer at that college, a new job which was paid for out of these designated tax funds.

Thorough research on your part will often reveal other ways in which *funding can be found for positions not yet created if you know exactly what it is you want to do,* and find someone who knows something about it.

3. What can I do if I want to create a job no-one has ever heard of, or otherwise go the route of self-employment?

Well, to begin with: you're probably *not* going to create a job no-one has ever heard of; in all likelihood you're only going to create a job that *most* people have never heard of. But someone, somewhere, in this world of endless creativity, has probably already put together the kind of job you're dreaming about. Your task: to go find her, or him, and interview them to death. Why should you have to invent the wheel all over again? They've already stepped on all the landmines for you. They know where all the pitfalls are in this business you're dreaming of starting.

But suppose you can't find such a person? Well, then, figure out who is doing something that is *close* to what you're dreaming of doing, and go interview *that* person. For example, let's suppose your dream is to use computers to monitor the growth of plants at the Arctic. And you can't find anybody who's ever done such a thing. Well, then, break it down into its parts: computers, plants, and Arctic. Try combining *two* parts with each other, and you'll see what your Informational Interviewing task is: to find someone who's used computers with plants, or computers at the Arctic, or someone who's worked with plants at the Arctic (yes, I know this is a moderately ridiculous example, but I wanted to stretch your imagination). My point is a simple one: you can ALWAYS find someone who has done something that approximates what it is you want to do, and from her or him you can learn a great deal. Better yet, they may lead you to others who have done something even closer to what it is you want to do.

How do you get funded for a new job no-one has ever heard of? Well, if it's a product or service you are offering, you get funded by convincing people to buy it. (And you ask people already offering a similar product or service how they got people to buy theirs, so you'll know what the general principles are, regarding what works and what doesn't work.)

But admittedly, this *can* be "the pits" if you have to go out and convince people, one by one, to buy your product, services, or whatever. No wonder, then, that a number of (hopefully) soon-to-be self-employed persons find the idea of a foundation grant or government grant, tremendously attractive and winsome. How, they ask—in letter after letter—can I find such a grant? Well, basically the same way you find a job. Thorough-going research. To get you started, consult your library (or else your banker) for one of the directories of grants (already) given. Such directories as:

Annual Register of Grant Support, published by Marquis Academic Media, 200 E. Ohio St., Room 5608, Chicago, IL 60611. If you have to buy it (ouch), it's $57.50, plus

$2.00 for postage and handling, plus state tax (where applicable). Makes your local library look absolutely *wonderful,* doesn't it? The directory or register covers 2300 current grant programs, and has four helpful indexes. There's also the *Foundation 500,* published by the Foundation Research Service, 39 E. 51st St., New York, NY 10022. Hopefully, your local library has this only-slightly-less expensive volume, too. There is also: Lefferts, Robert, *Getting a Grant.* Prentice-Hall, Spectrum. 1979. $4.95.

The following four books are available from Public Service Materials Center, 111 N. Central Ave., Hartsdale, NY 10530: Dermer, Joseph, *New Ways to Succeed with Foundations—A Guide for the Reagan Years.* 1982. $19.50, plus $1.50 postage. *The Corporate Fund Raising Directory,* 1983–84 edition. 1982. $34, plus $1.50 postage. Guide to 550 corporations and their grant programs. Pulling, Lisa, *The KRC Desk Book for Fund Raisers/with Model Forms and Records.* 1982. $37.95, plus $1.50 postage. Describes the everyday operation of a fund-raising organization. Dermer, Joseph, and Wertheimer, Stephen, ed., *The Complete Guide to Corporate Fund Raising.* 1982. $16.75, plus $1.50 postage. Describes the entire corporate fund-raising process. If you want further help, you can get a catalog of books and materials related to fund-raising and proposal-writing by contacting the Public Service Materials Center.

The Foundation Center, 888 Seventh Ave., New York, NY 10019, is an independent, non-profit organization offering assistance in locating grants. There are four reference collections operated by the Center, in New York, Washington, DC, Cleveland, and San Francisco. There are also dozens of cooperating collections nation-wide. For information on locations nearest you, call 800-424-9836.

If your idea of self-employment runs in the direction of *the arts (writing, etc.)* you may be interested in a $13.95 listing of operating foundations, businesses, unions, associations, educational and professional institutions, which give support (thru grants or other kinds of aid) to *writers, painters, filmmakers, musicians,* etc.: "Grants and Aid to Individuals in the Arts" from *Washington International Arts Letter,* 325 Pennsylvania Ave., Box 9005A, Washington, DC 20003. They have other lists (private foundations active in the arts, federal monies available, etc.) and their *Letter* itself is $13.95/yr. (or see your local library to see if it has it).

On the other hand, if you've always dreamed about being a consultant there are books about consultancy available through the mails, or at your library, or at your bookstore, such as Shenson, Howard, *How to Establish and Operate Your Own Consulting Practice.* Prentice-Hall, Spectrum. 1979. $17.50. OR: Bermont, Hubert, *How to Become a Consultant in Your Own Field.* Bermont Books, 815 15th St. NW, Washington, DC 20005. $20.00. Money-back guarantee available. But I need to tell you that some of our readers have not found books very helpful. We recommend, in such a case, that you go talk to some consultants of the type which interest you (see the yellow pages in your phone book) to see what they regard as the virtues and pitfalls of your intended profession. If you like to do consulting or training, but prefer to hitch up with an already established firm, go to your library and peruse Wasserman, Paul, and Watson, Marlene A., eds., *Training and Development Organizations Directory.* Second edition. $125.00. OR: *New Training and Development Organizations,* Supplement. $48.00. Gale Research Co., Book Tower, Detroit, MI 48226. These are reference works describing many individuals, institutions, firms, and other agencies offering training programs for business, industry, etc.

IF YOU WANT TO BUY IN ON YOUR OWN BUSINESS, there are roughly 1.5 million franchises in this country (you put up thousands of dollars of your own, and in return you get equipment, know-how, and—sometimes—national advertising campaigns to help you). You also can get taken to the cleaners by supposedly reputable companies.

For a sampling of the kind of franchises available you may want to get your hands on *Franchise Opportunities Handbook*. Produced by the U.S. Dept. of Commerce, Industry and Trade Admin. and Office of Minority Business Enterprise, (1978). Available from: Supt. of Documents, U.S. Govt. Printing Off., Washington, DC 20402.

For a more complete, and more up-to-date, directory, see *1982 Directory of Franchising Organizations*, S.T. Small, ed., Pilot Books, New York, NY, 1982. $3.95, paper. For some guidance on how to run a franchise, see Finn, Richard P., *Your Fortune In Franchises*. Contemporary Books, 1979. $9.95. Details the steps involved in acquiring a franchise, including financing, site selection, franchisor's rights, and promotion.

Caution: Some experts warn that the successful entrepreneur and the successful organization person are two entirely different breeds of cat, and the longer a man or woman has been at one, the less likely he or she will succeed at the other. Think about it!

Mechanics of funding and other issues aside, I would like to say a word about the whole idea in general of working for yourself. Here it is: the self-employment route is exceedingly attractive to the unemployed, because it is a beautiful way to avoid the job-hunt. It becomes even more attractive during Hard Times, of course. If you doubt me, look at the statistics. 1982 was a record year for businesses failing (26,000 expected, at this writing); BUT it was also a record year for businesses starting up. In 1981, 581, 661 new businesses were incorporated—up to that time a record high. 1982, at this writing, promised to exceed it. In other words, Recessions/Depressions are times when record numbers of people try starting up their own (small) business: doing home repairs, landscape gardening, making musical instruments, running taxi services, or whatever. Unable to find work, they figure they have nothing to lose.

But of course you do. Your shirt (or blouse). The statistics on new businesses are depressing. You've probably heard them already, but just in case you haven't: the average new business lasts three years; only one out of every ten new businesses makes it through five years or so. That's the bad news.

The good news, if you want the bright side of things, is that there are about 28 old businesses in this country, for every new business that starts up. This keeps the bankruptcy/failure rate *for the country* much lower than most people think. In Good Times, out of every 10,000 businesses, only 62 fail in a given year. In Hard Times (as currently), out of every 10,000 businesses, 186 fail. That means 9,814 out of every 10,000 survive even during a tough Recession year. So, *if* you make it through the first few very difficult years in your new business (say, the first seven, to be safe) you'll probably survive.

EVERYTHING therefore depends on how you start up. That's why you must not even for a moment think that the self-employment route is a good way to avoid the job-hunt. On the contrary, you'll have to work harder at your Informational Interviewing, harder at setting up your business, harder at finding customers (should you be offering a service or product) than you ever would in a normal job-hunt if your experience is at all like the self-employed from whom I regularly hear. You will look back at the job-hunt as an elementary school exercise by comparison.

If you're determined to try it anyway (it's just in your blood to do this), read up all you can *first*. The books are listed in section 12, Appendix B. I'd certainly read Levinson's book, especially the first part on "modular economics." I'd also browse my library to see if they have a copy of Peter Weaver's 1973 book, *You, Inc. A detailed escape route to being your own boss*.

Secondly, I'd go do Informational Interviewing (were I in your shoes) until I'd interviewed everyone in my geographical area who had done anything remotely like what it is I'm thinking of doing.

And thirdly, if I could move *gradually* into self-employment, doing it as a moonlighting activity first of all, I certainly would. Test out your enterprise, as you would a floorboard in a very old run-down house, stepping on it cautiously without putting your full weight on it, at first, to see whether or not it will hold you. If you're not presently employed, and you're determined to go the self-employment or franchise route, for heaven sakes have a plan B. "I'm going to try out this self-employment, and my plan B is that if after a certain number of months it doesn't look like it's going to make it, then I'm going to...... (fill in the blank)." And give some time to the exploration of that alternative before you start your self-employment thing, so that plan B is "all in place," as they say.

And: good luck.

4. What do I do if I want to work in the education field, but there are no jobs for teachers in the local schools or colleges?

Teachers teach in schools. That has been the assumption that has dominated teacher-training for ages. Thus, when teachers run into a 'tight' labor market, as has been the case for the last dozen years or so, they often quickly conclude they must abandon their desire to teach, and go hunting for some some kind of employment altogether.

You would do well not to make this error. The range of places that use people with teaching skills is mind-boggling: but as just a sampling, there are—as experts like John Crystal point out—training academies (like fire and police); corporate training and education departments; local and state councils on higher education; designers and manufacturers of educational equipment; teachers associations; foundations; private research firms; regional and national associations of universities, etc.; state and congressional legislative committees on education; specialized educational publishing houses; professional and trade societies. An indication of some of the possibilities you may want to research, can be found in *Education Directory: Education Associations*. It's available in your local library, or from the Superintendent of Documents, U.S. Govt. Printing Off., Washington, DC 20402.

Moreover, the range of jobs that are done under the broad umbrella of Education is multitudinous and varied; just for openers, there is: *teaching* (of course), *counseling* (an honorable teaching profession, where it isn't just used by a school system as the repository for teachers who couldn't 'cut it' as teachers), *general administration, adult education programs, public relations, ombudsman, training, human resource development*, and the like. If the latter—i.e., training and development—is of particular interest to you, you will find that the Ontario Society for Training and Development has put out a very helpful guide, entitled *Competency Analysis for Trainers: A Personal Planning Guide*. It is available for O.S.T.D., Box 537, Postal Station K, Toronto, M4P 2G9, Ontario, Canada, for $5.00, plus $1.50 for postage and handling. It outlines the kinds of skills which people who are entering this field ought to possess, and provides a checklist against which one can compare one's own skills.

All of which is to say, just because you have defined your dream of life for yourself as "teacher" doesn't mean you have even begun to narrow the territory down sufficiently for you to start looking for a job. You still have more research, and information gathering to do, before you have defined exactly *what kind* of teaching, *with what* kind of *groups, in what* kind of *place*. In other words, chapters 4–7 in this manual apply to you as much as, or even more than, anyone else.

If you decide to look elsewhere than teaching, there are aids produced for various teaching specialties, that you may want to seek out, e.g., for history majors there is: *Careers for Students of History*, from the American Historical Association, 400 A St. SE, Washington, DC 20003. 1977. $3.50, paper. While, for English majors, there is: *Aside from Teaching English, What in the World Can You Do?* by Dorothy K. Bestor, available from: University of Washington Press, Seattle, WA 98105. 1982, revised. $5.95, paper.

There are other more general guides for faculty who have decided to become career-changers; new ones are produced each year, as the publishing industry has lately (very lately) become aware of the problem; these are, in reverse order of publication:

Krannich, Ronald L., and Banis, William J., *Moving Out of Education: The Educator's Guide to Career Management and Change*. Progressive Concepts, Inc., 4212 Gadwall Pl., Virginia Beach, VA 23462. 1981. $14.95, postpaid.

Baldwin, Roger, et al., *Expanding Faculty Options: Career Development at Colleges and Universities*. American Association for Higher Education, One Dupont Circle, Suite 780, Washington, DC 20036. 1981. Paper.

Furniss, W. Todd, *Reshaping Faculty Careers*. American Council on Education, One Dupont Circle, Washington, DC 20036. 1981. Paper.

Miller, Jean M., and Dickinson, Georgianna M., *When Apples Ain't Enough: Career Change Techniques for Teachers, Counselors and Librarians*. Jalmar Press, Inc., 6501 Elvas Ave., Sacramento, CA 95819. 1980. $4.95, paper.

Miller, Anne, *Finding Career Alternatives for Teachers: A Step-by-Step Guide to Your New Career*. Apple Publishing Co., Inc., Box 2498, Dept. R., Grand Central Sta., New York, NY 10017. 1979. $7.95 plus $.75 postage and handling. Paper.

Pollack, Sally, *Alternative Careers for Teachers*, Harvard Common Press, Inc., The Common, Harvard, MA 01451. 1979. $6.95, paper.

5. What do I do if I want to get a government job?

The diversity of jobs in government (or public service) is very great. You must decide, first of all, whether you want to work for *Federal, State, County, Municipal,* or *Other Agencies of a quasi-governmental nature* (redevelopment agencies, regional councils of governments, special district governments, etc.).

Each of these employs personnel in a great variety of occupations, including *administrative assistant, human relations specialist,* and others. You've got to decide *where* it is you want to work, what skills you want to be able to use, and what it is you want to do (in other words, chapters 5 and 6 in this book apply to you as much as to non-governmental workers).

If you are new to the idea of the government as your employer, you will of course suppose that Informational Interviewing is not for you, for you are going to have to take a Civil Service examination of one kind or another. Well, eventually you probably *are* going to have to take that exam. But all the principles in chapter 7 apply just as much to government managers as they do to other employers. Government managers, too, are tired of hiring people ill-suited for the job. Civil service exams don't give these managers any better clues than resumes do for non-governmental employers. So if, in the course of your Informational Interviewing you happen to visit the government person who has the power to hire you, and if he or she takes a real liking to you, you can bet your bottom dollar they will do everything *they can* to guide you through the examination maze, so that you can end up in their office. Any government manager worth her or his salt knows how to manipulate—ah, excuse me, creatively use—standard operating procedures, so that it all works out to their best advantage.

You will observe that as of this writing government budgets are suffering from tight constraints, the like of which have not been encountered in many years (seems like I've been writing that sentence every year since 1970, and it just keeps getting truer and truer). Many people will therefore caution you that this is no time to be thinking of government work. But, hey, listen: people retire, quit, die every month—and not *all* of the positions they held get obliterated after their departure. The government, in its various forms and levels, still employs millions of people. When the market gets tight, it doesn't mean necessarily that you should turn elsewhere. It only means that traditional job-hunting methods are *less and less effective*, and you are going to have to be *more and more creative* in your own job-hunting techniques. In other words, the tighter the job-market, the more slavishly you should follow chapters 4–7 here in *Parachute*.

When you hit chapter 6, you will be beginning your Informational Interviewing. It couldn't hurt to have some places with which to start, in gathering your information. So, here are some clues:

Federal Jobs: The U.S. Office of Personnel Management (formerly called the U.S. Civil Service Commission) has a *Guide to Federal Career Literature*. Order it from the Superintendent of Documents, U.S. Govt. Printing Off., Washington, DC 20402. For other information, see your nearest Office of Personnel Management (it's in all large cities), and ask them what else they've got about working for the U.S. of A.

And, incidentally, when doing your Informational Interviewing about salaries, once it's come down to that, it is helpful to know that unless you are up for an occupation for which there is an extremely limited supply of job-hunters, your government Personnel Officer will rarely have the authority to negotiate salary. If it *is* fixed, you can probably find it in the Temporary box, on a Federal SF-171. (Yes, I know you probably don't know what a Federal SF-171 is, at the moment; but you should know by the time you get to this stage of your research.)

State jobs: Contact your State Personnel Board for beginning clues for your research. Do your research extensively. Follow the Techniques of chapter 6.

County jobs: Personnel departments of the individual counties, again for beginning clues. Lots of interviewing, done by you, to find out what you want to know, is essential before deciding what field you want to aim at and *campaign for.*

Municipal jobs: Personnel departments of individual cities. Also your state may have some association of them (California has the League of California Cities, 1108 O St., Sacramento, CA 95814—for example), where you can pick up clues. Some regions have organizations or "house organs," for municipalities, e.g., the western part of the country has *Western City Magazine*—see your local library, or 702 Hilton Center Bldg., Los Angeles, CA 90017.

Do remember how broad government employment is. If there's anything done in the private sector, the chances are that the government hires such people, too.

Government fields, for example, include antipollution enforcement, education, welfare, day care, beautification, probation and parole, public works, recreation and parks, health and hospitals, urban renewal, and countless others.

For books to help, see Appendix B, Section 15, p. 264.

6. What do I need to know if I want to get into the business world?

In filling management positions, most companies have a penchant for *generalists* who can see " the whole picture" rather than for *specialists* who may suffer from "tunnel vision." Thus, they often prefer 'outsiders,' rather than 'insiders'-who-have-been-booted-upstairs!

What the businesses need are executives with *people skills*. First of all, this is the way history has moved. The history of the industrial enterprise has focused successively on Production, Marketing, and Distribution, and finally (these days) on the needs of the people making up the organization or being served by the organization.

Most of the problems that an organization faces today are *people problems*. A survey revealed that, in 177 organizations, for every manager who failed to make the grade because of insufficient knowledge, seven failed because of personality problems. Or, as we might prefer to say, because of a lack of "self-management skills" for that particular environment.

The higher position a man or woman holds, the more he or she has to deal with people. A top executive's major job is to organize resources for the accomplishment of goals. Two-thirds of the average company's resources, are *human resources*, i.e., people. It is hardly surprising, therefore, that experts say top executives rarely have more than five minutes to themselves in between their dealing with *people*, and their major task is—in the end—passing judgment upon people.

What exactly are "people skills"? Well, they include such skills as the following:

- authority—the only authority which succeeds, today, being comprised of (overall) competence + compassion;
- ability to work with others;
- communicative skills—studies have shown that effectiveness is directly correlated with the extent to which a man or woman can express his or her own convictions and feelings and at the same time also express consideration for the thoughts and feelings of others;
- intelligence and ability to solve problems;
- perseverance—the ability to deliver continuously, and not just in spurts; inner-motivation; *and*
- character, dependability, integrity, maturity.

Beyond people skills, managers and executives who are going to succeed in business will need the following:

- clear thinking;
- flexibility;
- the ability to deal with increasing complexity and ambiguity in the world in which we live;
- the ability to get others to accomplish results.

While situations may differ from one company to another, you may well find that these are the skills you should stress (assuming you *do* have them) in your interviewing for hire.

During your prior Informational Interviewing, you will probably find your search (eventually) narrowing down to some particular companies—about which you would like to know more. If they are public companies, the Securities Exchange Commission in Washington, DC (with SEC reference centers in New York, Chicago and Los Angeles) will have their Form 10-K (their annual report), their Form 10-Q (their quarterly report), and their form 8-K (important current developments). You write to the SEC, 500 N. Capitol, Washington, DC 20549, stating which company or companies you are interested in, and which reports you want. They will bill you if you state in your letter that you understand the cost of this service is $.10 a page, with a minimum of $5.00 for the service, and that you promise to pay upon receiving their bill. If you have any difficulty in getting these from the Commission, there are firms which will acquire them for you—at a somewhat higher price. Disclosure, Inc., for example (10960 Wilshire Blvd., Ste. 1710, Los Angeles, CA 90024 or 5161 River Rd., Washington, DC 20016) will supply you with the 10-K and other reports, for any company you are interested in checking out, at the cost of $.35 a page. If you want to check out how many pages that will be, you can always call them at 213-478-4441 in the West, or 301-951-1350 in the East.

If you prefer to do most of this kind of checking on your own, get your hands on *How to Find Information About Companies*, Donna M. Jablonski, editor. Washington Researchers, 918 16th St. NW., Washington, DC 20006. 1979.

For further resources, see section 11 in the Bibliography (p. 261) that you will find in Appendix B.

7. What do I do if I decide I want to work overseas?

Well, first of all, talk to everyone you possibly can who has in fact been overseas, most especially to the country or countries that interest you. A nearby large university will probably have such faculty or students (ask). Companies in your city which have overseas branches (your library should be able to tell you which they are) should be able to lead you to people also—possibly to the names and addresses of personnel who are still "over there" to whom you can write for the information you are seeking. Alternatively, try asking every single person you meet for the next week (at the supermarket checkout, at your work, at home, at church or synagogue, etc.) if they know someone who used to live overseas and now is in your city or town. By doing your Informational Interviewing with such people, you will learn a great deal.

Talking to the consulate of the country in question (should you live in or near a major city) may also be very enlightening. Books from your local library or local bookstore (in the travel section), if they are recent, may also tell you much.

To supplement such research, there is Sherman, Margaret E., ed., *Whole World Handbook: A Guide to travel, study and work abroad*, 1981–82, published by Elsevier-Dutton Publishing Co., Inc., Two Park Ave., New York, NY 10016. 1981. $5.75, paper. And: Beckmann, David M., and Donnelly, Elizabeth Anne, *The Overseas List, Opportunities for Living and Working in Developing Countries*, published by the Augsburg Publishing House, 426 S. Fifth St., Minneapolis, MN 55415. 1979. $4.95, paper.

As for the general facts about living overseas, books on this subject keep getting regularly published, regularly flourish for a season, and then regularly die. But currently these are:

Phelps, Cathy S., *The Guide to Moving Overseas*. Guide, Box 236, Lemont, PA 16851. 1978. $4.95, paper.

Shrank, Robert, ed., *American Workers Abroad*. The MIT Press, 28 Carleton St., Cambridge, MA 02142. 1979. $13.50, postpaid.

Kocher, Eric, *International Jobs: Where They Are, How to Get Them*. Addison-Wesley, Jacob Way, Reading, MA 01867. $11.45, paper, postpaid.

Your library should also have books such as Angel, Juvenal, *Dictionary of American Firms Operating in Foreign Countries*. (World Trade Academy Press.)

And to research overseas public companies which sell stock in this country, the Securities Exchange Commission will have their Form 6-K, which they filed in order to be able to sell that stock.

In general, the principles found in chapter 6, in the section on how to research cities at a distance (pp. 138 to 144) will apply here with equal or greater force.

Index

A

Ability Potentials, Inc., 63
Accomplishments. *See also* Achievements; Skills
  analyzing, for career, 99-100
Achievements. *See also* Skills
  analyzing, as skills, 86-87
Advertisements, newspaper, 30-32. *See also* Newspapers
  efficacy of, 21, 23
  for job club, 146
  placing, as job-seeker, 23
  questionable, 22
  using, 20-23
Agencies, government, as resources, 143
Alaska, 189
Alumni, as contacts, 144-45
American Almanac of Jobs and Salaries, 187
American Coalition of Citizens with Disabilities, 260
American Dreams, 96n.
American Friends Service Committee, 109
American Men and Women of Science, 148
American Society of Training and Development Directory, 148
Americans in Transition, 44n.
Annual reports. *See* Reports, annual
Appearance, importance of, 108, 183
Appointments, for informational interviewing, 165
Aptitude. *See also* Skills
  testing, 63
Art, selling, 263-64
Arts, support for, 318
Association of Executive Recruiting Consultants, 1981 Directory, 18
Association of Interpretative Naturalists, 34
Associations, professional, 108
  and salaries, 189
At A Journal Workshop, 305
Attitudes, mental, and failure, 201-204
Azrin, Nathan, 58-60, 197

B C

BBB. *See* Better Business Bureau
Benchmarks, for skills, 104
Better Business Bureau, 148, 278, 283
Bibliography. *See also* Books; Resources, publications as
  of alternative careers, 248-50
  of being fired, 271
  of being laid-off, 271
  of being published, 263
  of the brain, 267-69
  of burnout, 270-71
  of business, 261, 324
  of career planning, 250-52
  of careers in education, 320-21
  of changing careers, 266, 310-21 *passim*
  about couples working, 259
  of creativity, 267-69
  of decision-making, 267-68
  of government employment, 264, 322
  of jobs: for college students, 254-55
    for the handicapped, 259-60
    for high-school students, 254
  of job-hunting, 252-53
    for the clergy, 267
    for college students, 254-55
    for executives, 261, 324
    for minorities, 259
    for women, 256-58
  of job keeping, 270-71
  of interviewing, 270
  of promotion, 270-71
  of resume writing, 270
  of retirement, 266
  of second careers. *See* Bibliography, of changing careers
  of self-employment, 261-62, 318-19
  of selling crafts, 263-64
  of skills analysis, 269-70
  of social service/change careers, 264-65, 314-17
  of volunteering, 264-65
  of working in America, 247-48
  of working overseas, 325
  of writing, as a career, 263
Boasting, 83, 87-88
Books. *See also* Bibliography; Resources, publications as
  highly recommended, 244-45
  as a job-hunting resource, 62
  for special reference on careers and job-hunting, 244-71
  using, 71
Brain, books about, 267-69
Brain/Mind Bulletin (periodical), 267
Brain and Strategy (periodical), 267
Briarpatch Book, The, 155n.
Brooks, Phillips, 198
Buddy system, 60, 64
Budget, 112-14. *See also* Salary
Bureau of the Census, 36
Bureau of Labor Statistics, 120, 121
Burnout, 303-304
  books on, 270-71
Business: books about, 261, 324
  buying. *See* Franchises
  changing careers to, 323-24
Business consultants, as resources, 63
Business Information Guidebook, 154n.
Business Information Services, 148

Canada: books obtainable in, 245, 255
  job options in, 104
Canadian Classification and Dictionary of Occupations, 104
Career counselors, 275-87. *See also* Help, paid professional
  catalogs listing, 286-87
Career Guide to Professional Associations, 148
Career Guide to Professional Organizations, 108
Career and Life Planning (Life/work Planning):
  cautions about, 47
  defined, 47, 73
  described, 46-47
  determining what you want to do, 46-115
  and second careers, 68-69
  scope of, 46
  synonyms for, 47
Career Placement Registry, 32
Career planning. *See also* Job-hunting
  books on, 250-52
  determining control of, 74-75
Career Satisfaction and Success, 86n.
Career transition, 198
Careers. *See also* Jobs; Occupations
  alternative, options for, 130-32
    books on, 248-50
  books on individual, 252
  changing. *See also* Careers, second
    and Career and Life Planning, 68-69
    in education, 320-21
    education system and, 45-46
    enforced, 44-46
    to government jobs, 322-23
    and job environments, 92
    and the numbers game, 12
    personal problems in, 303-307
    rearranging blocks and, 73
    research on, 134-35
  counter-cultural, 109-10
  defined, 102-104
  information about, in libraries, 151. *See also* Research; Resources
  mid-life. *See* Careers, changing; Careers, second
  second. *See also* Careers, changing
    books about, 266
    necessity for, 44
    resumes and, 12, 14
    and traditional job-hunting, 40
  public service, books on, 316
Cassettes on job-hunting, 244-45, 260
Catalogs of career counselors, 286-87
Catalogue of Federal Domestic Assistance, 315
CETA, 58, 59
Chamber of Commerce, 142, 148
Change: and Career and Life Planning, 101
  bibliography of social, 264-65
Changing internal vs. external furniture, 61, 91-93, 101, 304-307
Character, importance of proving, 199
Child Care Personnel Clearinghouse, 34
Children, jobs with, 34
Christian perspective, books with, 267
Church. *See also* Clergy
  clearinghouse for vacancies in, 32-33
Chusid, Frederick & Co., 277
City Directory, 144
City Hall, as a resource, 142
Clearinghouses, for educational information, 314
Clergy, changing careers of, 299-300
  books about, 267
  help for, 63, 282-83
  and salaries, 113n.
Clubs, job-seekers', 58-60, 89n., 146. *See also* Group support
Coaching: professional help for, 274-87
  as a skill, 79
  sources of, 283-87
College graduates, clearinghouse for jobs for, 32
College placement centers, 28
College Placement Council, 188
College students. *See* Students, college
Colorado Outward Bound School, 34
Committee, identifying power in, 156
Common Body of Knowledge for Management Consultants, 147n.
Companies: and the numbers game, 13-14
  obtaining information about, 324
  surveys of, 151
"Compen$ation in the Guidance and Counseling Field," 189
Competition for jobs, 122-26
  gauging, 105
Competitors, and salary research, 192
Conflict, resolving internal, 101. *See also* Psychotherapy
Constancy, in the face of change, 75
Consultants as resources, 105. *See also* Counselors; Help, professional
Consultants News, 18, 19
Consulting, 79
  books about, 318
  as a career, 318
Contact: The First Four Minutes, 107
Contacts, 152, 156, 157
  finding, 142-43, 144-46
  for informational interviewing, 166
  as resources, 166
  salary research and, 191
  using, 144-46, 166, 172
Contacts Influential, 149
Contracts, career-counselors', 281-83
Counseling, personal, 304-307
Counselors. *See also* Consultants; Help, professional
  choosing, 276-78, 279-83

paid, 72
psychological. *See* Psychotherapy
State Employment, 105
Couples, books about working, 259
Courses, academic, analyzing for skills, 86
Crafts, books about selling, 263-64
Creative minority. *See* Minority, creative
Creativity, books about stimulating, 267-69
Credentials: of career counselors, 281
for a second career, 101, 130-31
Crystal, John, 153, 189, 193, 285, 320
Cullen, Albert, 58

D E F

Damn Good Resume Guide, 180n.
Data, skills dealing with, 77, 80
Deciding, 89
Deciding: A Leader's Guide, 89n.
Decision making: books about, 89, 267-68
as a skill, 89
Decisions, 89
Decisiveness, 43
Degrees, academic, 312
Demand for labor, 119
Diary: analyzing in terms of skills, 85
and raises, 195
writing, as an aid to Career and Life Planning, 83-85
Dictionary of Occupational Titles (D.O.T.), 77, 78, 80, 103-104, 244
Diligence, in job-hunting, 50-57, 65
Directory of Corporate Affiliations, 149
Directory of Counseling Services, 307
Directory of Directories, 151
Directory of Executive Recruiters, 18
Directory of Information Resources in the United States, 149
Directory of Internships, Work Experience Programs and On-The-Job Training Opportunities, 315
Directory of Personal Image Consultants (1979), 183n.
Disclosure, Inc., 324
Diverting, as a skill, 79
Divorce, and job-hunting, 15
D.O.T. *See Directory of Occupational Titles*
Dreams and Career and Life Planning, 96-99
Dress code. *See* Appearance
Dress for Success, 183n.
Drucker, Peter, 73
Dunn & Bradstreet's Middle Market Directory, 149
Dunn & Bradstreet's Million Dollar Directory, 149
Dunn & Bradstreet's Reference Book of Corporate Managements, 149

Earnings, average weekly (tables), 187, 188. *See also* Salary
Education, changing careers in, 320-31
financing, 314-15
for multiple careers, 45-46
overseas, 315
pursuing, 312-14
Education Directory, 313
Effective Executive, 101n.
Employees: former, as resources, 161
number of new, 55
Employers: approaching, 51, 55
of the handicapped, 260
informational interviewing and, 167, 175
scheduling, 106n., 167
mistakes of, in hiring, 173-74
and the power to hire, 139, 170, 172-76
Employment: government services for, (USES), 26-27, 59
private agencies for, 24-25
value of, to job-seeker, 70-71
"Employment and Earnings," 114
Empowerment, defined, 299
Encyclopedia of Associations, 149, 189
Encyclopedia of Business Information Sources, 149
Enjoyment. *See also* Tropisms
and aptitude, 89-90
as a benchmark, 85
and self-awareness, 93-94, 95
virtue in, 87
and work places, 147
Everybody's Business, An Almanac, 151
Exchanging information, as a skill, 79
Executive Employment Guide, 18
Executive Manpower Directory, 35
Executive search firms (Headhunters), 18-20
helpful, 20
lists of, 18
statistics on, 19
Executives, business: qualities of, 324
books for, about job-hunting, 261, 324
Exercises: for checking progress, 100
in completing a work autobiography, 85-87
for determining what makes you unhappy, 90-91
for finding help, 64, 72
for goal analysis, 98
on goal setting, 90
for identifying functional skills, 210-30
on identity, 93-95
for inventorying skills, 82-100
for seeking an answer to larger contexts, 101
Ex-offenders, job-hunting books for, 259-60
Experience, 130-32
Exploration, personal, professional help for, 304-306

Failure, causes and cures of, 201-204
F & S Index of Corporations and Industries, 149
Federal Information Center, 150
Feedback in job-hunting, 60
Feelings. *See also* Enjoyment; Tropisms
practical exercises analyzing, 82, 89-95
use of, in inventorying skills, 89-95

Fees: private employment agencies and, 24
for professional help, 277, 281-82
registries of vacancies and, 29
Field survey, directions for, 238-39
"Final Report to U.S. Department of Labor: The Job-Finding Club," 59
Finding Facts Fast, 111
Finding Your Best Place to Live in America, 129n.
Fine, Sidney, 103
Fired, being, 71
books on, 271
Fischer, Joseph, 58
Fitch Corporation Manuals, 149
Flexibility in job requirements, 41-42. *See also* Realism
Flower, The, 236, 238
Focusing down, 133, 144-48. *See also* Funneling
principles of, 232-235
Fortune Magazine, 149
Fortune's Plant & Product Directory, 149
Forty Million Americans in Career Transition, 44n.
Forty-Plus Clubs, 35, 58, 288
Foundation Center, 318
Foundation Directory, 149
Franchises: books about, 318-19
buying, 318-19
Free Spirit (directory), 265
Friends: as counselors, 63-65
as resources, 105, 161
Fringe benefits, 194
Frustration, relieving, 101
Function. *See* Skills
Funding for creating jobs, 317-18
Funneling, job-hunting as, 129-33. *See also* Focusing down
Future, the: and Career and Life Planning, 81, 95-100
dealing with, 73-75
dreaming about, 96-98
Future Directions for a Learning Society (an organization), 44
Future Shock, 75

G H I

Gambling, job-hunting as, 11-37, 62
Getting A Job, 145n.
Getting Organized, 71
Goals, and Career and Life Planning, 46-47, 69, 70, 73, 98-100, 101
exercises on, 90, 98
Government, books about employment in, 264, 322
changing careers to, 322-23
information from, 150
Grants, finding, 318
Group: counseling for personal growth, 305-308
informational interviewing, 167
professional, as a resource, 63
support, for job-hunting, 57-60, 264-66, 288-89. *See also* Clubs, job-seekers'
Grow Your Roots Anywhere, Anytime, 129n.
Guide to American Directories, 151
Guilt, while job-hunting, 57
Haldane, Bernard, 86, 87, 180, 198, 289, 300
Handbook of Business Problem Solving, 155n.
Handbook for Job Restructuring, 104
Handbook for Nonsexist Writing, xiii
Handicapped, books about jobs for the, 259-60
Headhunters. *See* Executive search firms
Help (assistance), determining requirements for, 61
Help, free, 62-63, 140
Help, professional/paid, 140
cautions against, 274-78
evaluating, 276-78, 279-83
for job-hunters, 63, 274-87. *See also* Coaching
for psychotherapy, 304, 306-307
sources of, 283-86
Helping, as a skill, 79
Help Kids, 34
High-school students. *See* Students, high-school
Hiring, 208
criteria for, 196-97
individual with the responsibility for. *See* Power to hire
Hobbies, analyzing as skills, 84, 86
Hoffman, Charles, 58
Holland, John L., 90, 92-93, 210
Homework. *See also* Research
for Career and Life Planning, 68-69, 70-71, 72-75
on inventorying skills, 165
Quick Job-Hunting Map as, 207
on salaries, 191-93
How To Beat the Employment Game, 21
How To Decide, 89
How To Find Information About Companies, 154n.
How To Make a Habit of Success, 195
How To Reach Anyone Who's Anyone, 149
How to Read a Financial Report, 154n.
How To Win With Information, 111n.
How to Write Your Own Life Story, 85n.
Human Engineering Laboratory, 63
Human service. *See* Social service
Human Service Organizations, 316
Identity, exercise on, 93-95
Impression, making an, 108. *See also* Appearance
Increase Your Employment Opportunities with the Audiovisual Portfolio, 180n.
Industrial Research Laboratories of the United States, 149
Inflation, recognition of, 195
Information, finding, 110-111, 135. *See also* Resources, published

Information, interviewing for, 100, 106-107, 132-33, 136-48, 181
in business, 324
cautions about, 106-107, 110-11
checklist for, 165-66
in choosing professional help, 279-83
contacts for, 153-54
in creating jobs, 317, 319-20
dealing with failure of, 165-66
about education, 315
employers and, 165, 167
example of, 317
and government jobs, 322-23
help for, 61
to identify problems, 153-63
initial results of, 153-54
and job-seeking, 165-66, 172-73
John Crystal on, 153
and the power to hire, 160-61
questions for, 237-40
and salary, 112
and self-employment, 319-20
and working overseas, 325
In-House Training and Development Programs Directory, 149
Initiative, job-hunters', 42
Instructing, as a skill, 79
Instruction, psychological counseling and, 304, 305
Intercristo, 32, 315
Intermatch, 32
Internships, 315
Interviewing: books on, 270
dress-code for, 183
employers' questions in, 182
guidelines for questions in, 182-84
informational. *See* Information, interviewing for
for a job, 136. *See also* Interviews, for a job
practice, 237
procedure for, 172-76
Interviews, for a job, 240-41
employers' questions, 241
essence of, 181-85
and illegal questions in, 184-85
negative information in, 180, 185
obtaining, 173-76, 178
statistics on, 14
stress in, 173-76
Investor, Banker, Broker Almanac, 150
Investors Information Kit, 154n.

J K

Job: clubs. *See* Clubs, job seekers'
defined, 100, 102
functional analysis of, 103-104
losing. *See* Fired, being
market, 119-33
hidden, 126-27
myths about, 119-26
researching, 127-64
victim mentality and, 119-22
titles, misleading, 100
Job Bank, 30, 286
Job Club Counselor's Manual, 59
Job Factory, 58
Jobfinder, 173
Job Hunt, 17
"Job-hunters anonymous," 60
Job-hunting. *See also* Career and Life Planning; Career planning
alternative methods of, 40-44
deficiencies in the accepted method of, 9-14
doomed, 2-7
while employed, 54-57
false assumptions about, 41-43
as a full-time job, 43, 50-54
as a gamble, 40
general books on, 252-53
help for, 203-204
homework for, 68-69, 70, 71
information required for, 138-39, 140
keys to, 43-44, 50-51, 68, 70, 118, 170
laser beam approach to, 129-33
and level of skills, 80-81
methods of (table), 36
numbers game in, 11-37
sources of help for, 60-63. *See also* Resources
successful, 43-44, 50-54
time spent on, 50-57
Job Opportunities in Social Work, 33
Job Power Now!, 86n.
Jobs: accepting, 185
books on keeping, 270-71
changing. *See* Careers, changing; Careers, second
creating, 122-23, 126-27, 317
handling offers of, 153, 173
identifying desirable, 129-54, 237-40. *See also* Careers; Occupations
"Job Search Assistance," 51n.
Johnson O'Connor, 63, 82
Journals, professional, 108
Justice, criminal, jobs in, 33

Kennedy, James H., 19
Keys to career planning and job-hunting, 50-54, 68, 70-71, 118, 170

L

Language, use of, in defining problems, 161-62, 175-76
Lay-offs, books dealing with, 271
Librarian, as a resource, 105, 173, 189
Libraries, as resources, 105, 107, 108, 140, 142, 148, 151, 161, 172, 188-89
Library of Congress, 150
Life in Organizations, 155n.

Life/work Planning. *See* Career and Life Planning
Listening, importance of, 160
Location, geographical: determining, 118, 129, 135, 141-48, 232
researching, 135, 138, 140-46

M N

MacRae's Blue Book, 150
Making Vocational Choices, 92
Management 158n.
Map, The Quick Job-Hunting, 198-233
references to, 87, 114, 118, 140, 165, 166, 179, 180n, 191
Memories, exercises using, 82-89
Mentoring, as a skill, 80
Military, the: career transition and, 303-304
and salaries, 113n.
Mind Test, 63n.
Minorities, job-hunting books for, 259
Minority, the creative, 40-44, 123, 173, 175
Money, budgeting, 112, 113. *See also* Salary
Moody's Industrial Manual, 150
Motivation for Career and Life Planning, 45, 69, 70-75
Moving, 129n.

Nader, Ralph, 315
Names and Numbers, 144n.
National Association of Social Workers, 33
National Career Development Project, 176
National Center for Educational Brokering, 314
National Directory of Addresses and Telephone Numbers, 143n., 150
National Job-Sharing Network, 249
National Office of Program Development, 59
National Recreational Sporting and Hobby Organization of the U.S., 150
National Trade and Professional Associations of the United States and Canada and Labor Unions, 108, 150
Natural Science for Youth Foundation, 34
Negotiating, as a skill, 80
NELS Monthly Bulletin, 33
Networking, 145n.
New Research Centers, 150
Newspapers: advertisements in. *See* advertisements, newspaper
as resources, 142
New Ways To Work (an organization), 249-50
Next Whole Earth Catalogue, 110
900,000 Plus Jobs Annually, 33
Nova University (Florida), 58
Numbers game, in job-hunting, 2-7, 11-36, 197
components of, 17
efficacy of, 11-14
understanding, 17
using, 16-36

O

Occupational Outlook Handbook, 105, 188
Occupational Outlook Handbook for College Graduates, 105
Occupational Outlook Quarterly, 36
Occupations. *See also* Careers; Jobs
alternative, 109-10
guides to, 103-106
identifying desirable, 208
research on, 135
salary ranges in (chart), 190
in terms of skills, 138
"Occupations Finder," 92-93
Opportunities, 34
Options, alternative, 46, 100, 104
Organizations: identifying desirable, 208, 237-40
information about, 139
researching, 139
Organizing Principle, The (an organization), 71
Outdoors, jobs in the, 34
Overseas: education, 315
working, 325
books on, 325

P Q

Parachute: color of, 70
success rate of the process, 172-73
Past, the, and Career and Life Planning, 81, 82, 83-89
Paychecks, 187
People: as resources, 134, 135
skills in dealing with, 323-24
People: environments, 92-93, 234
People Functions Scale, 78-80
People in Places, 148n.
"People's Yellow Pages," 109
Perfect Resume, 180n.
Periodicals, 151
Personal image consultancy, 183n.
Personnel department, 139, 170-72, 174
Persuading, as a skill, 79
Peter Principle, 195
Places Rated Almanac, 129n.
Plan Purchasing Directory, 150
Planning: and alternatives (Plan B), 100-101
attitude toward, 101, 102
futurity of present decisions, 73
risk in, 75
Pound, Ezra, 102
Power: to hire, individual with, 139, 156, 160-61, 162, 170-76
knowledge as, 127-29
Present, the, and Career and Life Planning, 81, 89-95
Problems, corporate/organizational: analyzing, 156-63

determining, 139
educated guesses about, 159-60
employer's perception of, 175-76
identifying from publications, 161
relative size of, 156
researching, 153-63
and responsibility for hiring, 170
Problem solving: ability in, and a second career, 132
importance of the employer's interpretation of, 158-59, 175-76
research to prove ability in, 132-63
Procrastination, 70-72
Professionals, as counselors, 274-87
Promotion: books on, 270-71
discussion of, in interviews, 196
Psychology of Vocational Choice, 90n.
Psychotherapy, professional counseling for, 304, 306-307
Publications as resources, 134, 135. *See also* Bibliography; Books
list of, 148-51
Public service. *See* Government; Social service
Published, books about being, 263
Puritanism, 87-88
Purpose. *See* Goals

Quality is Free, 155n.
Questions: for choosing organizations, 147-48
for choosing paid professional help, 280-81
for identifying problems, 159-61
illegal, in interviews, 184-85
for informational interviewing, 106, 154, 157
personal, in defining a career, 148

R

Rainbook: Resources for Appropriate Technology, 315
Raises, negotiating, 194-95
Ratings: climatic, 129n.
geographical, 129n.
Realism, vs. flexibility: in choosing a career, 96-100
in job-hunting, 118
Recession, and unemployment figures, 120-21
Recruiters, executive. *See* Executive search firms
Referrals. *See also* Contacts
obtaining, 152-53
using, 152-53, 172
Registers: of manufacturers, 150
of job vacancies, 29-34
Rejection shock in job-hunting, 14-16
Religious, help for, 299-300
Reports, annual, 149, 154n., 192
Research. *See also* Information, interviewing for
defining the scope of, 135
drawing analogies from, 143-44
first-hand, 134-35
geographical, 138, 140-46
help for, 61. *See also* Resources
to identify responsibility for hiring, 172
local, 143-44
need for detailed, 43-44
object of, 135
personal, in job-hunting, 62
program of, in job-hunting, 134-63
on salaries, 186-94
on social change careers, 314-17
Research Centers Directory, 150
Resources: competitors as, 160-61
consultants as, 105
contacts as, 161
ex-employees as, 161
friends as, 63-65, 105, 161
for geographical research, 141-48
government agencies as, 143
for job-hunting, 57-63, 107, 111
libraries as. *See* Libraries
people as, 134, 135
personal research as, 61, 110-11
professional groups as, 58, 63
publications as, 134-35, 241. *See also* Bibliography
university as, 63
Resumes, 11-14, 177-81, 202-203
in booklets, 35
books on writing, 270
defined, 177
for executive search firms, 18-20
screening, 13-14
and second careers, 12, 14
uses of, 177-80
writing, and success, 42-43
Resumes That Work, 180n.
Retirement: books about, 266
and career change, 45
Retraining, 45-46, 76-77, 130-32. *See also* Credentials; Education
Risk: acknowledging, 100-101
and Career and Life Planning and, 75
Risking, 73n.

S

Salary, 64-65, 182. *See also* Budget; Money
annual ranges in (chart), 190
average, 114
of college graduates, 188
determining ranges for, 112-14, 189-94
government, 322
graphing a history of, 113
level, choosing, 235
in major industries (table), 187

negotiating, 185-95
researching, 186-94
Salary Guide and Job Outlook, 187
Salesman, for career counselors, 281
Savings, using while job-hunting, 56-57
Screenee, 136, 166
Screener, 136-37, 166
Secrets of a Corporate Headhunter, 20n.
Securities Exchange Commission, 324, 325
Self, defining for oneself, 93-94, 95
Self-awareness and vocational choice, 90-95
Self-confidence, acquiring through research, 134
Self-Directed Job Search, 58n.
"Self-Directed Search," 92-93
Self-employment: 317-20
books on, 261-62, 318-19
cautions about, 319-20
changing careers and, 317-20
Self-esteem, 75
and career planning, 68
and Puritanism, 87-88
Sense of Place, 148n.
Serving, as a skill, 79
Shyness, 107
Shyness, What It Is, 107
Shyness Workbook, 107
Sick-leave, 56
Skills. *See also* Accomplishments; Achievements
accounting, 216
acquiring, for second careers, 76-77
analytic, 229-30
analyzing, 118, 135, 140, 202
books on, 269-70
checking, 100-102
feelings and, 89-95
instruments for, 86-87
artistic, 227-28
athletic, 214
in communications, 221-22
described, 78-80
in detailed work, 215-16
in education, 222-23
erroneous ideas about, 77
evaluation, 229-30
financial, 216
of following through, 215-16
guiding, 222-23
helping, 223-25
hierarchy of, 77-80
in human relations, 223-25
identifying (exercises), 85-87, 210-30
in innovation, 225-26
in instructing, 222-23
in interpretation, 222-23
interpreting: for employers, 175-76
as occupations, 208, 209
as problems, 182
of intuition, 225-26
inventory of, 212-30
inventorying, 75-76, 208, 209-30
aids for, 103-15
investigative, 229-30
language, 221-22
leadership, 218-19
in learning, 228-29
levels of, 79, 123-26
in management, 219-20
manual, 213-14
mechanical, 213-14
money management, 216
numerical, 216
object of research on, 133
of observation, 228-29
and occupations, 103-11
outdoor, 214
performing, 218
of persuasion, 217
prioritizing, 100, 118, 138, 231, 233
in reading, 221-22
relative to job opportunities, 80-81
in research, 134, 229-30
secondary, 118
in serving, 223-25
in speaking, 221-22
of systematization, 229-30
translation of, into problem solving, 161-62
in writing, 221-22
Social Casework, 33
Social change, careers in, 314-17
Social service: changing careers to, 314-17
books on, 314-16
vacancies in, 33
So This is Where You Work, 148n.
Specialists, doomed, 45-46
Standard and Poor's Corporation Records, 150
Standard and Poor's Industrial Index, 150
Standard and Poor's Listed Stock Reports, 150
Standard and Poor's Register of Corporations, Directors, and Executives, 150, 173
Statement of where you are going. *See* Resume
Statistics: of employed job-hunters, 54
on government employment services, 26-27
on job-hunting, 207
on vacancies, 119-22, 199
on new employees, 55
on private employment agencies, 24
on unemployment, 119-22
Stewardship, 64, 68
Storybook, 85n.
Stress, employers', in interviews, 173-76
Students: college, books on jobs for, 254-55
professional help for, 289
high-school, 93
books on jobs for, 254
career counseling for, 289

Study, alternatives for, 314
Success, chances of, 197-98
of the *Parachute* process, 172-73
Summer jobs, books on, 254
Supervising, as a skill, 80

T

Talents, parable of, 68, 147, 163
Targeting, systematic, 133, 138-43
Task. *See* Skills
Taskmaster, need for, 72
Teachers, changing careers, 320-21
job listings for, 32
Telephone Contacts for Data Users, 150
Test Your Own Job Aptitude, 63n.
Testimonials, deficiencies of, 277-78
Testing, vocational, 65
Thank-you letters, 164, 180
Therapists, psychology, choosing, 306-307
Things, skills dealing with, 77, 80
Thomas' Register of American Manufacturers, 150
Three Boxes of Life, 206n., 314
Time: for Career and Life Planning, 69, 70-71
for job-hunting, 64-65, 141, 202
limits of, for informational interviewing, 166
lines, 73
spans, 101
Titles, misleading, 276
Tools for Career and Life Planning, 69, 70, 80-115. *See also* Resources
Training and Development Directory, 105
Transition, career, and burnout, 303-304
Traveling, for research, 141, 144-46
Treating, as a skill, 79
Tropisms, 89, 101, 131
negative, 90-91
Truth About You, 87n.
Turnover, statistics on, 54-55

U V

Underemployment, 15-16, 41, 44, 94, 198
Understanding Financial Statements, 154n.
"Understanding Yourself and Your Career," 93
Unemployed, sources of group support for the, 288-89
Unemployment: among men, 16
and Career and Life Planning, 71
revolving, 122-23
statistics, 120-22
and your value as a worker, 71
Unhappiness, as an indicator of vocation, 90-91
United States Government Manual, 150
University, as a resource, 63
USES. *See* Employment service, government
Vacancies, and unemployment statistics, 122-24
Vacations, 56
Value Line Investment Survey, 150
Values. *See also* Goal setting
choosing organizational, 234
personal, 101
Victim mentality, 74-75
about geography, 118
about the job market, 119-22
Visualization, ability in, 82
Vocation: choice of, and feelings, 89-95
determining, 62
Vocational planning. *See* Career planning
Vocations for Social Change, 314
Volunteering, books about, 264-65, 316-19

W Y

Walker's Manual of Far Western Corporations and Securities, 150
Wall Street Journal, 31-32, 184
Washington International Arts Letter, 318
Weather Almanac, 129n.
Western City Magazine, 323
Western Governmental Research Association, 316-17
What Color Is Your Parachute? 146
What Else Can Financial Statements Tell You? 154n.
"Where," 135, 141, 144-48, 232
Where Do I Go From Here With My Life? 85, 115, 144n., 191, 193, 271
What Women Earn, 186
Who's Hiring Who, 180
Who's Who directories, using, 172
Who's Who in Finance and Industry, 151
Windowshopping, interviews as, 175
Winning the Salary Game, 193n.
Wishcraft, 96, 98
Women: books on job-hunting for, 256-58
effect of unemployment on, 124n.
help for, in job-hunting, 290-99
promotion for, 195
Women's Dress for Success Book, 183n.
Work, 100. *See* Jobs; Occupations
Work and Love, 92n.
Work autobiography, exercise in compiling, 85-87
Workbooks for inventorying skills, 86, 87
Work in America, 158n.
Working conditions, choosing, 235
Workplaces, research on, 135
Worksteads, 148n.
Work-time options, 301
World of work, books on American, 247-48
World Paychecks, 188
Writing, books about, 263

"Yellow Pages," 144
Youth, vacancies of jobs with, 33

Author Index

A

Adams, R.L., 286
Adams, S., 306
Aero, R., 63n.
Albert, K.J., 155n.
Albin, J.R., 287
Albrecht, K., 268
Albrecht, M., 256
Ali, K., 265
Altekruse, M., 253
American Association of Retired Persons, 266
American Historical Association, 321
American Management Association, 18
Anderson, B.F., 268
Andresen, G., 268
Angel, J., 325
Applebaum, J., 263
Appleby, J.A., 260
Aptakin, K., 315
Arbeiter, S., 44n.
Arieti, S., 269
Arnold, P., 241, 245
Artists Foundation, Inc., 264
Asimov, I., 268
Aslanian, C.B., 44n., 266
Association of Executive Recruiting Consultants, 18
Avrutis, R., 271
Azrin, N.H., 58, 59, 245

B

Babson, S., 250, 316
Bachuber, T.D., 253
Bailey, G., 256
Bailyn, L., 266
Bair, F.E., 129n.
Bair, M., 268
Baldwin, C., 269
Baldwin, R., 321
Ballenger, S.M., 267
Banis, W.J., 270, 321
Bao, R., 255
Baranov, A.B., 262
Barrett, J., 63n.
Bass, J.A., 262
Basso, J.L., 251
Bear, J., 313
Becker, B., 89
Beckmann, D.M., 325
Behn, R.D., 271
Belitsky, A.H., 245
Bennett, V., 262
Berg, I., 312
Berlye, M.K., 264
Bermont, H., 111n., 318
Bern, P., 256
Berson, L.E., 247
Best, F., 248, 249
Bestor, D.K., 321
Biegeleisen, J.I., 270
Billhartz, C., 253
Billingsley, E., 166, 245
Bingham, N., 316
Bird, C., 259
Black Resources Guide, Inc., 259
Bloomfield, W.M., 250
Blue, M., 263
Blue Cross/Blue Shield, 271
Boisen, A., 304
Boll, C.R., 261
Bolles, R.N., 85, 115, 241, 244-45
Borchard, D.C., 250
Bowman, T.F., 129n.
Boyer, R., 129n.
Brady, J., 263
Brennan, D., 265
Briarpatch Community, 155n.
Brickell, H.M., 44n., 269
Bridges, W., 305
Brigham, N., 250
Brill, P., 266
Brodsky, A., 271
Brohaugh, W., 263
Broida, P., 108
Bruck, L., 260
Bry, A., 268
Burack, E.H., 256
Bureau of Labor Statistics, 247
Business and Professional Women's Foundation, 257
Buskirk, R.H., 256
Butler, P.E., 256
Buzan, T., 269

C

Calano, J., 254
Calvert, R., Jr., 257
Cameron, C.T., 251
Campbell, D.P., 247, 261, 269
Cannon, C., 265
Carkhuff, R., 254
Carney, T.F., 255
Casewit, C.W., 268
Catalyst (an organization), 256, 270
Catalyst Press, 265
Chastain, S., 193n.
Chung, E.Z., 263
Clagett, C., 262
Clark, L.W., 262
Cluster, D., 248
Cochrane, D., 264
Cohen, B.S., 261
Cole, K.W., 259
Colgate, C., Jr., 108
Community Publications Cooperative, 265
Connaughton, H.W., 263
Cook, P.F., 260
Cook, W.A., 255
Corporate Action Project, 316
Cosgrave, G., 252
Cowle, J., 271
Crites, J.O., 250
Crosby, P.B., 155n.
Cross, W., 313
Crystal, J., 85, 115, 241, 244

D

Dahl, P.R., 260
Daitzman, R.J., 268
Daniel, L., 85n.
Daniels, L.M., 148
Darrow, C.N., 266
Datcher, L., 259
Davidson, M., 263
DeBono, E., 262
DeKay, J.T., 268
Dermer, J., 318
Deutsch, A.R., 251
Deutsch, G., 268
Dickinson, G.M., 321
Donaho, M.W., 270
Donnelly, E.A., 325
Donnis, M., 287
Dooling, D.M., 263
Doss, M.M., 258
Douglas, D., 259
Douglas, M.C., 254
Downs, H., 266
Drucker, P.F., 101n., 158n., 261
Dubin, J., 256
Dunlop, E., 255
Durkin, J., 266
Duval, R.J., 259

E

Edelwich, J., 271
Edlund, M., 245
Edlund, S., 245
Edwards, B., 268
Edwards, P.B., 248
Ehrenberg, M., 306
Ehrenberg, O., 306
Eisenberg, M.G., 259
Ekstrom, R.B., 258
Eliot, S.V., 129n.
Ericson, K., 252
Eternity Magazine, 267
Evans, N., 263

F

Family Service Association of America, 33
Farbstein, J., 148n.
Farley, J., 258
Farnsworth, K., 267
Federal Research Service, Inc., 264
Feingold, S.N., 33, 253, 255
Feldman, B.N., 251
Ferber, E., 263
Ferguson, M., 267, 268
Ferguson, S., 261
Ferguson, S.D., 261
Figler, H.E., 245, 255, 269
Figueroa, O., 154n.
Fine, S.A., 78, 103, 270
Finn, R.P., 319
Ford, G.A., 251
Foundation Research Service, 318
Fox, M.R., 255
Fracchia, C.A., 148n.
Freudenberger, H.J., 271
Friedman, B., 260
Fulton, L., 263
Furniss, W.T., 321

G

Gale, B., 250
Gale, L., 250
Gale, M.A., 260
Garrett Park Press, 259
Garrison, C.B., 254
Garry, W., 261
Gartley, W., 255
Gartner, A., 265
Garvin, A.P., 111n.
Gawain, S., 269
General Services Administration, 256
Germann, R., 241, 245
Ghezzi, B., 267
Giuliana, G.A., 129n.
Goldfein, D., 256
Gonyea, J.C., 255
Goodman, C.J., 264
Goodman, F.J., 264
Gottlieb, A., 98n.
Gould, R.L., 266
Goulet, T., 254
Gracie, D. McI., 247
Granovetter, M.S., 145n.
Greenfield, H., 263
Greenfield, S.R., 143n., 150
Gregory, R.L., 268
Greiner, P., 244
Grieff, B.S., 259
Griggins, C., 259
Gross, R., 312

H

Hagberg, J., 250
Hahn, A., 260
Haldane, B., 86n., 195, 241, 245, 261
Haldane, J., 86n., 241, 245
Half, R., 253
Hall, D.T., 259
Hall, F.S., 259
Hallock, R.L., 262
Hansard-Winkler, G.A., 33
Hapunski, W.C., 313
Hardigree, P., 254
Harding, James S., 250
Harms, S., 287
Harragan, B.L., 258
Harris, A.M., 258
Harris, J.C., 267
Harrop, D., 187, 188
Harvey, B., 269
Hawes, G.R., 313
Hawkins, J.E., 264
Hayes, J.P., 266
Healy, C., 250
Herzberg, F., 248, 261
Hewes, J.J., 148n.
Hoge, C.C., Sr., 262
Holland, J.L., 90n., 92-93, 241, 244
Holt, N., 262
Honigsberg, P.J., 271
Hopke, W.E., 252
Hoppock, R., 252
Houston, J., 268, 269
Howard, Alfred, 262
Howard, Alice, 262
Hoyt, K., 251
Hughes, K., 265
Hull, R., 261
Human Resources Corp., 316
Hunt, M., 267

I

Irish, R.K., 245, 259, 271

J

Jablonski, D.M., 154n., 324
Jackson, T., 180n., 245, 253
Jameson, R.J., 261
Jacques Cattell Press, 252
Jastrow, R., 267
Jelinek, M., 251
Johnson, A.W., 85n.
Johnson, W.L., 259
Jones, B.G., 251
Journal of Employment Counseling, 259

K

Kandel, T., 187
Kanter, R.M., 155n., 261, 271
Kantrowitz, M., 148n.
Kaplan, G., 261
Karmos, A., 253
Karmos, J., 253
Katz, J.A., 252
Katz, M., 151
Kelley, R.E., 262
Kelly, J.J., 250
Kendall, N.P., 251
Kennedy, J.L., 254
Kennedy, M.M., 270
Kidron, M., 247
King, D., 258
Kingstone, B., 255
Kirn, A.G., 251
Kirn, M. O'D., 251
Kleiman, C., 256
Klein, B., 151
Klein, E.B., 266
Kocher, E., 325
Komar, J.J., 253
Krannich, R.L., 264, 270, 321
Kravette, S., 253
Krumboltz, J.D., 251

L

Landau, S., 256
Lang, C., 261
LAOS/ASF, 265
Lapin, L., 263
Lathrop, R.C., 180, 241, 244, 248
Lawhead, W., 267

LeBoeuf, M., 268
Lederer, M., 258
Lee, N., 256
Lefferts, R., 262, 318
Leider, R., 250
Lesko, M., 261
Levering, R., 151
Levine, K., 258
Levine, M., 149
Levine, R., 287
Levinson, D.J., 266
Levinson, H., 261
Levinson, J.C., 249, 262, 319
Levinson, M.H., 266
Lewis, F., 287
Libby, B., 260
Lichty, R., 262
Lipe, D., 260
Lipnack, J., 145n.
Lippitt, G.L., 251
Lockheed, M.E., 258
Long, C., 261
Loughary, J.W., 255
Lynch, D., 267

M

McBurney, W.J., 255
McCabe, C.E., 313
McClure, L., 251
McClure, R.M., 255
McCormick, E.J., 269
McKee, B., 266
McRobie, G., 265
Mainstream Access, Inc., 252, 263
Malcolmson, W.L., 267
Malnig, L.R., 255
Malveaux, J., 259
Mancuso, A., 262
Mann, D., 265
Marquis Academic Media, 263, 317
Martin, L., 86n., 241, 245
Martin, P., 253, 270, 271
Martin, R.K., 267
Masters, R., 269
Mathieu, A., 263
Matson, F., 268
Mattson, R.T., 87n., 245
Maurer, H., 248
May, J., 271
Mayleas, D., 253
Medley, H.A., 270
Meier, G., 249
Meranus, L.S., 263
Mercer, M., 129n.
Midwest Academy, 316
Miguel, R.J., 269
Miles, B., 256
Miller, Ann, 321
Miller, Anne R., 248
Miller, Arthur F., 245
Miller, C., *xiii*
Miller, D.B., 251
Miller, D.S.M., 251
Miller, G., 248
Miller, G.P., 258
Miller, Jean M., 321
Miller, Jeffery M., 249
Miller, S., 252
Minge, M.R., 129n.
Mishara, B., 306
Mitchell, A.M., 251
Mitchell, J.S., 251, 254, 255, 258, 260
Molloy, J.T., 183n.
Montagu, A., 268
Moore, C.G., 253
Moore, D.J., 264
Moran, P.J., 267
Morgan, R.L., 255
Morrisey, G., 251
Morrow, S.L., 255
Moskowitz, M., 151
Mouat, L., 256
Muchnick, S., 256
Mullinack, W., 287
Munch, G.R., 253
Munschauer, J.L., 254
Munter, P.K., 259
Myers, I.B., 269
Myers, P., 269

N

Nadler, B.J., 254
National Career Development Project, 260
National Center for Citizen Involvement, 264-65
National Council for Alternative Work Patterns, 250
National Home Study Council, 313
National University Extension Association, 313
Nicholas, T., 262
Noer, D., 245
Nordland, R., 144n.

O

O'Brien, B., 254
O'Callaghan, D., 287
Odell, C.E., Sr., 266
Odell, L.M., 266
Office of Human Development Services, 260
Olson, R.P., 267
Omstead, B., 249
Ontario Society for Training and Development, 269, 320
Orgel, M., 306
O'Toole, J., 247
Ouchi, W., 247

P

Parker, G.T., 313
Parker, Y., 180n.
Patterson, R., 306
Paul, R.H., 269
Peacock, R., 256
Pearson, H.J., 269
Pedolsky, A., 149
Peskin, D.B., 271
Peter, L.F., 261
Petit, R.E., 253
Phelps, C.S., 325
Phillips, C., 256
Pietsch, P., 268
Pilder, R.J., 251
Pilder, W.F., 251
Polking, K., 263, 265
Pollack, S., 321
Potter, B.A., 271
Prince, J.S., 258
Progoff, I., 268
Pulling, Lisa, 318

R

Rabby, R., 259
Raders, S., 287
Radl, S.L., 107
Raelin, J.A., 247
RAIN (an organization), 315
Rainer, T., 269
Raines, J.C., 247
Rashad, H.M., 264
Raymond, R.J., Jr., 129n.
Ready Reference Press, 258, 259
Reardon, P., 245
Regal, M.L., 262
Revel, C., 262
Richelson, G., 271
Riessman, F., 265
Rightor, H.H., 267
Rinella, R.J., 251
Ripley, T.M., 255
Robbins, C.C., 251
Robbins, P.I., 266
Robertson, J., 270

Robinson, D., 249
Rockcastle, M.T., 250
Rogers, E.J., 270
Rohrlich, J.B., 92n.
Roll, R.J., 266
Root, M., 260
Rosenthal, E., 262
Rosenthal, S.M., 252
Rucker, T.D., 252
Ruffner, J.A., 129n.
Russell, P., 268
Russell, P.A., 250
Rust, H.L., 261
Rustad, R., 85n.
Rutter, N., 248

S

Saff, J., 287
Salzman, J., 254
Sampson, D., 287
Savageau, R.B.D., 129n.
Scheele, A., 269
Scheiber, J.L., 247
Schein, E.H., 251, 266
Schemenauer, P.J., 263
Schepps, S.J., 262
Schmelter, H.B., 266
Schmidt, P.J., 255
Scholz, N.T., 258
Schrank, R., 248
Scientific American, 268
Seitler, H., 256
Shedd, C., 254
Sheehy, G., 266
Shenson, H., 318
Shephard, H.A., 251
Sheppard, H.L., 245
Sher, B., 96
Sherman, M.E., 325
Shields, L., 256
Shingleton, J., 255
Shmerbeck, F.A., 44n.
Shrank, R., 325
Shuchat, J., 262
Simon, S.B., 271
Sjogren, D., 269
Small, S.T., 319
Smith, S., 249
Special Task Force to the Secretary of Health, Education and Welfare, 248
Spradley, J.P., 270
Springer, S., 268
Stafford, E., 253
Stamps, J., 145n.
Stanat, K.W., 245
Stanton, T., 265
Steele, F., 148n.
Stein, B.A., 155n., 271
Stern, E.L., 187
Straub, J.T., 253
Super, D.E., 252
Superintendent of Public Documents, 251, 320
Swift, K., *xiii*

T

Taylor, G.R., 268
Terkel, S., 96n., 248
Thain, R.J., 255
Thomas, M., 253
Tiedeman, D.V., 251
Todd, A., 111
Toffler, A., 75
Tough, A., 250
Townley, J., 251
Townsend, R., 261
Trahey, J., 258
Triere, L., 256
Trower-Subira, 259
Turner, C.H., 268

U

United States Department of Commerce, 319
United States Department of Health, Education and Welfare, 266
United States Department of Labor, 247, 248, 250
United States Employment and Training Administration, 58n.
United States Office of Personnel Management, 258, 322
Upjohn, W.E., Institute for Employment Research, 270

V

Vaillant, G.E., 266
Van Roden, A.C., 253
Vash, C.L., 271
Vaupel, J.W., 271
Vegso, K.A., 250
Veninga, R.L., 270
Viscott, D., 73n.
Vocations for Social Change, 250
Volunteers for Educational and Social Services, 33
von Klemperer, L., 314

W

Waelde, D.E., 264
Waitley, D., 271
Wallace, P., 259
Wallace, W., 254
Wallach, E.J., 260
Walz, G., 260
Wareham, J., 20n.
Wasserman, P., 105, 318
Watson, M.A., 318
Wayne, B., 313
Weaver, N.P.K., 250
Weaver, P., 266, 319
Weiner, E., 63n.
Weinhold, B., 268
Welch, M.S., 256
Wertheimer, S., 318
White, J., 271
Wiener, D.N., 306
Wiley, W.W., 270
Williams, E., 180n., 270
Williams, G., 63n.
Winkler, C., 154n.
Winkler, G., 253
Winston, S., 71
Wiseberg, L.S., 259
Wood, L.C., 247
Wood, O.G., Jr., 261
Woodworth, D.J., 254
Wright, J.W., 187

Z

Zehring, J.W., 264, 267
Zimbardo, P.G., 107
Zunin, L., 107
Zunin, N., 107

Update 1983

To: PARACHUTE
P. O. Box 379
Walnut Creek, CA 94597

☐ I think that the information in the '83 edition needs to be changed, in your next revision, regarding (or, the following resource should be added):

____

____

____

____

____

____

☐ I cannot find the following resource, listed on page ______:

____

____

____

____

____

____

Name ____

Address ____

____

Please Read This Before Writing To Hotline

Inasmuch as people buy *Parachute* at the rate of between 10,000 and 90,000 copies per month, we receive a lot of HOTLINES from readers, as you may imagine.

We answer them as rapidly as possible, but sometimes it can take up to three weeks. Added to the time it takes your letter to get to us, and our letter to get back to you, we can save you a lot of time by telling you the most common answers that we usually have to send out. So, please study this checklist, before deciding if you still need to send us your HOTLINE:

1. Are you devoting at least six hours a day, five days a week to your job-hunt?
   IF NOT, *THAT* IS YOUR DIFFICULTY. GO DO IT.
2. If you're having trouble in getting going, are you recruiting some other job-hunters to meet with you regularly, in a group as described in chapter 4?
   IF NOT, *THAT* IS YOUR DIFFICULTY. GO DO IT.
3. Are you clear exactly what your skills are (having used the Quick Job-Hunting Map in Appendix A)?
   IF NOT, *THAT* IS YOUR DIFFICULTY. GO DO IT.
4. Have you put your skills in their order of priority for you (as we described in Appendix A)?
   IF NOT, *THAT* IS YOUR DIFFICULTY. GO DO IT.
5. Have you got your skills described with more than one word – e.g., not just "organizing" but, say, "organizing data into meaningful groups" or "organizing people into motivated small groups"?
   IF NOT, *THAT* IS YOUR DIFFICULTY. GO DO IT.
6. Have you decided just exactly where it is you want to use your skills, in terms of factors (see Appendix A, again)?
   IF NOT, *THAT* IS YOUR DIFFICULTY. GO DO IT.
7. Have you gone out and done Informational Interviewing, seeing at least two or three people a day, for 20 days, as described in chapter 6?
   IF NOT, *THAT* IS YOUR DIFFICULTY. GO DO IT.
8. Are you looking for exceptions, rather than the rule (e.g., most employers may be prejudiced against someone over 40, but are you looking for those who *aren't)*?
   IF NOT, *THAT* IS YOUR DIFFICULTY. GO DO IT.
9. If you're getting in to be interviewed for hire, after finishing your Informational Interviewing, and getting turned down, are you going back to ask them for helpful feedback as to how you could improve the way in which you are presenting yourself?
   IF NOT, *THAT* IS YOUR DIFFICULTY. GO DO IT.
10. Are you really determined to find that job that fits you, no matter what, rather than just giving this an idle push, so you can say, Well, I knew it wouldn't work?
    IF NOT, *THAT* IS YOUR DIFFICULTY. GO DO IT.

Now you know what to work on, without even sending in the HOTLINE. If however your answer to all ten was emphatically "Yes," or if you have determined already that you just want the name of a good counselor in your area, then by all means send that HOTLINE in.

Hotline

Please read, mark, learn, and inwardly digest the page to the left before you send us this Hotline page!

To: PARACHUTE
P.O. Box 379
Walnut Creek, CA 94597

(1) I HAVE READ YOUR ENTIRE BOOK AND HAVE COMPLETELY FILLED IN *THE QUICK JOB-HUNTING MAP* EXERCISE IN APPENDIX A, but I am still having trouble with the following part of the career-change/job-hunting process:

____

____

____

____

____

____

____

____

____

(2) I have studied all the resources in Appendix C, but I need additional names or suggestions for my geographical area. If there are additional counselors you could suggest, from whom I could get help with the above difficulty, please let me know.

Name ____

Address ____

City, State, Zip __________________________________

Mailing List & Newsletter

The author of *Parachute*, Richard Bolles, is the Director of the National Career Development Project (a program of United Ministries in Education), headquartered in Walnut Creek, California (26 minutes due East of San Francisco).

The Project maintains a mailing list. If you wish to be on the mailing list, please fill out the form below, and enclose a check for $10, payable to "National Career Development Project." People on the mailing list receive notification of new books or other creations from the pen of Richard Bolles, as well as of the workshops which he conducts twice a year, in various parts of the country or Canada.

You will also receive a Newsletter, published randomly six times during the year, written and edited by him, containing his latest thoughts on various subjects. It contains articles about special problems that job-hunters or career-changers are encountering; plus descriptions of new research or publications; plus more of Bolles' philosophy; plus news of the Project, and what we are up to lately (three new books are currently wending their way toward 1984-1985 publication dates). Subscriptions *must* run from January through December, for a given year. So, if you send us a check in, say, June, we will send you all the issues that have already come out in the period January–June of this year, and then continue your subscription through the end of December, only. Then you have to re-subscribe, if you wish the Newsletter for the next year.

TO: Mailing List & Newsletter
NCDP
P. O. Box 379
Walnut Creek, CA 94597

Dear Folks:
Please add me to your mailing list for the next twelve months, so that I may receive periodic announcements of your newly-published works, your workshops, etc., and your Newsletter six times a year. My check for $10 is enclosed.

Name ____________________________________

Address ____________________________________

City, State, Zip ____________________________________

____

Organization (optional) ____________________________________

Other Books by Richard N. Bolles

THE THREE BOXES OF LIFE
And How To Get Out Of Them
"Parachute" has reshaped the way people think about jobs and how to find them. *The Three Boxes of Life* calls for as much change in the way we look at school, work, and retirement.
". . . a rich and rewarding guidebook that provides literally hundreds of resources and opportunities for growth." – *Library Journal.* "Why aren't learning, working, and playing, lifelong – simultaneous – activities rather than boxes or blocks of time as we traditionally have been taught they must be?" – *American School Board Journal.* ". . . truly a monumental work which provides a wealth of information." – *Journal of College Placement.* ". . . an eloquent plea for the restructuring of our work lives." – *Career Planning and Adult Development Newsletter.*

Contains hundreds of resources, exercises, charts, illustrations and the complete *Beginning Quick Job-Hunting Map.* 6 x 9 inches, 480 pages, $8.95 paper. $14.95 cloth

WHERE DO I GO FROM HERE WITH MY LIFE?
by John C. Crystal and Richard N. Bolles

Here is *the workbook* for the self-motivated individual, student, professional or anyone who has an interest in a systematic approach to job-hunting and career mobility, bringing together two of the leading people in the field. "A master work in career literature." – *Washington Star-News*
9 x 7 inches, 272 pages, $9.95 paper

THE QUICK JOB-HUNTING MAP
Advanced Version

A practical book of exercises designed to give job seekers detailed help in analyzing their skills, finding the right career field, and knowing how to find job openings and get hired. This is a 32-page version, 8½ x 11 inches, of the *Map* printed in this book (see page 206). $1.25 paper

THE QUICK JOB-HUNTING MAP
FOR BEGINNERS
Offers special help to new job seekers and others looking for their first jobs. 8½ x 11 inches, 32 pages, $1.25 paper

TEA LEAVES: A New Look At Rēsumēs
A leader in the field of career guidance takes a look at effective preparation and use of résumés. 6 x 9 inches, 24 pages, $.50

Available at your local book store, or when ordering direct from the publisher please include $.75 additional per clothbound copy for postage and handling, or $.50 additional per paperback copy for postage and handling.

 TEN SPEED PRESS • Box 7123, Berkeley, California 94707